Translator
Mystie Cho

Editors
Martin Earle
Duncan Cameron
Gina Kim

Marketing Editor
Nicole Curry

Production Artists
Walter Tsai
Janet Shiao
Kelly Lin

US Cover Design
Eric Lin

Lettering Fonts
Comicraft
www.comicbookfonts.com

President
Robin Kuo

Redmoon V6 © Mina Hwang
Originally published in Korea in 1988 by Seung-chul Pack
English translation rights arranged through
World Netgames, Inc.

Publisher
ComicsOne Corporation
48531 WarmSprings Blvd., Suite 408
Fremont, CA 94539
www.ComicsOne.com

First Edition: February 2002
ISBN 1-58899-098-2

Long ago a prophet foretold that man's sins would one day pierce the sky, allowing evil to spill forth across the land and punish man for his wickedness.

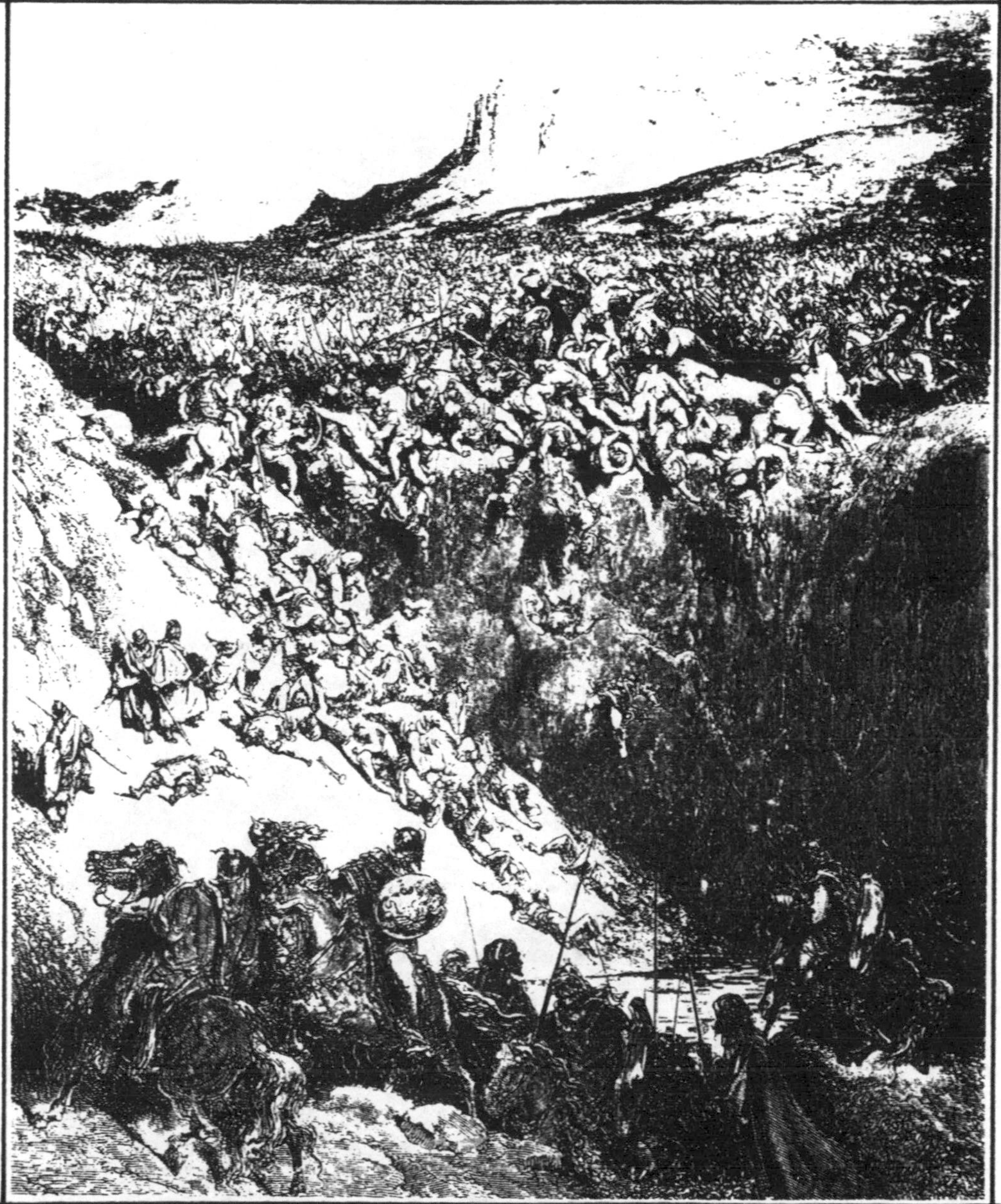

A pillar of fire and overflowing oceans would separate the lands, causing man to fall to his knees, repenting in frantic prayer.

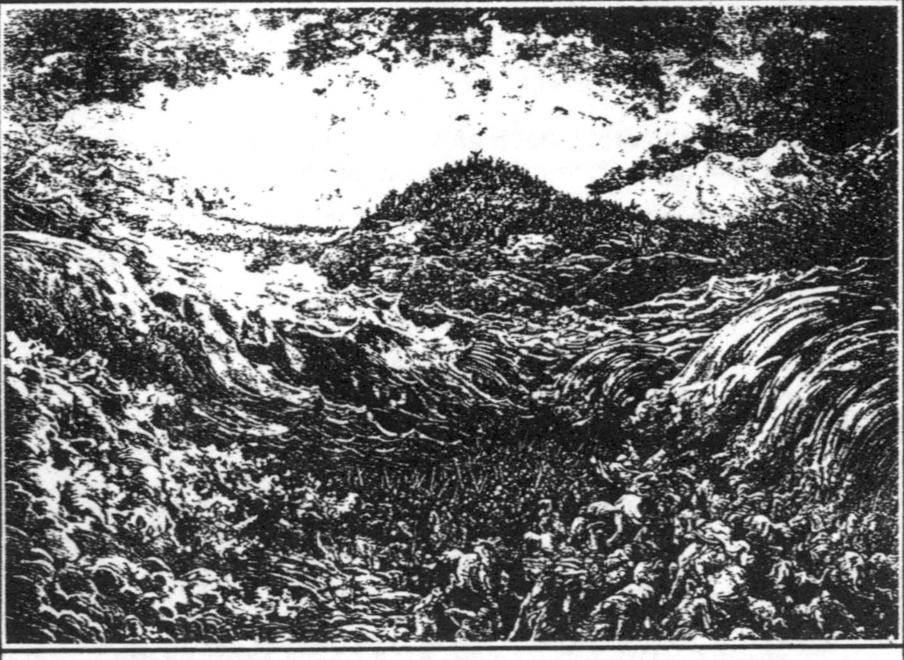

A Sun, bearing the mark of his ancestors would be born, and he would bring an end to man's suffering.

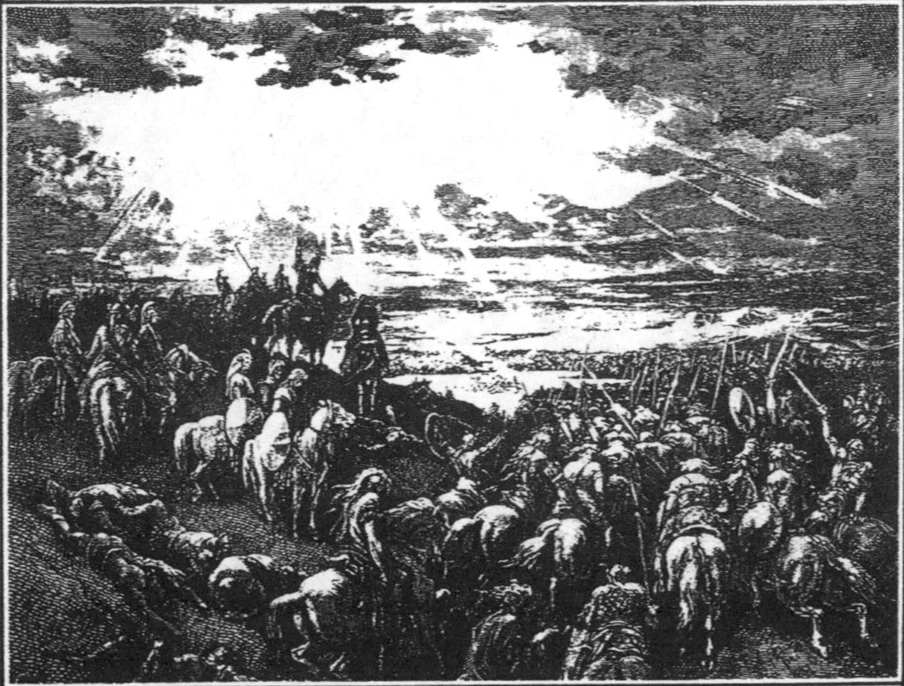

The savior's name would be "Philaro Volcanes Inferno", meaning, the light, the fire, the one and the only.

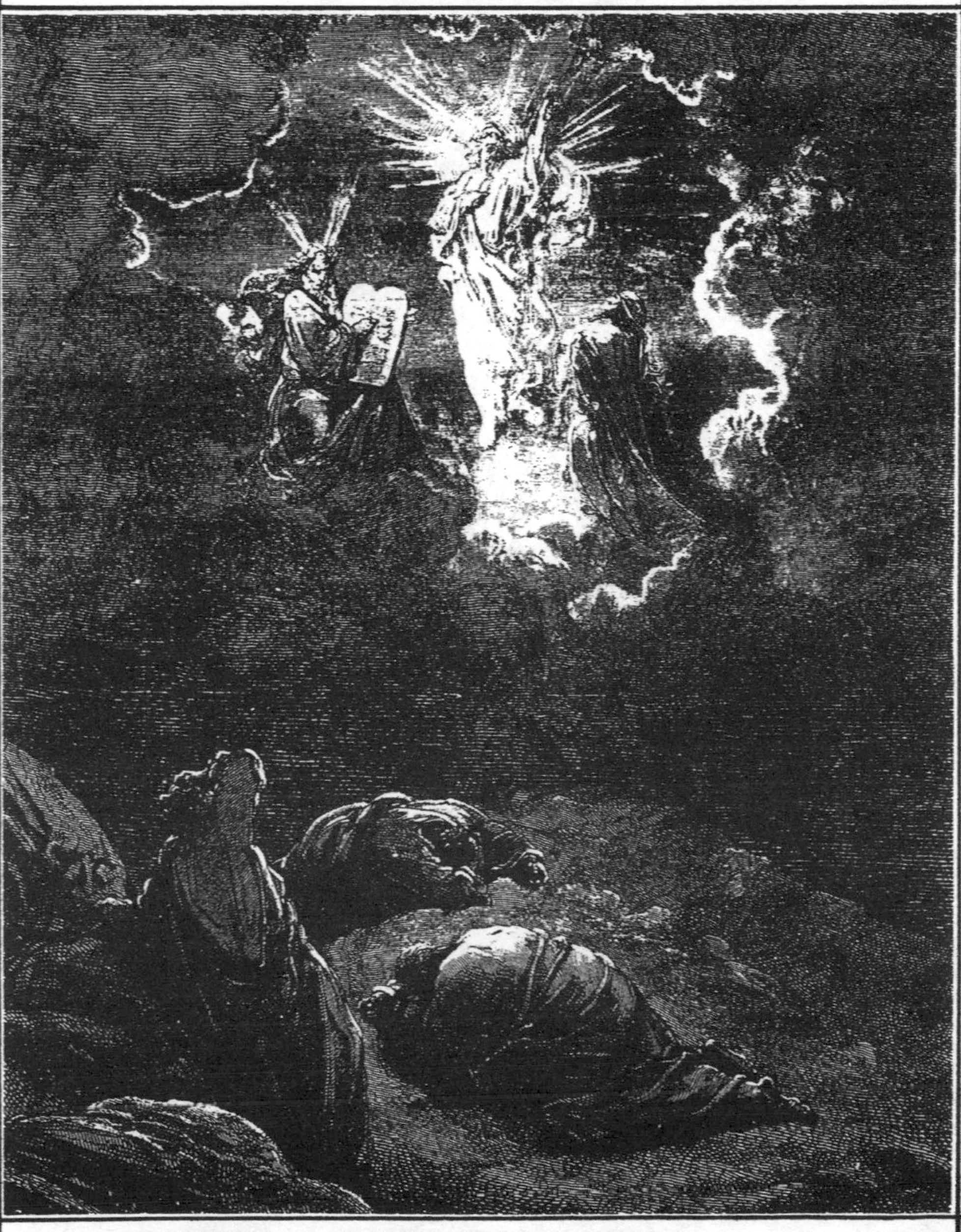

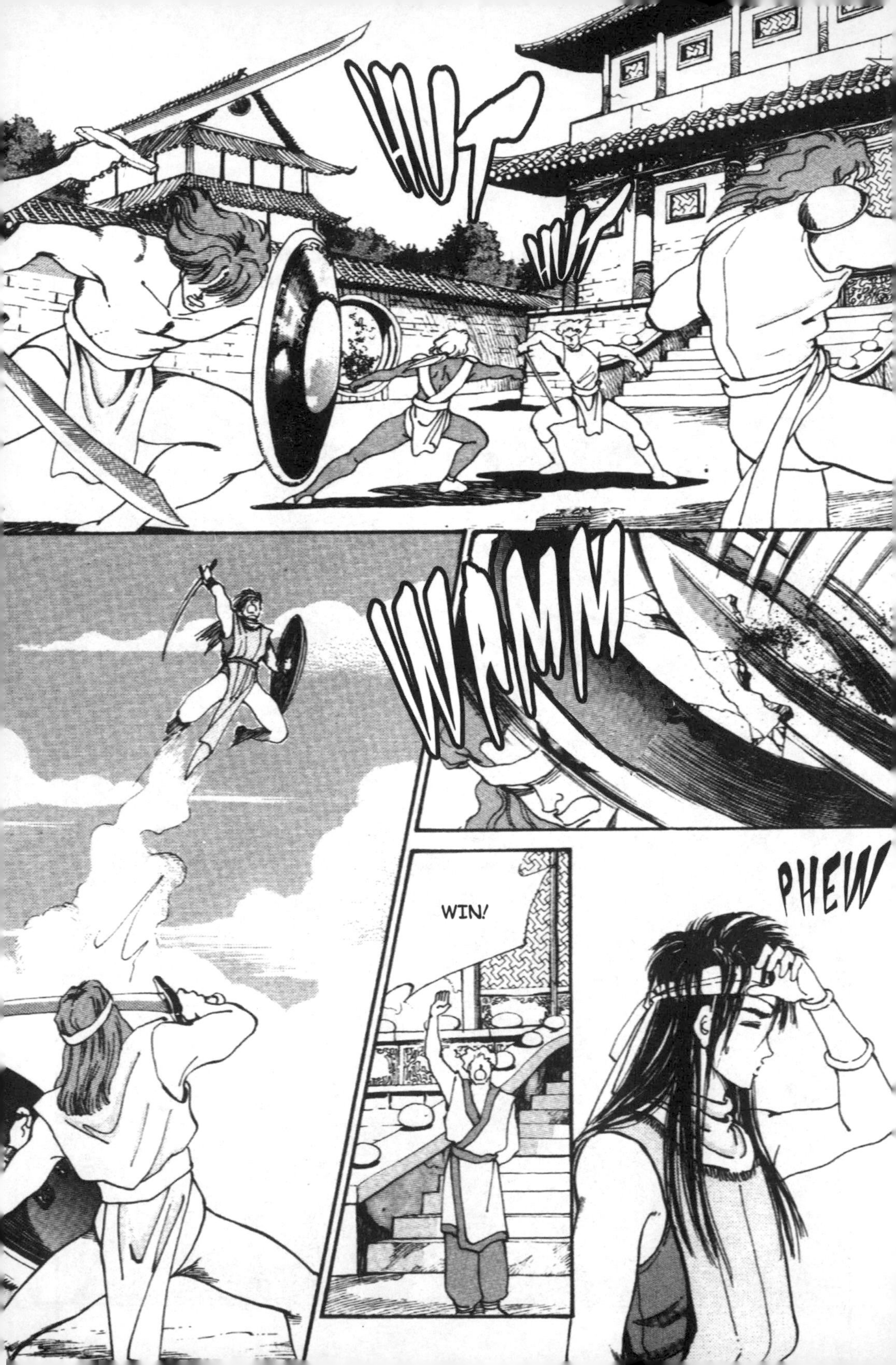
HUT
HUT
WAMM
WIN!
PHEW

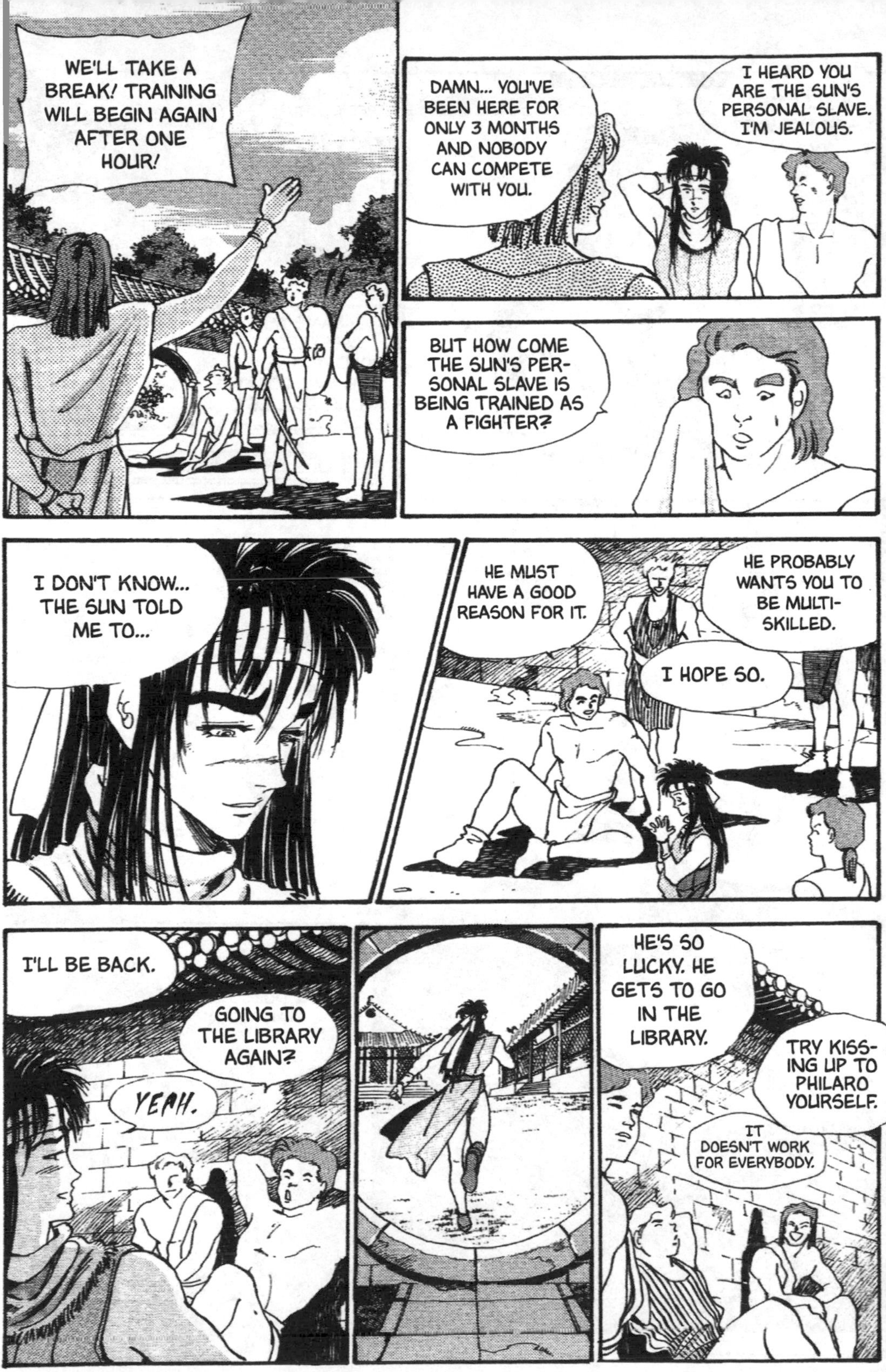
WE'LL TAKE A BREAK! TRAINING WILL BEGIN AGAIN AFTER ONE HOUR!
DAMN... YOU'VE BEEN HERE FOR ONLY 3 MONTHS AND NOBODY CAN COMPETE WITH YOU.
I HEARD YOU ARE THE SUN'S PERSONAL SLAVE. I'M JEALOUS.
BUT HOW COME THE SUN'S PER-SONAL SLAVE IS BEING TRAINED AS A FIGHTER?
I DON'T KNOW... THE SUN TOLD ME TO...
HE MUST HAVE A GOOD REASON FOR IT.
HE PROBABLY WANTS YOU TO BE MULTI-SKILLED.
I HOPE SO.
I'LL BE BACK.
GOING TO THE LIBRARY AGAIN?
YEAH.
HE'S SO LUCKY. HE GETS TO GO IN THE LIBRARY.
TRY KISS-ING UP TO PHILARO YOURSELF.
IT DOESN'T WORK FOR EVERYBODY.

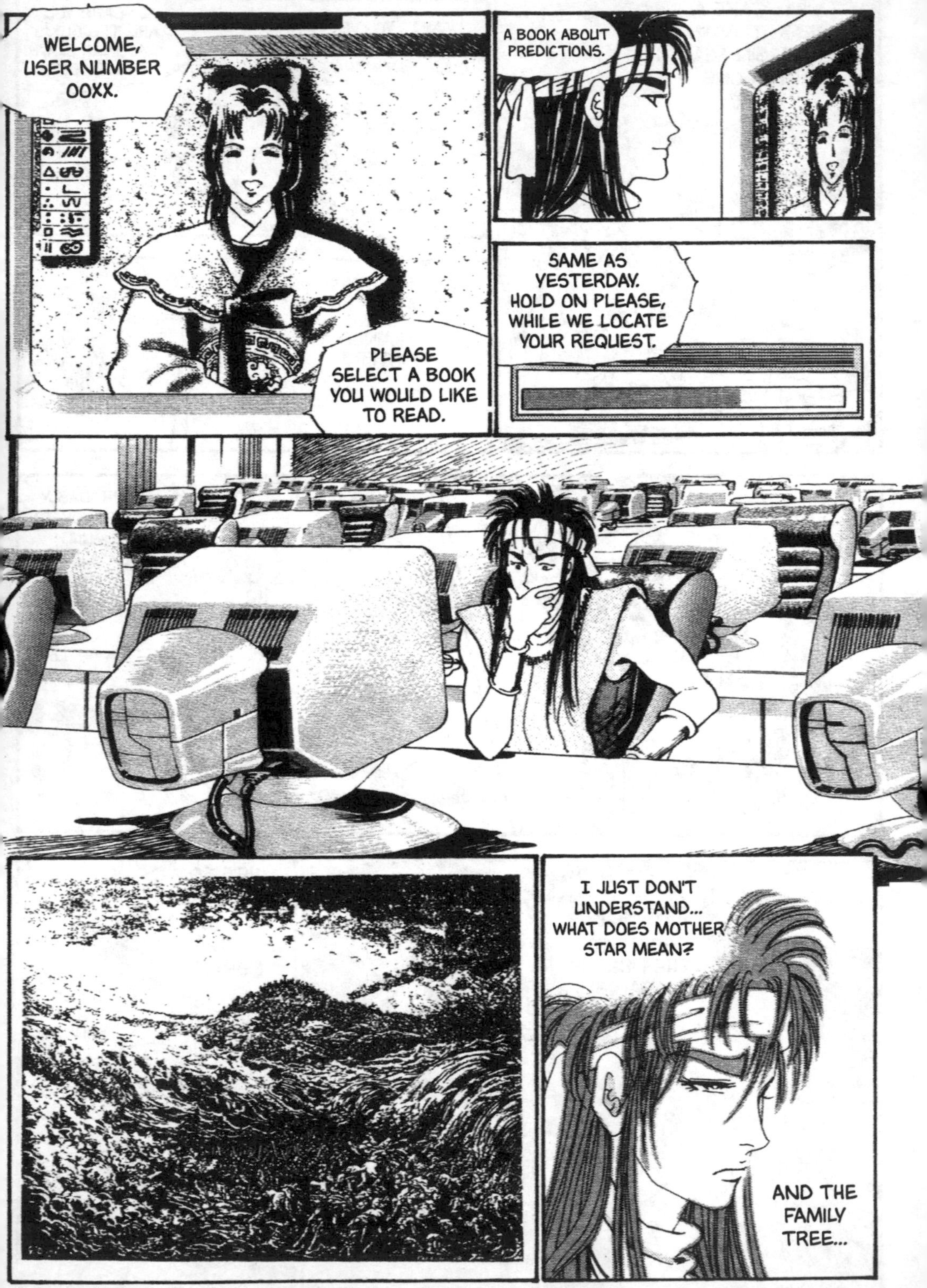
WELCOME, USER NUMBER OOXX.
A BOOK ABOUT PREDICTIONS.
SAME AS YESTERDAY. HOLD ON PLEASE, WHILE WE LOCATE YOUR REQUEST.
PLEASE SELECT A BOOK YOU WOULD LIKE TO READ.
I JUST DON'T UNDERSTAND... WHAT DOES MOTHER STAR MEAN?
AND THE FAMILY TREE...

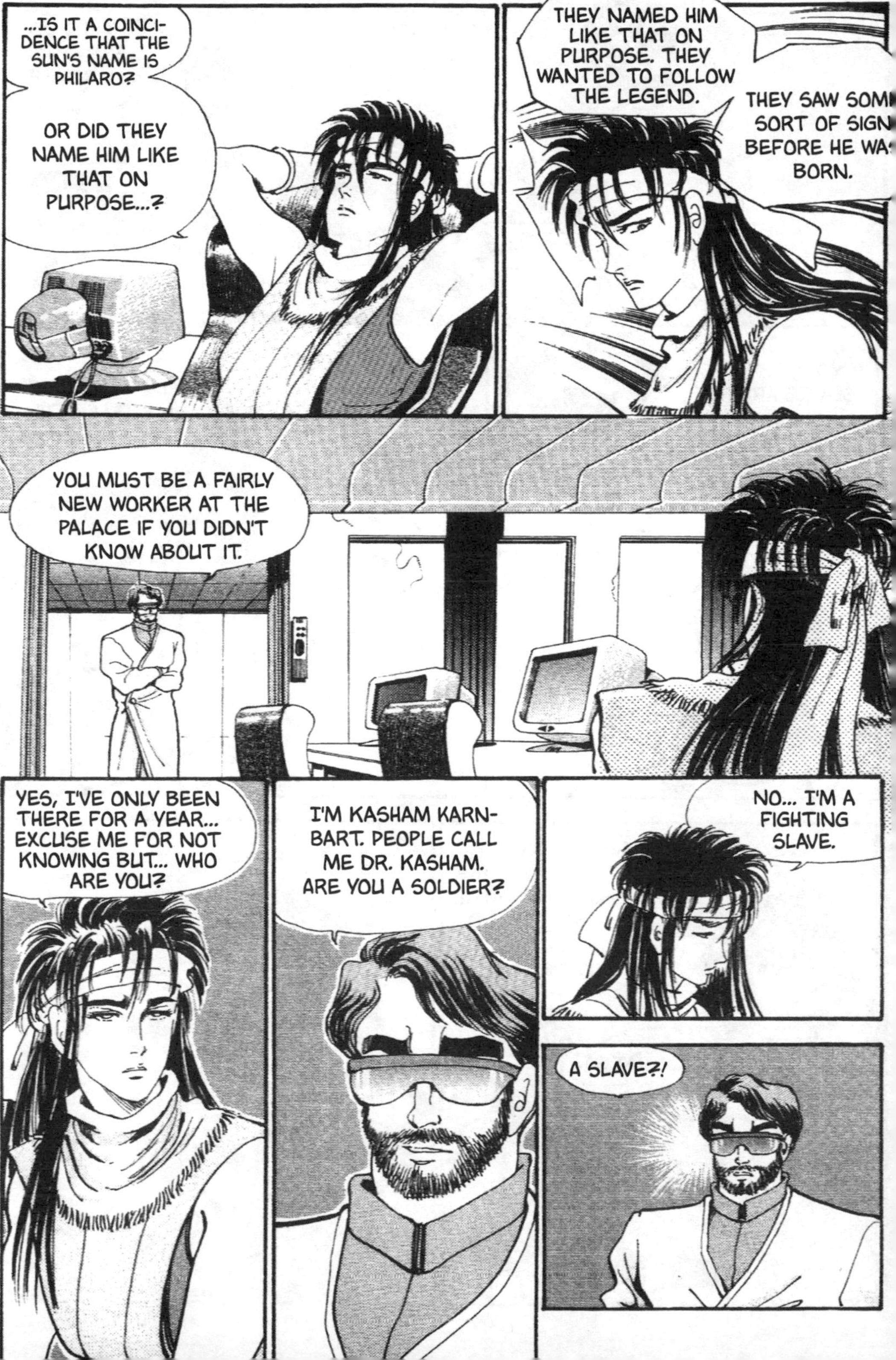
...IS IT A COINCIDENCE THAT THE SUN'S NAME IS PHILARO?
OR DID THEY NAME HIM LIKE THAT ON PURPOSE...?
THEY NAMED HIM LIKE THAT ON PURPOSE. THEY WANTED TO FOLLOW THE LEGEND.
THEY SAW SOM SORT OF SIGN BEFORE HE WA BORN.
YOU MUST BE A FAIRLY NEW WORKER AT THE PALACE IF YOU DIDN'T KNOW ABOUT IT.
YES, I'VE ONLY BEEN THERE FOR A YEAR... EXCUSE ME FOR NOT KNOWING BUT... WHO ARE YOU?
I'M KASHAM KARNBART. PEOPLE CALL ME DR. KASHAM. ARE YOU A SOLDIER?
NO... I'M A FIGHTING SLAVE.
A SLAVE?!

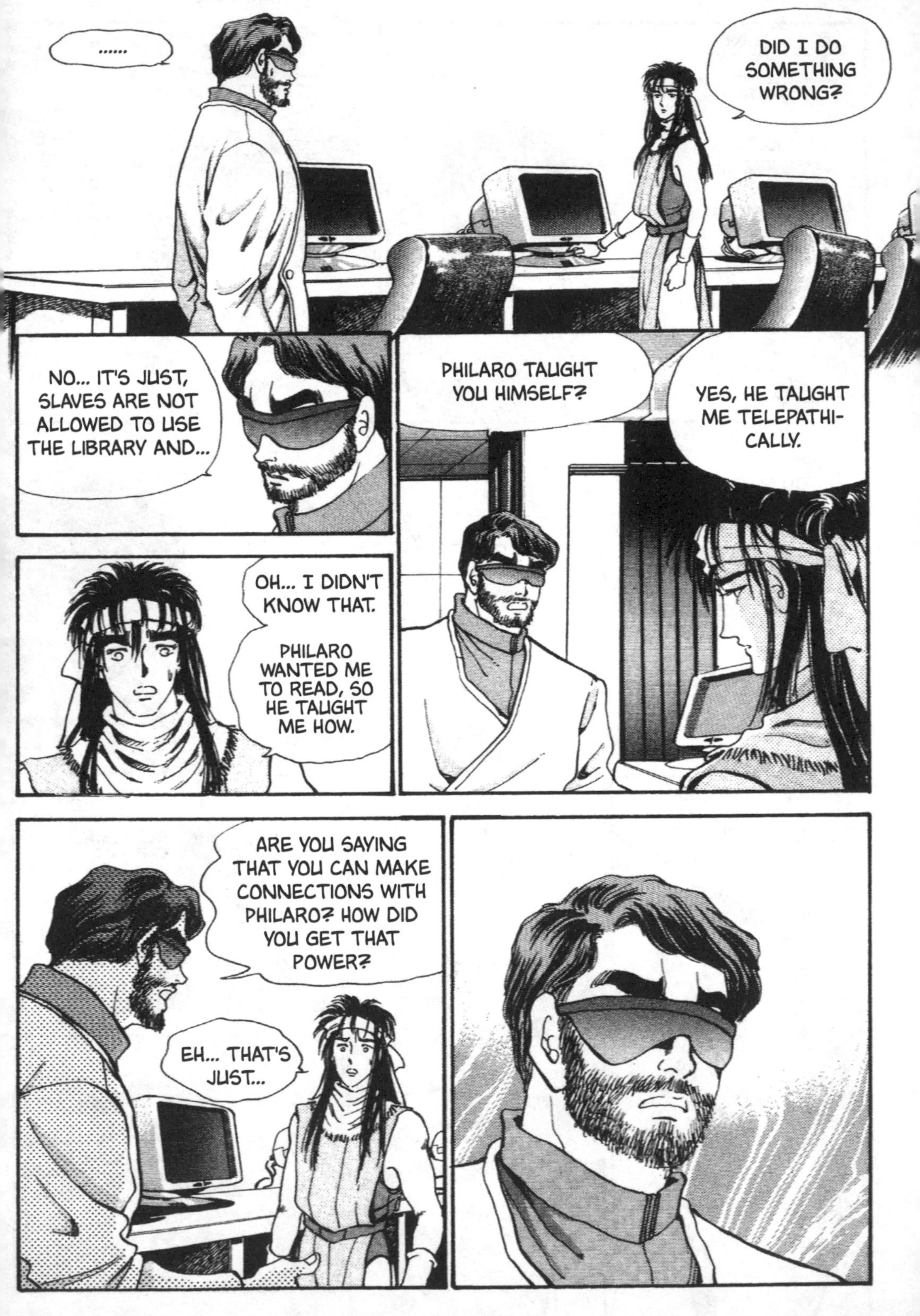
......
DID I DO SOMETHING WRONG?
NO... IT'S JUST, SLAVES ARE NOT ALLOWED TO USE THE LIBRARY AND...
PHILARO TAUGHT YOU HIMSELF?
YES, HE TAUGHT ME TELEPATHI-CALLY.
OH... I DIDN'T KNOW THAT.
PHILARO WANTED ME TO READ, SO HE TAUGHT ME HOW.
ARE YOU SAYING THAT YOU CAN MAKE CONNECTIONS WITH PHILARO? HOW DID YOU GET THAT POWER?
EH... THAT'S JUST...

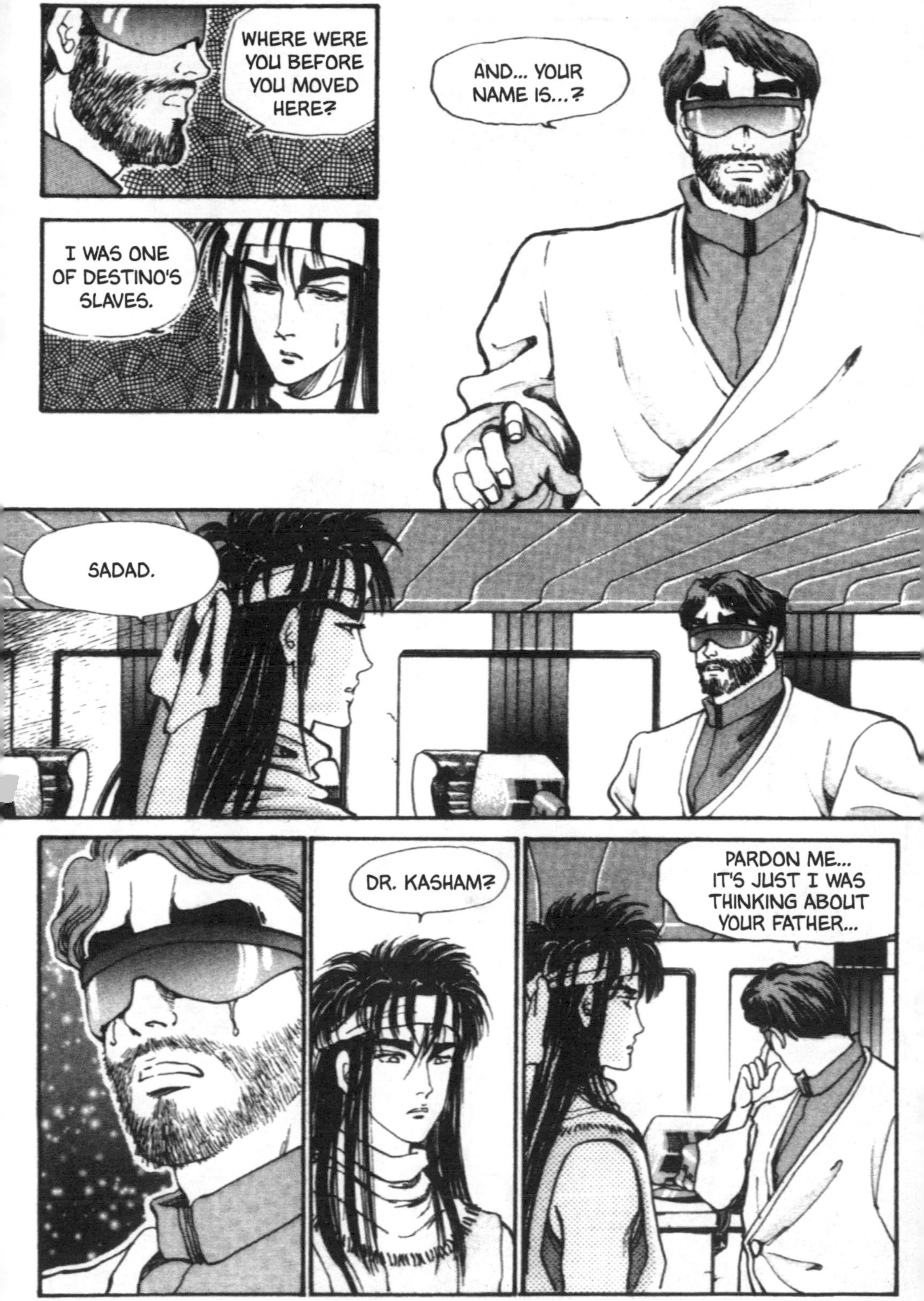

WHERE WERE YOU BEFORE YOU MOVED HERE?
AND... YOUR NAME IS...?
I WAS ONE OF DESTINO'S SLAVES.
SADAD.
DR. KASHAM?
PARDON ME... IT'S JUST I WAS THINKING ABOUT YOUR FATHER...

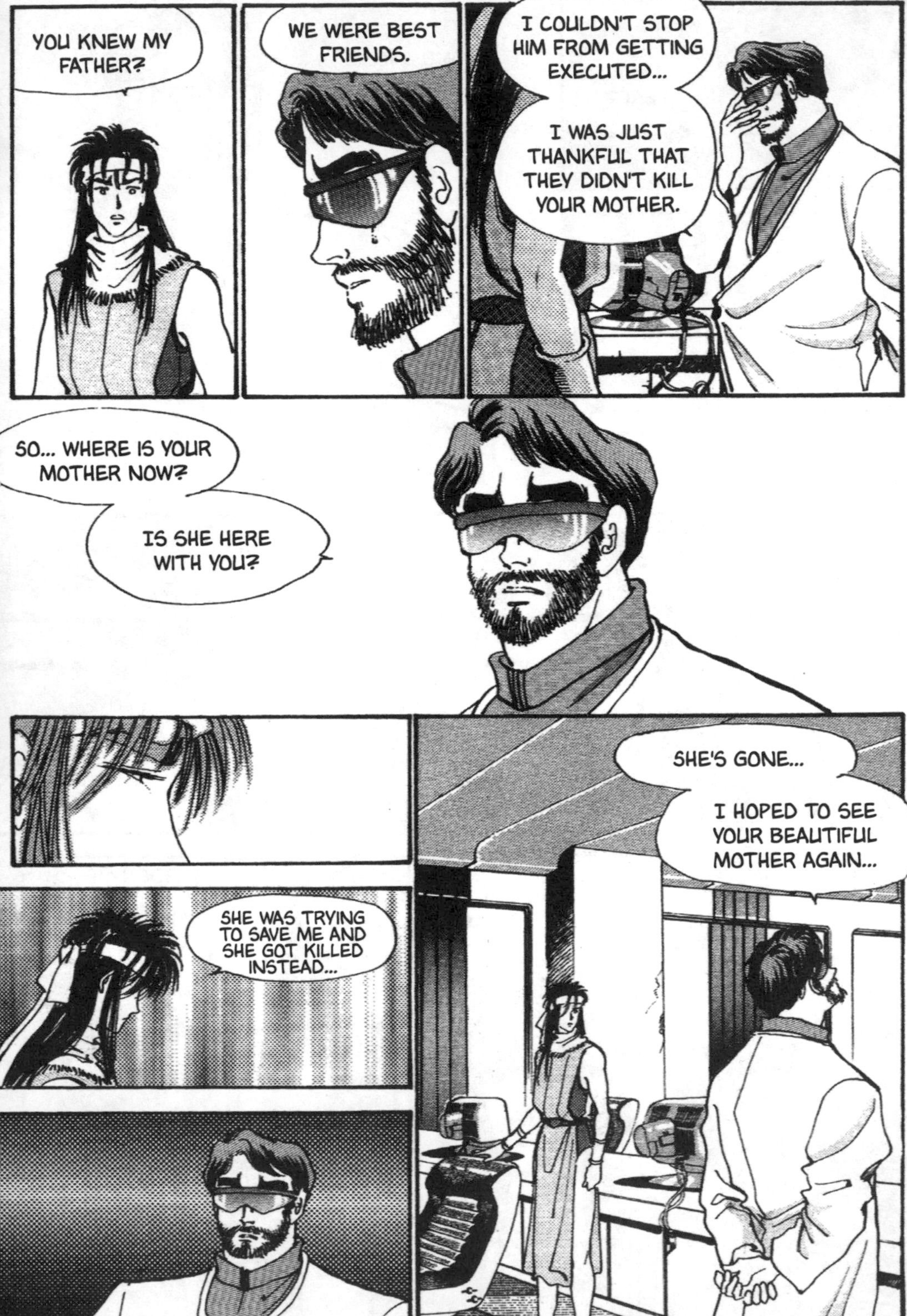
YOU KNEW MY FATHER?
WE WERE BEST FRIENDS.
I COULDN'T STOP HIM FROM GETTING EXECUTED...
I WAS JUST THANKFUL THAT THEY DIDN'T KILL YOUR MOTHER.
SO... WHERE IS YOUR MOTHER NOW?
IS SHE HERE WITH YOU?
SHE WAS TRYING TO SAVE ME AND SHE GOT KILLED INSTEAD...
SHE'S GONE...
I HOPED TO SEE YOUR BEAUTIFUL MOTHER AGAIN...

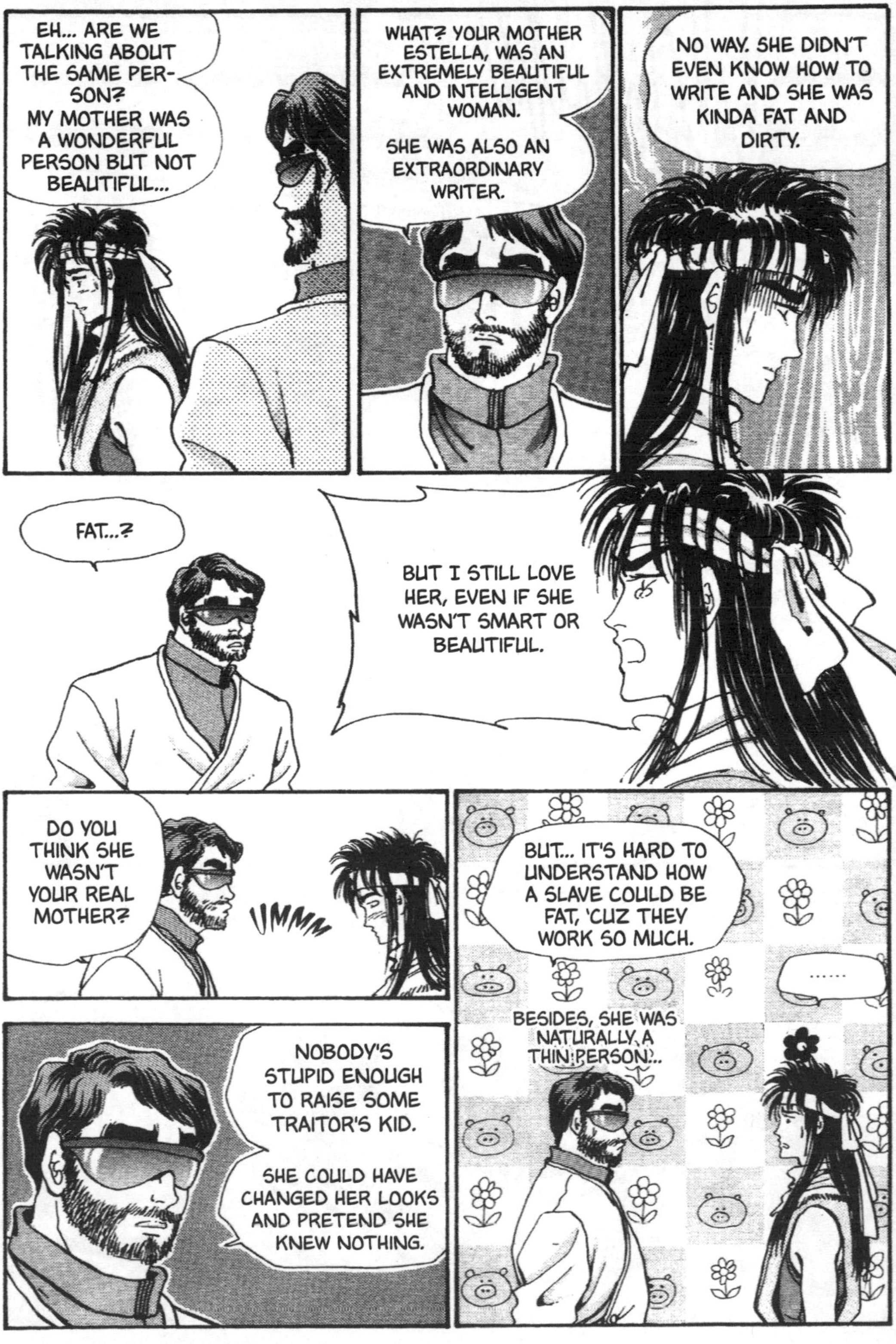
EH... ARE WE TALKING ABOUT THE SAME PER-SON? MY MOTHER WAS A WONDERFUL PERSON BUT NOT BEAUTIFUL...
WHAT? YOUR MOTHER ESTELLA, WAS AN EXTREMELY BEAUTIFUL AND INTELLIGENT WOMAN.
SHE WAS ALSO AN EXTRAORDINARY WRITER.
NO WAY. SHE DIDN'T EVEN KNOW HOW TO WRITE AND SHE WAS KINDA FAT AND DIRTY.
FAT...?
BUT I STILL LOVE HER, EVEN IF SHE WASN'T SMART OR BEAUTIFUL.
DO YOU THINK SHE WASN'T YOUR REAL MOTHER?
UMMM
NOBODY'S STUPID ENOUGH TO RAISE SOME TRAITOR'S KID.
SHE COULD HAVE CHANGED HER LOOKS AND PRETEND SHE KNEW NOTHING.
BUT... IT'S HARD TO UNDERSTAND HOW A SLAVE COULD BE FAT, 'CUZ THEY WORK SO MUCH.
......
BESIDES, SHE WAS NATURALLY A THIN PERSON...

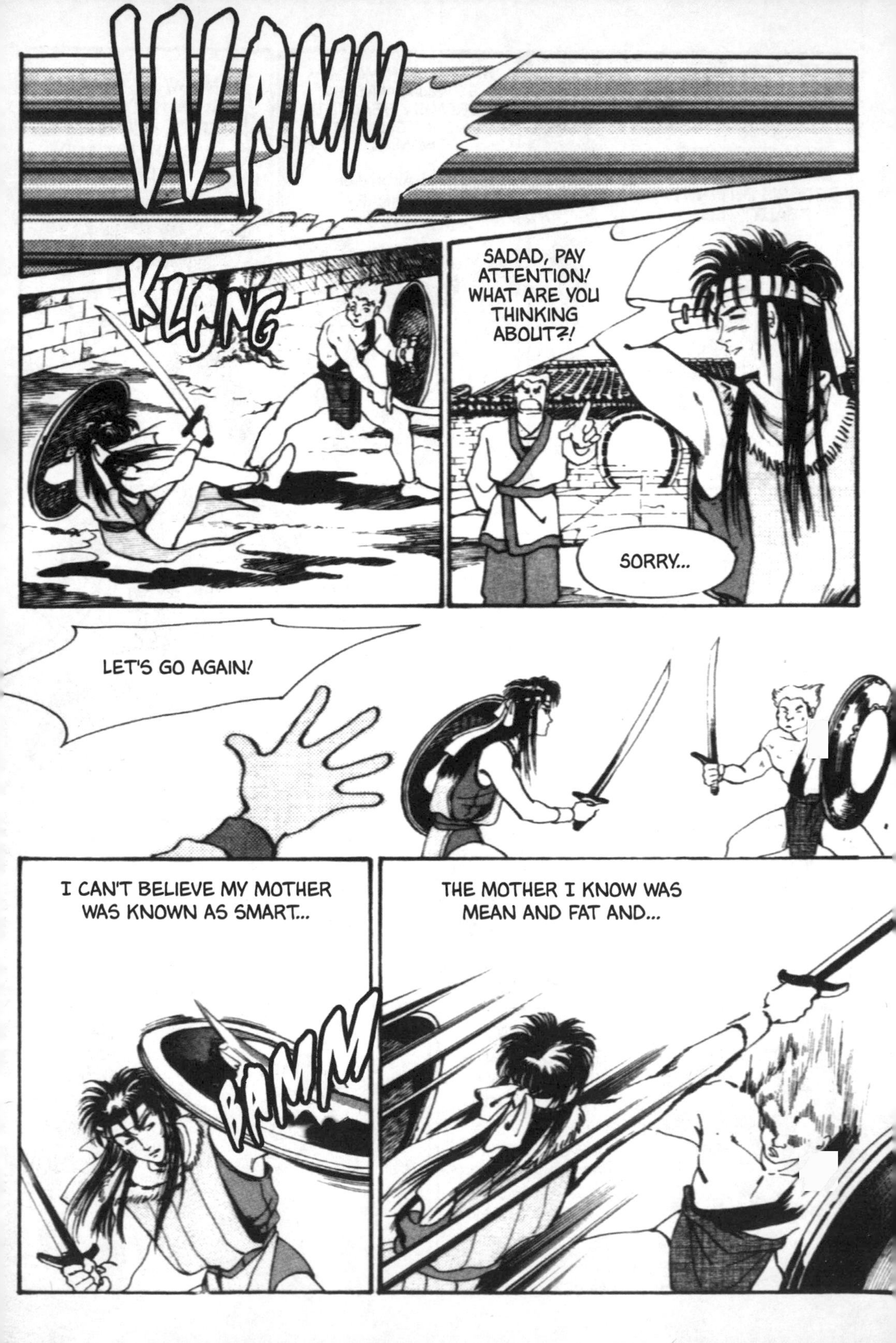
WAMM
KLANG
SADAD, PAY ATTENTION! WHAT ARE YOU THINKING ABOUT?!
SORRY...
LET'S GO AGAIN!
I CAN'T BELIEVE MY MOTHER WAS KNOWN AS SMART...
BAMM
THE MOTHER I KNOW WAS MEAN AND FAT AND...

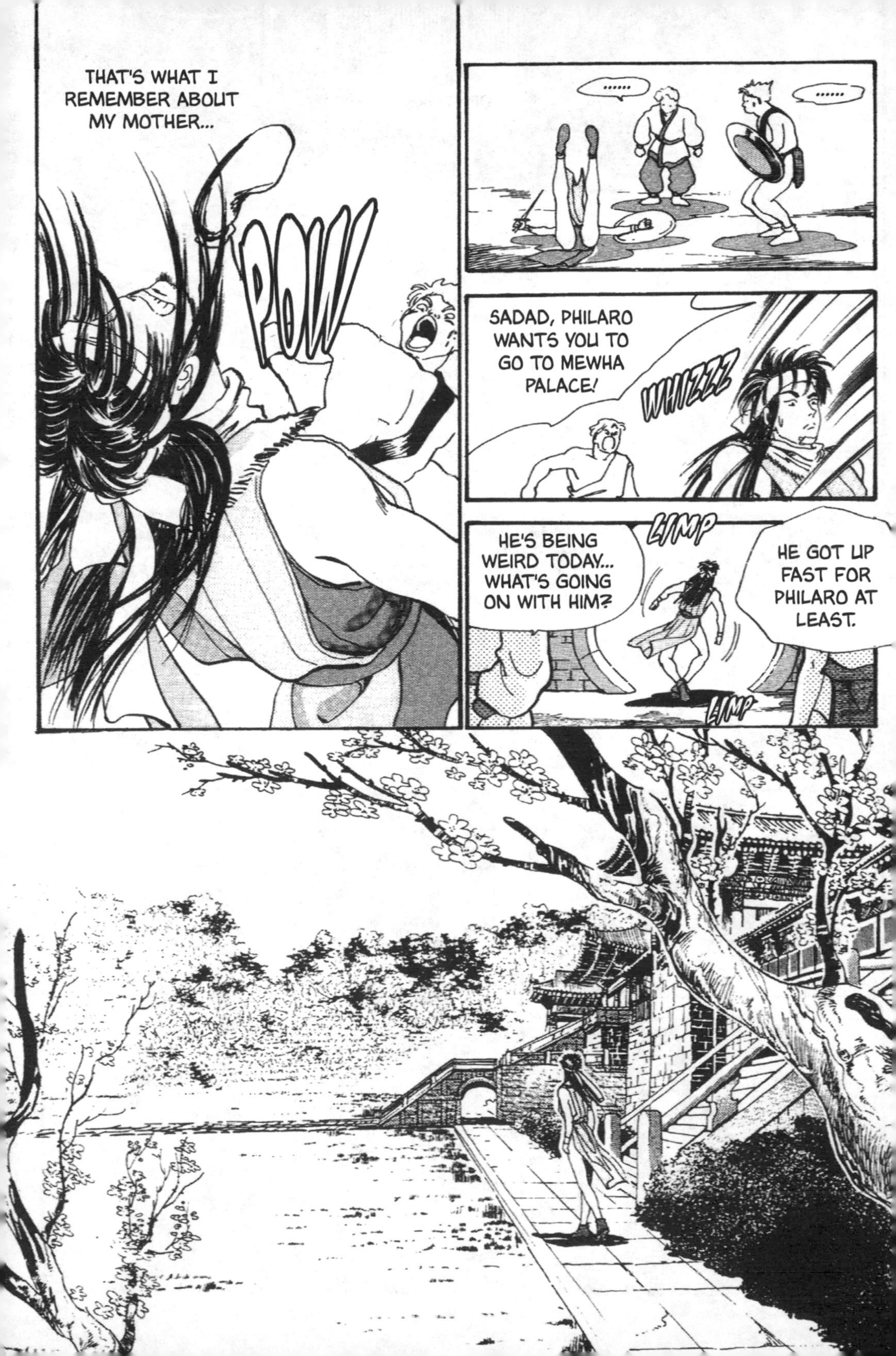
THAT'S WHAT I REMEMBER ABOUT MY MOTHER...
POW
......
......
SADAD, PHILARO WANTS YOU TO GO TO MEWHA PALACE!
WHIZZZ
HE'S BEING WEIRD TODAY... WHAT'S GOING ON WITH HIM?
LIMP
HE GOT UP FAST FOR PHILARO AT LEAST.
LIMP

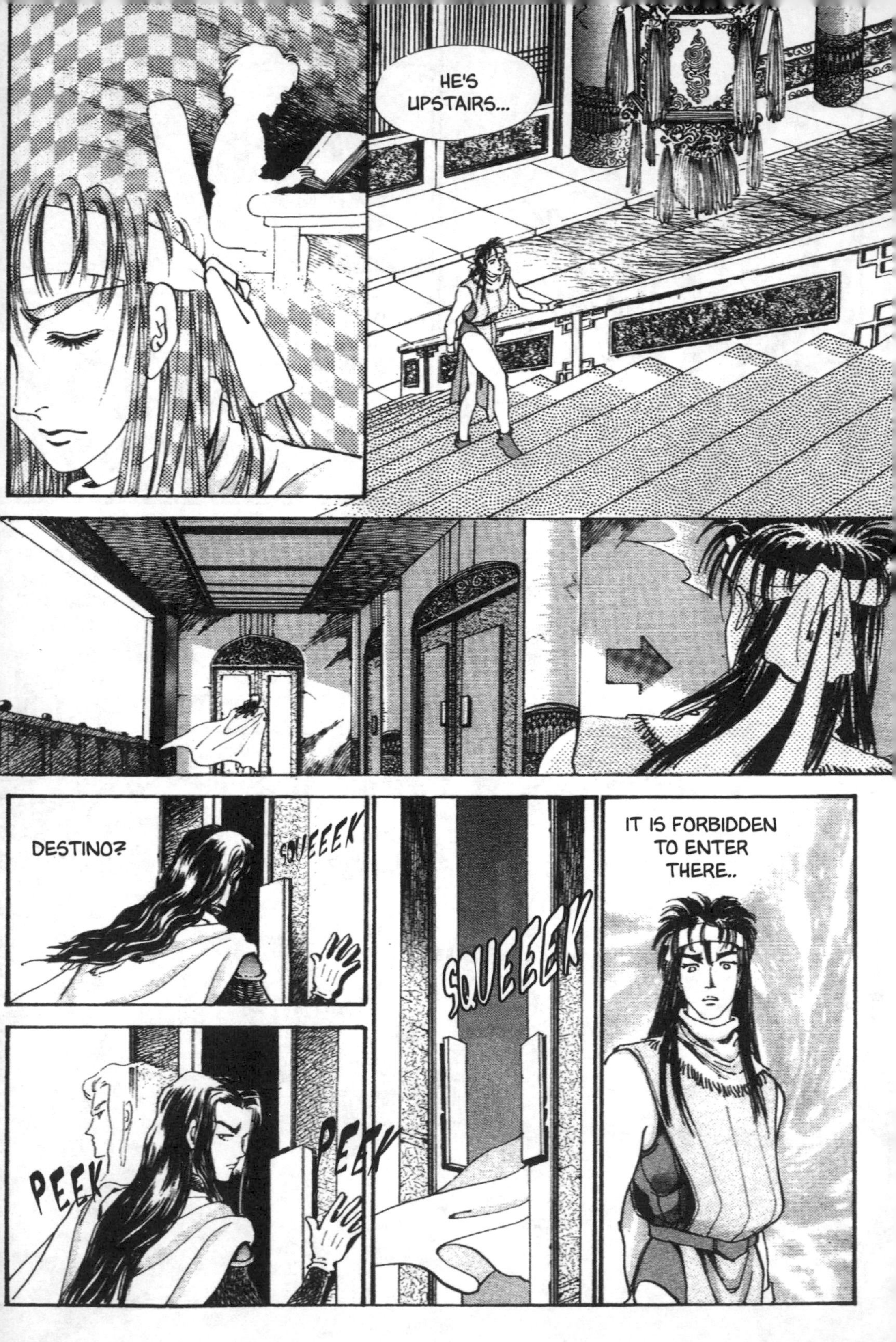
HE'S UPSTAIRS...
DESTINO?
SQUEEEK
SQUEEEK
PEEK
PEEK
IT IS FORBIDDEN TO ENTER THERE..

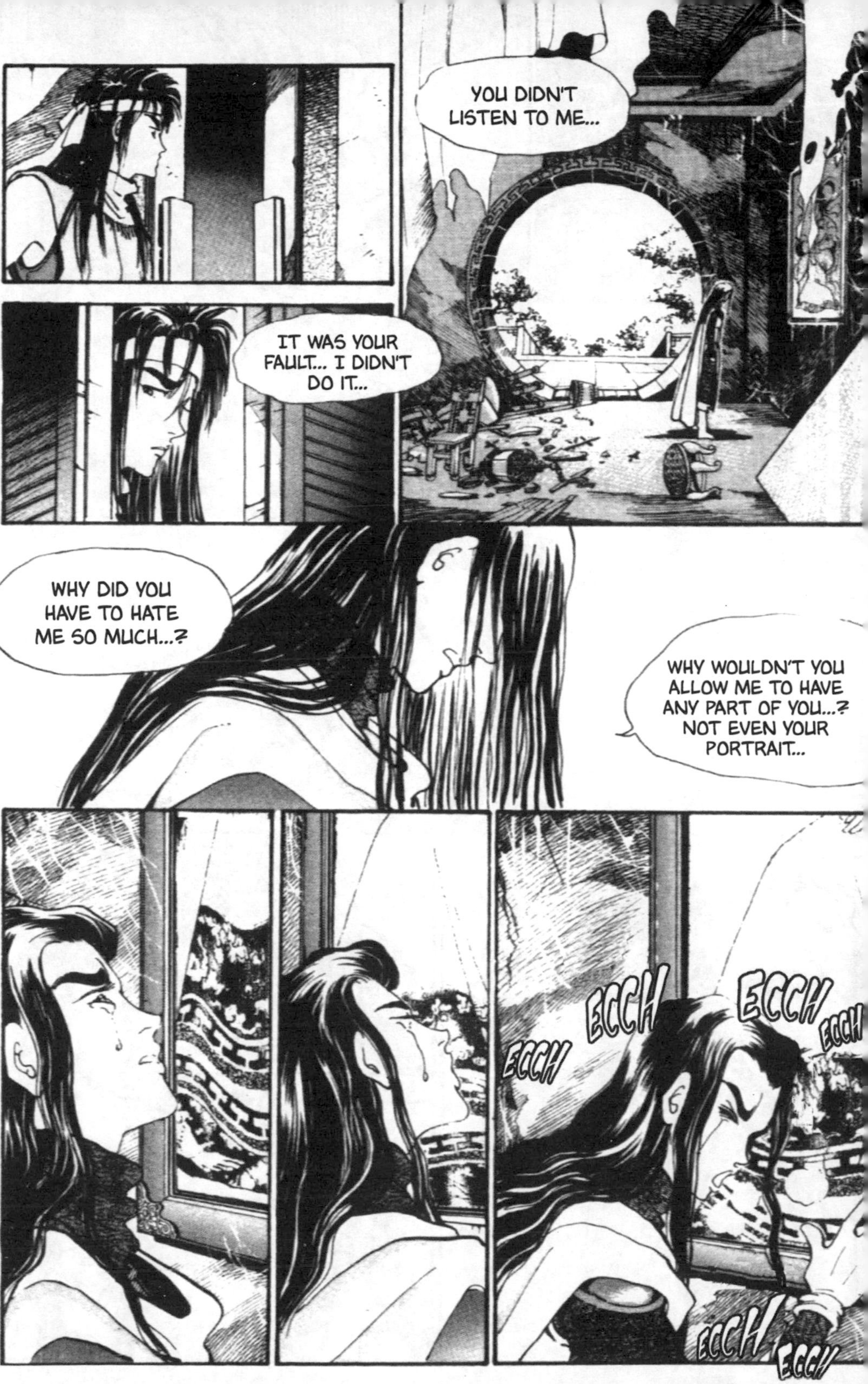
YOU DIDN'T LISTEN TO ME...
IT WAS YOUR FAULT... I DIDN'T DO IT...
WHY DID YOU HAVE TO HATE ME SO MUCH...?
WHY WOULDN'T YOU ALLOW ME TO HAVE ANY PART OF YOU...? NOT EVEN YOUR PORTRAIT...
ECCH
ECCH
ECCH
ECCH
ECCH
ECCH

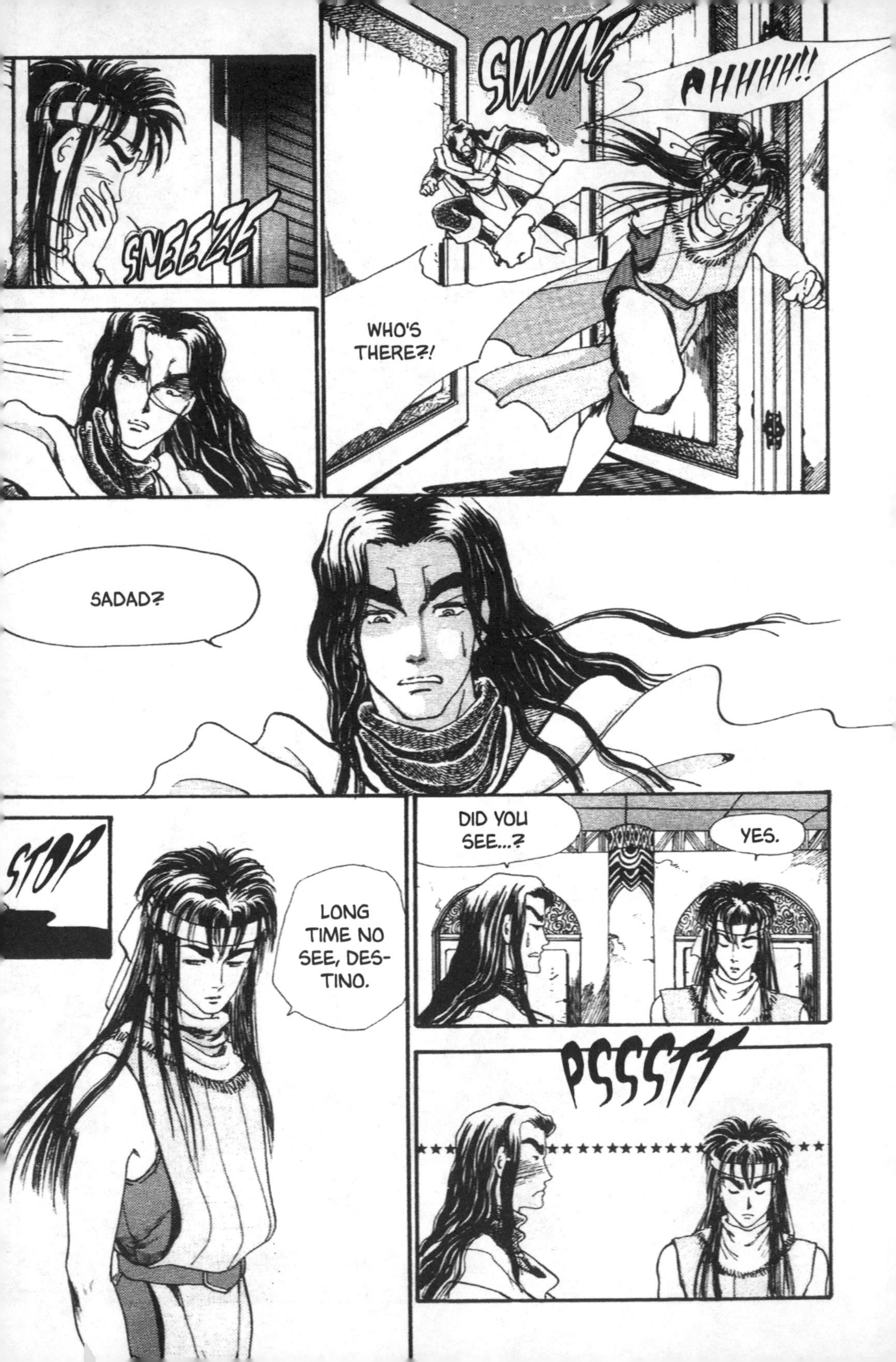
SNEEZE
SWING
AHHHH!!
WHO'S THERE?!
SADAD?
STOP
LONG TIME NO SEE, DES-TINO.
DID YOU SEE...?
YES.
PSSSTT

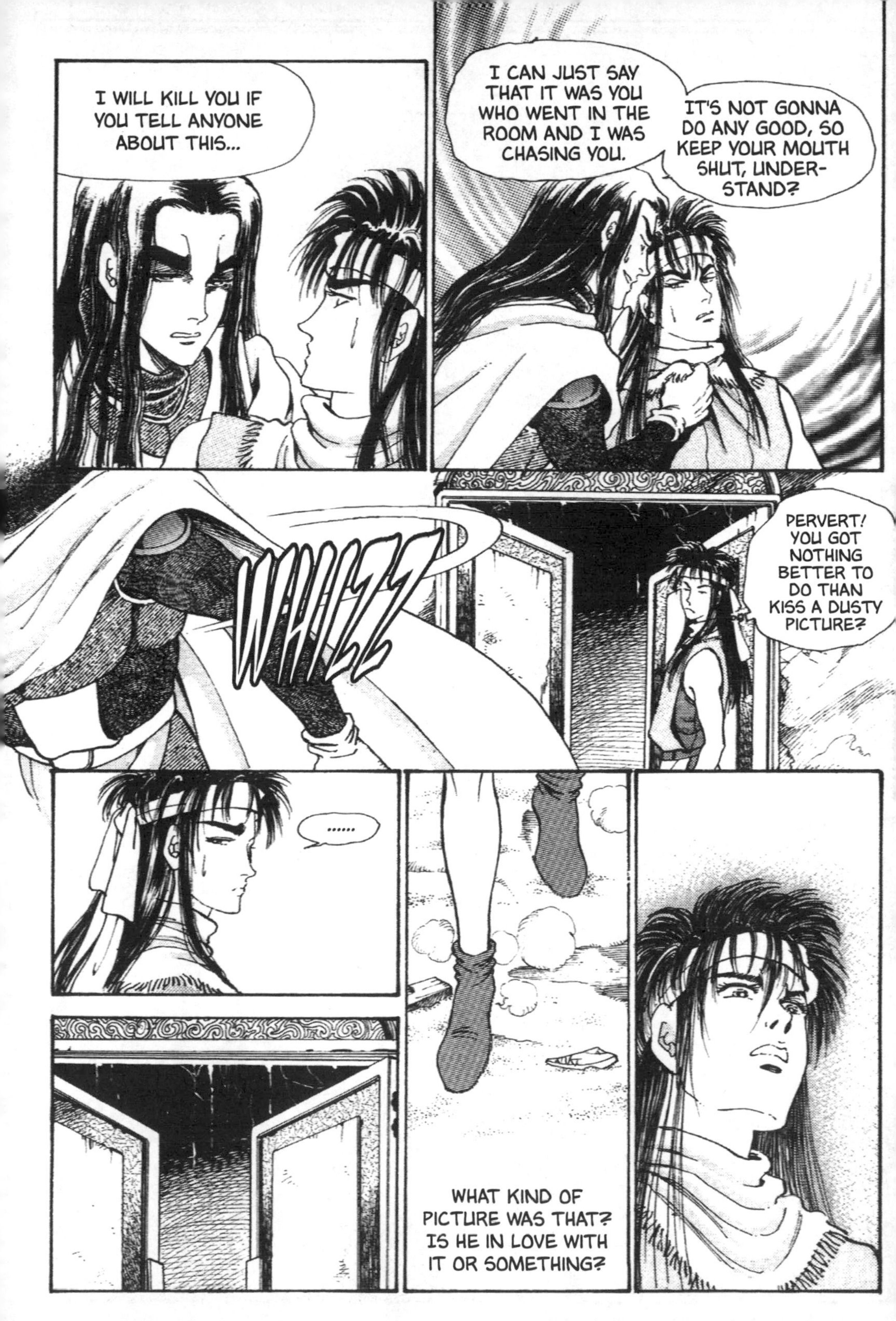
I WILL KILL YOU IF YOU TELL ANYONE ABOUT THIS...
I CAN JUST SAY THAT IT WAS YOU WHO WENT IN THE ROOM AND I WAS CHASING YOU.
IT'S NOT GONNA DO ANY GOOD, SO KEEP YOUR MOUTH SHUT, UNDER-STAND?
WHIZZ
PERVERT! YOU GOT NOTHING BETTER TO DO THAN KISS A DUSTY PICTURE?
......
WHAT KIND OF PICTURE WAS THAT? IS HE IN LOVE WITH IT OR SOMETHING?

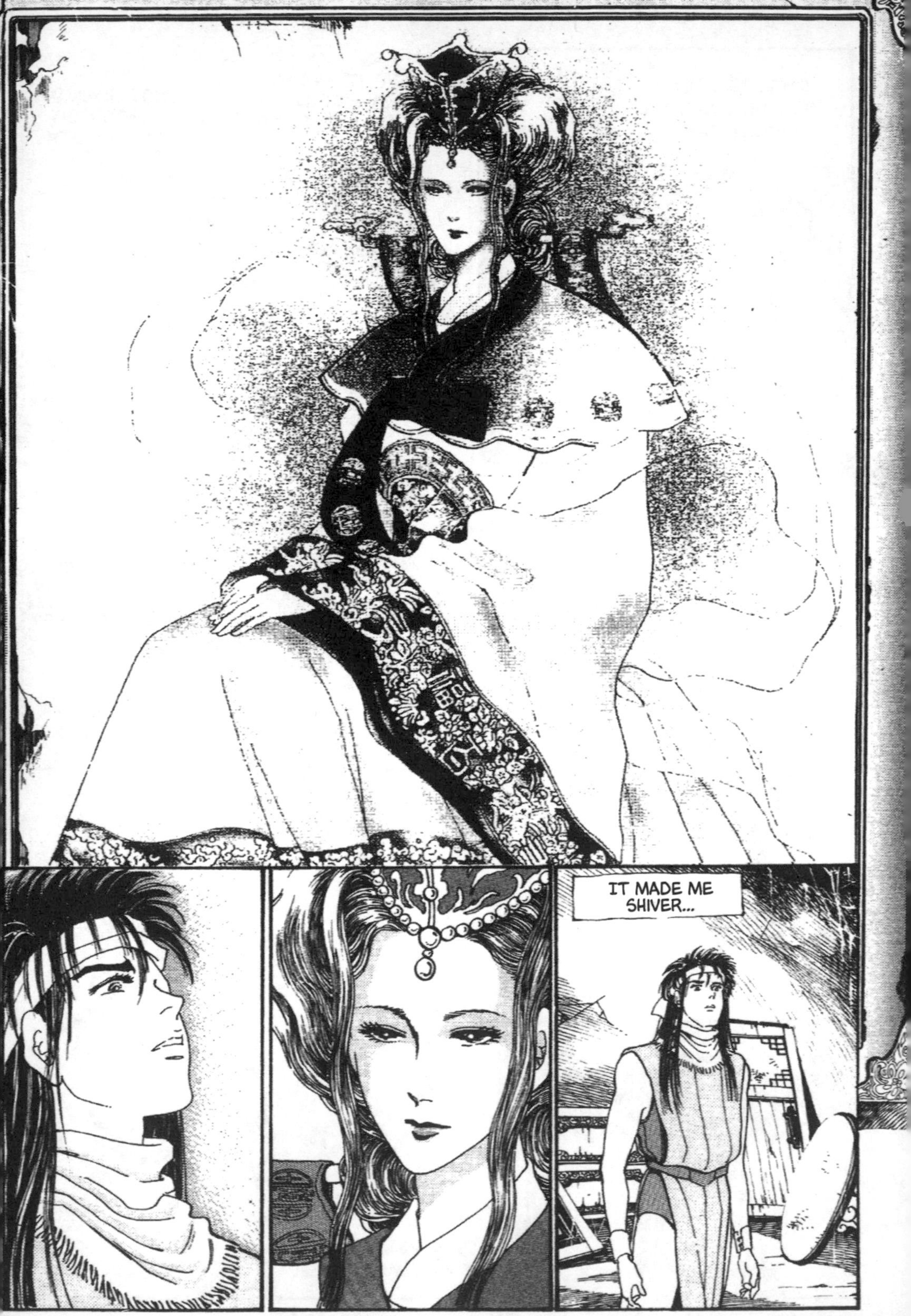
IT MADE ME SHIVER...

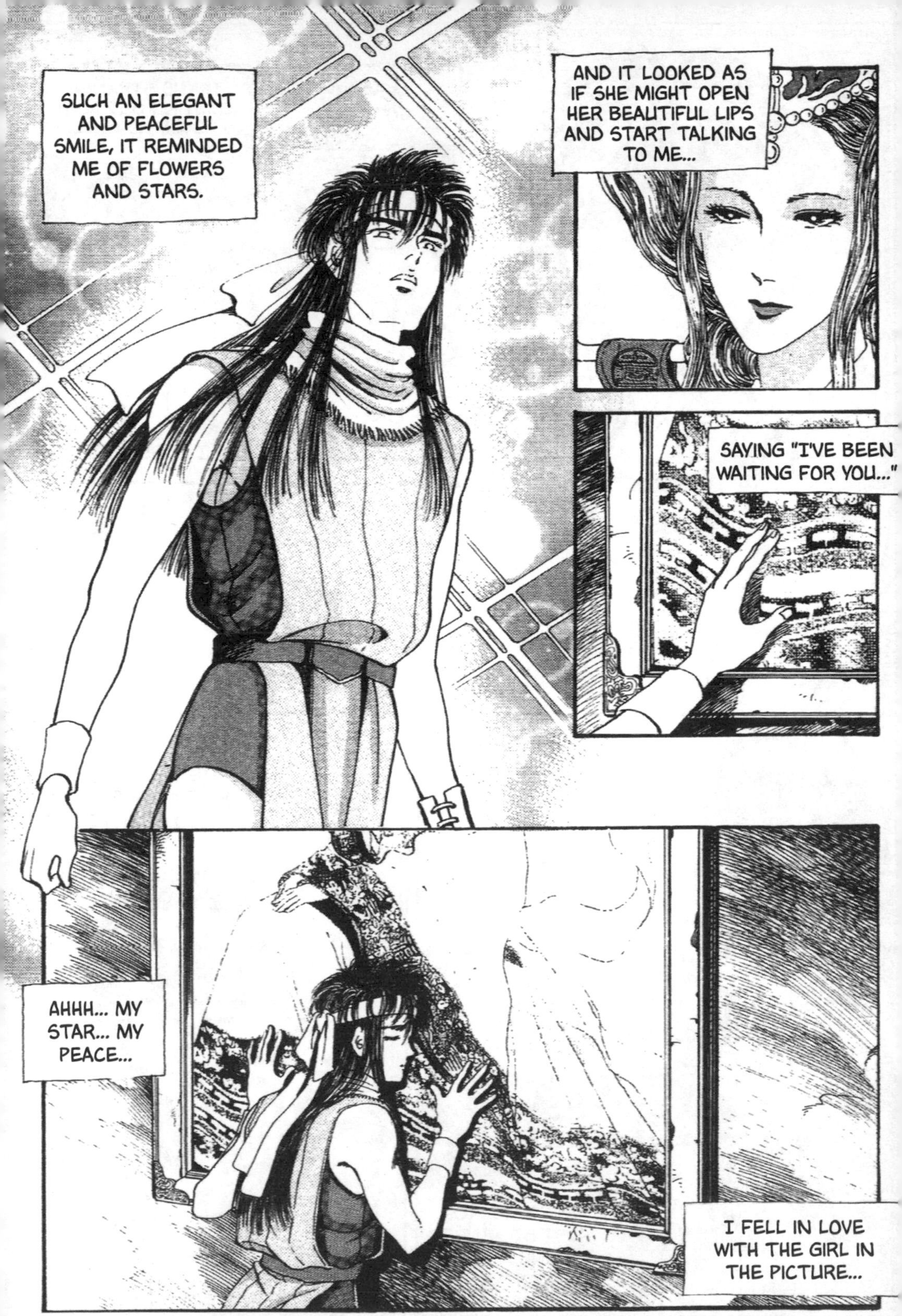
SUCH AN ELEGANT AND PEACEFUL SMILE, IT REMINDED ME OF FLOWERS AND STARS.
AND IT LOOKED AS IF SHE MIGHT OPEN HER BEAUTIFUL LIPS AND START TALKING TO ME...
SAYING "I'VE BEEN WAITING FOR YOU..."
AHHH... MY STAR... MY PEACE...
I FELL IN LOVE WITH THE GIRL IN THE PICTURE...

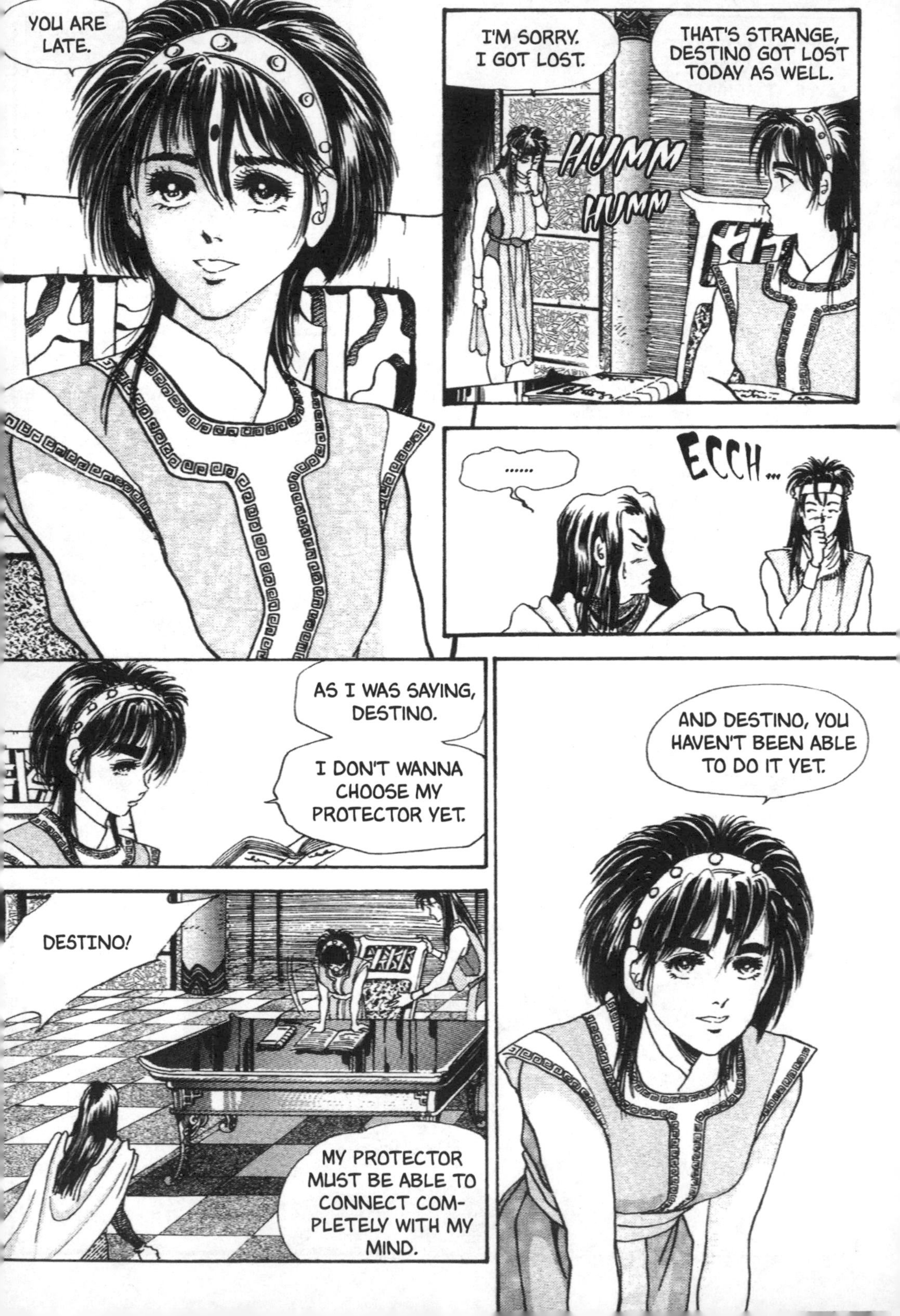
YOU ARE LATE.
I'M SORRY. I GOT LOST.
THAT'S STRANGE, DESTINO GOT LOST TODAY AS WELL.
HUMM HUMM
......
ECCH...
AS I WAS SAYING, DESTINO.
I DON'T WANNA CHOOSE MY PROTECTOR YET.
AND DESTINO, YOU HAVEN'T BEEN ABLE TO DO IT YET.
DESTINO!
MY PROTECTOR MUST BE ABLE TO CONNECT COMPLETELY WITH MY MIND.

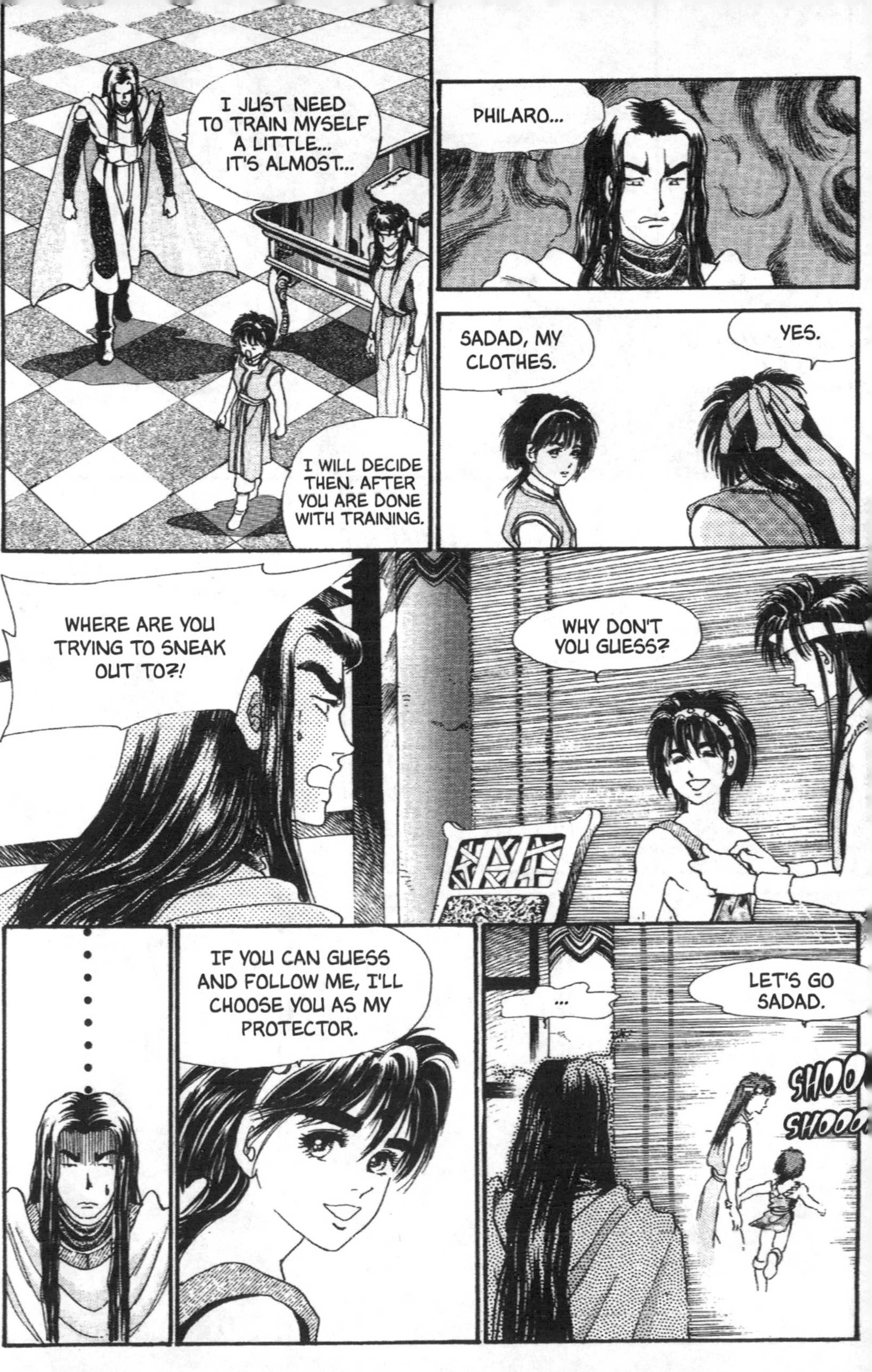
I JUST NEED TO TRAIN MYSELF A LITTLE... IT'S ALMOST...
I WILL DECIDE THEN. AFTER YOU ARE DONE WITH TRAINING.
PHILARO...
SADAD, MY CLOTHES.
YES.
WHERE ARE YOU TRYING TO SNEAK OUT TO?!
WHY DON'T YOU GUESS?
......
IF YOU CAN GUESS AND FOLLOW ME, I'LL CHOOSE YOU AS MY PROTECTOR.
...
LET'S GO SADAD.
SHOO
SHOOO

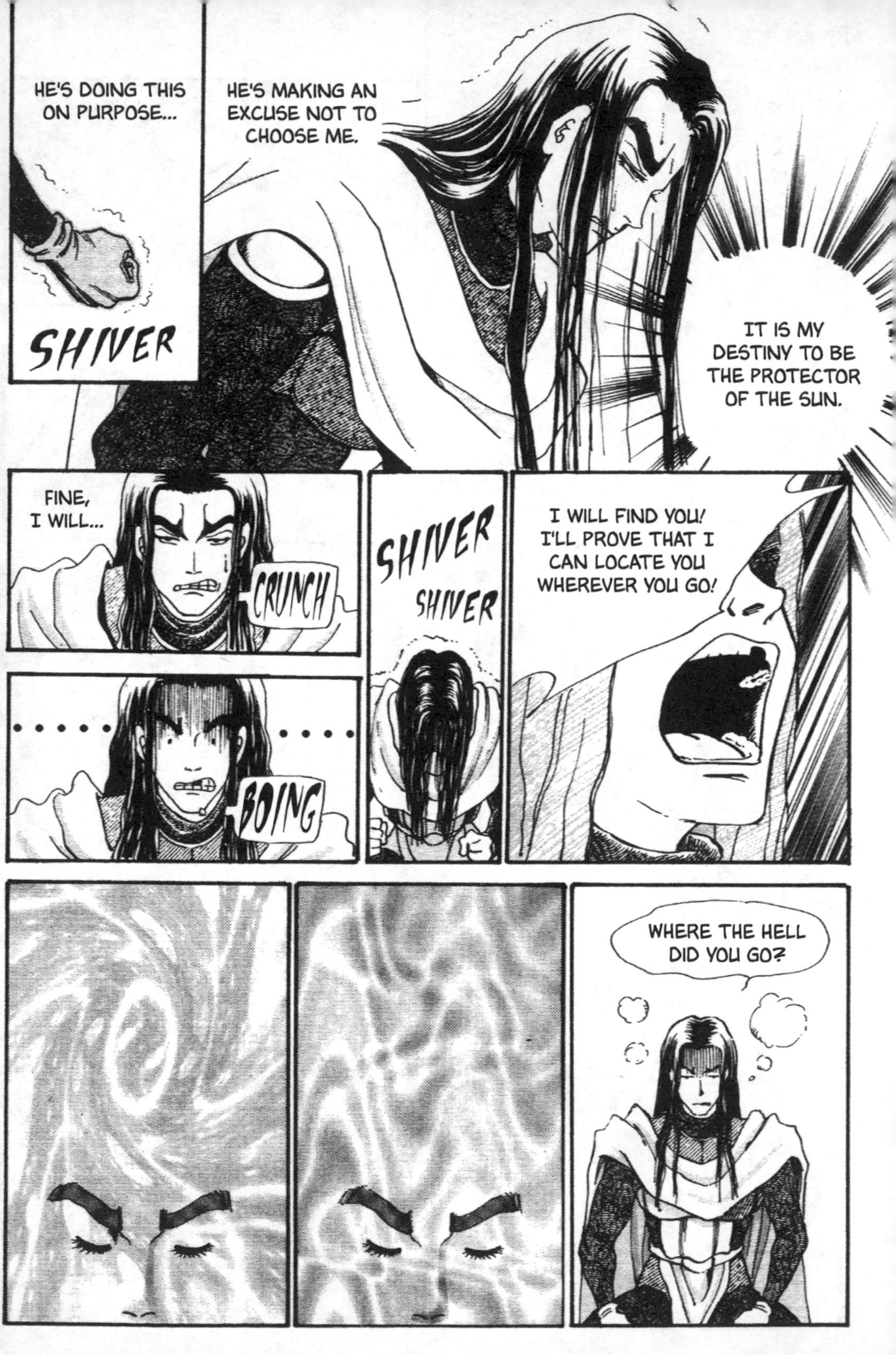

HE'S DOING THIS ON PURPOSE...
HE'S MAKING AN EXCUSE NOT TO CHOOSE ME.
SHIVER
IT IS MY DESTINY TO BE THE PROTECTOR OF THE SUN.
FINE, I WILL...
CRUNCH
SHIVER
SHIVER
I WILL FIND YOU! I'LL PROVE THAT I CAN LOCATE YOU WHEREVER YOU GO!
.....
.....
BOING
WHERE THE HELL DID YOU GO?

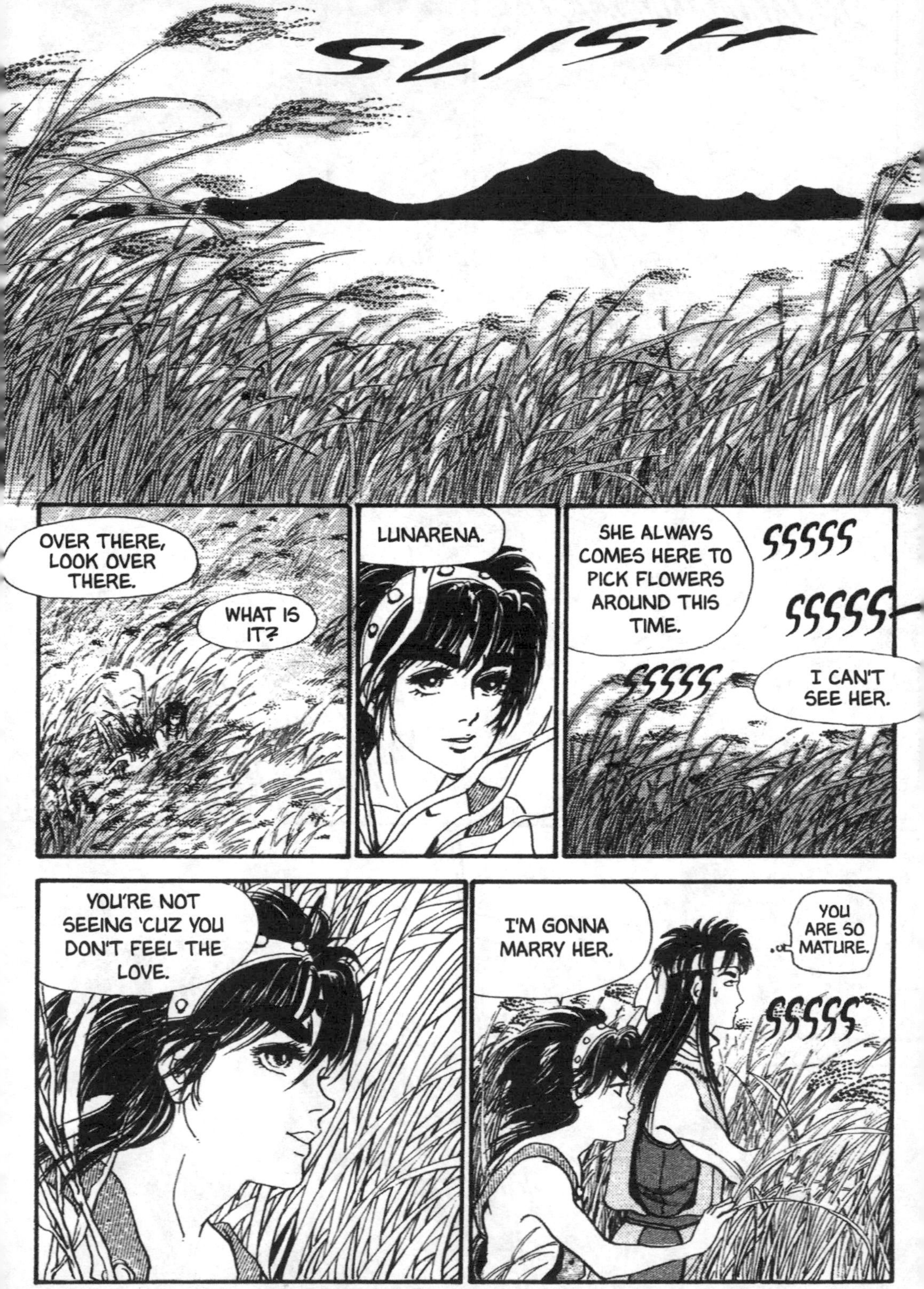
SLISH
OVER THERE, LOOK OVER THERE.
WHAT IS IT?
LUNARENA.
SHE ALWAYS COMES HERE TO PICK FLOWERS AROUND THIS TIME.
SSSSS
SSSSS
SSSSS
I CAN'T SEE HER.
YOU'RE NOT SEEING 'CUZ YOU DON'T FEEL THE LOVE.
I'M GONNA MARRY HER.
YOU ARE SO MATURE.
SSSSS

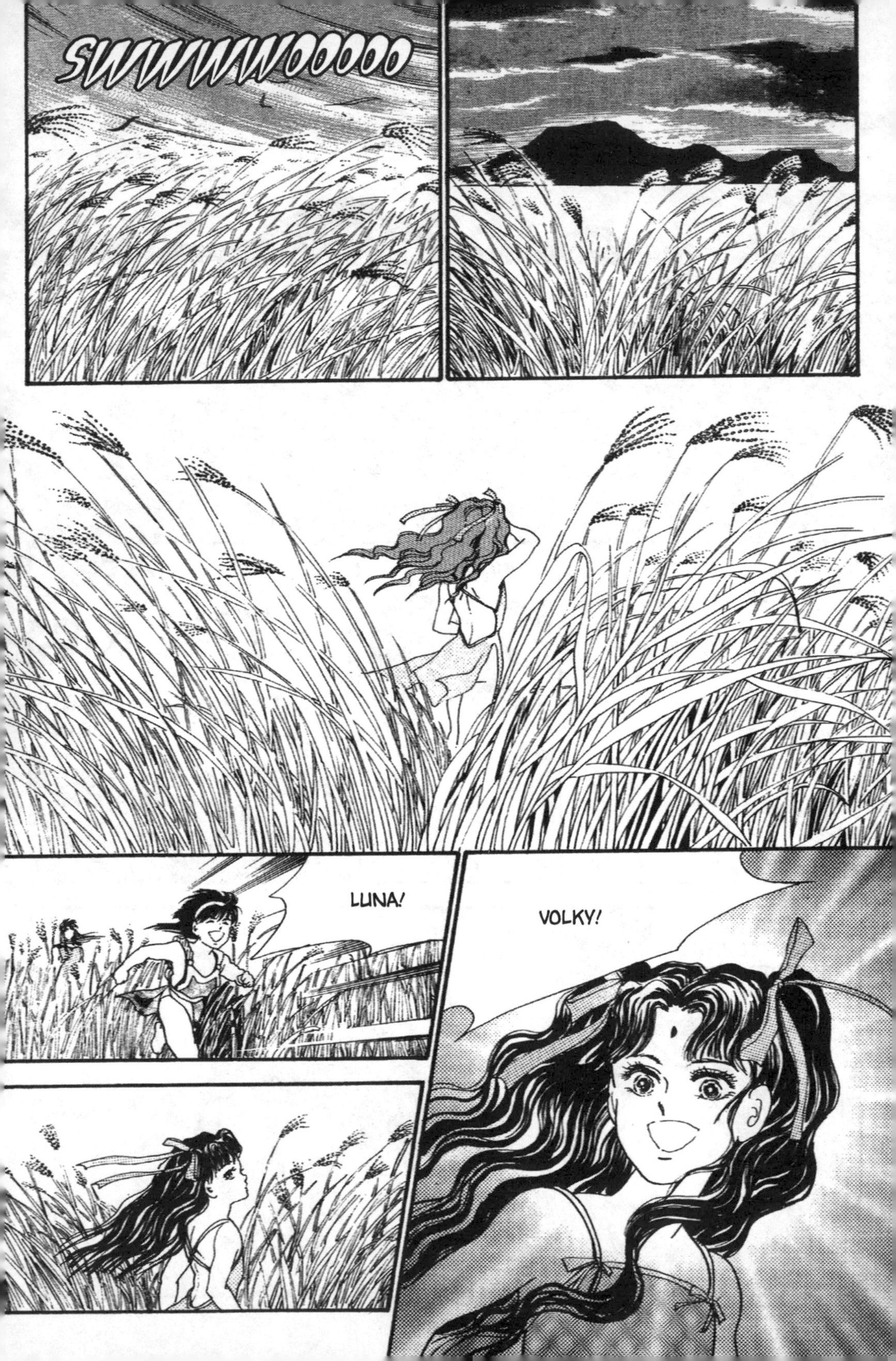
SWWWWOOOOO
LUNA!
VOLKY!

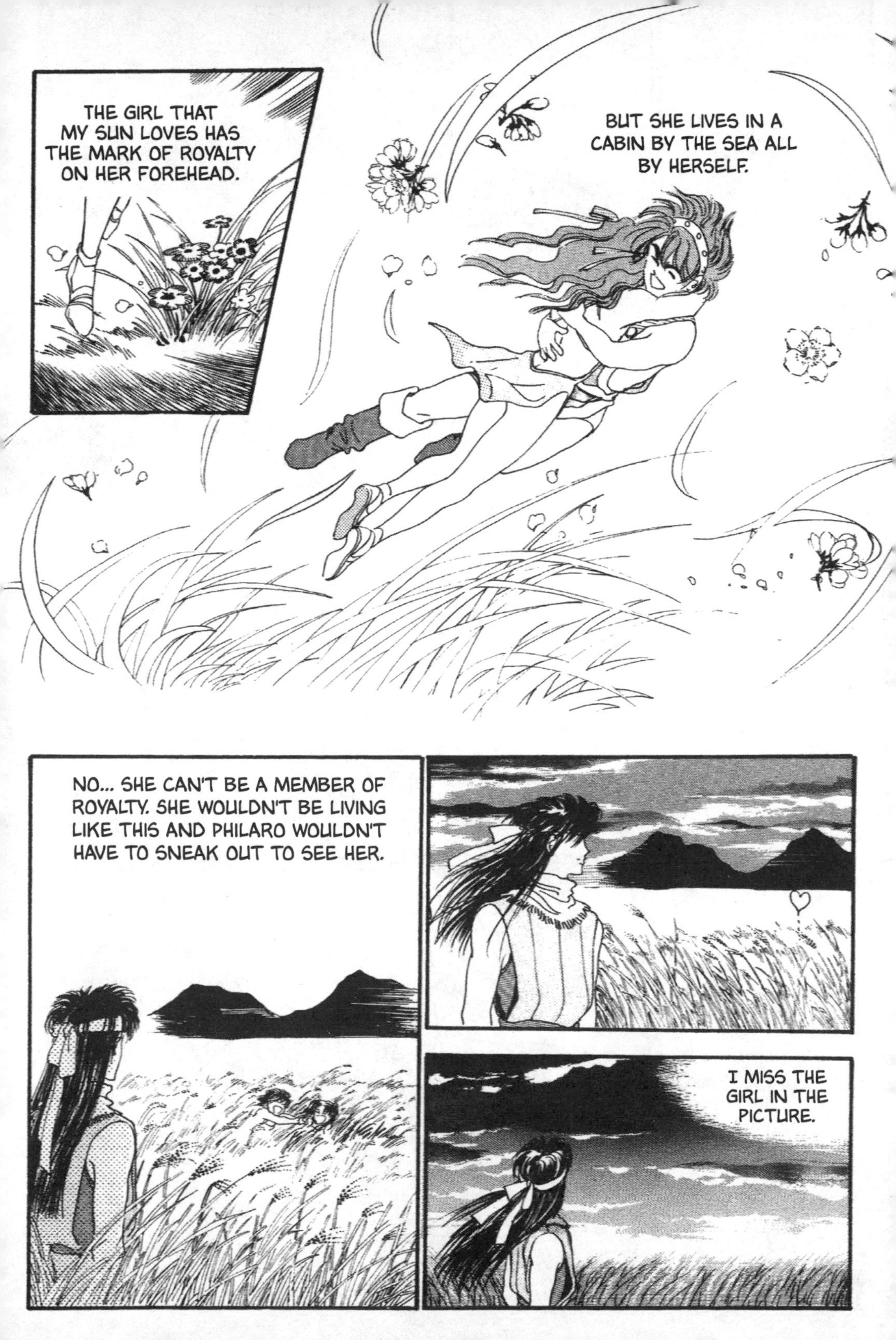
THE GIRL THAT MY SUN LOVES HAS THE MARK OF ROYALTY ON HER FOREHEAD.
BUT SHE LIVES IN A CABIN BY THE SEA ALL BY HERSELF.
NO... SHE CAN'T BE A MEMBER OF ROYALTY. SHE WOULDN'T BE LIVING LIKE THIS AND PHILARO WOULDN'T HAVE TO SNEAK OUT TO SEE HER.
I MISS THE GIRL IN THE PICTURE.

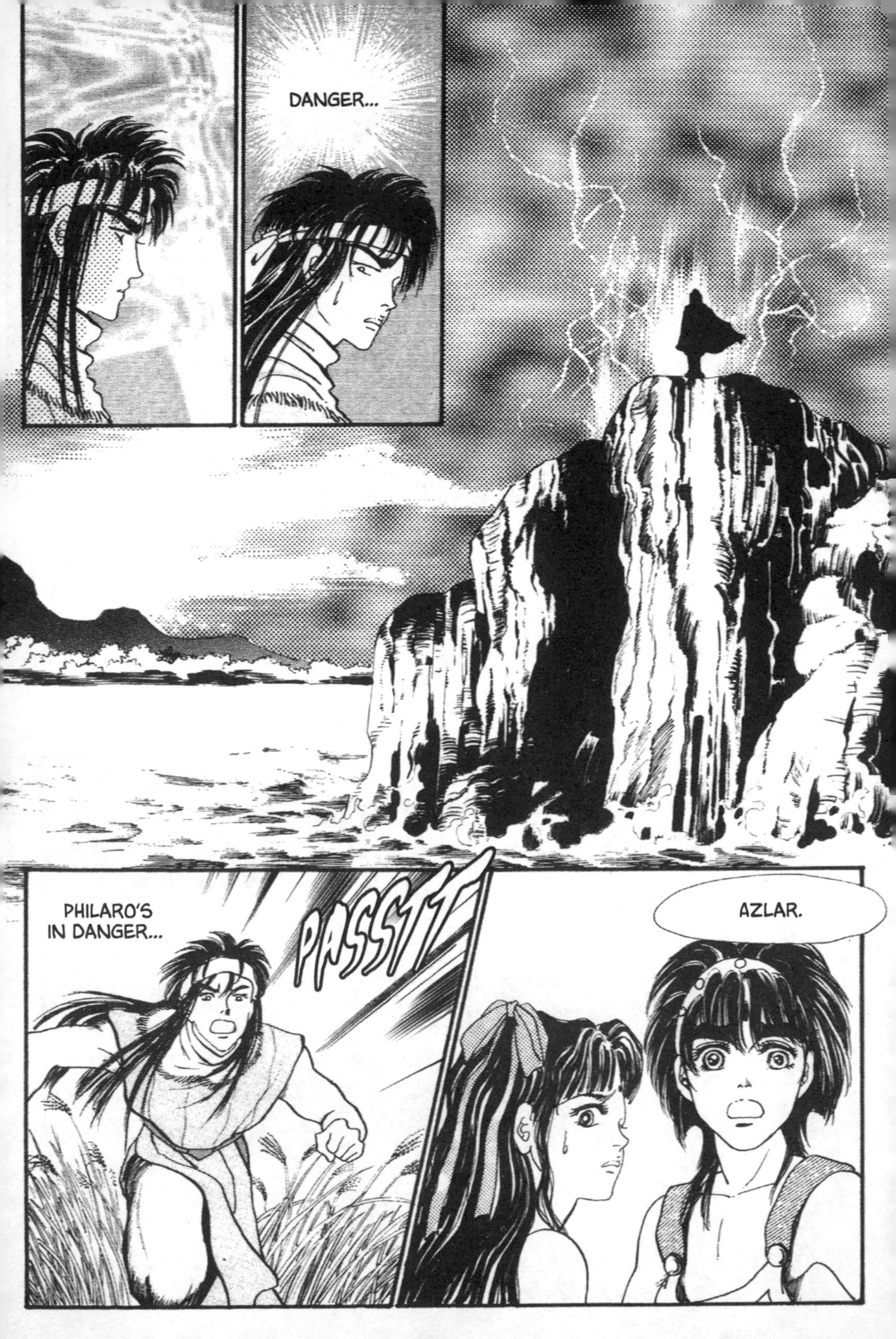
DANGER...
PHILARO'S IN DANGER...
PASSTT
AZLAR.

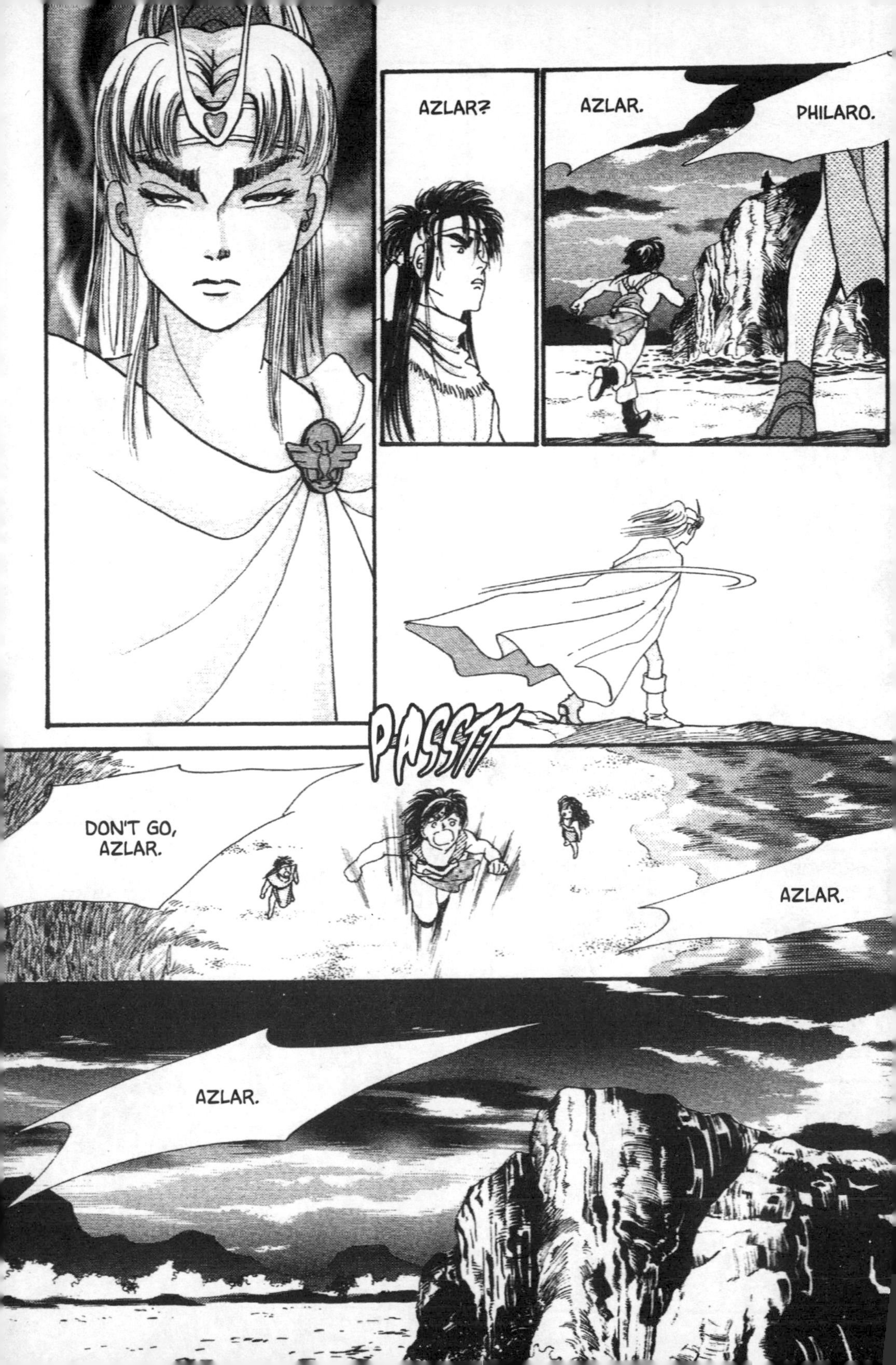
PHILARO.
AZLAR.
AZLAR?
PASSTT
AZLAR.
DON'T GO, AZLAR.
AZLAR.

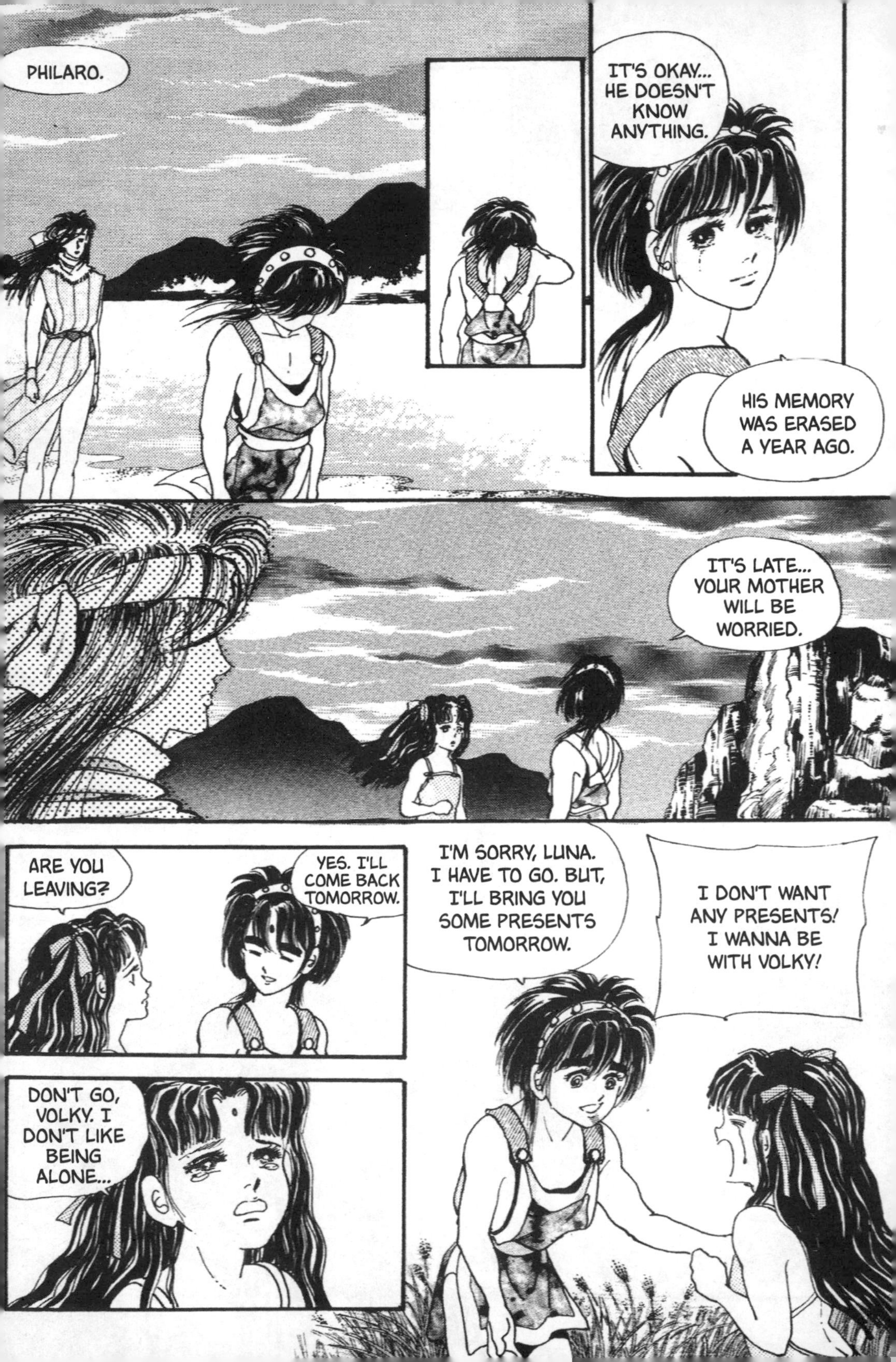
PHILARO.
IT'S OKAY... HE DOESN'T KNOW ANYTHING.
HIS MEMORY WAS ERASED A YEAR AGO.
IT'S LATE... YOUR MOTHER WILL BE WORRIED.
ARE YOU LEAVING?
YES. I'LL COME BACK TOMORROW.
DON'T GO, VOLKY. I DON'T LIKE BEING ALONE...
I'M SORRY, LUNA. I HAVE TO GO. BUT, I'LL BRING YOU SOME PRESENTS TOMORROW.
I DON'T WANT ANY PRESENTS! I WANNA BE WITH VOLKY!

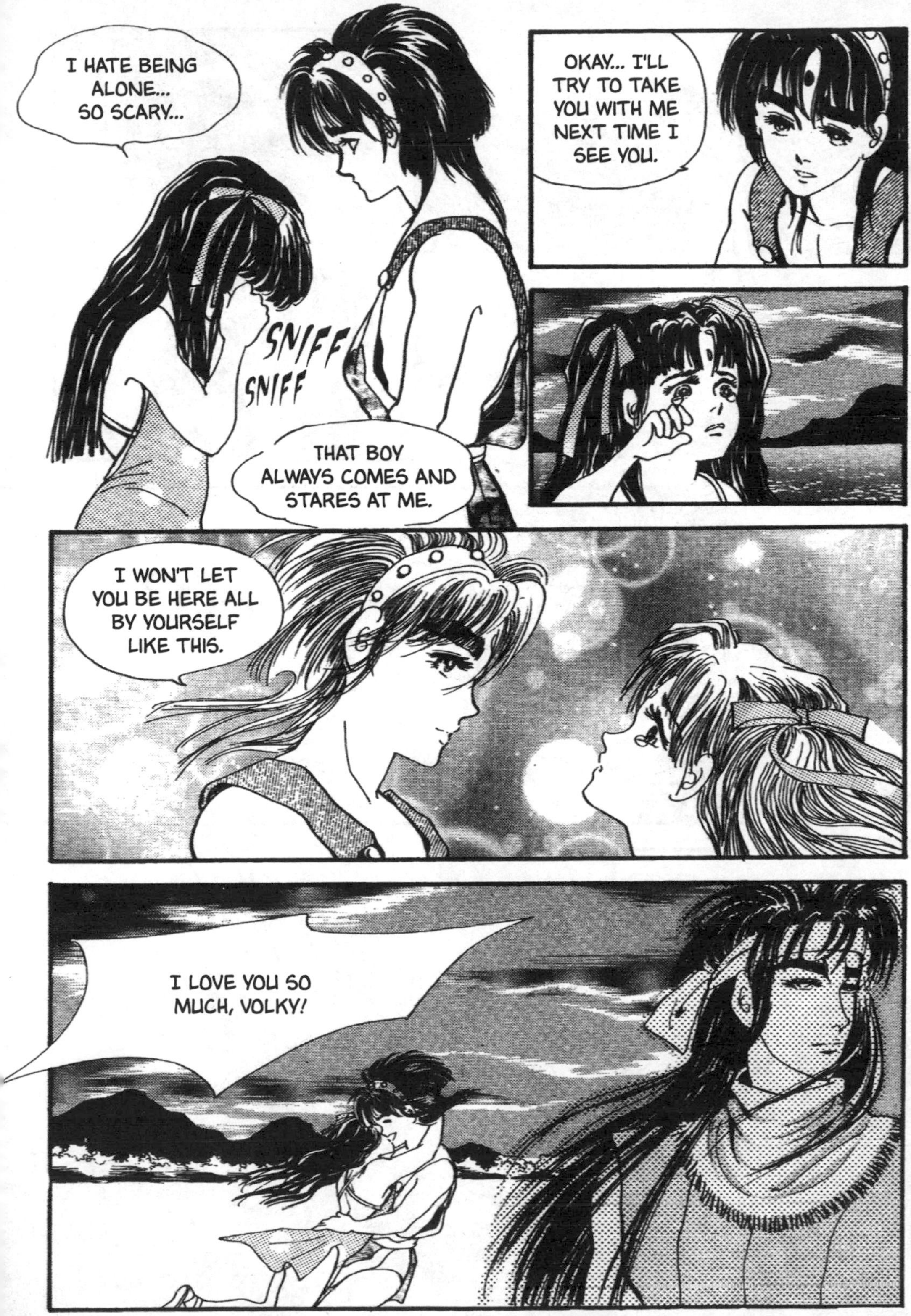

I HATE BEING ALONE... SO SCARY...
SNIFF SNIFF
THAT BOY ALWAYS COMES AND STARES AT ME.
OKAY... I'LL TRY TO TAKE YOU WITH ME NEXT TIME I SEE YOU.
I WON'T LET YOU BE HERE ALL BY YOURSELF LIKE THIS.
I LOVE YOU SO MUCH, VOLKY!

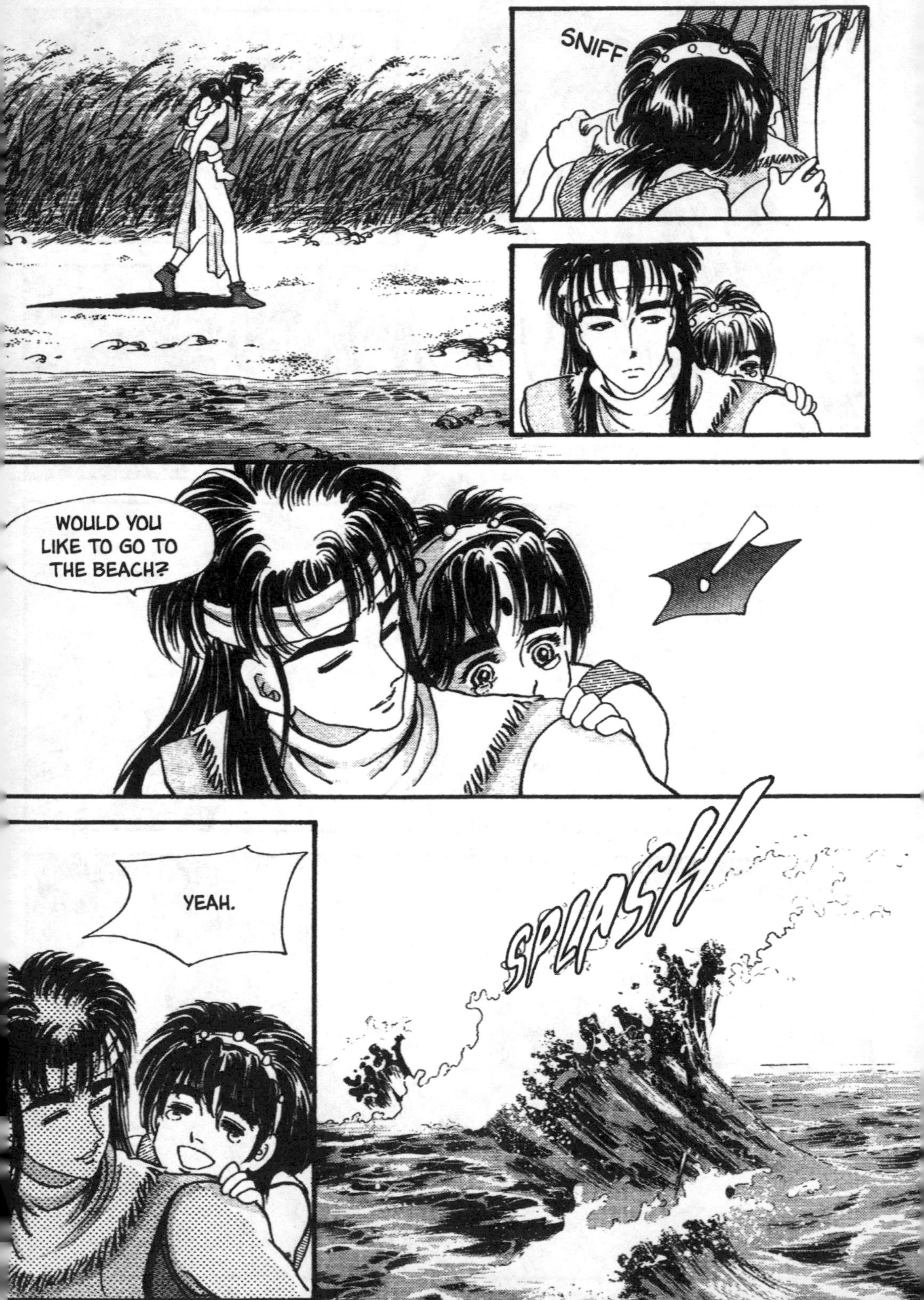
SNIFF
WOULD YOU LIKE TO GO TO THE BEACH?
!
YEAH.
SPLASH

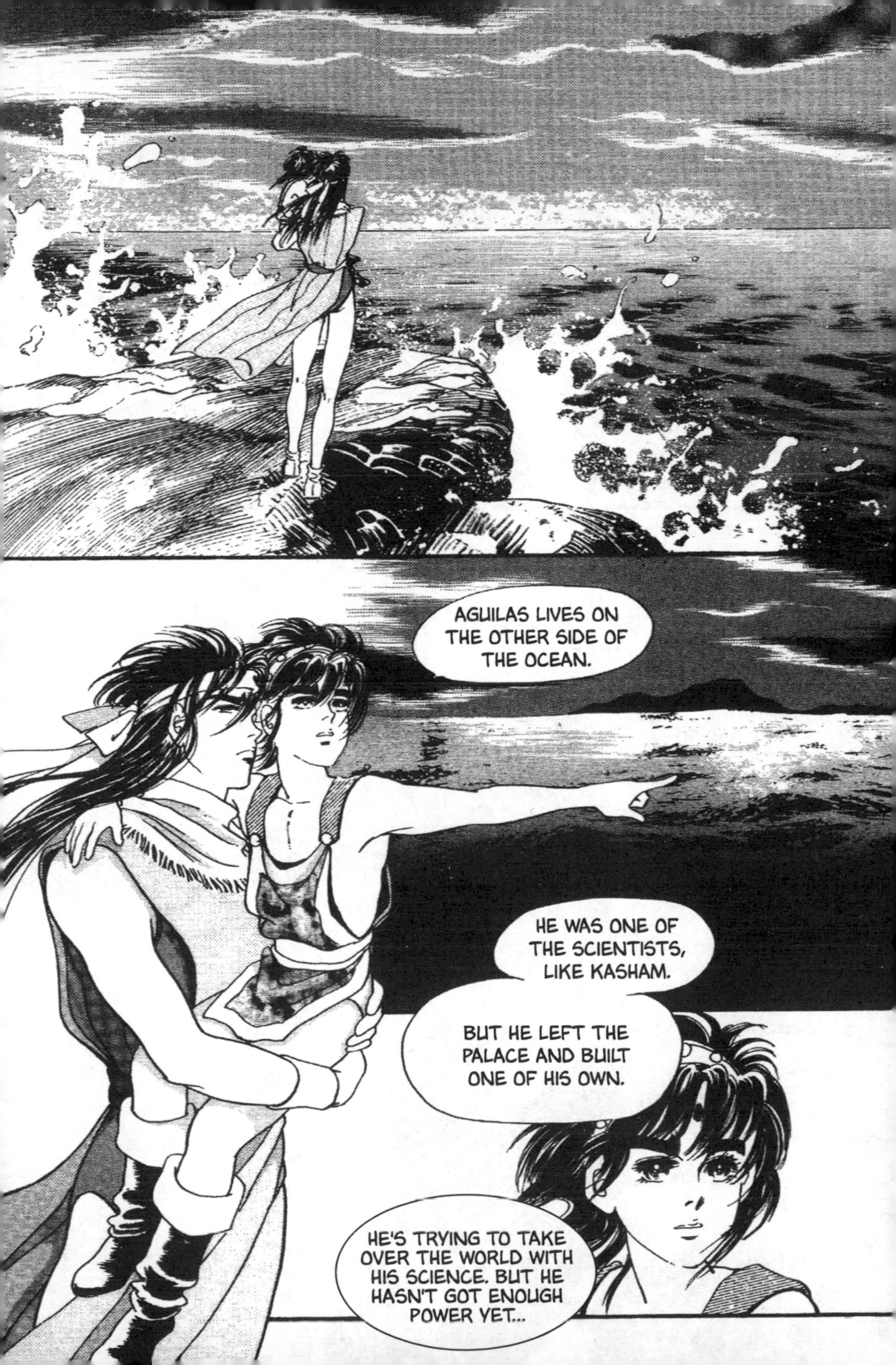
AGUILAS LIVES ON THE OTHER SIDE OF THE OCEAN.
HE WAS ONE OF THE SCIENTISTS, LIKE KASHAM.
BUT HE LEFT THE PALACE AND BUILT ONE OF HIS OWN.
HE'S TRYING TO TAKE OVER THE WORLD WITH HIS SCIENCE. BUT HE HASN'T GOT ENOUGH POWER YET...

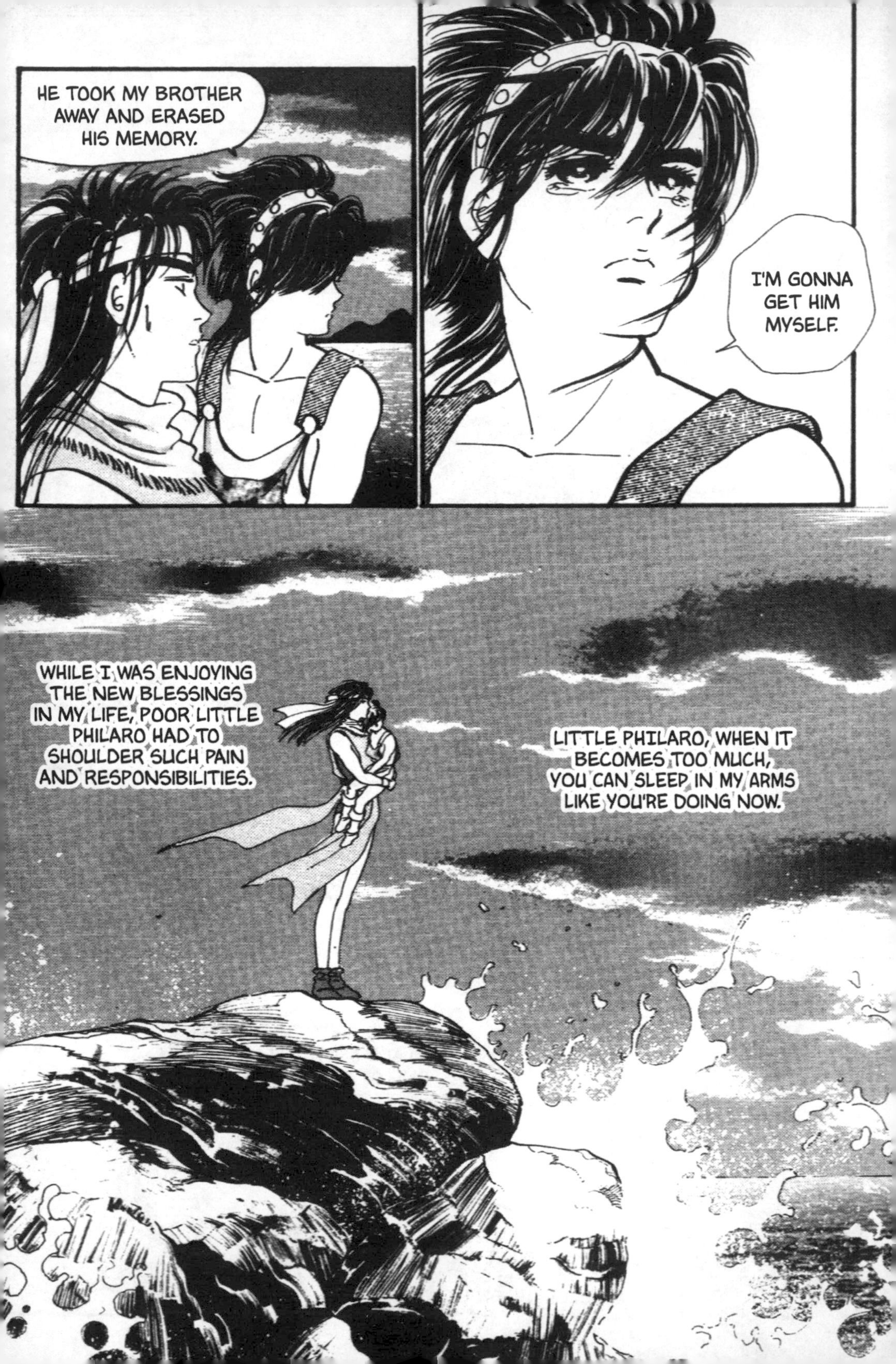
HE TOOK MY BROTHER AWAY AND ERASED HIS MEMORY.
I'M GONNA GET HIM MYSELF.
WHILE I WAS ENJOYING THE NEW BLESSINGS IN MY LIFE, POOR LITTLE PHILARO HAD TO SHOULDER SUCH PAIN AND RESPONSIBILITIES.
LITTLE PHILARO, WHEN IT BECOMES TOO MUCH, YOU CAN SLEEP IN MY ARMS LIKE YOU'RE DOING NOW.

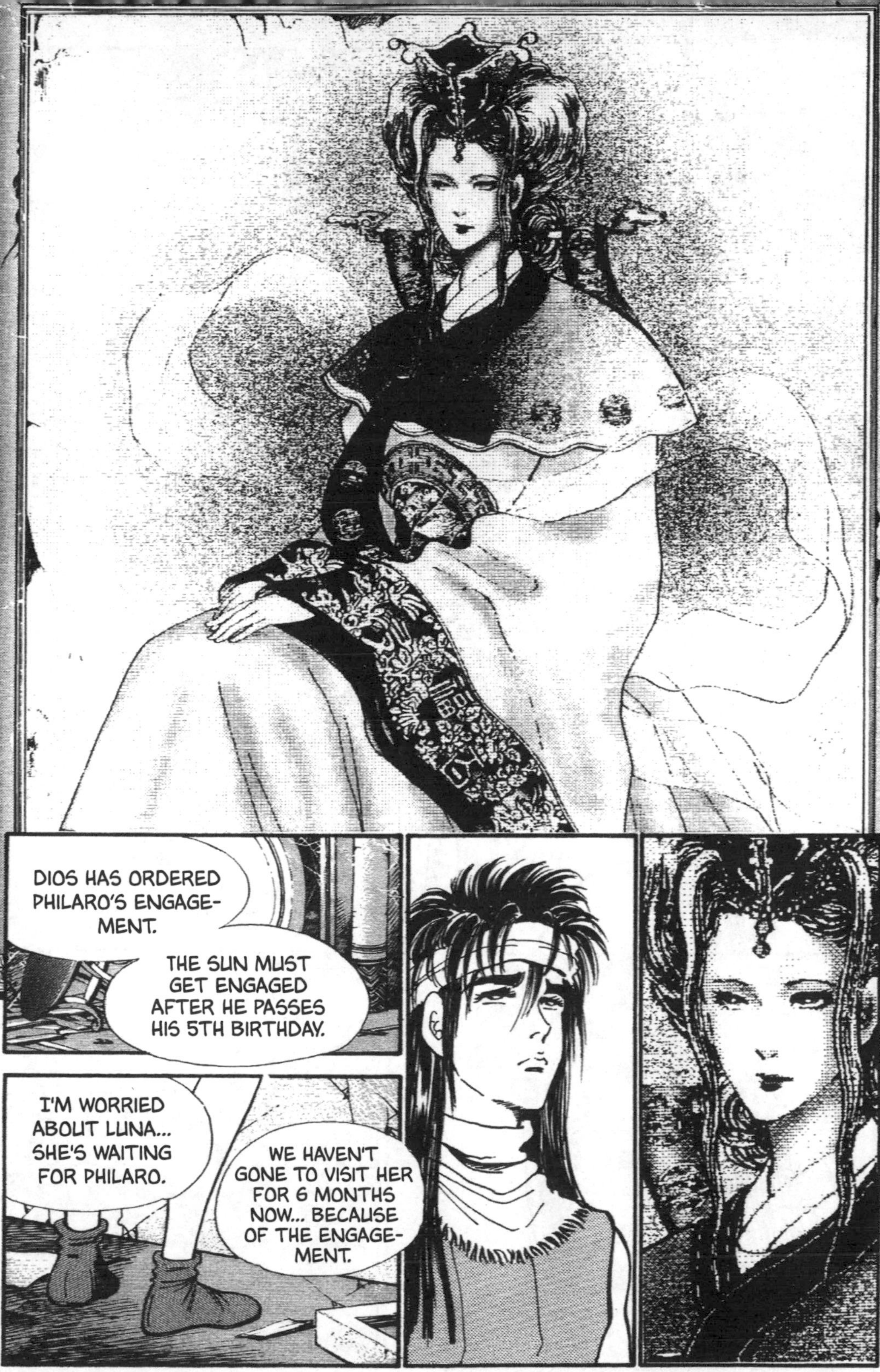
DIOS HAS ORDERED PHILARO'S ENGAGEMENT.
THE SUN MUST GET ENGAGED AFTER HE PASSES HIS 5TH BIRTHDAY.
I'M WORRIED ABOUT LUNA... SHE'S WAITING FOR PHILARO.
WE HAVEN'T GONE TO VISIT HER FOR 6 MONTHS NOW... BECAUSE OF THE ENGAGEMENT.

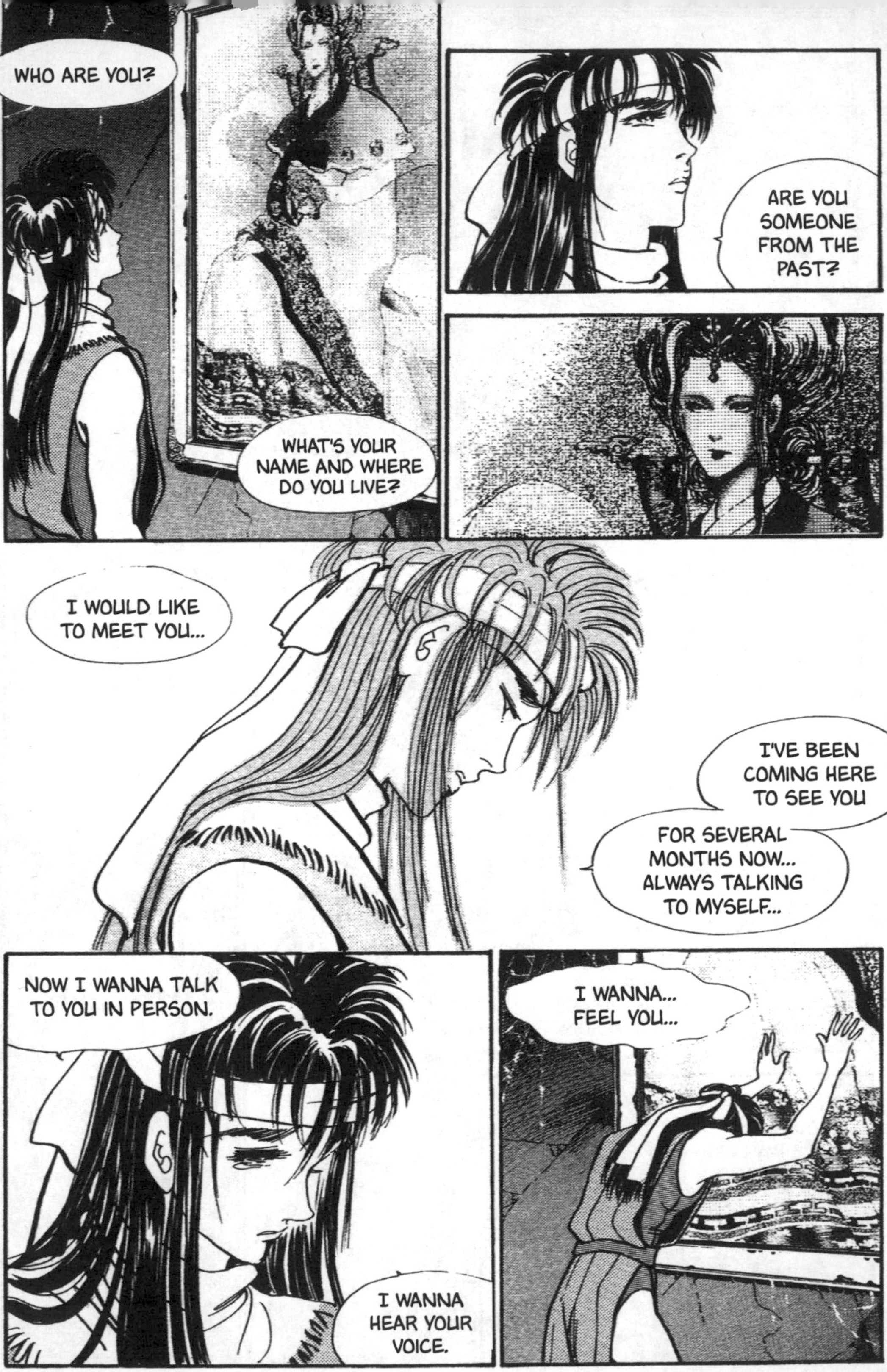
WHO ARE YOU?
WHAT'S YOUR NAME AND WHERE DO YOU LIVE?
ARE YOU SOMEONE FROM THE PAST?
I WOULD LIKE TO MEET YOU...
I'VE BEEN COMING HERE TO SEE YOU
FOR SEVERAL MONTHS NOW... ALWAYS TALKING TO MYSELF...
NOW I WANNA TALK TO YOU IN PERSON.
I WANNA HEAR YOUR VOICE.
I WANNA... FEEL YOU...

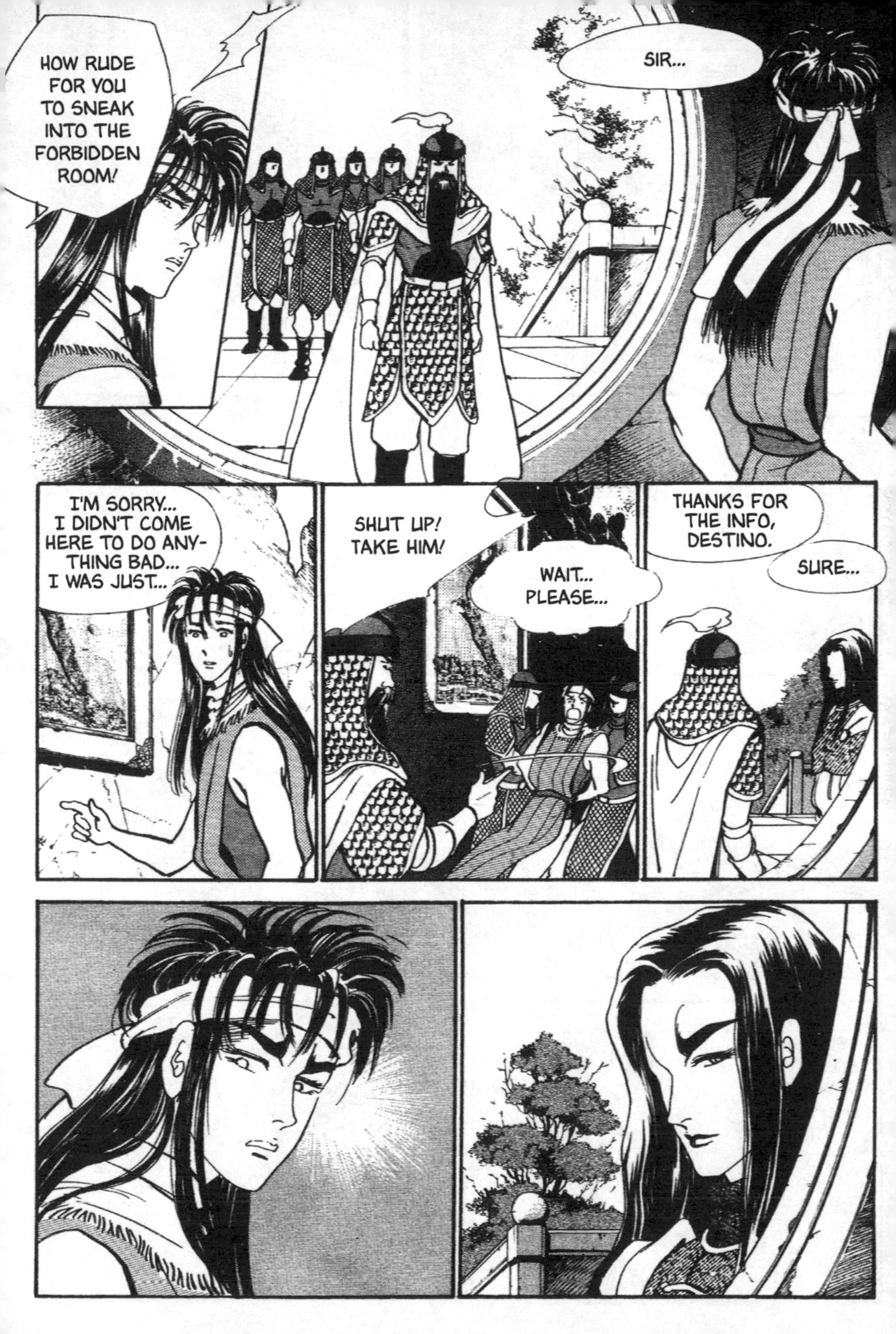
HOW RUDE FOR YOU TO SNEAK INTO THE FORBIDDEN ROOM!
SIR...
I'M SORRY... I DIDN'T COME HERE TO DO ANYTHING BAD... I WAS JUST...
SHUT UP! TAKE HIM!
WAIT... PLEASE...
THANKS FOR THE INFO, DESTINO.
SURE...

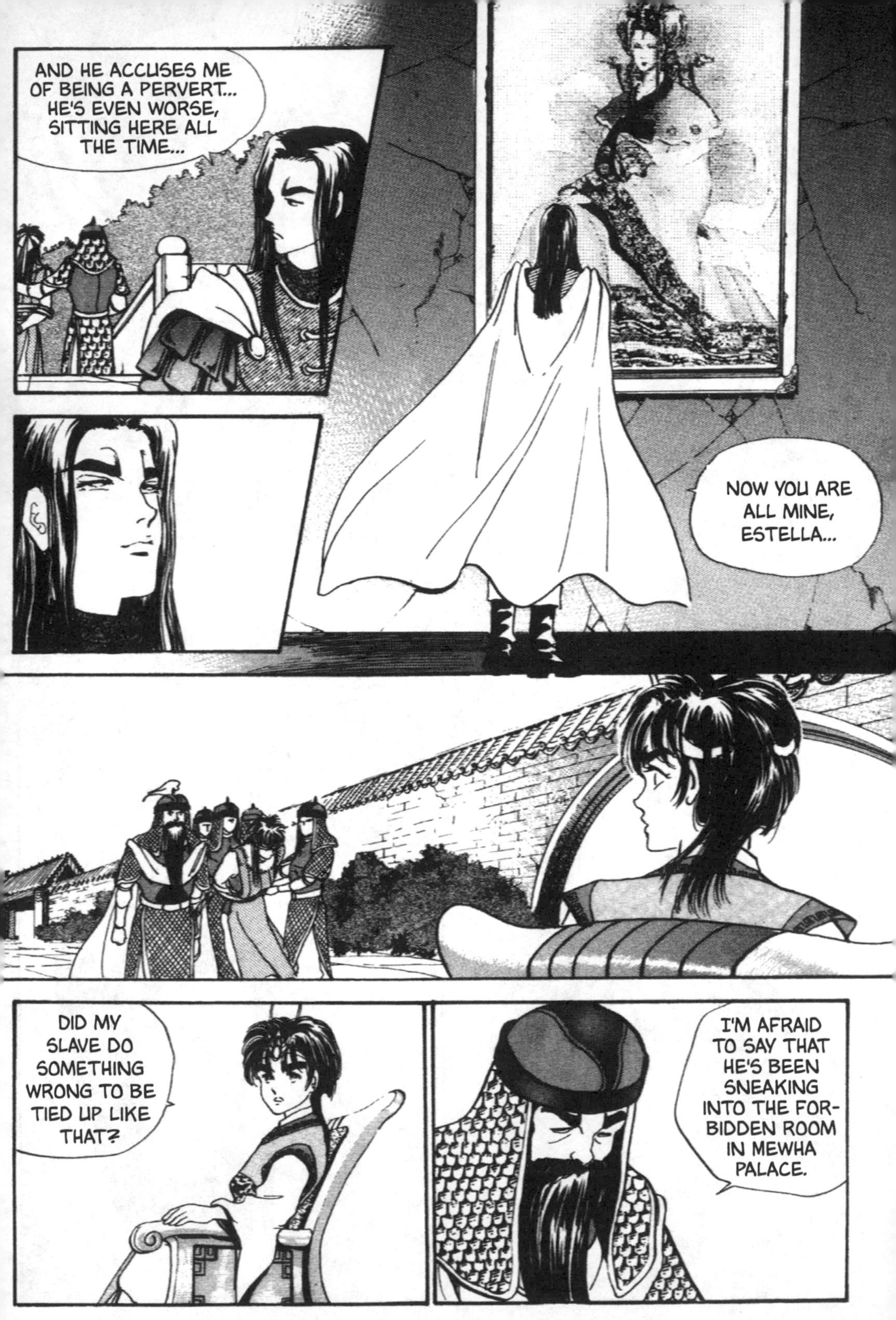
AND HE ACCUSES ME OF BEING A PERVERT... HE'S EVEN WORSE, SITTING HERE ALL THE TIME...
NOW YOU ARE ALL MINE, ESTELLA...
DID MY SLAVE DO SOMETHING WRONG TO BE TIED UP LIKE THAT?
I'M AFRAID TO SAY THAT HE'S BEEN SNEAKING INTO THE FOR-BIDDEN ROOM IN MEWHA PALACE.

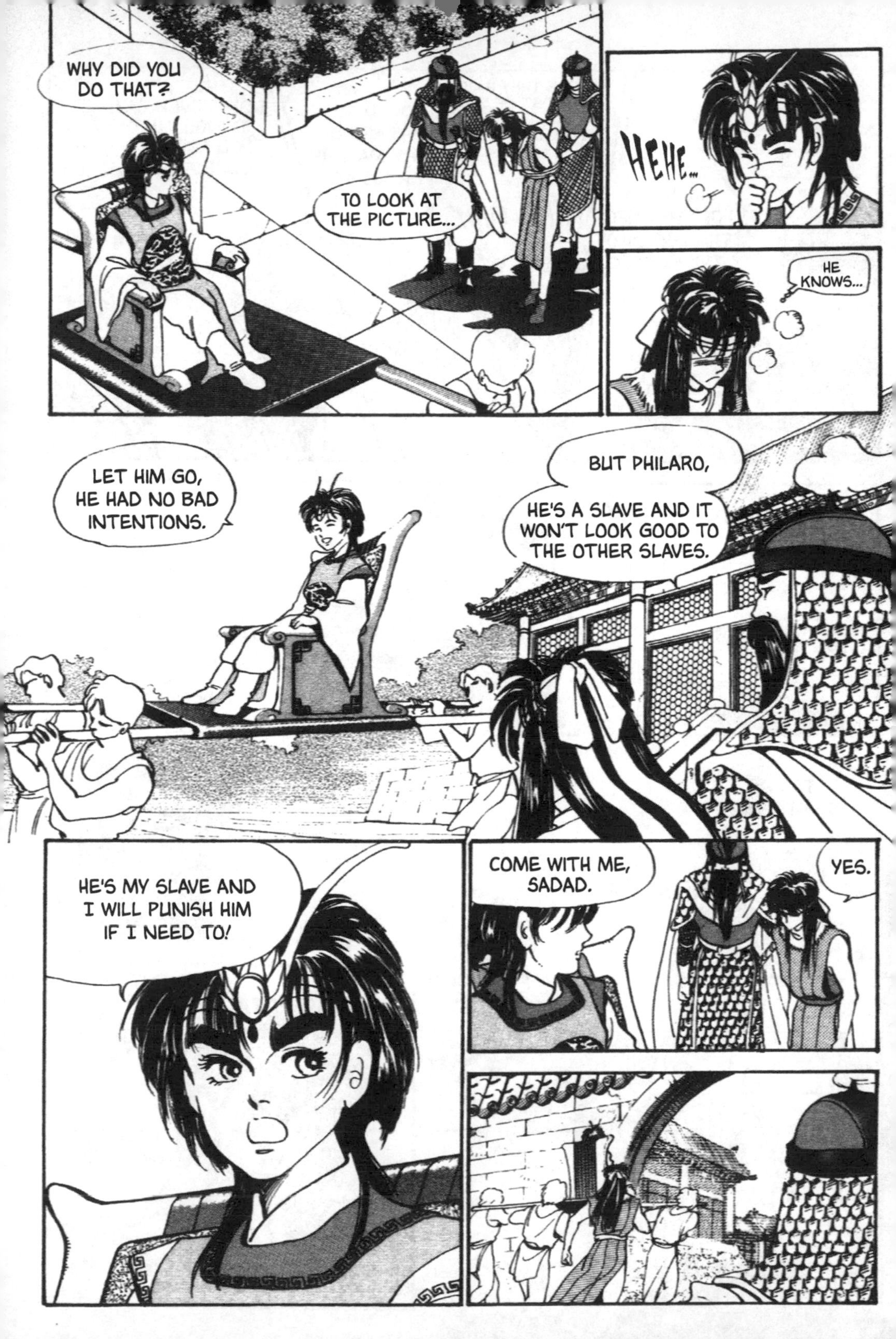
WHY DID YOU DO THAT?
TO LOOK AT THE PICTURE...
HEHE...
HE KNOWS...
LET HIM GO, HE HAD NO BAD INTENTIONS.
BUT PHILARO,
HE'S A SLAVE AND IT WON'T LOOK GOOD TO THE OTHER SLAVES.
HE'S MY SLAVE AND I WILL PUNISH HIM IF I NEED TO!
COME WITH ME, SADAD.
YES.

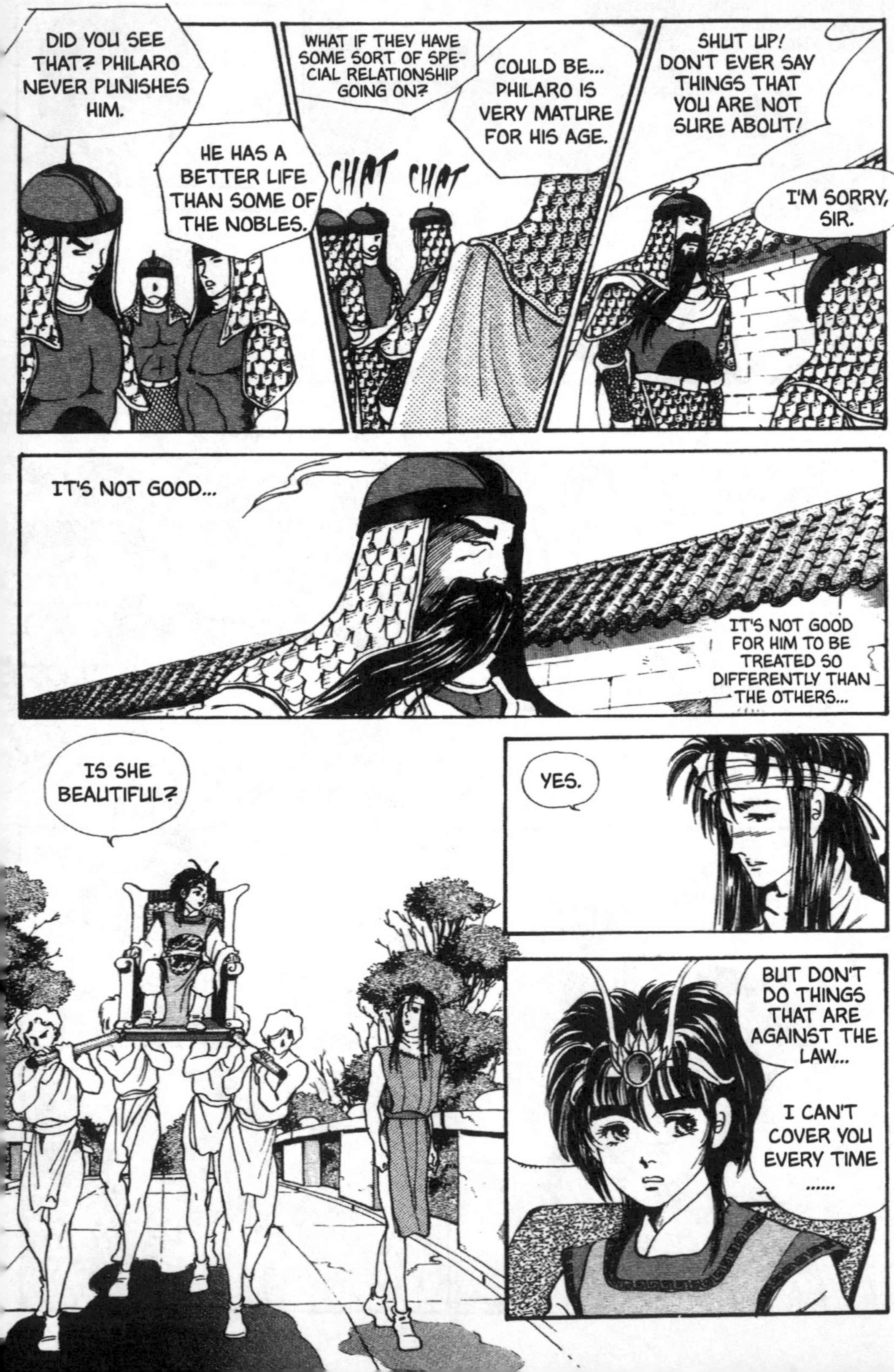
DID YOU SEE THAT? PHILARO NEVER PUNISHES HIM.
HE HAS A BETTER LIFE THAN SOME OF THE NOBLES.
WHAT IF THEY HAVE SOME SORT OF SPE-CIAL RELATIONSHIP GOING ON?
CHAT CHAT
COULD BE... PHILARO IS VERY MATURE FOR HIS AGE.
SHUT UP! DON'T EVER SAY THINGS THAT YOU ARE NOT SURE ABOUT!
I'M SORRY, SIR.
IT'S NOT GOOD...
IT'S NOT GOOD FOR HIM TO BE TREATED SO DIFFERENTLY THAN THE OTHERS...
IS SHE BEAUTIFUL?
YES.
BUT DON'T DO THINGS THAT ARE AGAINST THE LAW...
I CAN'T COVER YOU EVERY TIME ......

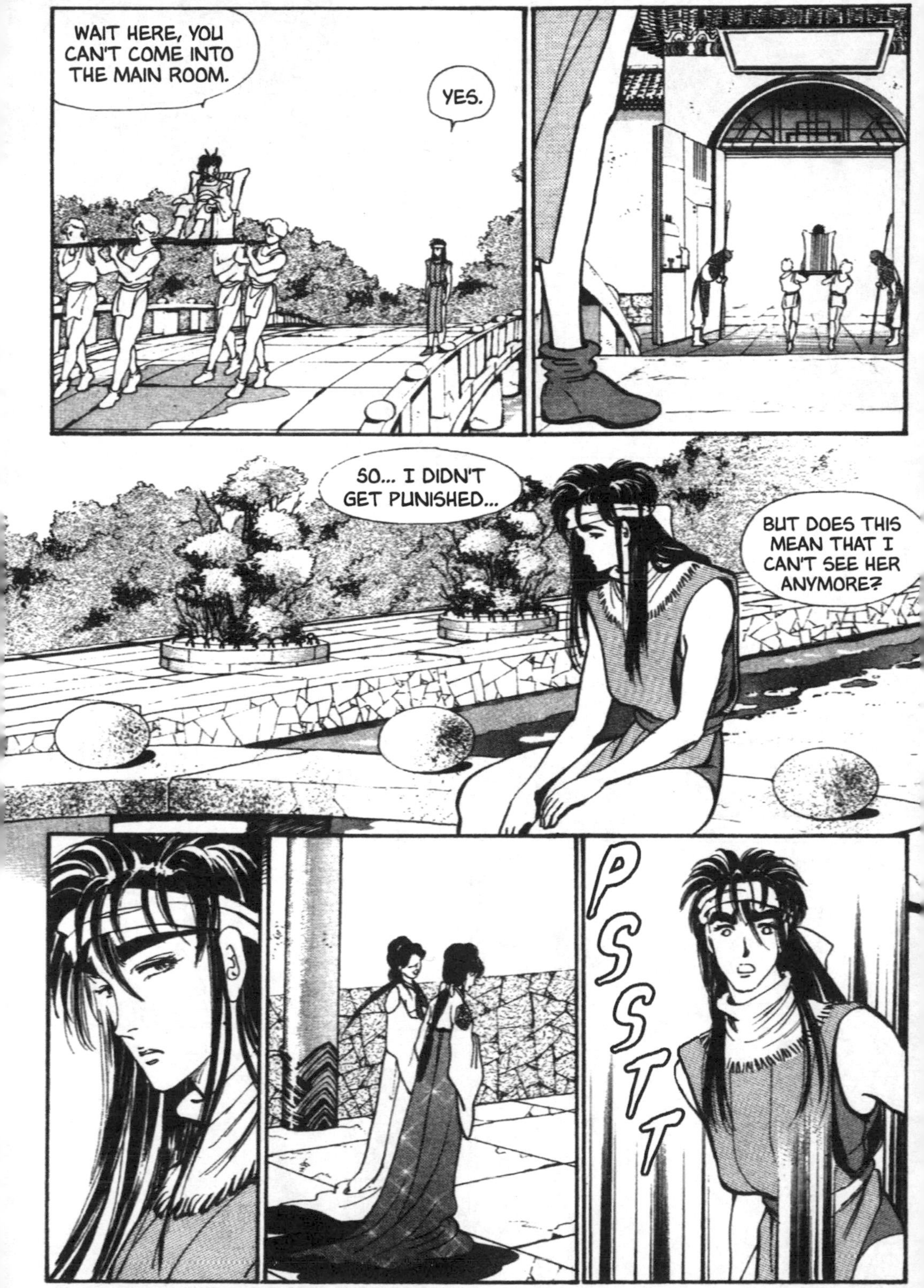
WAIT HERE, YOU CAN'T COME INTO THE MAIN ROOM.
YES.
SO... I DIDN'T GET PUNISHED...
BUT DOES THIS MEAN THAT I CAN'T SEE HER ANYMORE?
PSSTT

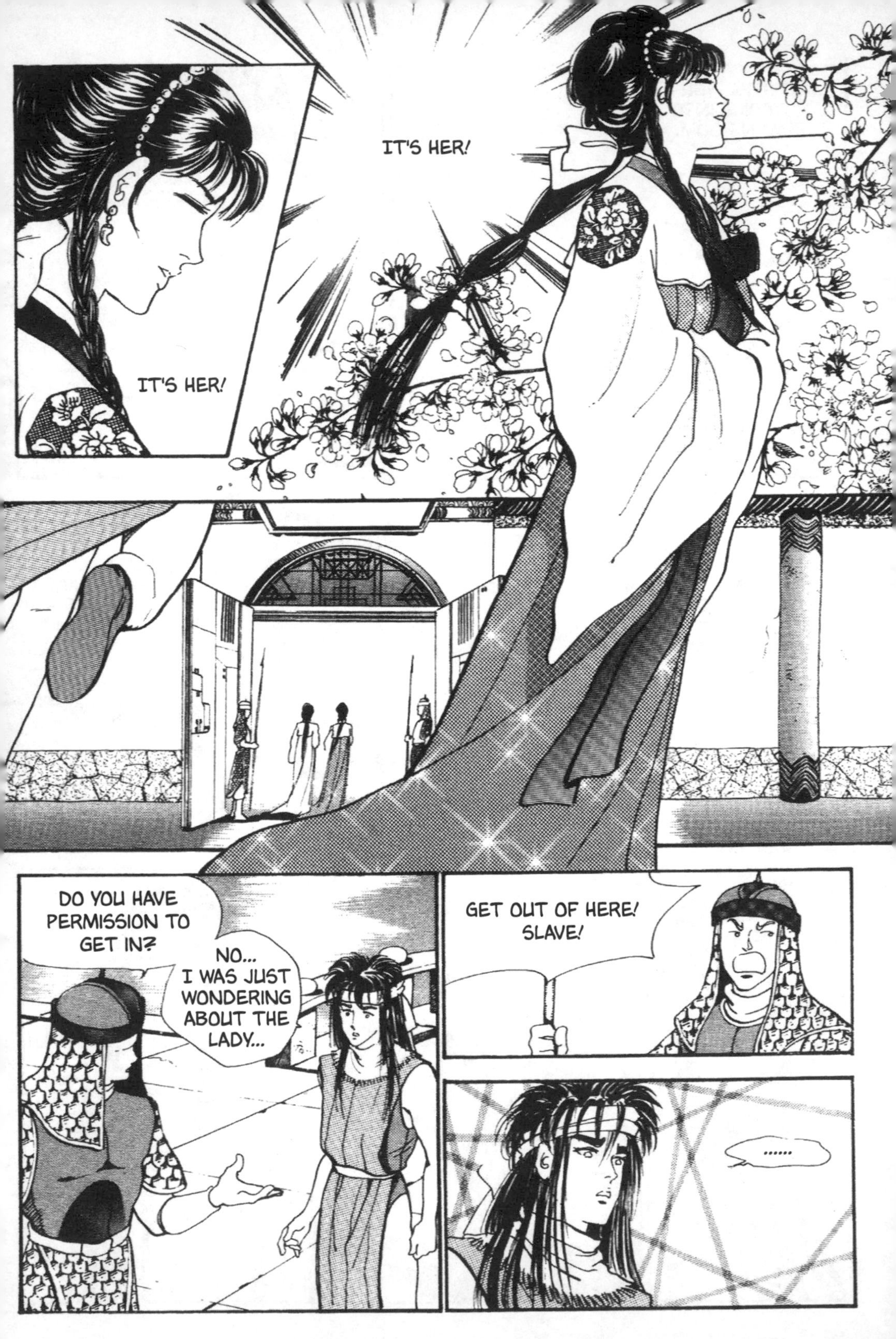
IT'S HER!
IT'S HER!
DO YOU HAVE PERMISSION TO GET IN?
NO... I WAS JUST WONDERING ABOUT THE LADY...
GET OUT OF HERE! SLAVE!
......

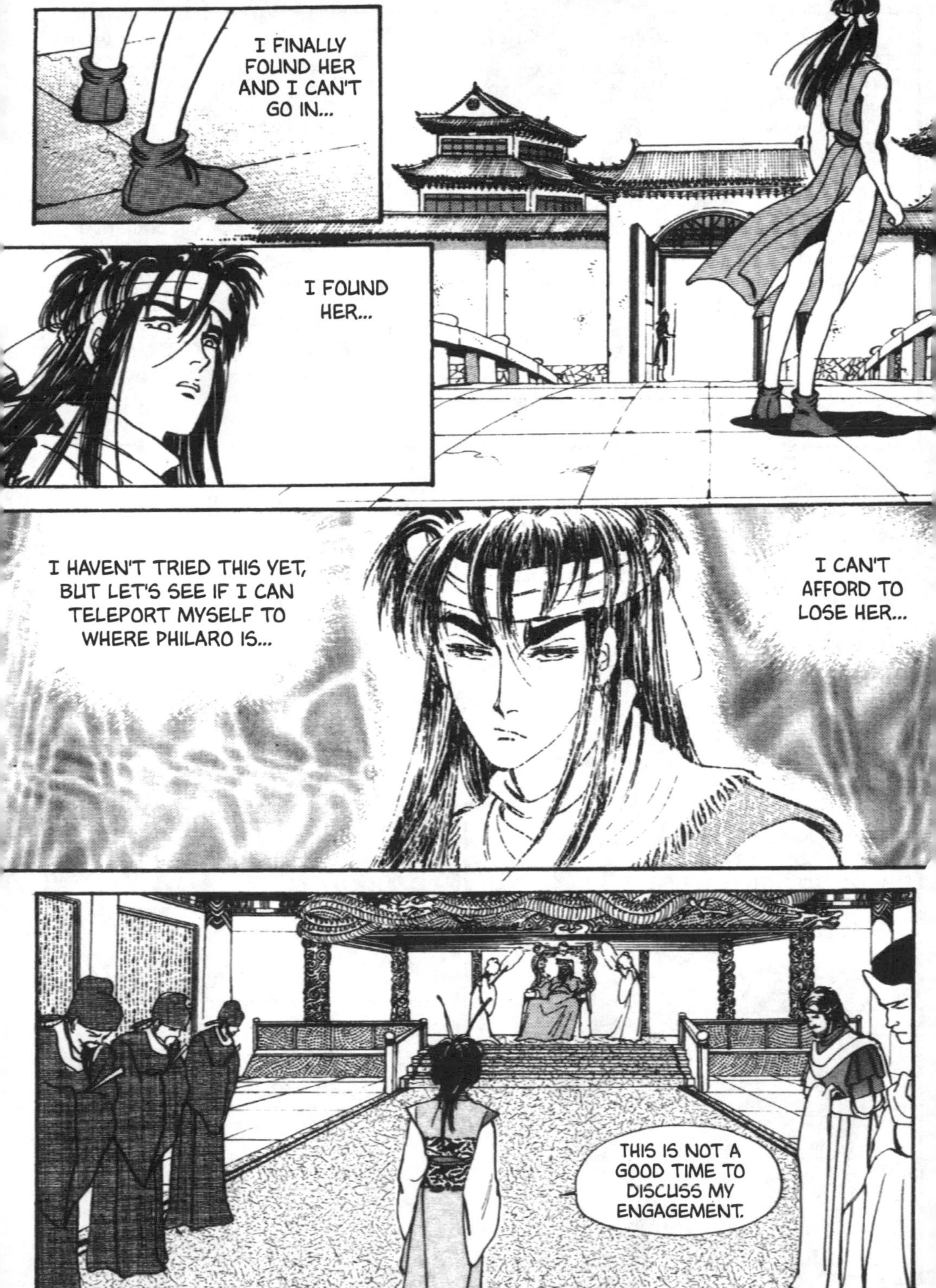
I FINALLY FOUND HER AND I CAN'T GO IN...
I FOUND HER...
I CAN'T AFFORD TO LOSE HER...
I HAVEN'T TRIED THIS YET, BUT LET'S SEE IF I CAN TELEPORT MYSELF TO WHERE PHILARO IS...
THIS IS NOT A GOOD TIME TO DISCUSS MY ENGAGEMENT.

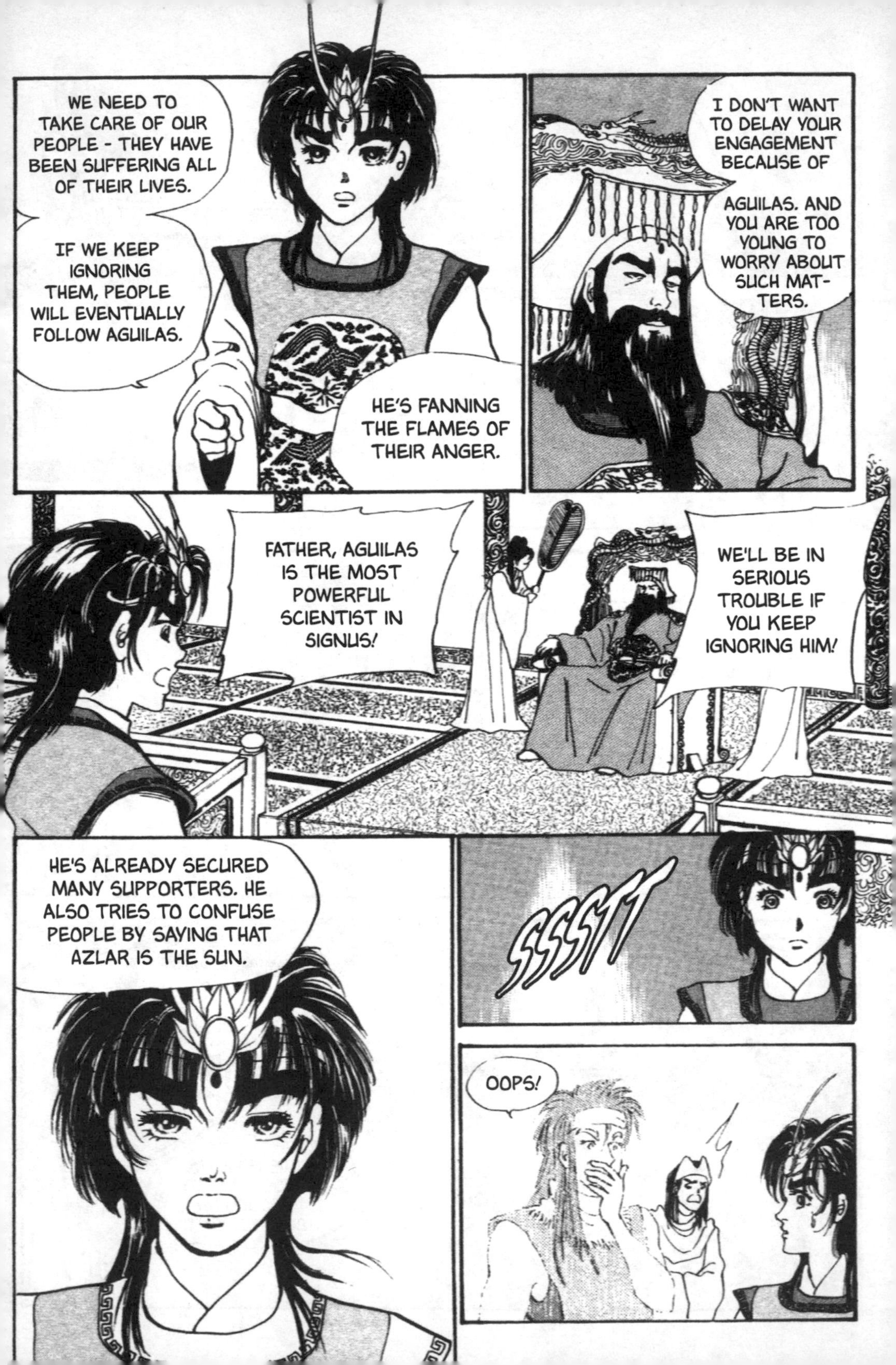
WE NEED TO TAKE CARE OF OUR PEOPLE - THEY HAVE BEEN SUFFERING ALL OF THEIR LIVES.
IF WE KEEP IGNORING THEM, PEOPLE WILL EVENTUALLY FOLLOW AGUILAS.
HE'S FANNING THE FLAMES OF THEIR ANGER.
I DON'T WANT TO DELAY YOUR ENGAGEMENT BECAUSE OF
AGUILAS. AND YOU ARE TOO YOUNG TO WORRY ABOUT SUCH MAT-TERS.
FATHER, AGUILAS IS THE MOST POWERFUL SCIENTIST IN SIGNUS!
WE'LL BE IN SERIOUS TROUBLE IF YOU KEEP IGNORING HIM!
HE'S ALREADY SECURED MANY SUPPORTERS. HE ALSO TRIES TO CONFUSE PEOPLE BY SAYING THAT AZLAR IS THE SUN.
SSSTT
OOPS!

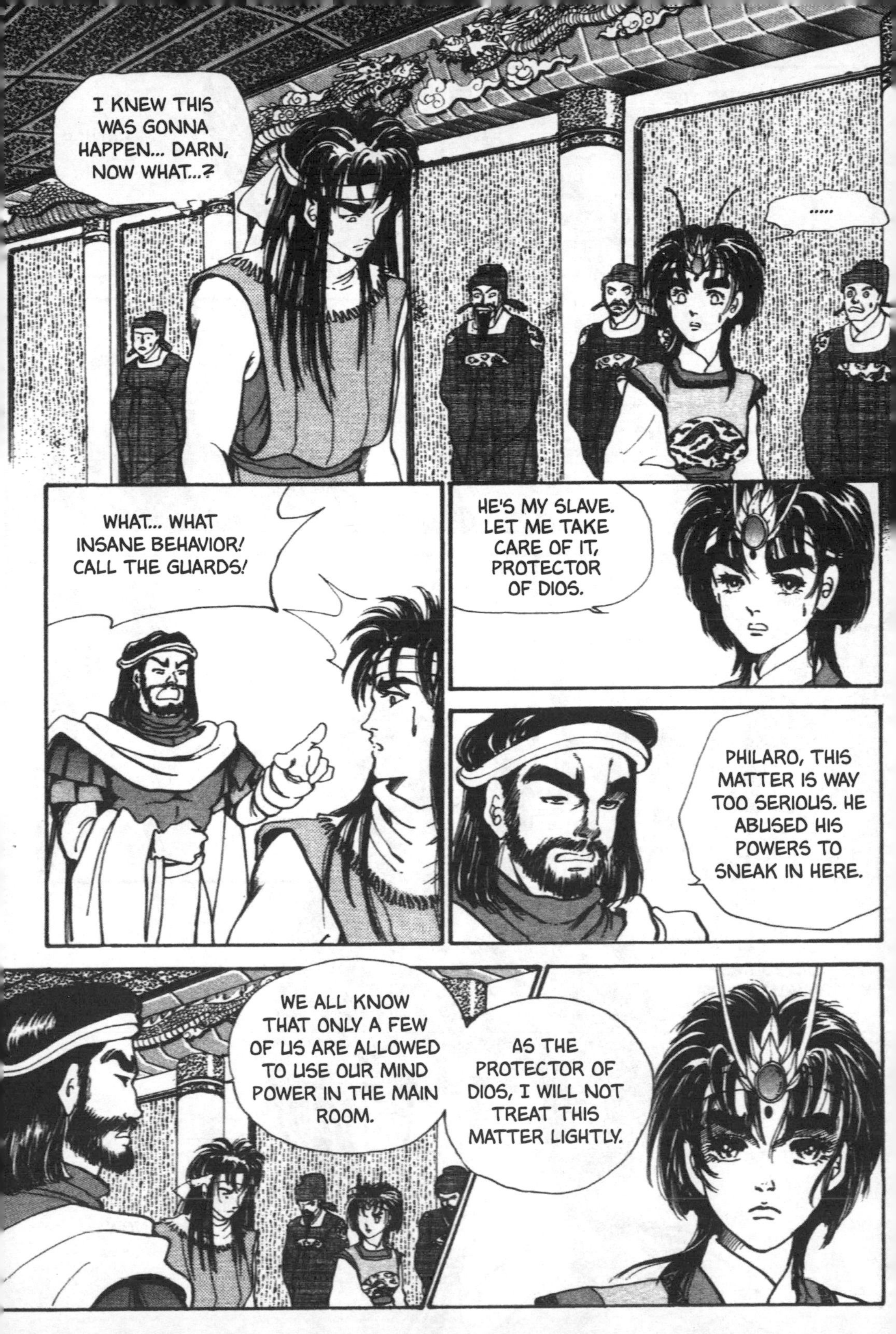
I KNEW THIS WAS GONNA HAPPEN... DARN, NOW WHAT...?
.....
WHAT... WHAT INSANE BEHAVIOR! CALL THE GUARDS!
HE'S MY SLAVE. LET ME TAKE CARE OF IT, PROTECTOR OF DIOS.
PHILARO, THIS MATTER IS WAY TOO SERIOUS. HE ABUSED HIS POWERS TO SNEAK IN HERE.
WE ALL KNOW THAT ONLY A FEW OF US ARE ALLOWED TO USE OUR MIND POWER IN THE MAIN ROOM.
AS THE PROTECTOR OF DIOS, I WILL NOT TREAT THIS MATTER LIGHTLY.

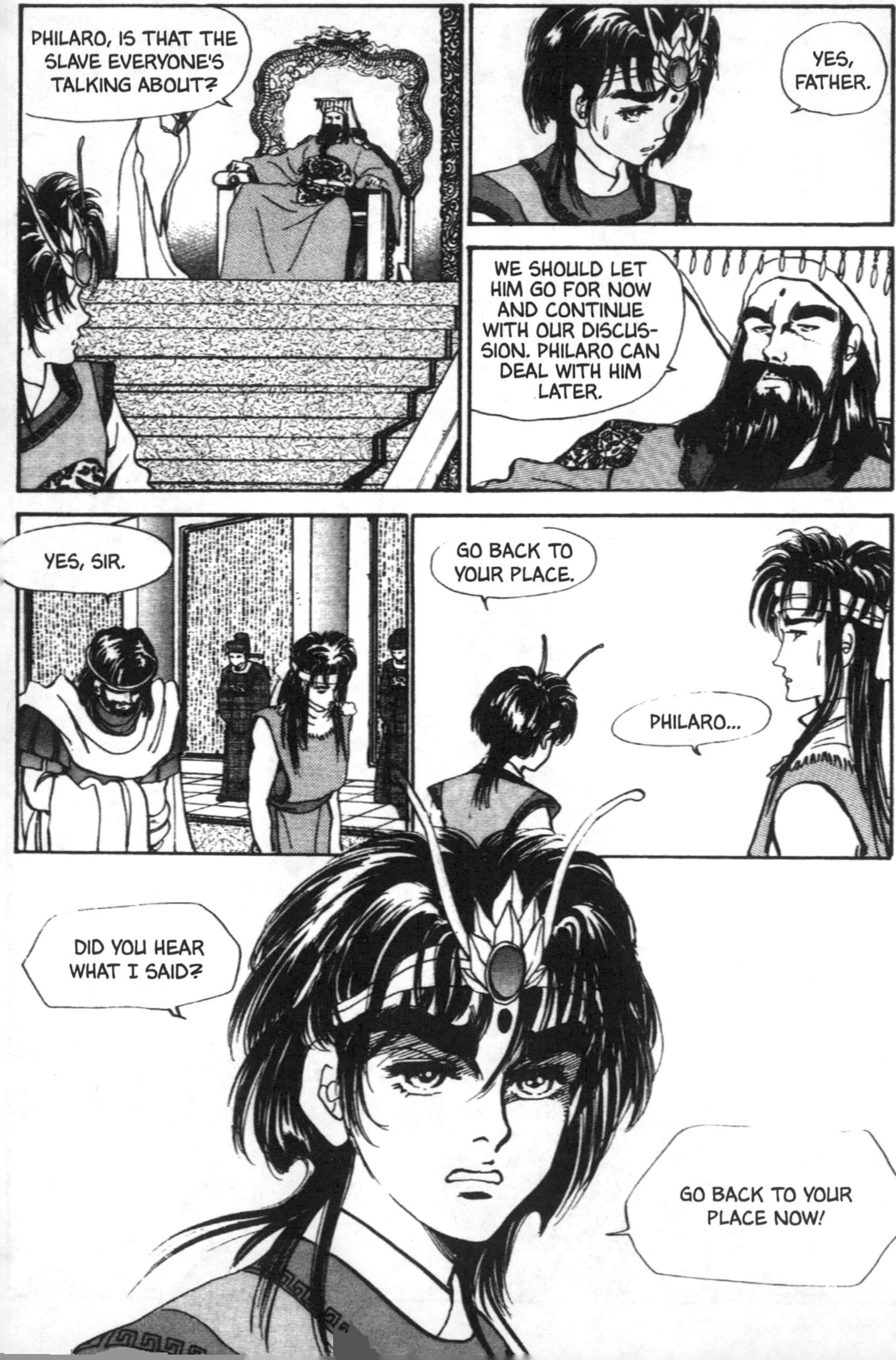
PHILARO, IS THAT THE SLAVE EVERYONE'S TALKING ABOUT?
YES, FATHER.
WE SHOULD LET HIM GO FOR NOW AND CONTINUE WITH OUR DISCUS-SION. PHILARO CAN DEAL WITH HIM LATER.
YES, SIR.
GO BACK TO YOUR PLACE.
PHILARO...
DID YOU HEAR WHAT I SAID?
GO BACK TO YOUR PLACE NOW!

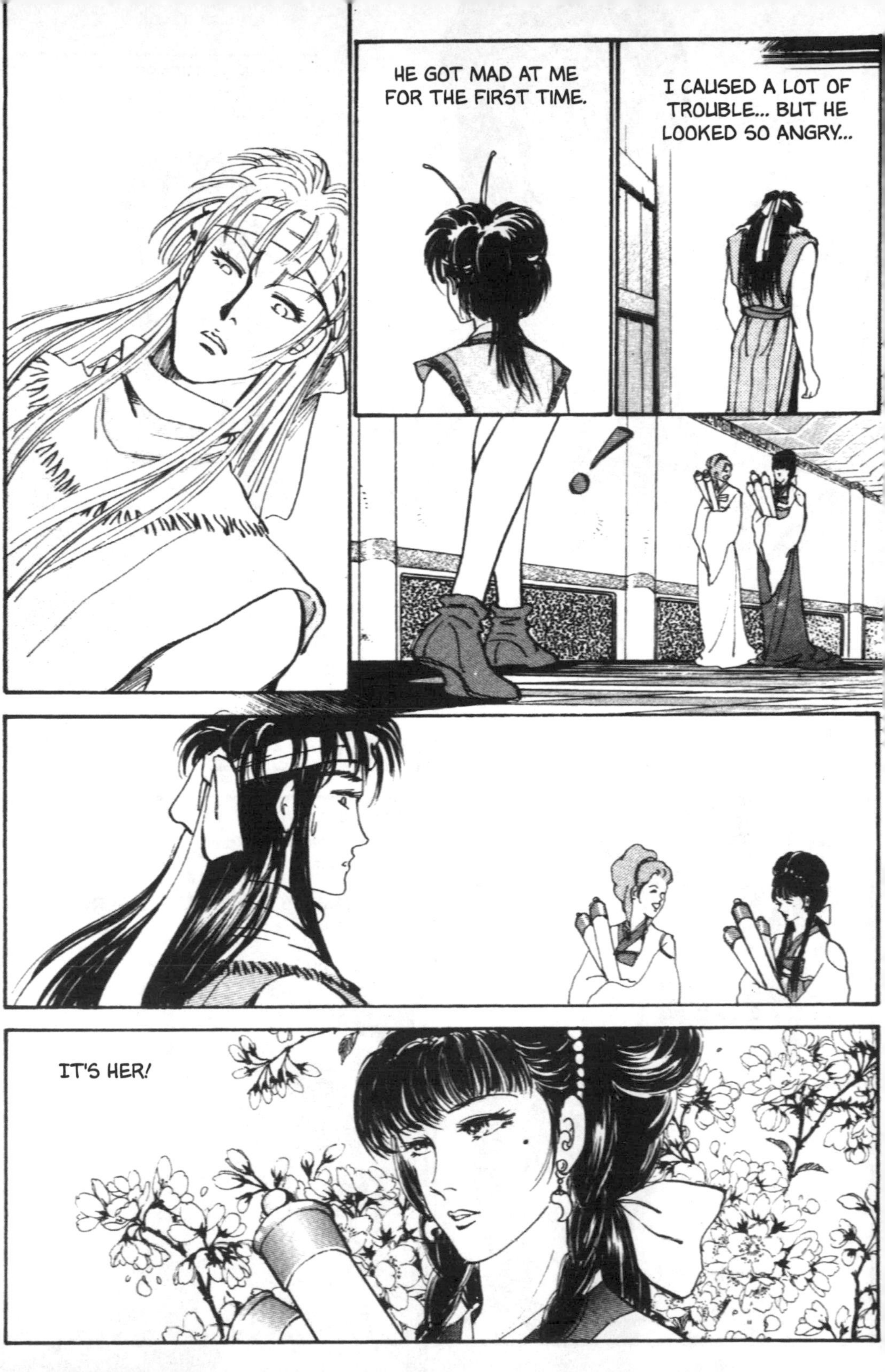
HE GOT MAD AT ME FOR THE FIRST TIME.
I CAUSED A LOT OF TROUBLE... BUT HE LOOKED SO ANGRY...
IT'S HER!

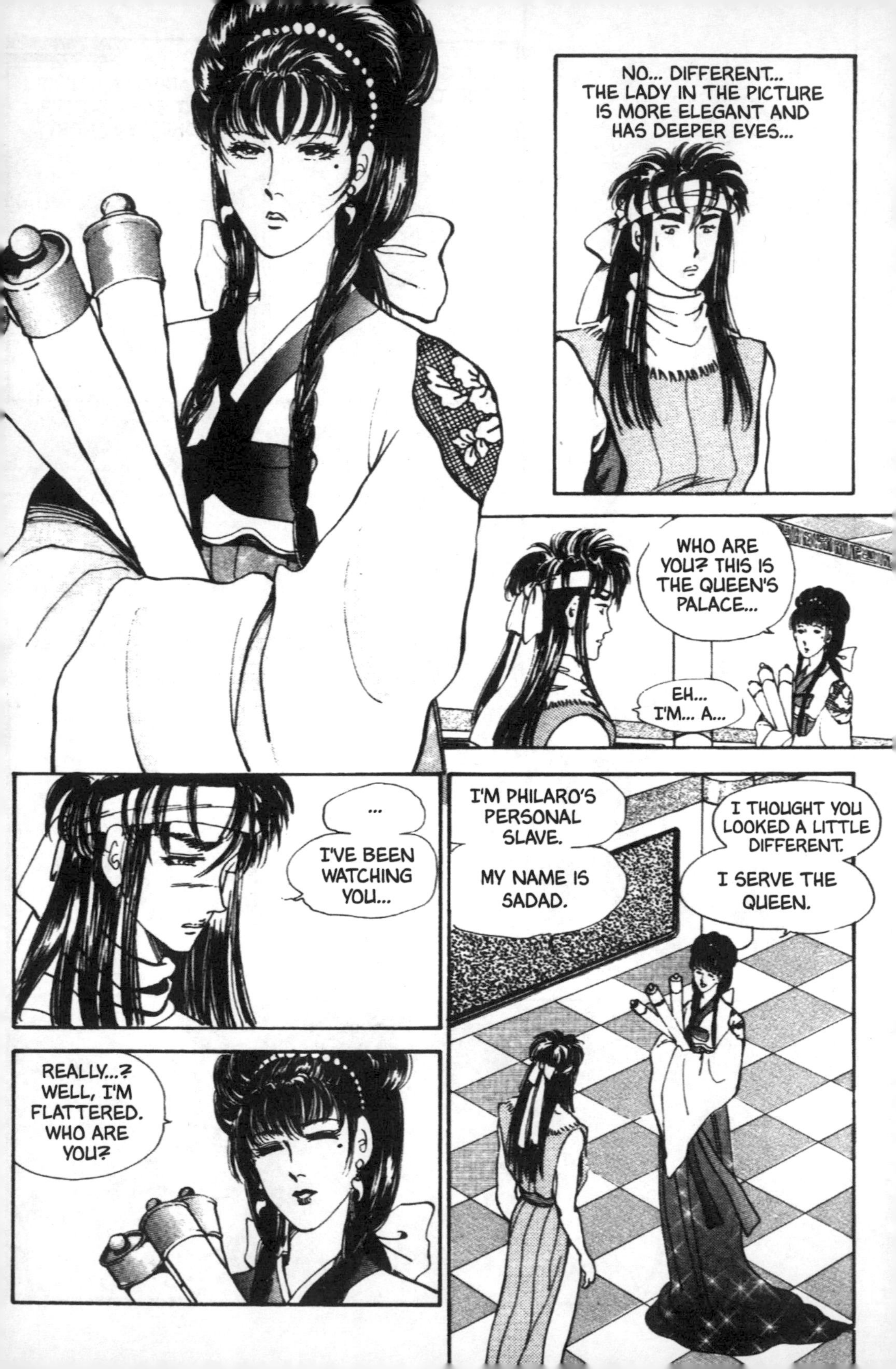
NO... DIFFERENT... THE LADY IN THE PICTURE IS MORE ELEGANT AND HAS DEEPER EYES...
WHO ARE YOU? THIS IS THE QUEEN'S PALACE...
EH... I'M... A...
...
I'VE BEEN WATCHING YOU...
I'M PHILARO'S PERSONAL SLAVE.
MY NAME IS SADAD.
I THOUGHT YOU LOOKED A LITTLE DIFFERENT.
I SERVE THE QUEEN.
REALLY...? WELL, I'M FLATTERED. WHO ARE YOU?

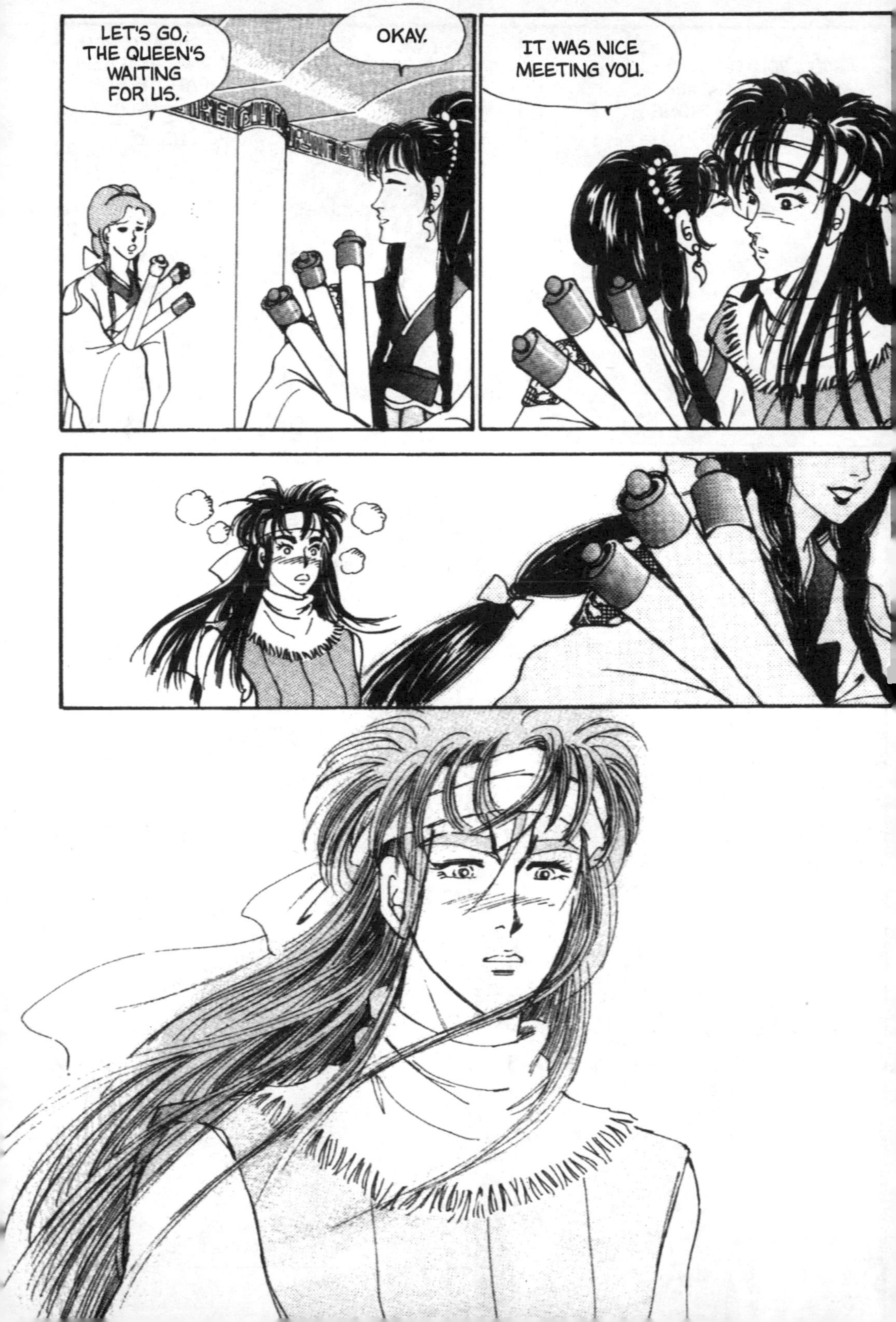
LET'S GO, THE QUEEN'S WAITING FOR US.
OKAY.
IT WAS NICE MEETING YOU.

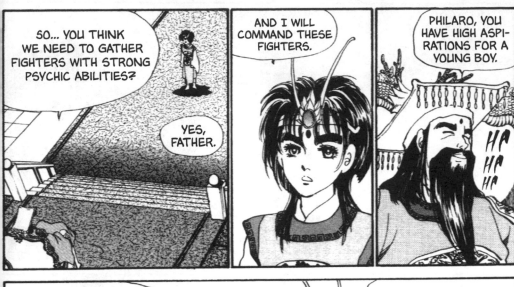

SO... YOU THINK WE NEED TO GATHER FIGHTERS WITH STRONG PSYCHIC ABILITIES?

YES, FATHER.

AND I WILL COMMAND THESE FIGHTERS.

PHILARO, YOU HAVE HIGH ASPIRATIONS FOR A YOUNG BOY.

HA HA HA

WE ALL KNOW THAT I'M TRULY CAPABLE OF THESE THINGS, EVEN THOUGH I'M STILL YOUNG.

POLITICAL SCIENCE, MILITARY SCIENCE, STRATEGY, LAW, TACTICS, CODE OF ETHICS... YOU CAN EVEN TEST MY PHYSICAL ABILITIES!

AGREED...

HE'S RIGHT...

AGUILAS KIDNAPPED MY BROTHER AND BRAINWASHED HIM. I WILL NOT FORGIVE HIM FOR THAT AND I WILL GET MY BROTHER BACK!

YOU NEVER HAD A BROTHER.

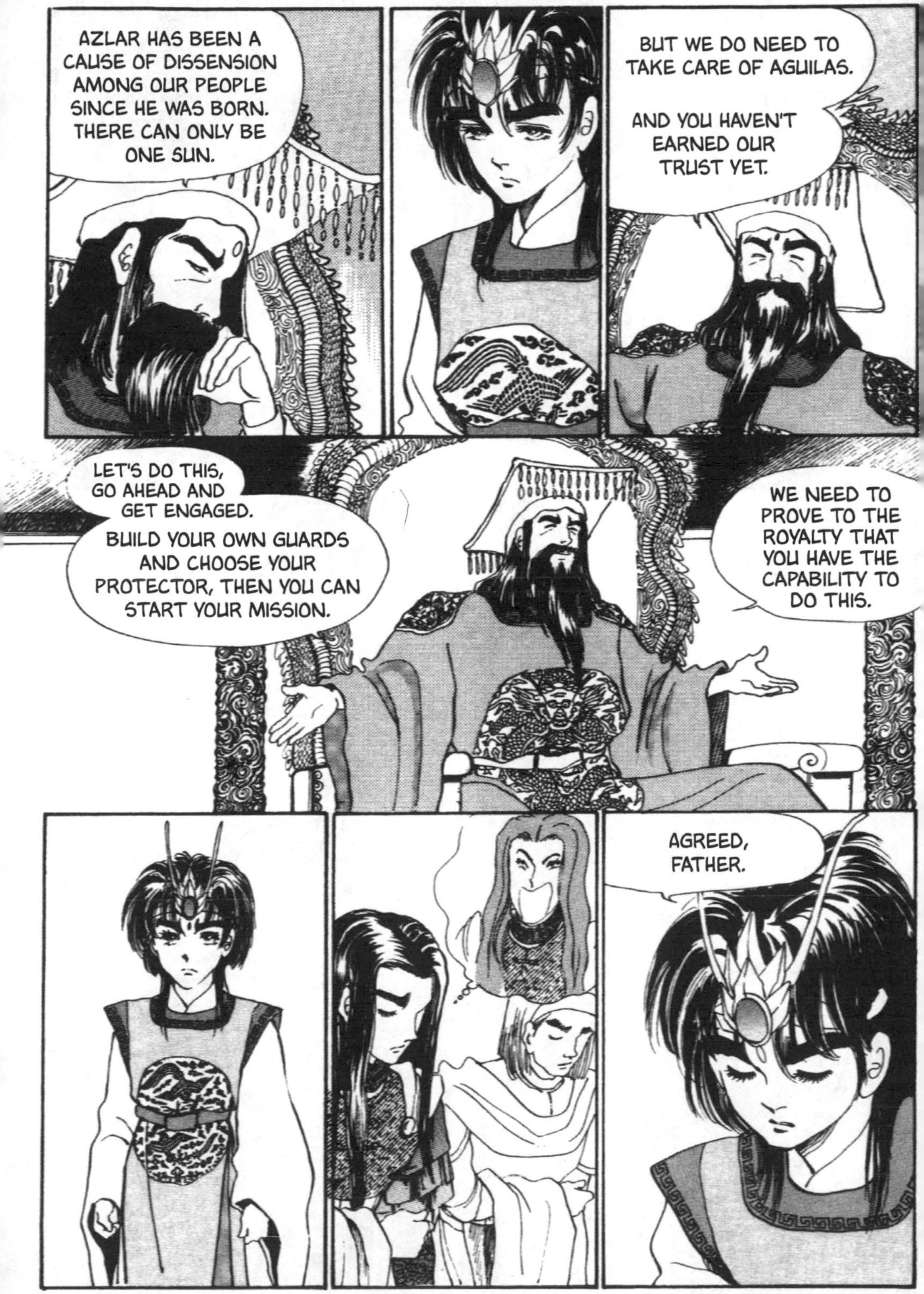
AZLAR HAS BEEN A CAUSE OF DISSENSION AMONG OUR PEOPLE SINCE HE WAS BORN. THERE CAN ONLY BE ONE SUN.
BUT WE DO NEED TO TAKE CARE OF AGUILAS.
AND YOU HAVEN'T EARNED OUR TRUST YET.
LET'S DO THIS, GO AHEAD AND GET ENGAGED.
BUILD YOUR OWN GUARDS AND CHOOSE YOUR PROTECTOR, THEN YOU CAN START YOUR MISSION.
WE NEED TO PROVE TO THE ROYALTY THAT YOU HAVE THE CAPABILITY TO DO THIS.
AGREED, FATHER.

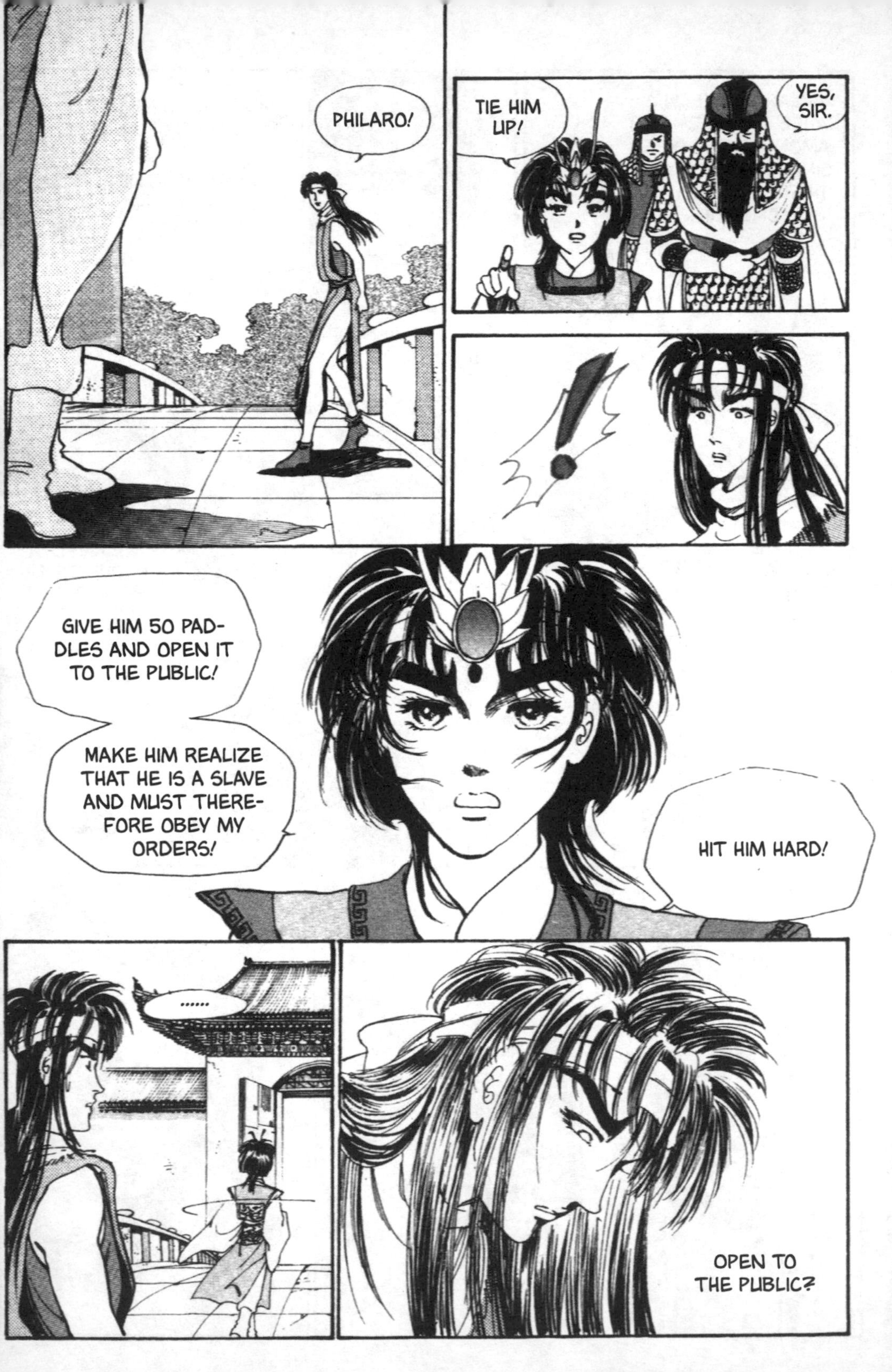
PHILARO!
TIE HIM UP!
YES, SIR.
!
GIVE HIM 50 PAD- DLES AND OPEN IT TO THE PUBLIC!
MAKE HIM REALIZE THAT HE IS A SLAVE AND MUST THERE- FORE OBEY MY ORDERS!
HIT HIM HARD!
......
OPEN TO THE PUBLIC?

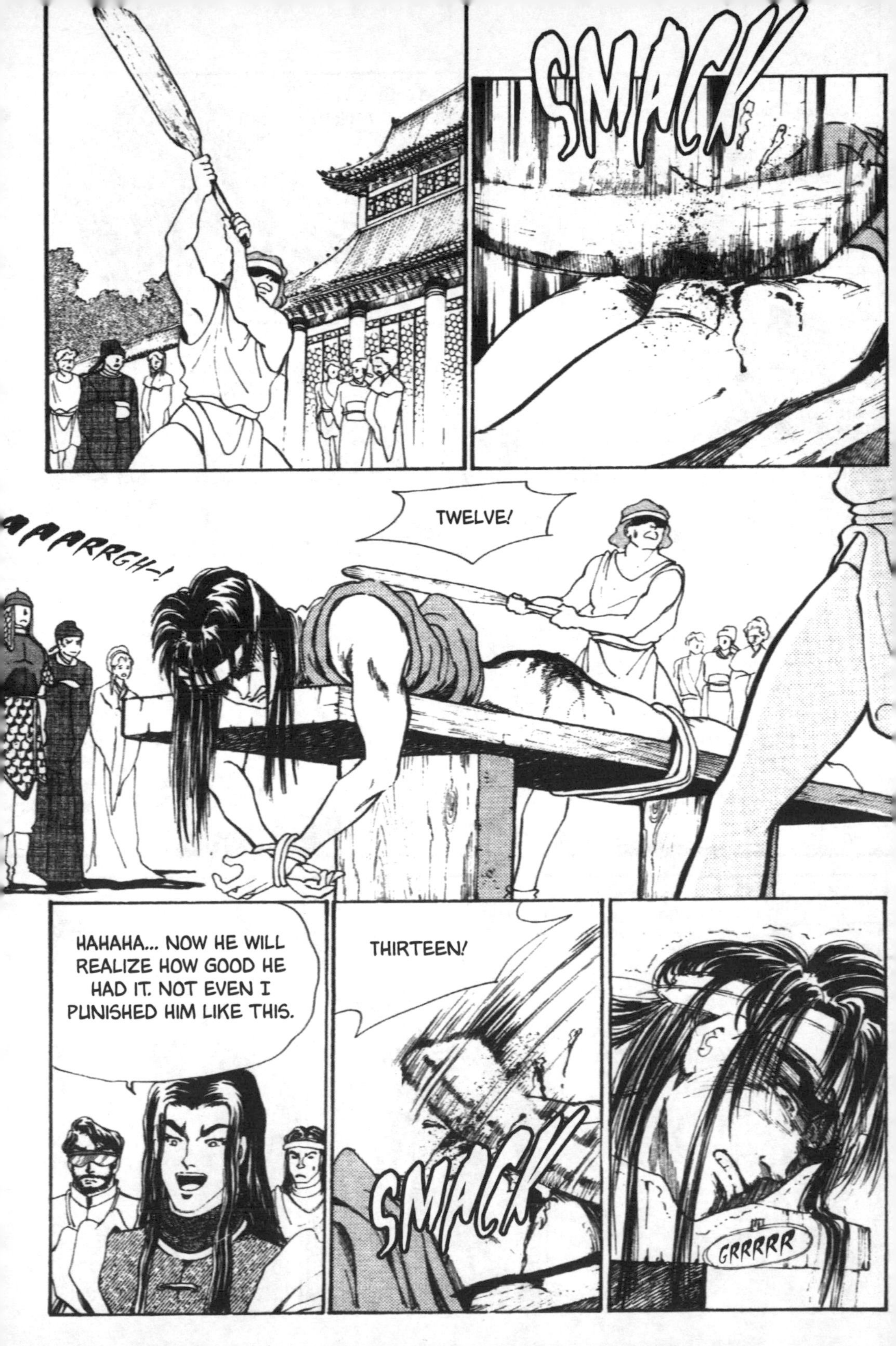
SMACK
AAAARRRGH—!
TWELVE!
HAHAHA... NOW HE WILL REALIZE HOW GOOD HE HAD IT. NOT EVEN I PUNISHED HIM LIKE THIS.
THIRTEEN!
SMACK
GRRRRR

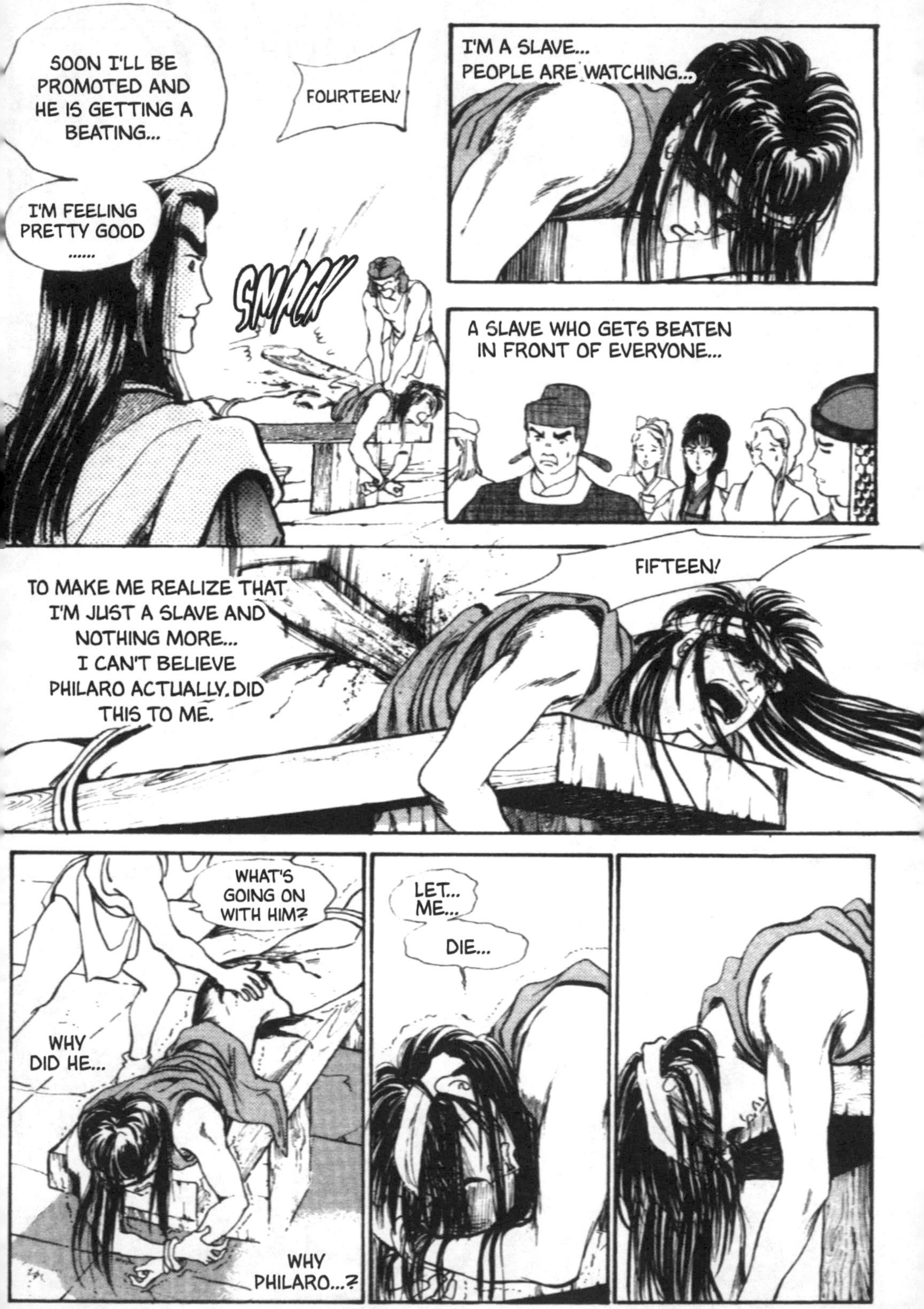
SOON I'LL BE PROMOTED AND HE IS GETTING A BEATING...
I'M FEELING PRETTY GOOD ......
FOURTEEN!
SMACK
I'M A SLAVE... PEOPLE ARE WATCHING...
A SLAVE WHO GETS BEATEN IN FRONT OF EVERYONE...
FIFTEEN!
TO MAKE ME REALIZE THAT I'M JUST A SLAVE AND NOTHING MORE... I CAN'T BELIEVE PHILARO ACTUALLY DID THIS TO ME.
WHAT'S GOING ON WITH HIM?
WHY DID HE...
WHY PHILARO...?
LET... ME...
DIE...

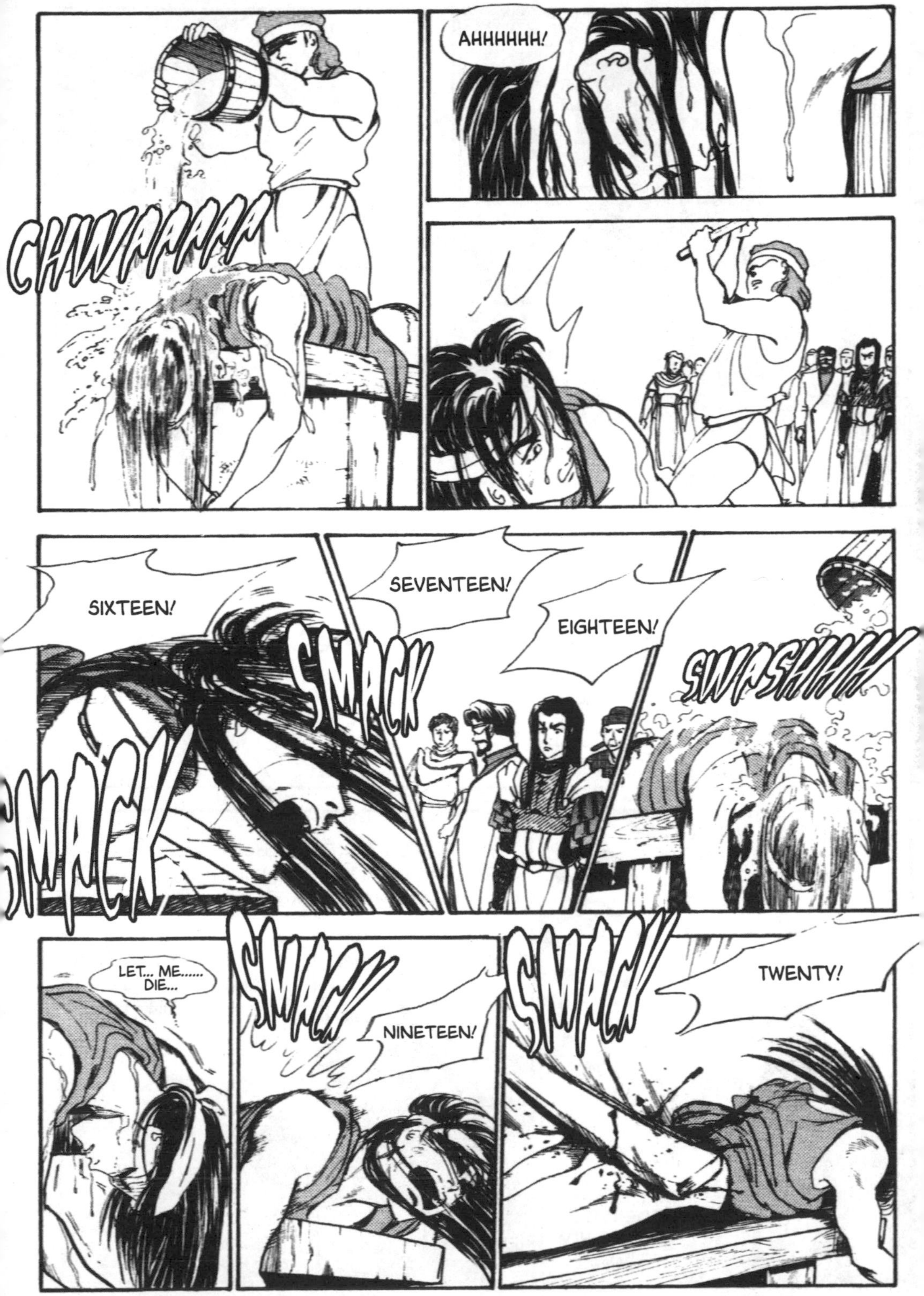
CHWAAAAAA
AHHHHHH!
SIXTEEN!
SMACK
SMACK
SEVENTEEN!
EIGHTEEN!
SWASHHH
LET... ME...... DIE...
SMACK
NINETEEN!
SMACK
TWENTY!

WHY? PHILARO....

......

WHY...?

UNNNF

SSSSS

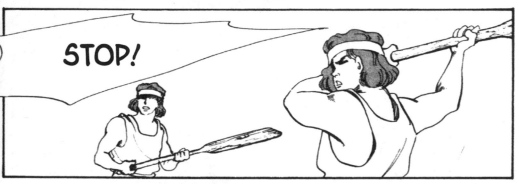

STOP!

HE'S PASSED OUT SO MANY TIMES ALREADY! YOU'RE GONNA KILL HIM IF YOU KEEP HITTING HIM!

BUT PHILARO ORDERED US TO GIVE HIM 50...

YOU CAN BE A BIT FLEXIBLE! PHILARO DIDN'T ORDER YOU TO KILL HIM, DID HE?!

LET HIM RECOVER AND THEN FINISH UP THE BEATING LATER!

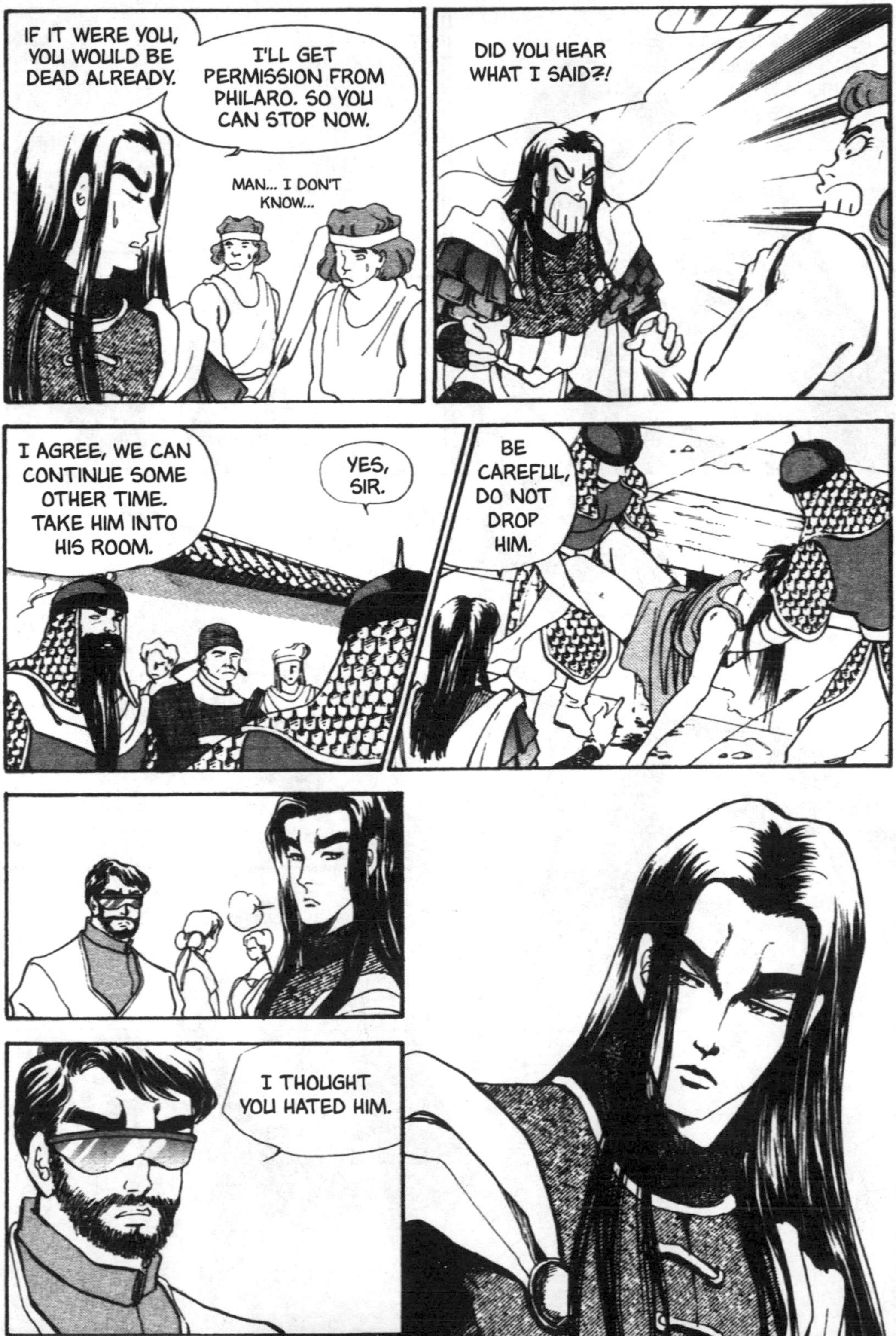
IF IT WERE YOU, YOU WOULD BE DEAD ALREADY.
I'LL GET PERMISSION FROM PHILARO. SO YOU CAN STOP NOW.
MAN... I DON'T KNOW...
DID YOU HEAR WHAT I SAID?!
I AGREE, WE CAN CONTINUE SOME OTHER TIME. TAKE HIM INTO HIS ROOM.
YES, SIR.
BE CAREFUL, DO NOT DROP HIM.
I THOUGHT YOU HATED HIM.

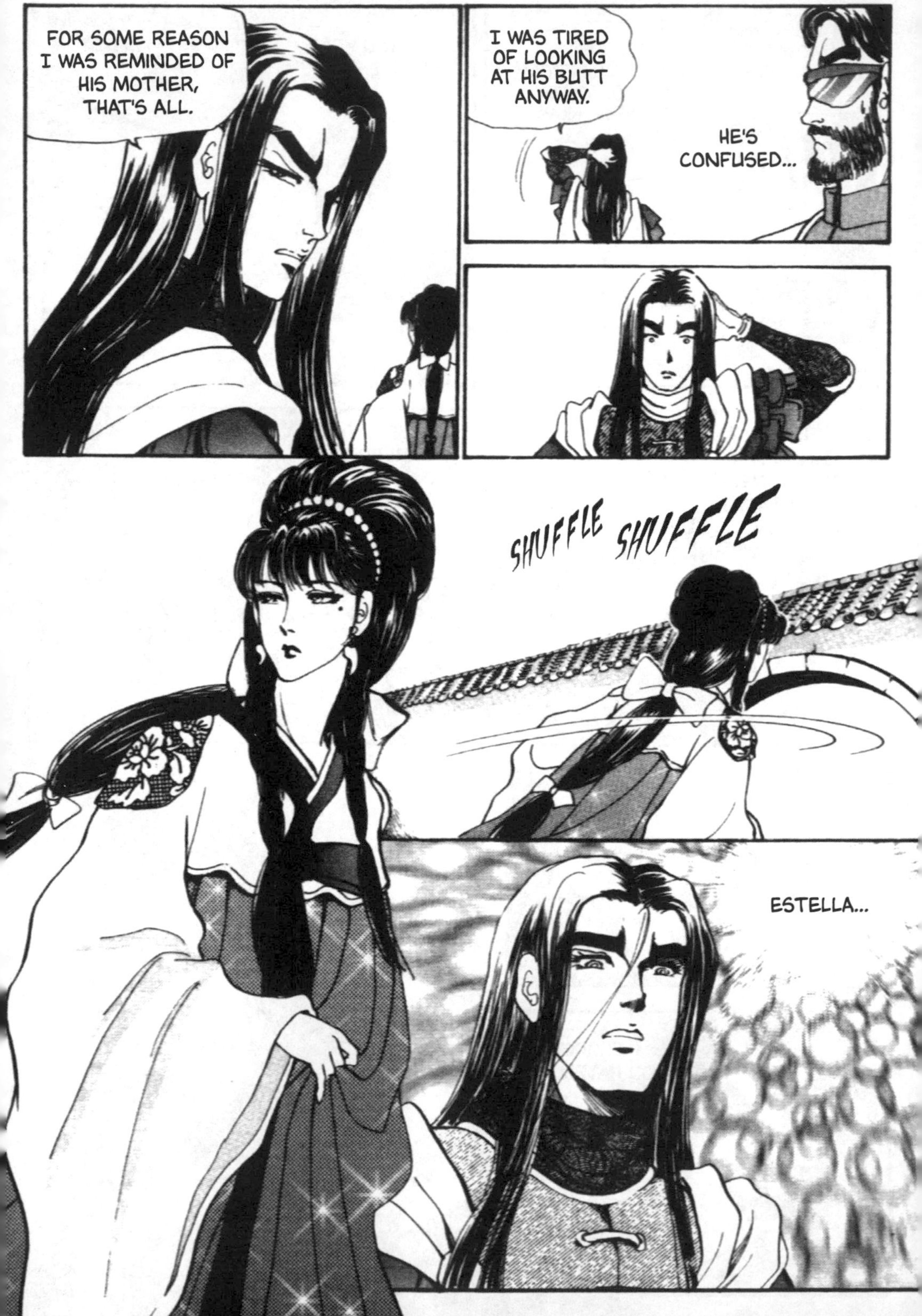
FOR SOME REASON I WAS REMINDED OF HIS MOTHER, THAT'S ALL.
I WAS TIRED OF LOOKING AT HIS BUTT ANYWAY.
HE'S CONFUSED...
SHUFFLE
SHUFFLE
ESTELLA...

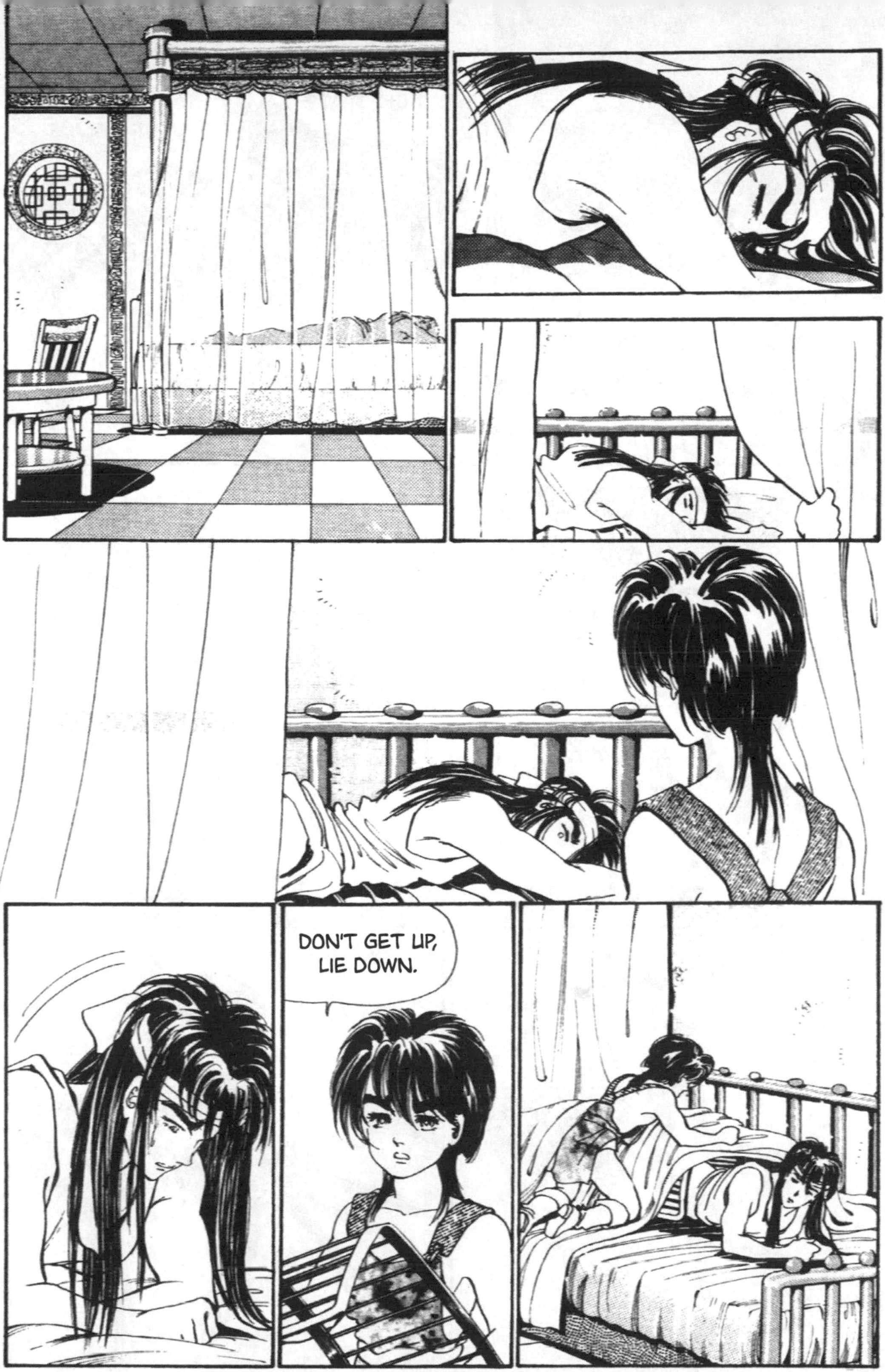
DON'T GET UP,
LIE DOWN.

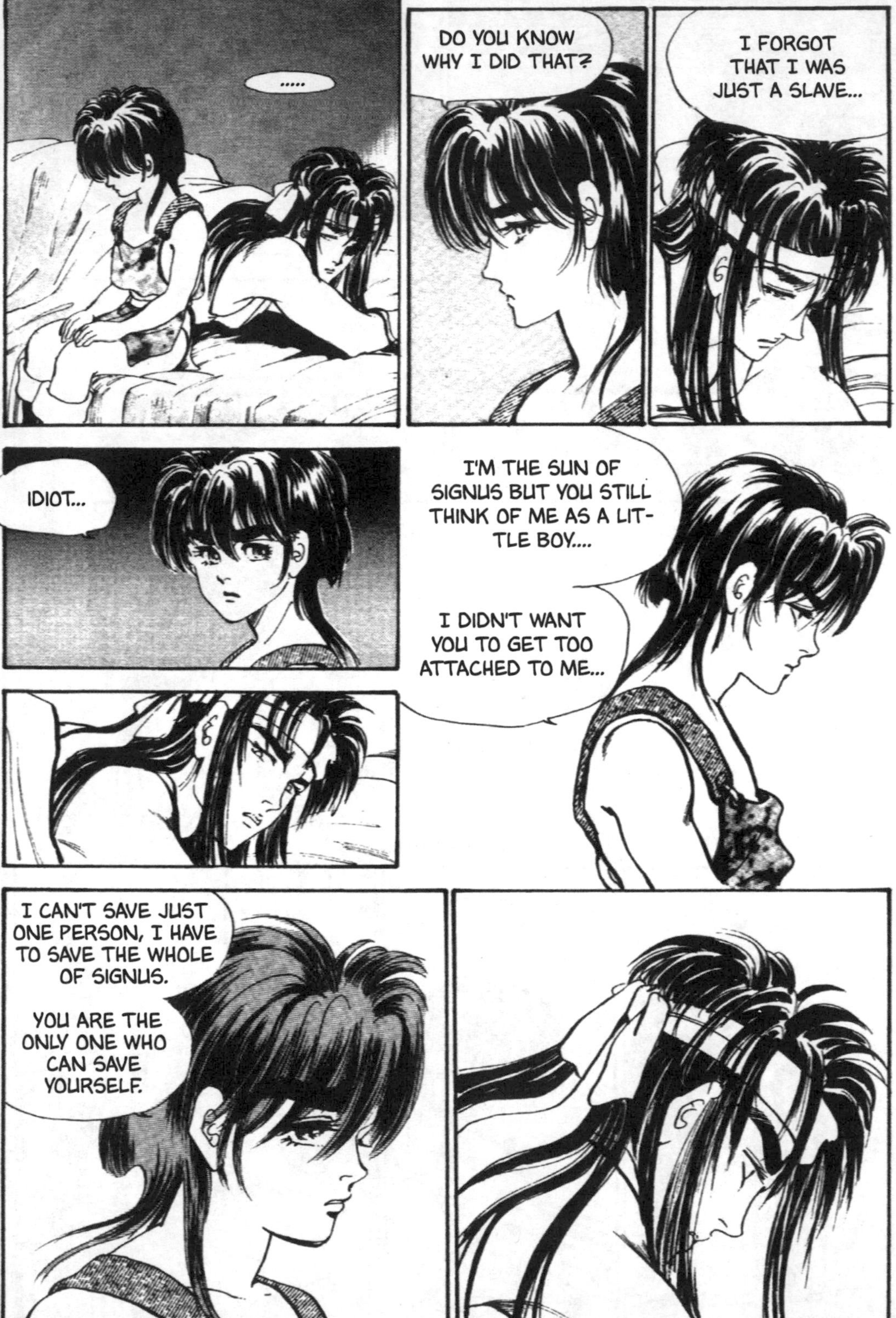
......
DO YOU KNOW WHY I DID THAT?
I FORGOT THAT I WAS JUST A SLAVE...
IDIOT...
I'M THE SUN OF SIGNUS BUT YOU STILL THINK OF ME AS A LIT-TLE BOY....
I DIDN'T WANT YOU TO GET TOO ATTACHED TO ME...
I CAN'T SAVE JUST ONE PERSON, I HAVE TO SAVE THE WHOLE OF SIGNUS.
YOU ARE THE ONLY ONE WHO CAN SAVE YOURSELF.

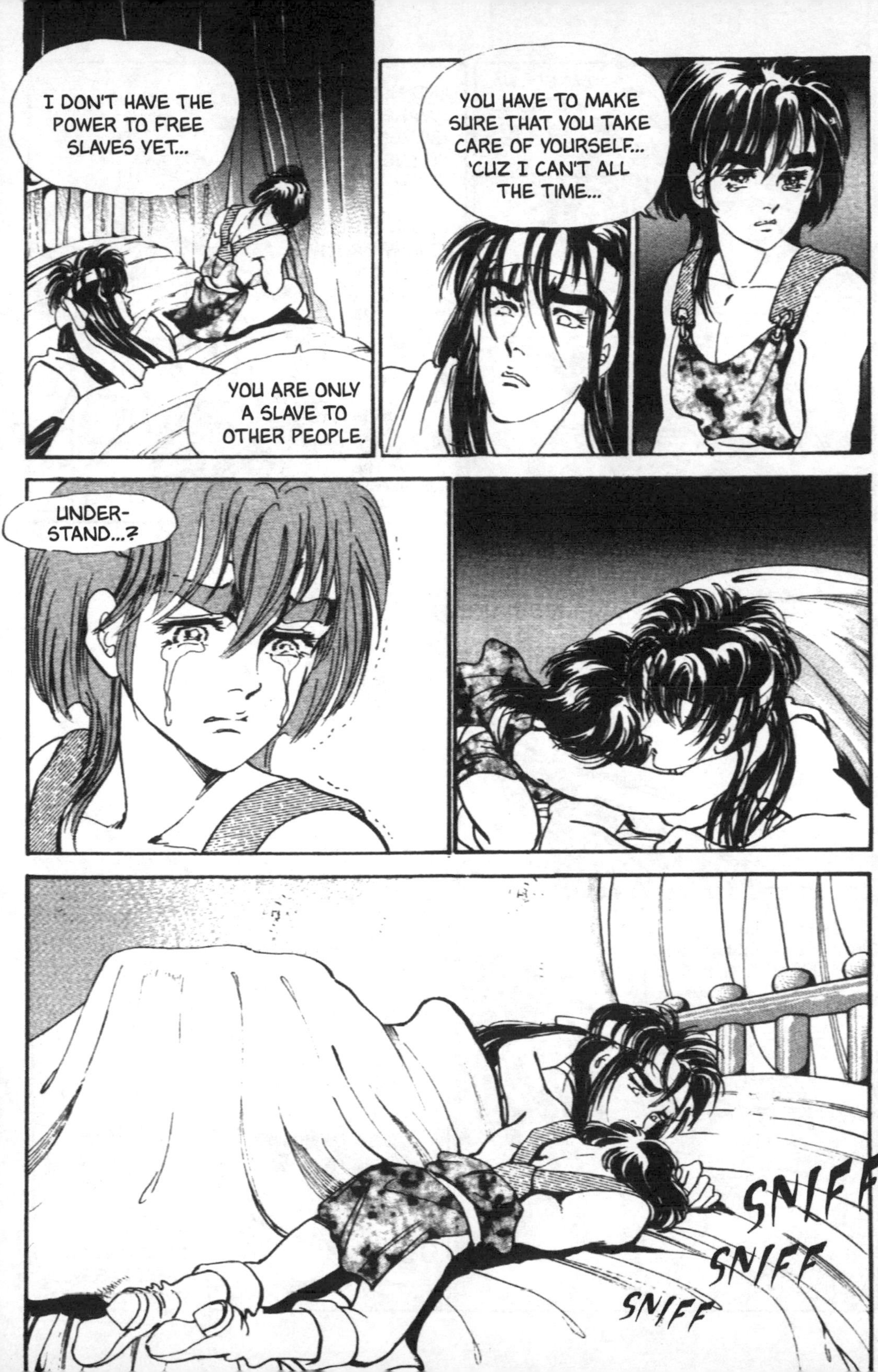
I DON'T HAVE THE POWER TO FREE SLAVES YET...
YOU ARE ONLY A SLAVE TO OTHER PEOPLE.
YOU HAVE TO MAKE SURE THAT YOU TAKE CARE OF YOURSELF... 'CUZ I CAN'T ALL THE TIME...
UNDER-STAND...?
SNIFF
SNIFF
SNIFF

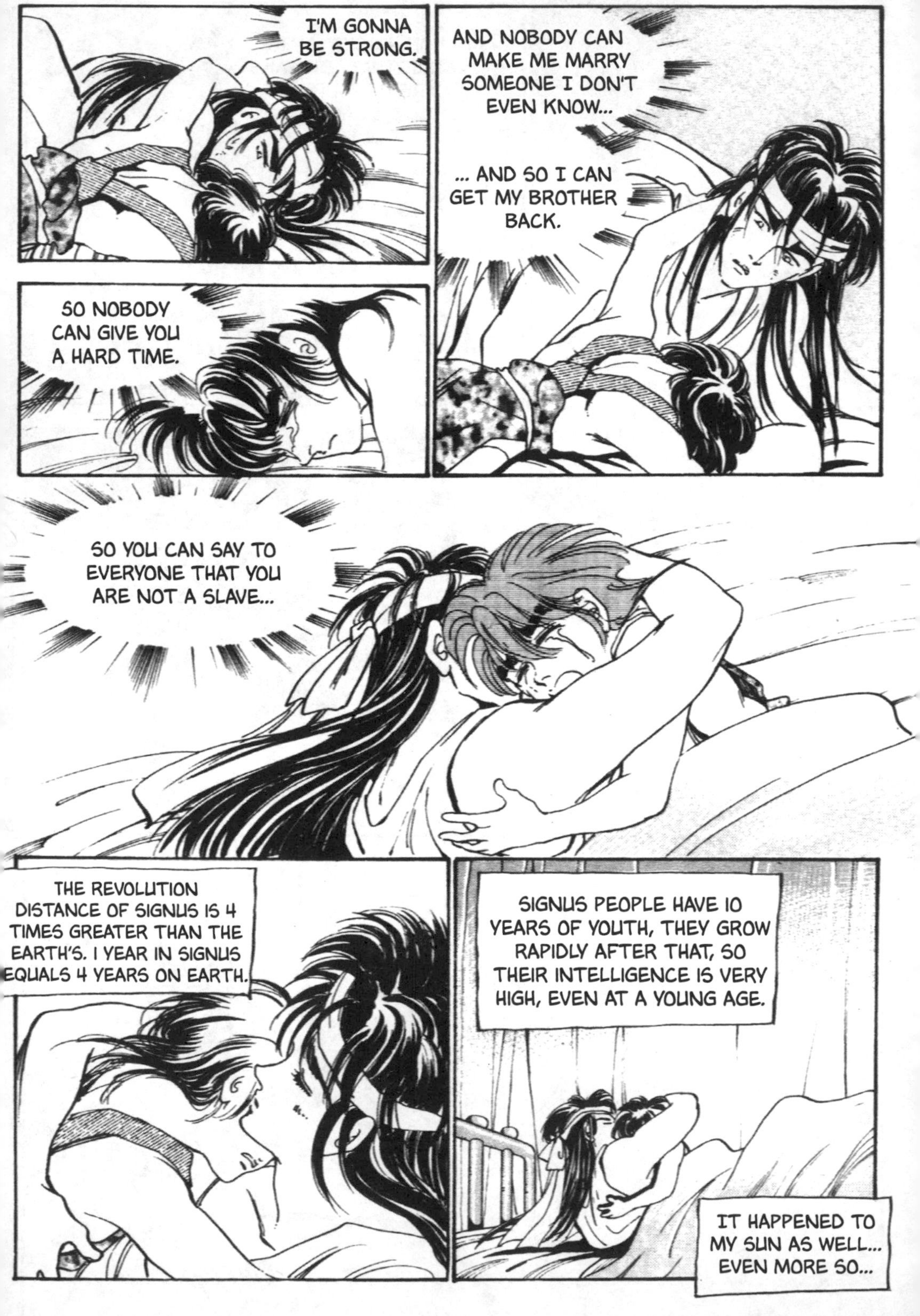
I'M GONNA BE STRONG.
AND NOBODY CAN MAKE ME MARRY SOMEONE I DON'T EVEN KNOW...
... AND SO I CAN GET MY BROTHER BACK.
SO NOBODY CAN GIVE YOU A HARD TIME.
SO YOU CAN SAY TO EVERYONE THAT YOU ARE NOT A SLAVE...
THE REVOLUTION DISTANCE OF SIGNUS IS 4 TIMES GREATER THAN THE EARTH'S. 1 YEAR IN SIGNUS EQUALS 4 YEARS ON EARTH.
SIGNUS PEOPLE HAVE 10 YEARS OF YOUTH, THEY GROW RAPIDLY AFTER THAT, SO THEIR INTELLIGENCE IS VERY HIGH, EVEN AT A YOUNG AGE.
IT HAPPENED TO MY SUN AS WELL... EVEN MORE SO...

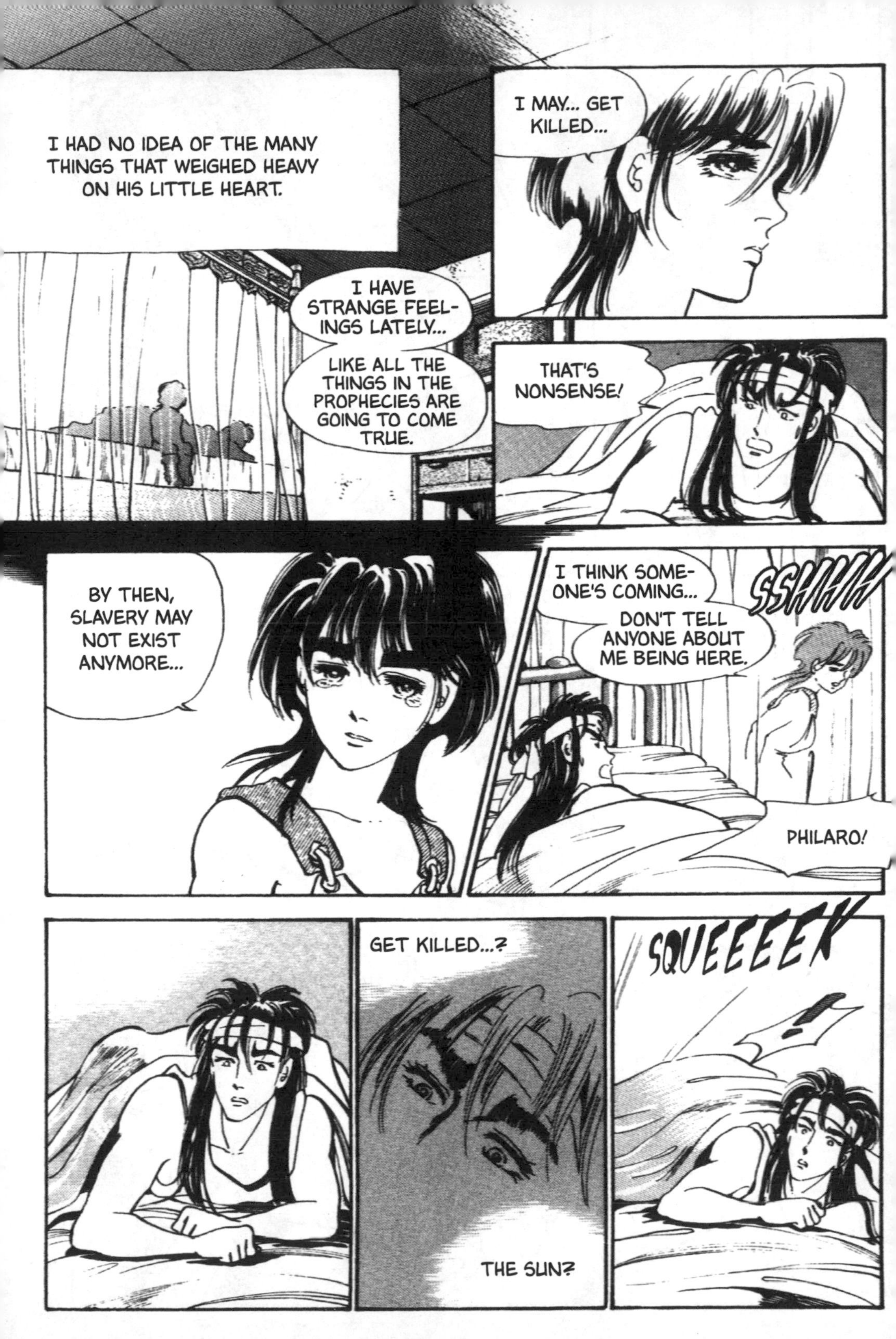
I HAD NO IDEA OF THE MANY THINGS THAT WEIGHED HEAVY ON HIS LITTLE HEART.
I MAY... GET KILLED...
I HAVE STRANGE FEEL-INGS LATELY...
LIKE ALL THE THINGS IN THE PROPHECIES ARE GOING TO COME TRUE.
THAT'S NONSENSE!
BY THEN, SLAVERY MAY NOT EXIST ANYMORE...
I THINK SOME-ONE'S COMING...
DON'T TELL ANYONE ABOUT ME BEING HERE.
SSHHH
PHILARO!
GET KILLED...?
THE SUN?
SQUEEEEEK
!

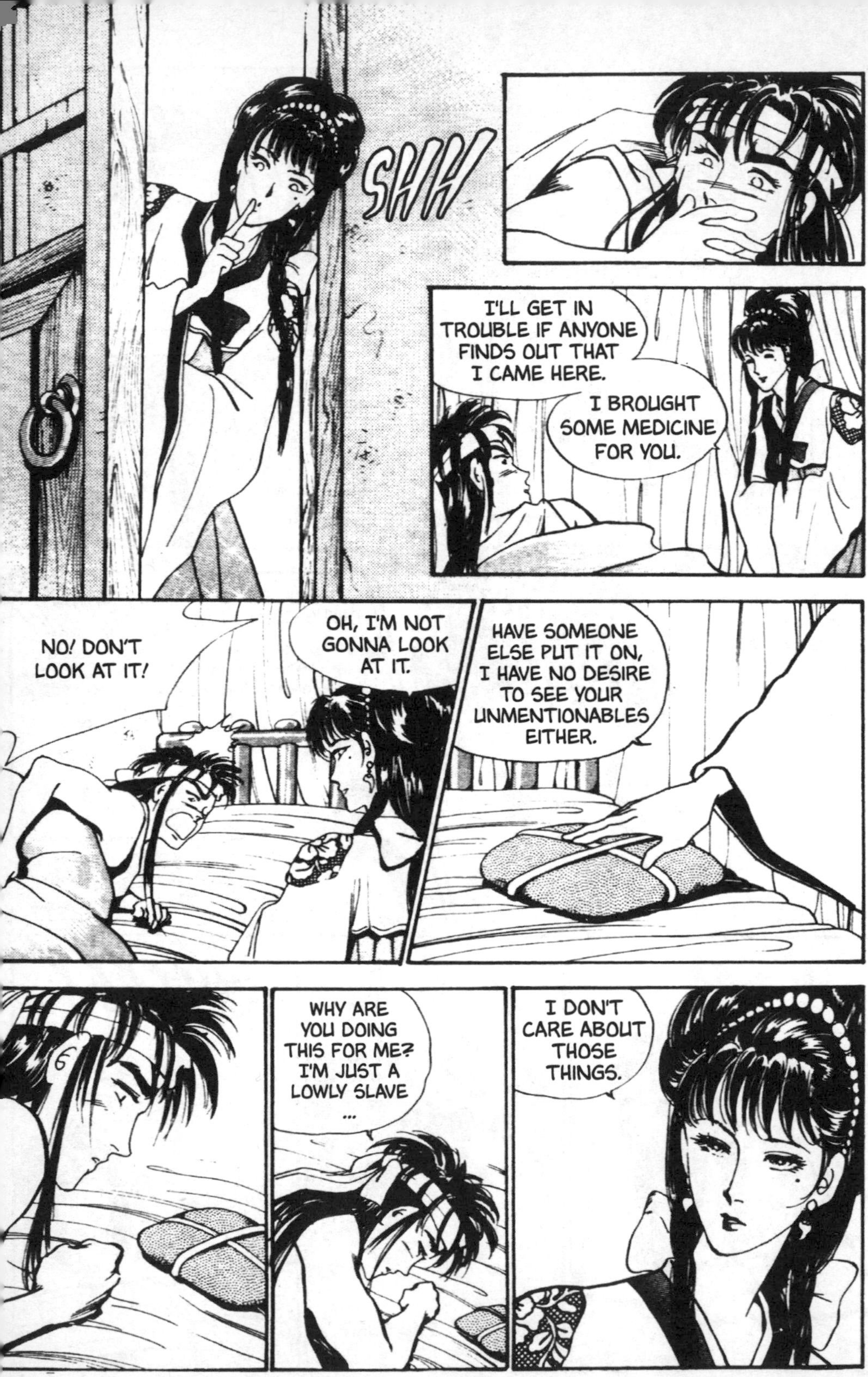
SHH
I'LL GET IN TROUBLE IF ANYONE FINDS OUT THAT I CAME HERE.
I BROUGHT SOME MEDICINE FOR YOU.
NO! DON'T LOOK AT IT!
OH, I'M NOT GONNA LOOK AT IT.
HAVE SOMEONE ELSE PUT IT ON, I HAVE NO DESIRE TO SEE YOUR UNMENTIONABLES EITHER.
WHY ARE YOU DOING THIS FOR ME? I'M JUST A LOWLY SLAVE ...
I DON'T CARE ABOUT THOSE THINGS.

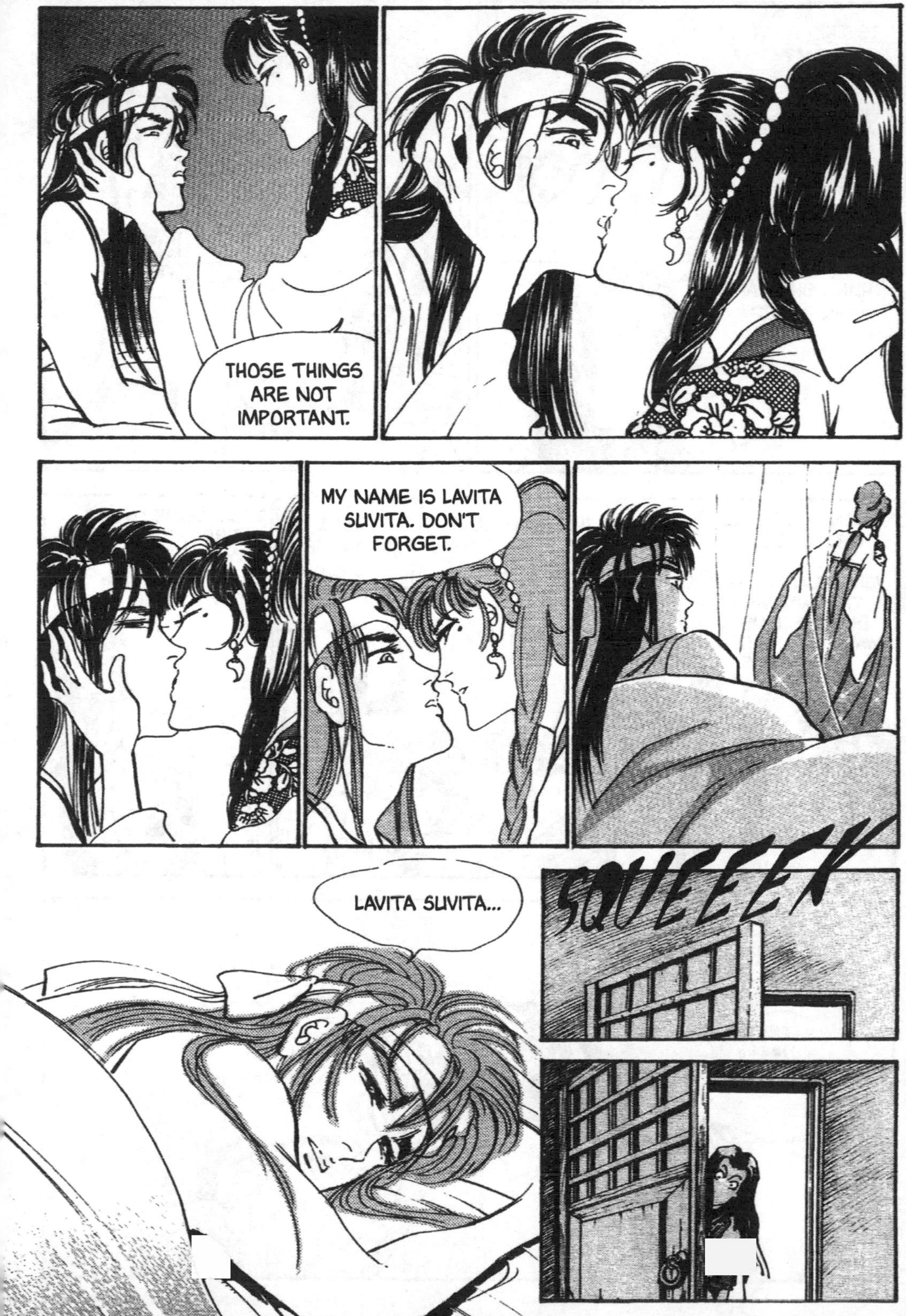
THOSE THINGS ARE NOT IMPORTANT.
MY NAME IS LAVITA SUVITA. DON'T FORGET.
LAVITA SUVITA...
SQUEEEEK

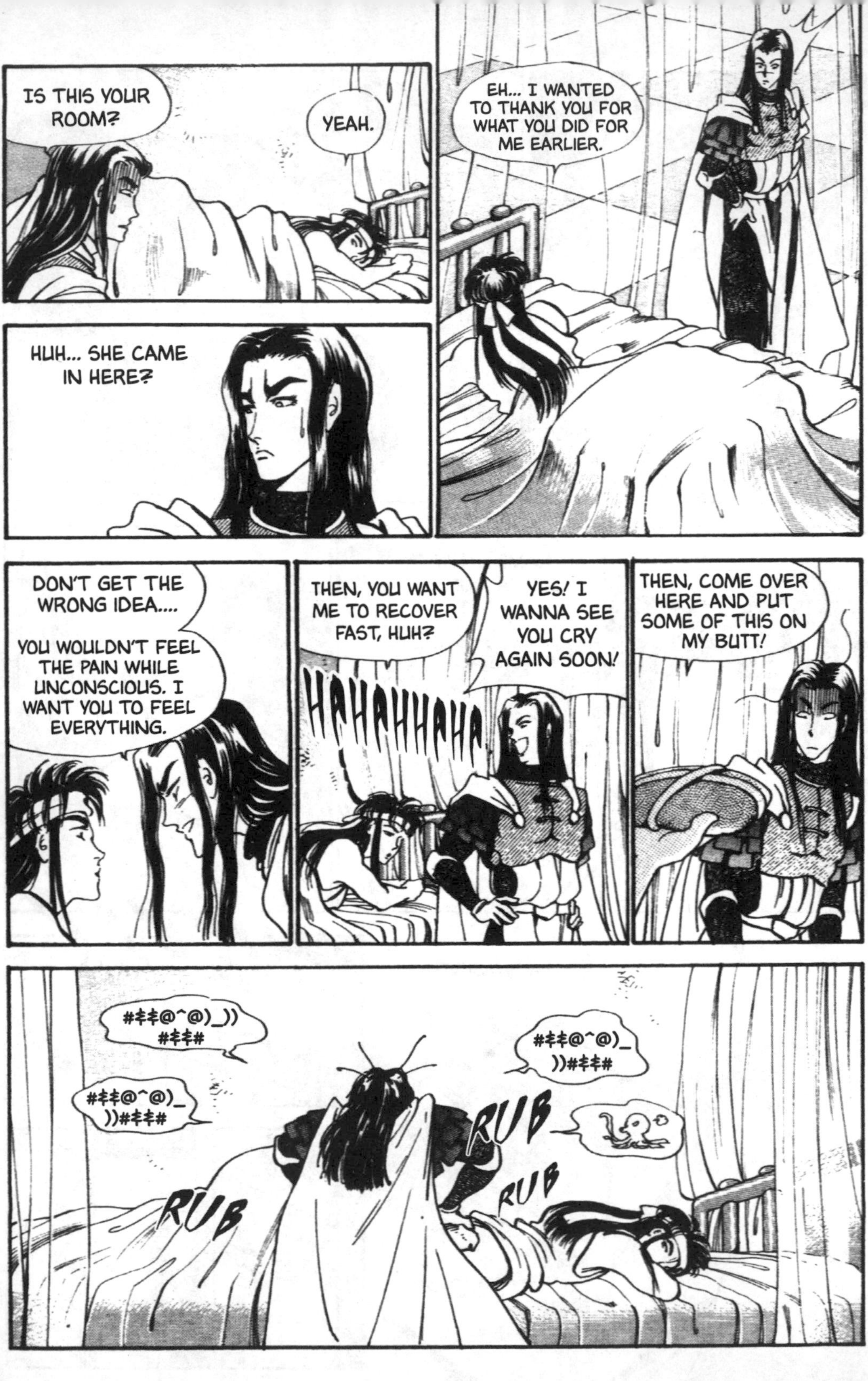
IS THIS YOUR ROOM?
YEAH.
EH... I WANTED TO THANK YOU FOR WHAT YOU DID FOR ME EARLIER.
HUH... SHE CAME IN HERE?
DON'T GET THE WRONG IDEA....
YOU WOULDN'T FEEL THE PAIN WHILE UNCONSCIOUS. I WANT YOU TO FEEL EVERYTHING.
THEN, YOU WANT ME TO RECOVER FAST, HUH?
HAHAHHAHA
YES! I WANNA SEE YOU CRY AGAIN SOON!
THEN, COME OVER HERE AND PUT SOME OF THIS ON MY BUTT!
#‡‡@^@)_))
#‡‡#
#‡‡@^@)_
))#‡‡#
#‡‡@^@)_
))#‡‡#
RUB
RUB
RUB

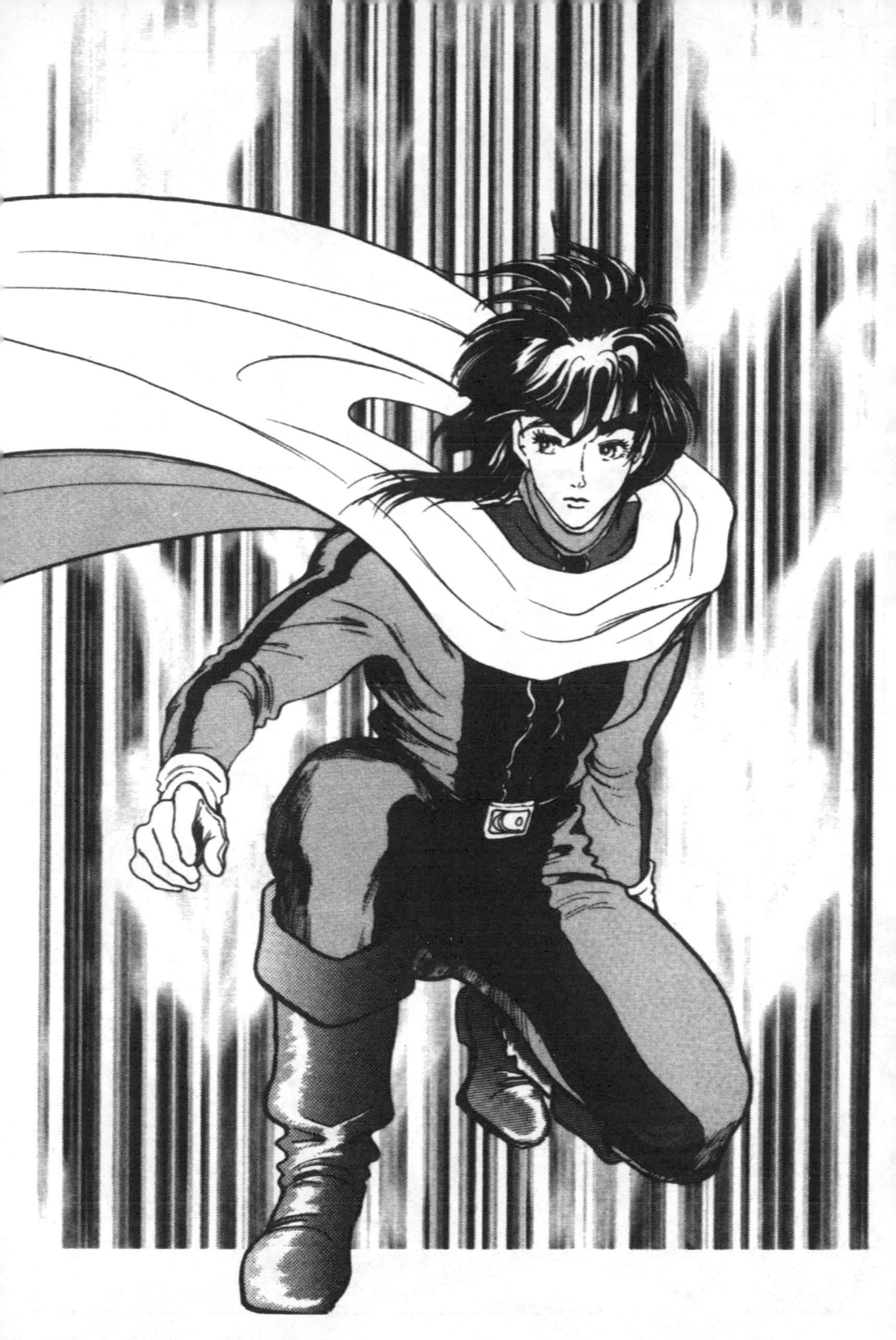

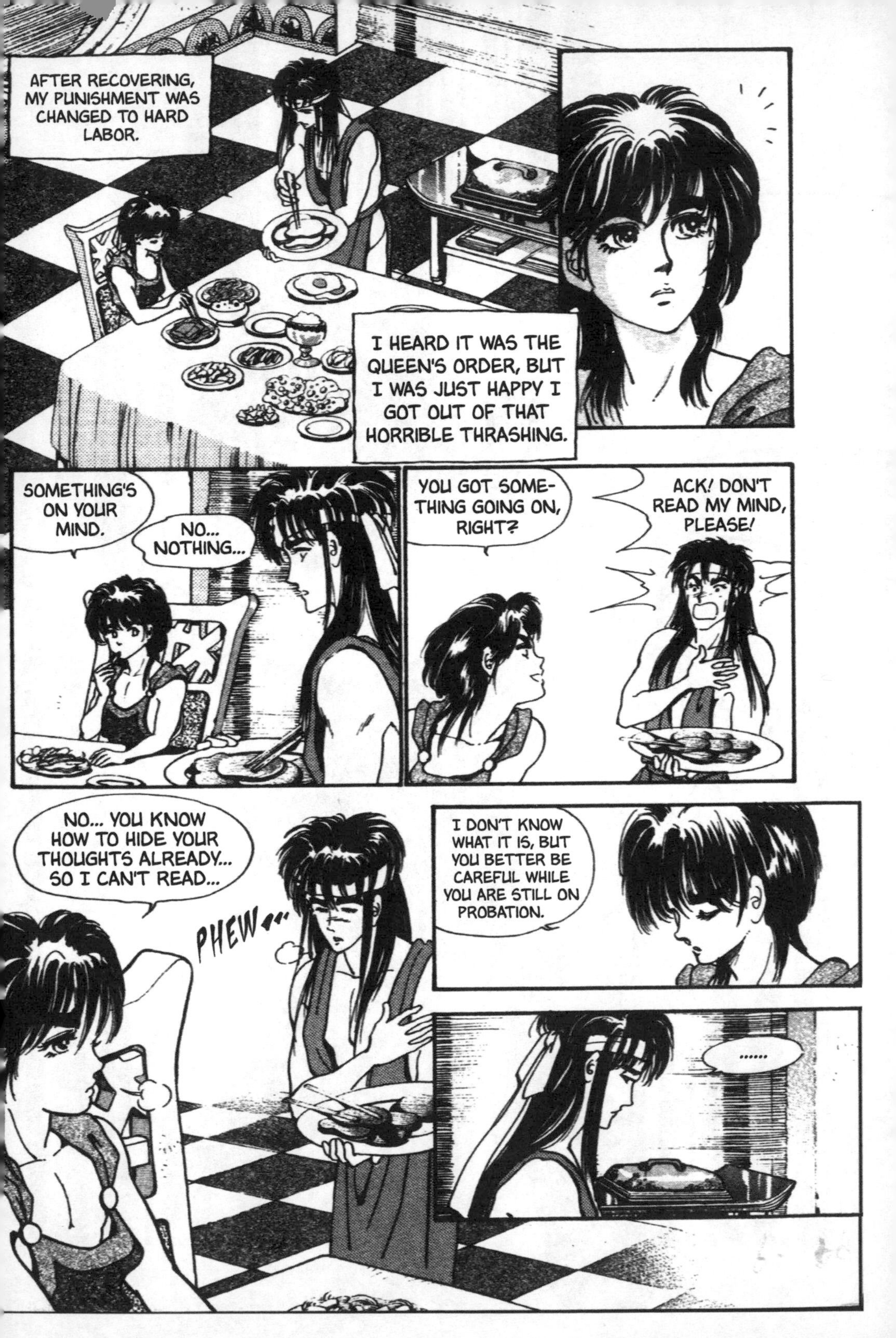
AFTER RECOVERING, MY PUNISHMENT WAS CHANGED TO HARD LABOR.
I HEARD IT WAS THE QUEEN'S ORDER, BUT I WAS JUST HAPPY I GOT OUT OF THAT HORRIBLE THRASHING.
SOMETHING'S ON YOUR MIND.
NO... NOTHING...
YOU GOT SOME-THING GOING ON, RIGHT?
ACK! DON'T READ MY MIND, PLEASE!
NO... YOU KNOW HOW TO HIDE YOUR THOUGHTS ALREADY... SO I CAN'T READ...
PHEW
I DON'T KNOW WHAT IT IS, BUT YOU BETTER BE CAREFUL WHILE YOU ARE STILL ON PROBATION.
......

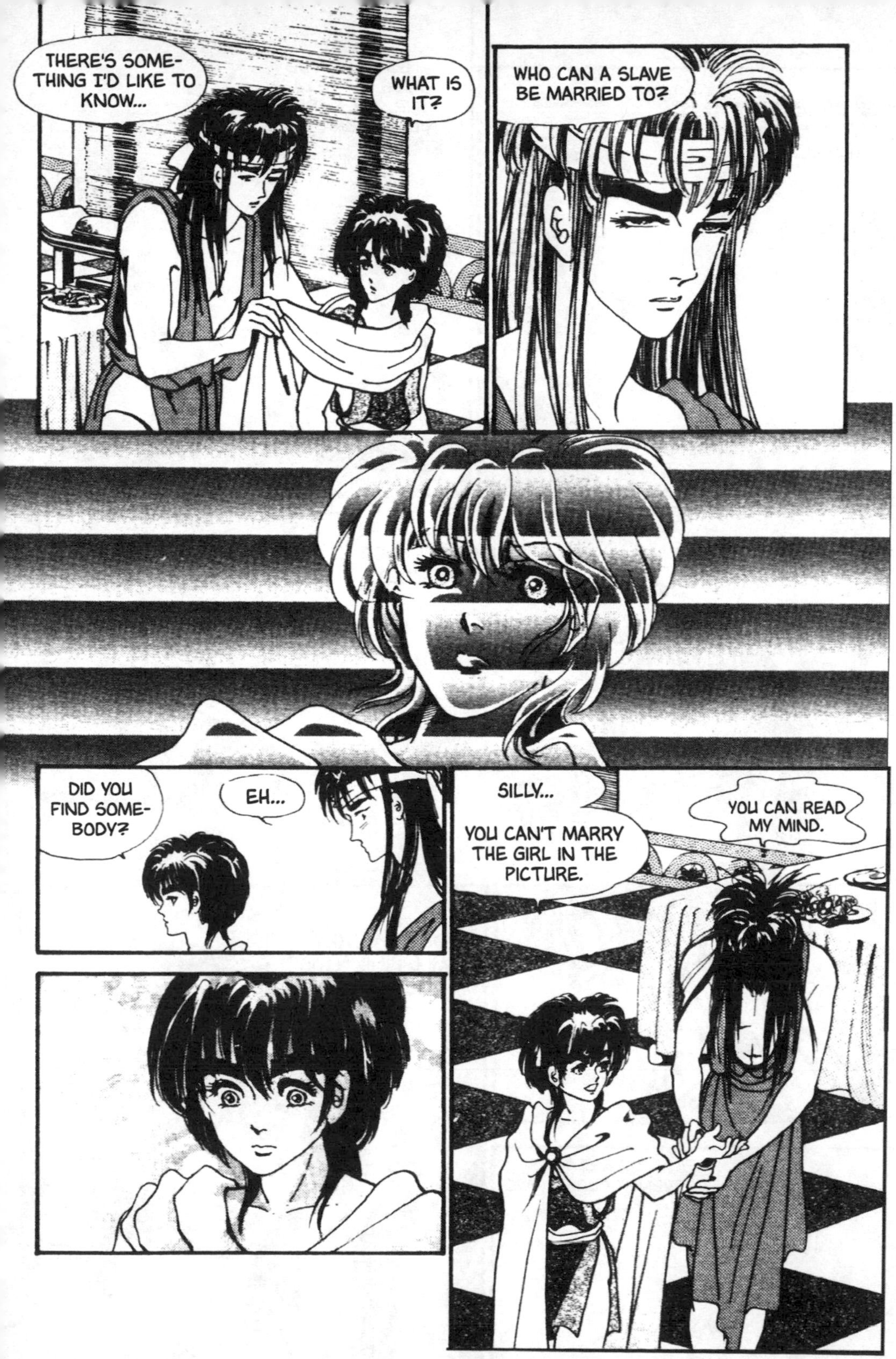
THERE'S SOME-THING I'D LIKE TO KNOW...
WHAT IS IT?
WHO CAN A SLAVE BE MARRIED TO?
DID YOU FIND SOME-BODY?
EH...
SILLY...
YOU CAN'T MARRY THE GIRL IN THE PICTURE.
YOU CAN READ MY MIND.

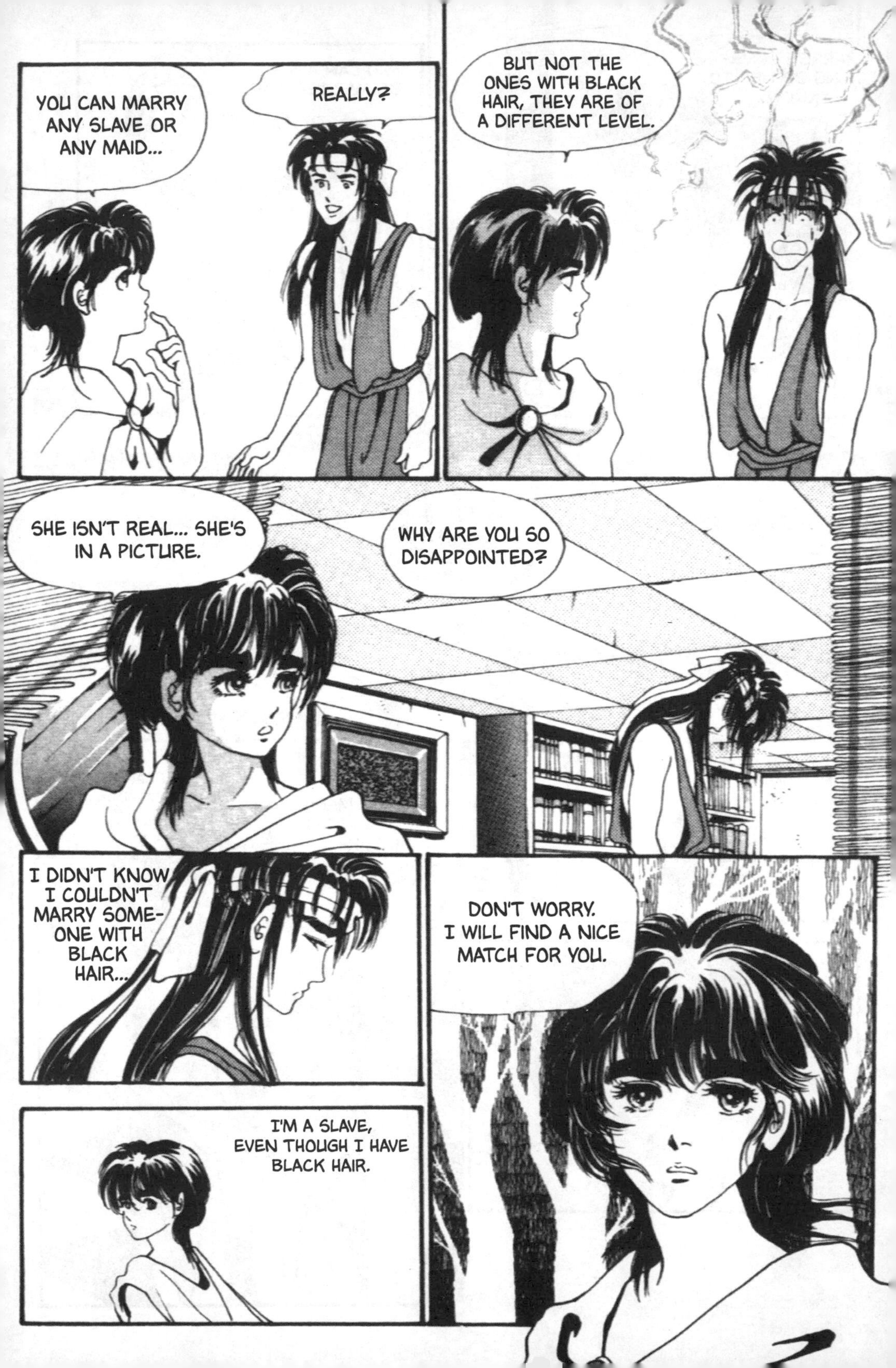
YOU CAN MARRY ANY SLAVE OR ANY MAID...
REALLY?
BUT NOT THE ONES WITH BLACK HAIR, THEY ARE OF A DIFFERENT LEVEL.
SHE ISN'T REAL... SHE'S IN A PICTURE.
WHY ARE YOU SO DISAPPOINTED?
I DIDN'T KNOW I COULDN'T MARRY SOME-ONE WITH BLACK HAIR...
DON'T WORRY. I WILL FIND A NICE MATCH FOR YOU.
I'M A SLAVE, EVEN THOUGH I HAVE BLACK HAIR.

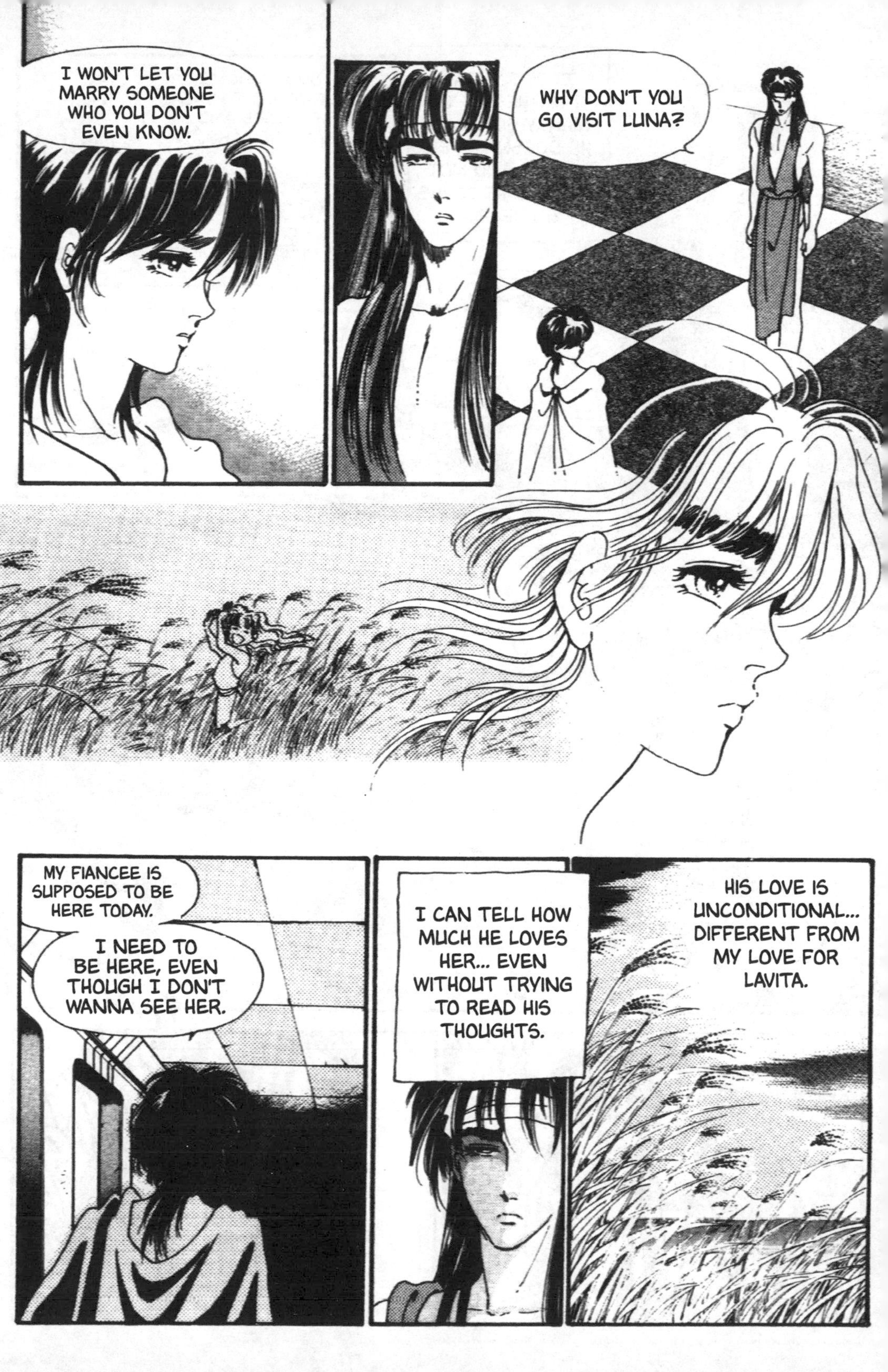
I WON'T LET YOU MARRY SOMEONE WHO YOU DON'T EVEN KNOW.
WHY DON'T YOU GO VISIT LUNA?
MY FIANCEE IS SUPPOSED TO BE HERE TODAY.
I NEED TO BE HERE, EVEN THOUGH I DON'T WANNA SEE HER.
I CAN TELL HOW MUCH HE LOVES HER... EVEN WITHOUT TRYING TO READ HIS THOUGHTS.
HIS LOVE IS UNCONDITIONAL... DIFFERENT FROM MY LOVE FOR LAVITA.

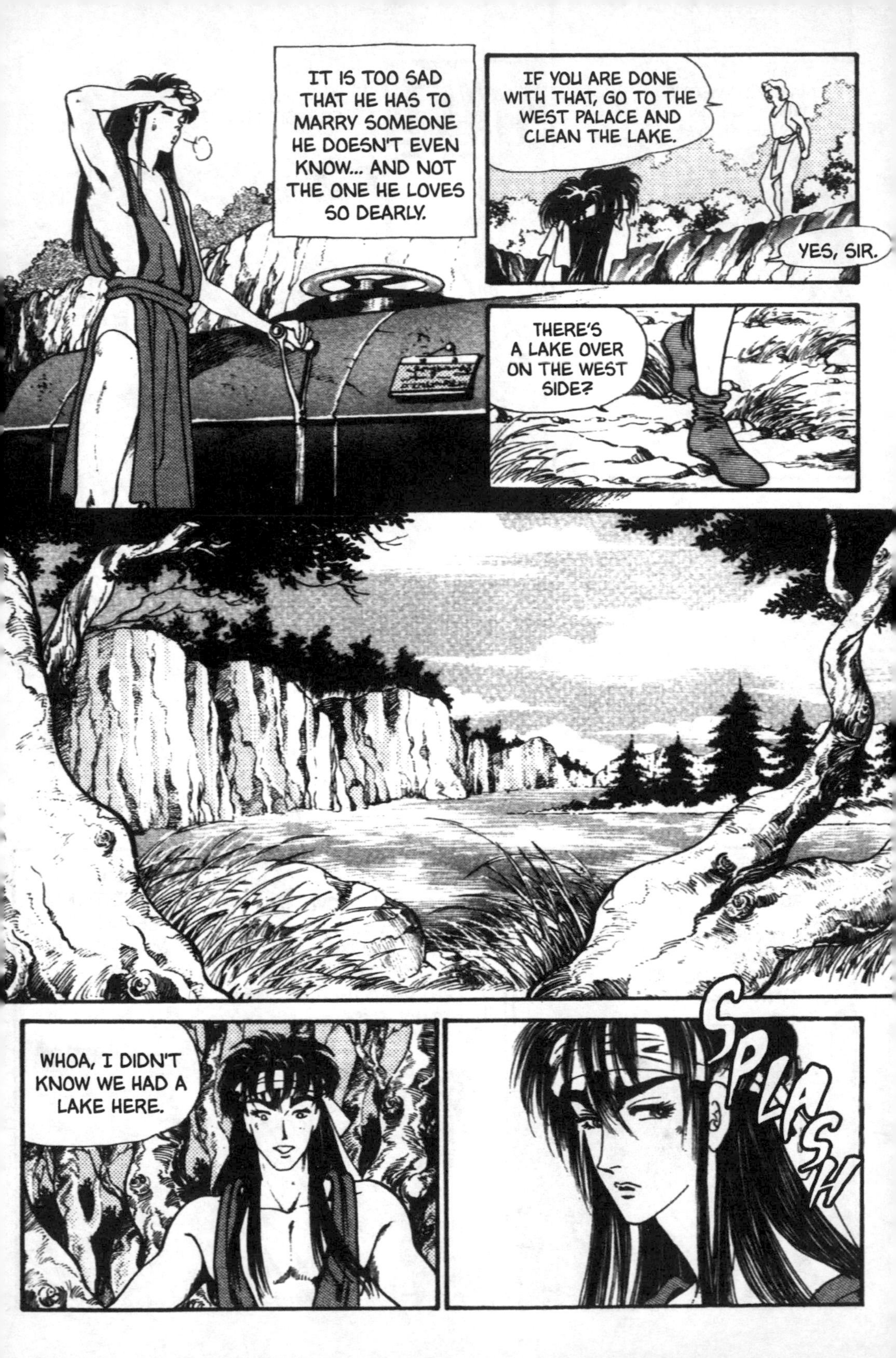
IT IS TOO SAD THAT HE HAS TO MARRY SOMEONE HE DOESN'T EVEN KNOW... AND NOT THE ONE HE LOVES SO DEARLY.
IF YOU ARE DONE WITH THAT, GO TO THE WEST PALACE AND CLEAN THE LAKE.
YES, SIR.
THERE'S A LAKE OVER ON THE WEST SIDE?
WHOA, I DIDN'T KNOW WE HAD A LAKE HERE.
SPLASH

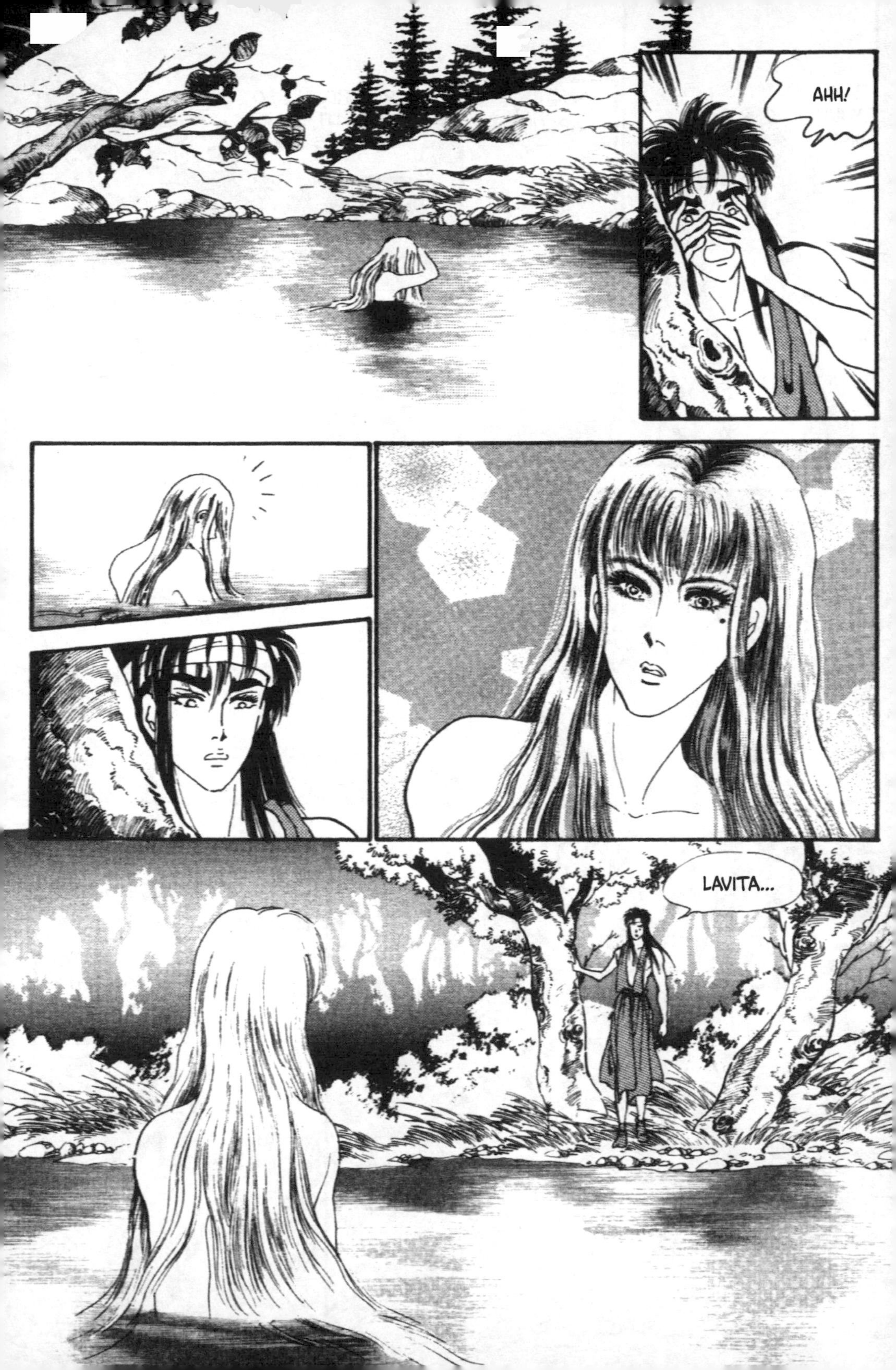
AHH!
LAVITA...

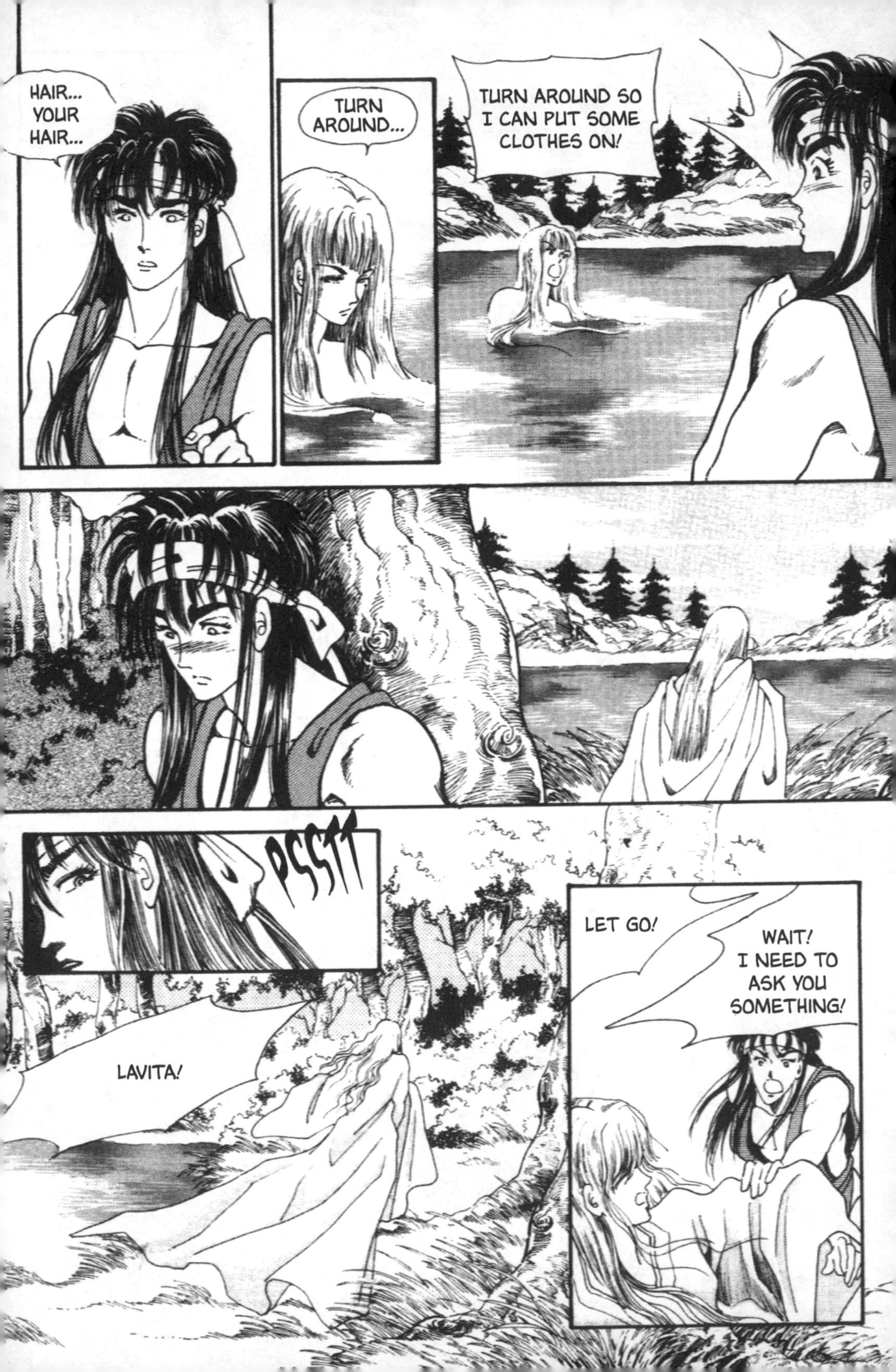
HAIR... YOUR HAIR...
TURN AROUND...
TURN AROUND SO I CAN PUT SOME CLOTHES ON!
PSSTT
LAVITA!
LET GO!
WAIT! I NEED TO ASK YOU SOMETHING!

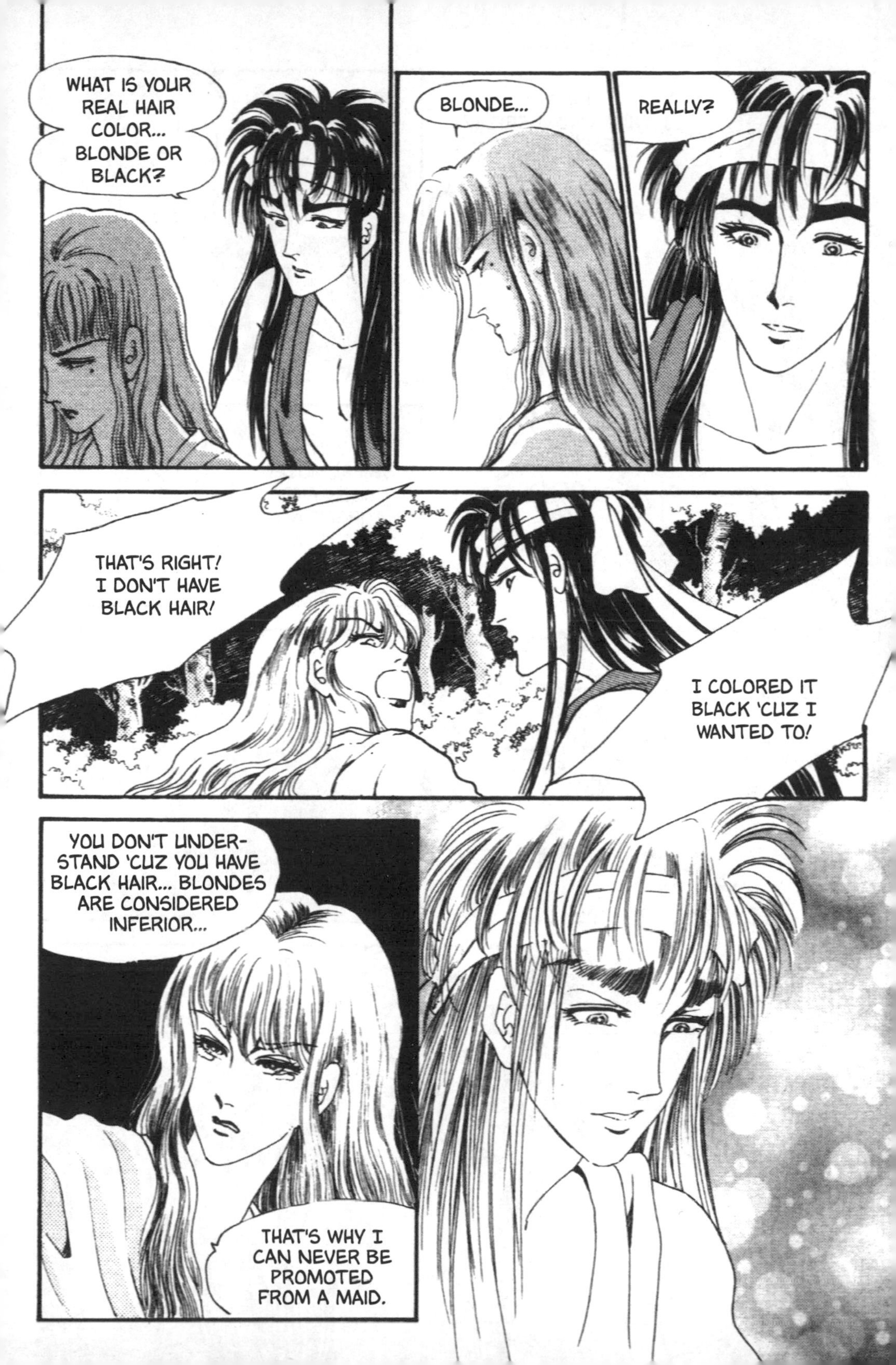
WHAT IS YOUR REAL HAIR COLOR... BLONDE OR BLACK?
BLONDE...
REALLY?
THAT'S RIGHT! I DON'T HAVE BLACK HAIR!
I COLORED IT BLACK 'CUZ I WANTED TO!
YOU DON'T UNDER-STAND 'CUZ YOU HAVE BLACK HAIR... BLONDES ARE CONSIDERED INFERIOR...
THAT'S WHY I CAN NEVER BE PROMOTED FROM A MAID.

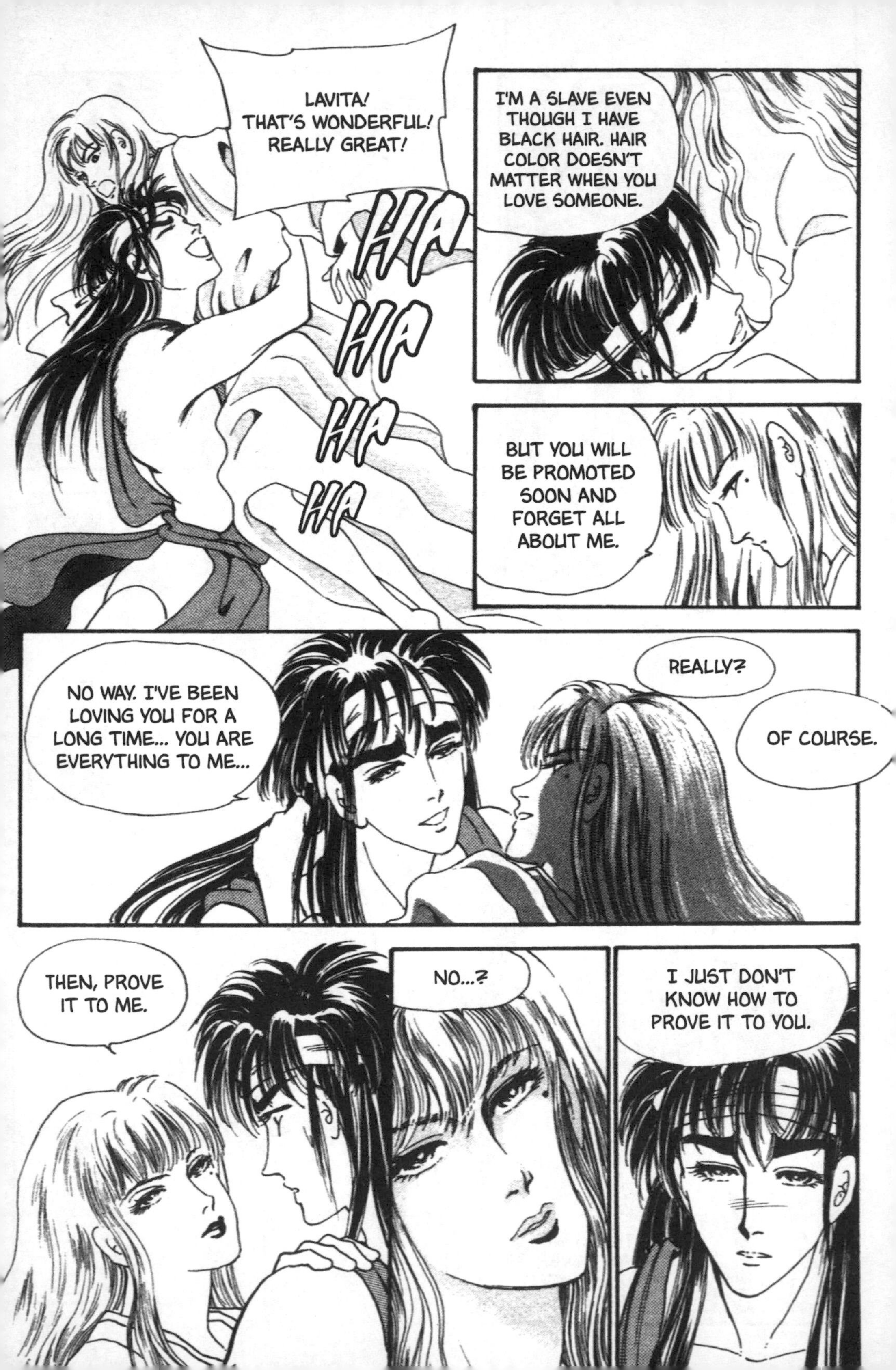
LAVITA! THAT'S WONDERFUL! REALLY GREAT!
HA HA HA HA
I'M A SLAVE EVEN THOUGH I HAVE BLACK HAIR. HAIR COLOR DOESN'T MATTER WHEN YOU LOVE SOMEONE.
BUT YOU WILL BE PROMOTED SOON AND FORGET ALL ABOUT ME.
NO WAY. I'VE BEEN LOVING YOU FOR A LONG TIME... YOU ARE EVERYTHING TO ME...
REALLY?
OF COURSE.
THEN, PROVE IT TO ME.
NO...?
I JUST DON'T KNOW HOW TO PROVE IT TO YOU.

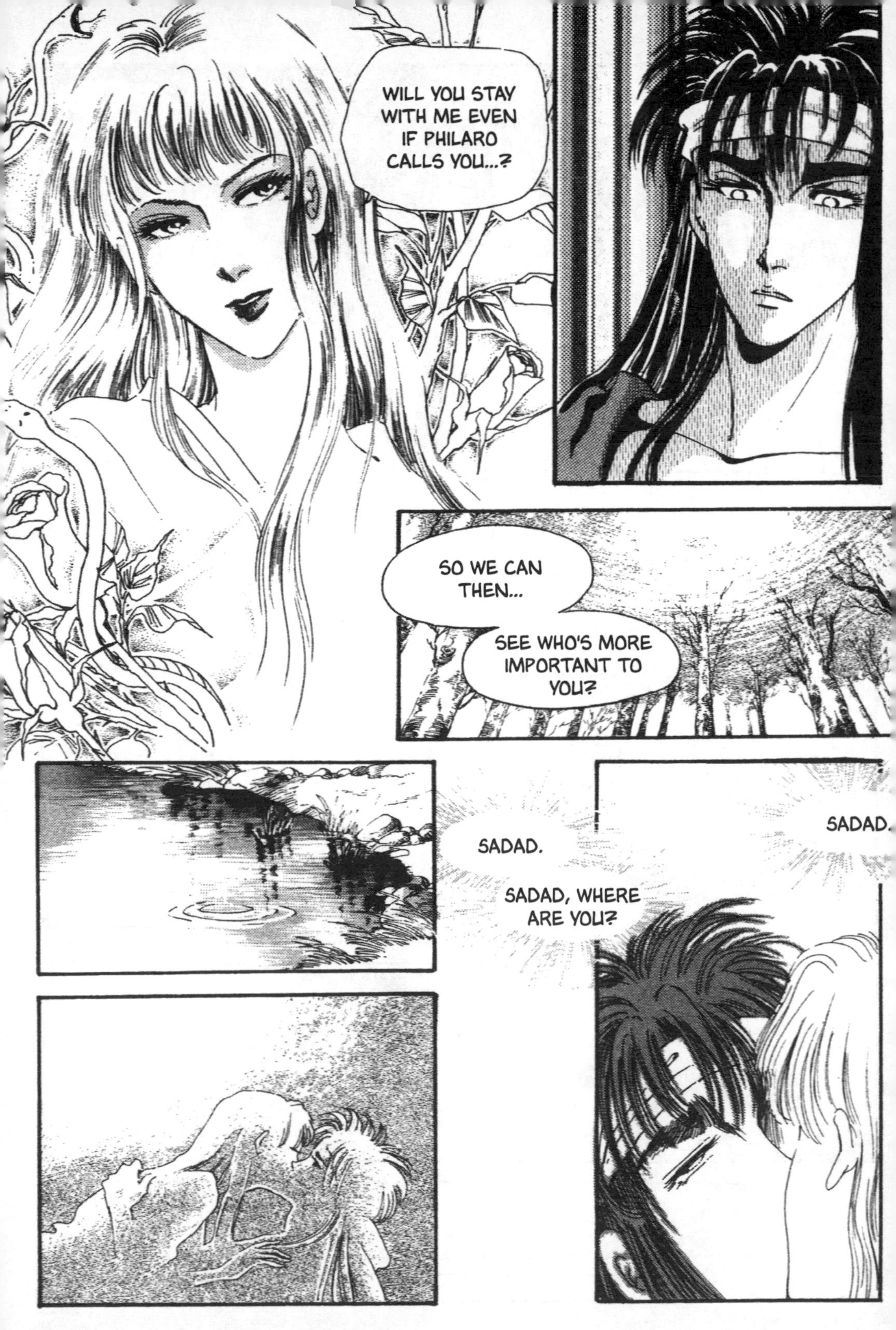

WILL YOU STAY WITH ME EVEN IF PHILARO CALLS YOU...?
SO WE CAN THEN...
SEE WHO'S MORE IMPORTANT TO YOU?
SADAD.
SADAD.
SADAD, WHERE ARE YOU?

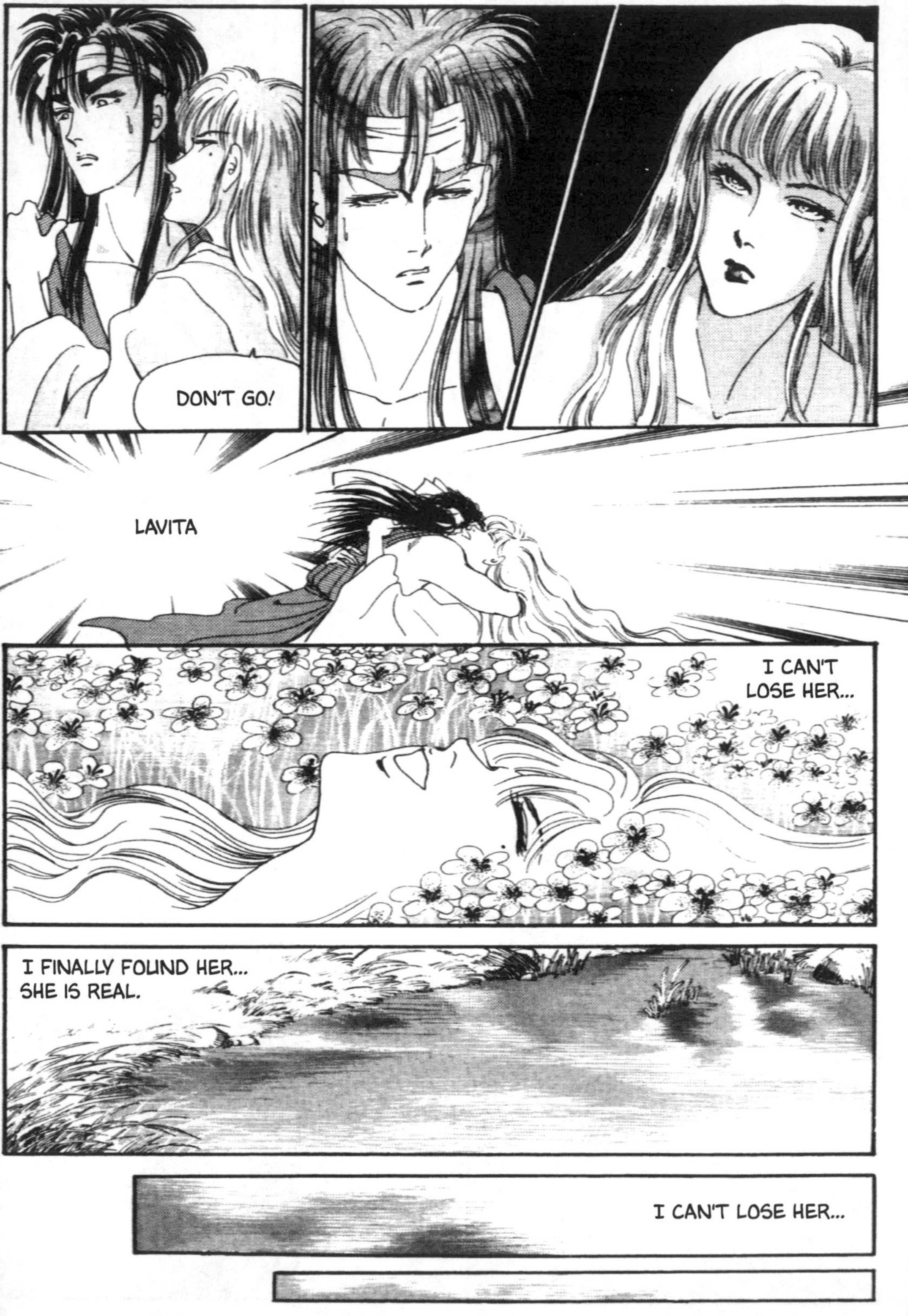
DON'T GO!
LAVITA
I CAN'T LOSE HER...
I FINALLY FOUND HER... SHE IS REAL.
I CAN'T LOSE HER...

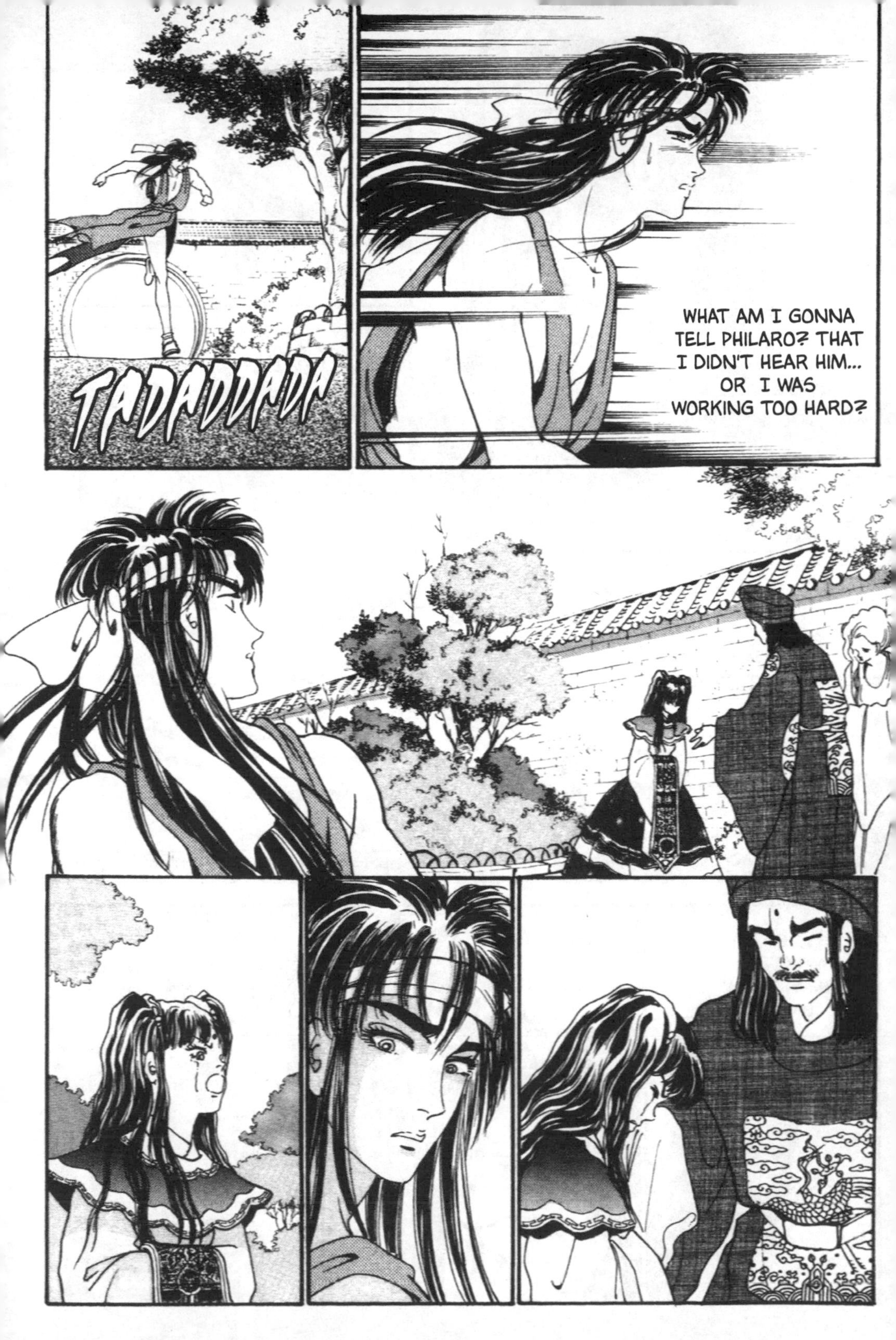

TADADDADA
WHAT AM I GONNA TELL PHILARO? THAT I DIDN'T HEAR HIM... OR I WAS WORKING TOO HARD?

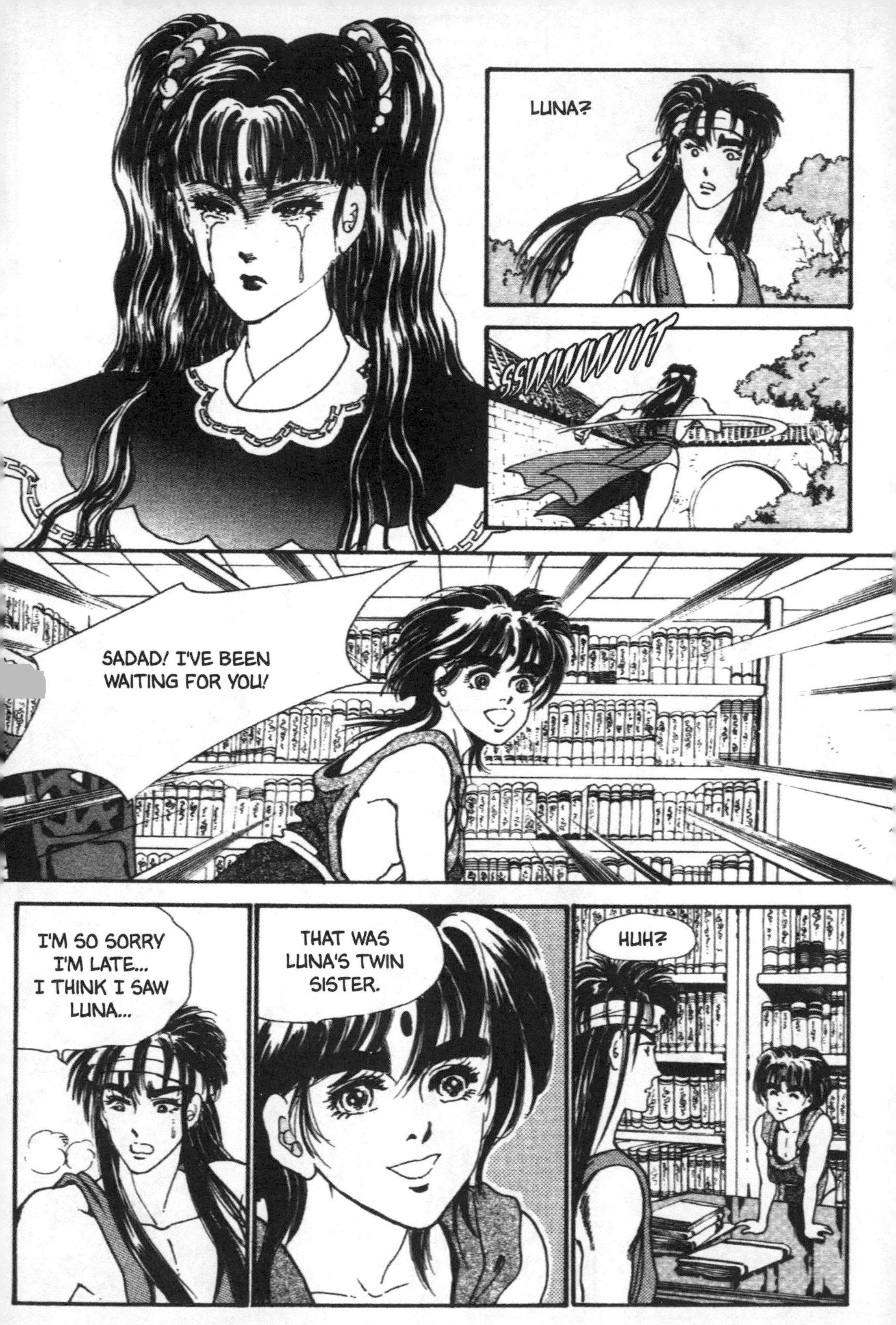
LUNA?
SSWAAAAAAIIIIT
SADAD! I'VE BEEN WAITING FOR YOU!
I'M SO SORRY I'M LATE... I THINK I SAW LUNA...
THAT WAS LUNA'S TWIN SISTER.
HUH?

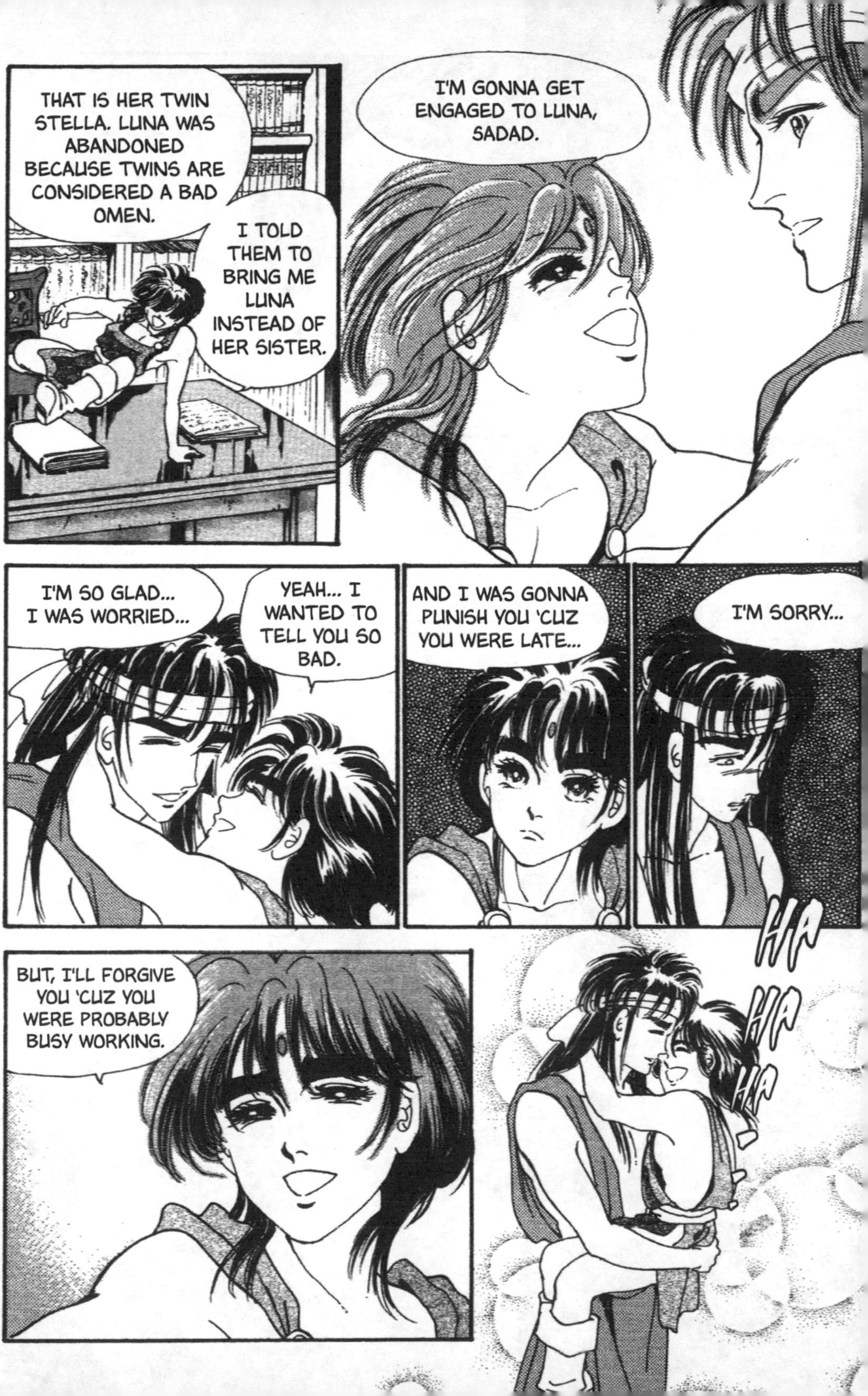
THAT IS HER TWIN STELLA. LUNA WAS ABANDONED BECAUSE TWINS ARE CONSIDERED A BAD OMEN.
I TOLD THEM TO BRING ME LUNA INSTEAD OF HER SISTER.
I'M GONNA GET ENGAGED TO LUNA, SADAD.
I'M SO GLAD... I WAS WORRIED...
YEAH... I WANTED TO TELL YOU SO BAD.
AND I WAS GONNA PUNISH YOU 'CUZ YOU WERE LATE...
I'M SORRY...
BUT, I'LL FORGIVE YOU 'CUZ YOU WERE PROBABLY BUSY WORKING.
HA
HA
HA

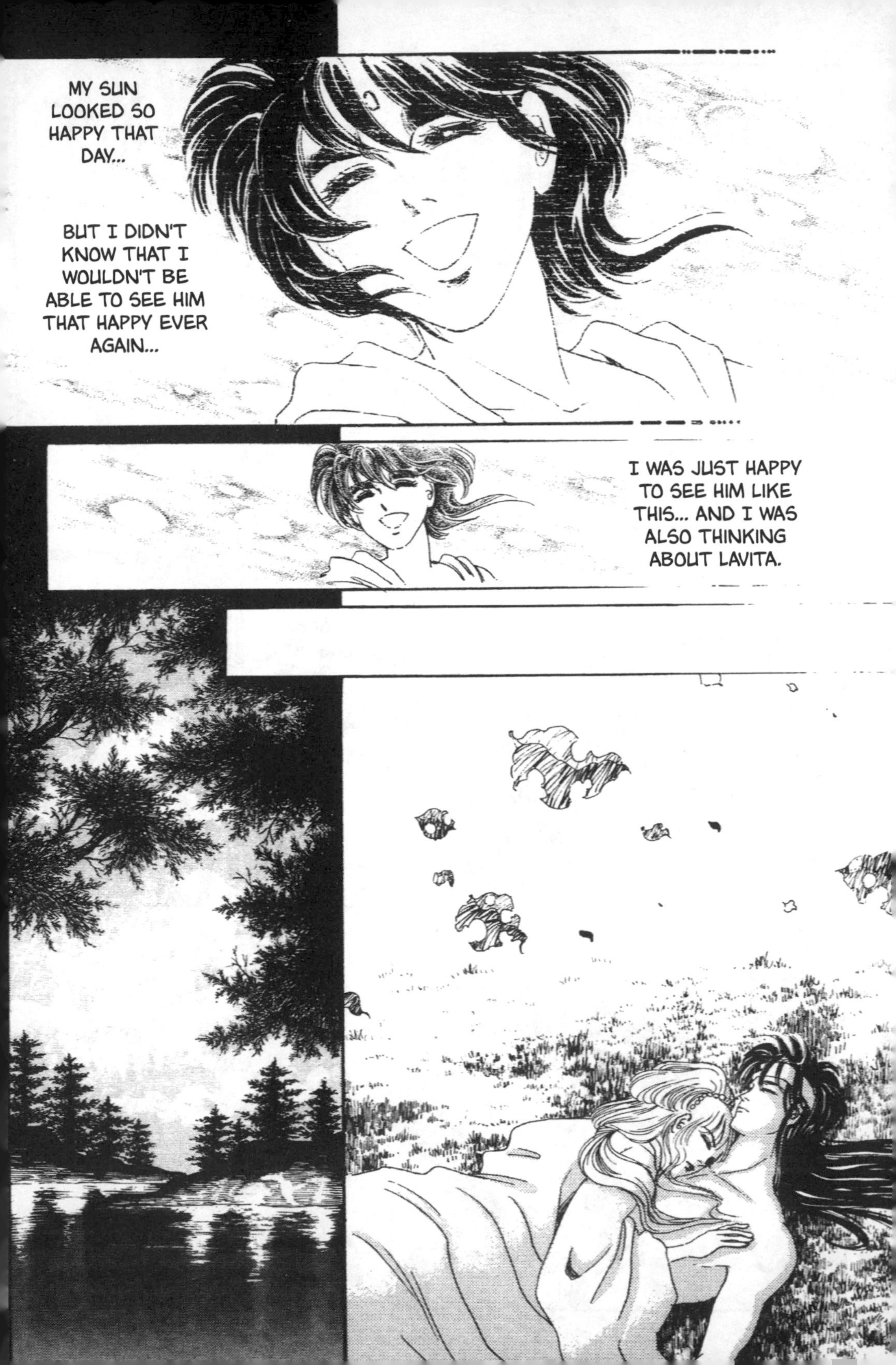
MY SUN LOOKED SO HAPPY THAT DAY...
BUT I DIDN'T KNOW THAT I WOULDN'T BE ABLE TO SEE HIM THAT HAPPY EVER AGAIN...
I WAS JUST HAPPY TO SEE HIM LIKE THIS... AND I WAS ALSO THINKING ABOUT LAVITA.

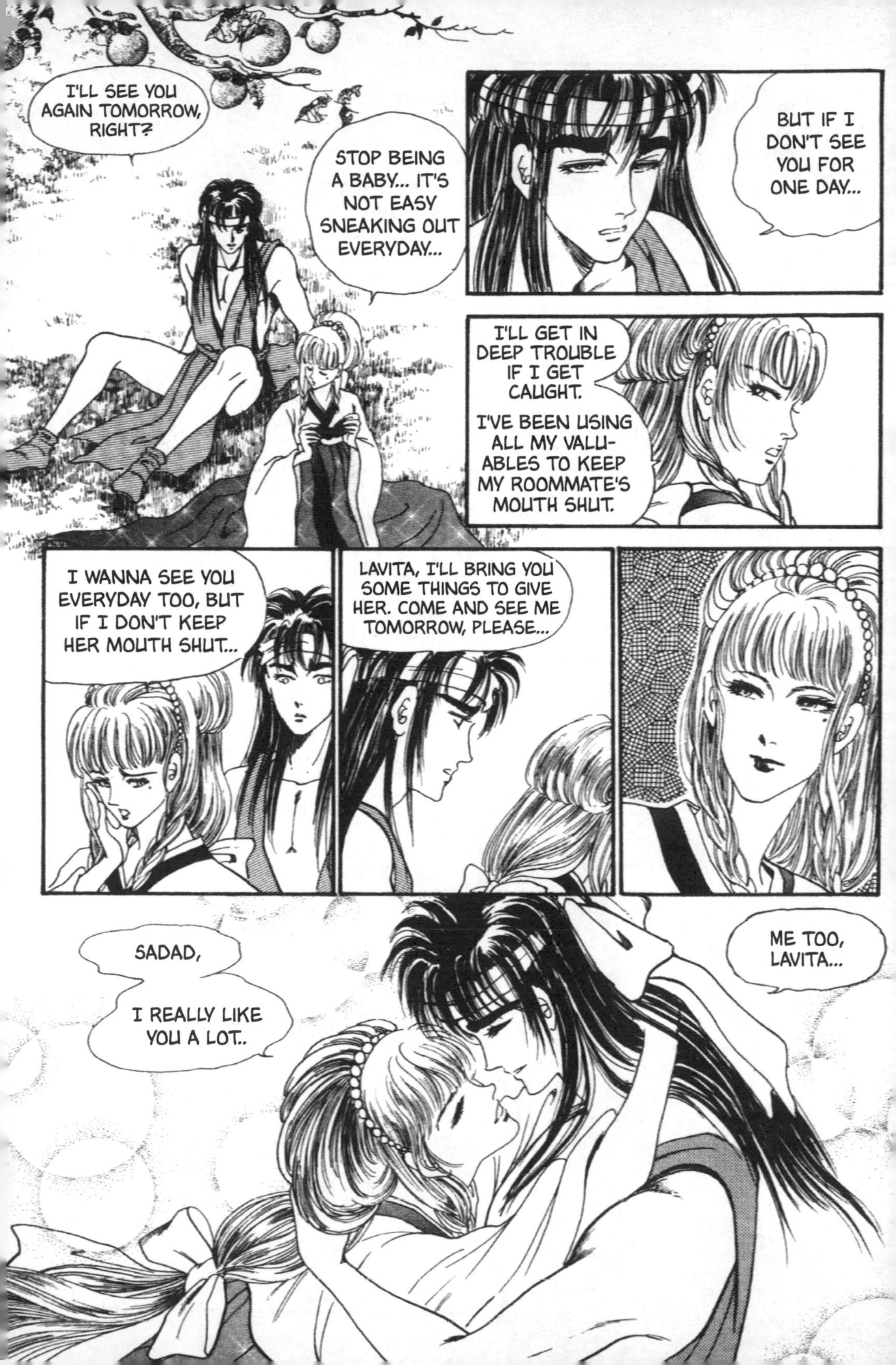
I'LL SEE YOU AGAIN TOMORROW, RIGHT?
STOP BEING A BABY... IT'S NOT EASY SNEAKING OUT EVERYDAY...
BUT IF I DON'T SEE YOU FOR ONE DAY...
I'LL GET IN DEEP TROUBLE IF I GET CAUGHT.
I'VE BEEN USING ALL MY VALU-ABLES TO KEEP MY ROOMMATE'S MOUTH SHUT.
I WANNA SEE YOU EVERYDAY TOO, BUT IF I DON'T KEEP HER MOUTH SHUT...
LAVITA, I'LL BRING YOU SOME THINGS TO GIVE HER. COME AND SEE ME TOMORROW, PLEASE...
SADAD,
I REALLY LIKE YOU A LOT..
ME TOO, LAVITA...

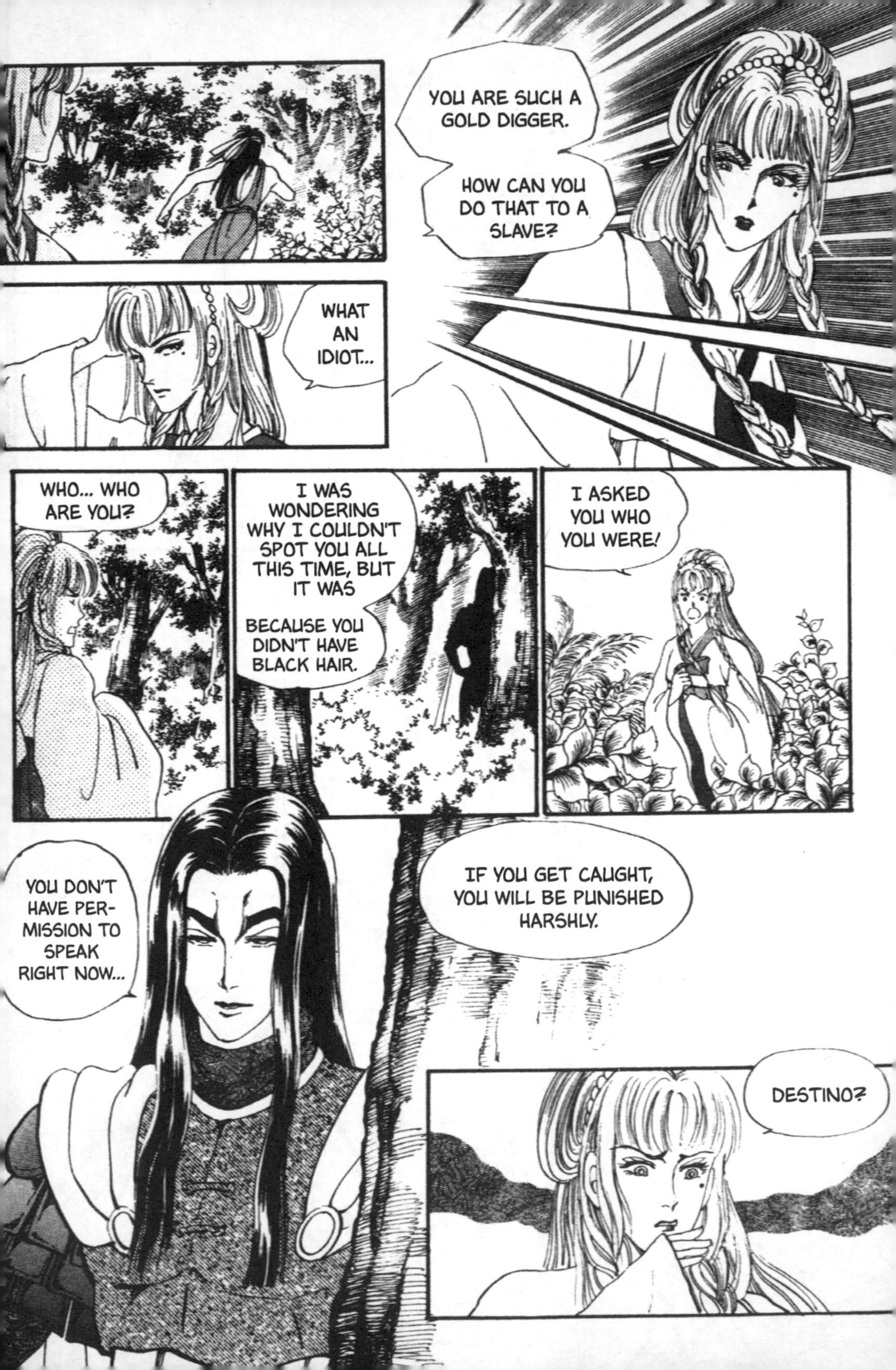
YOU ARE SUCH A GOLD DIGGER.
HOW CAN YOU DO THAT TO A SLAVE?
WHAT AN IDIOT...
WHO... WHO ARE YOU?
I WAS WONDERING WHY I COULDN'T SPOT YOU ALL THIS TIME, BUT IT WAS
BECAUSE YOU DIDN'T HAVE BLACK HAIR.
I ASKED YOU WHO YOU WERE!
YOU DON'T HAVE PER-MISSION TO SPEAK RIGHT NOW...
IF YOU GET CAUGHT, YOU WILL BE PUNISHED HARSHLY.
DESTINO?

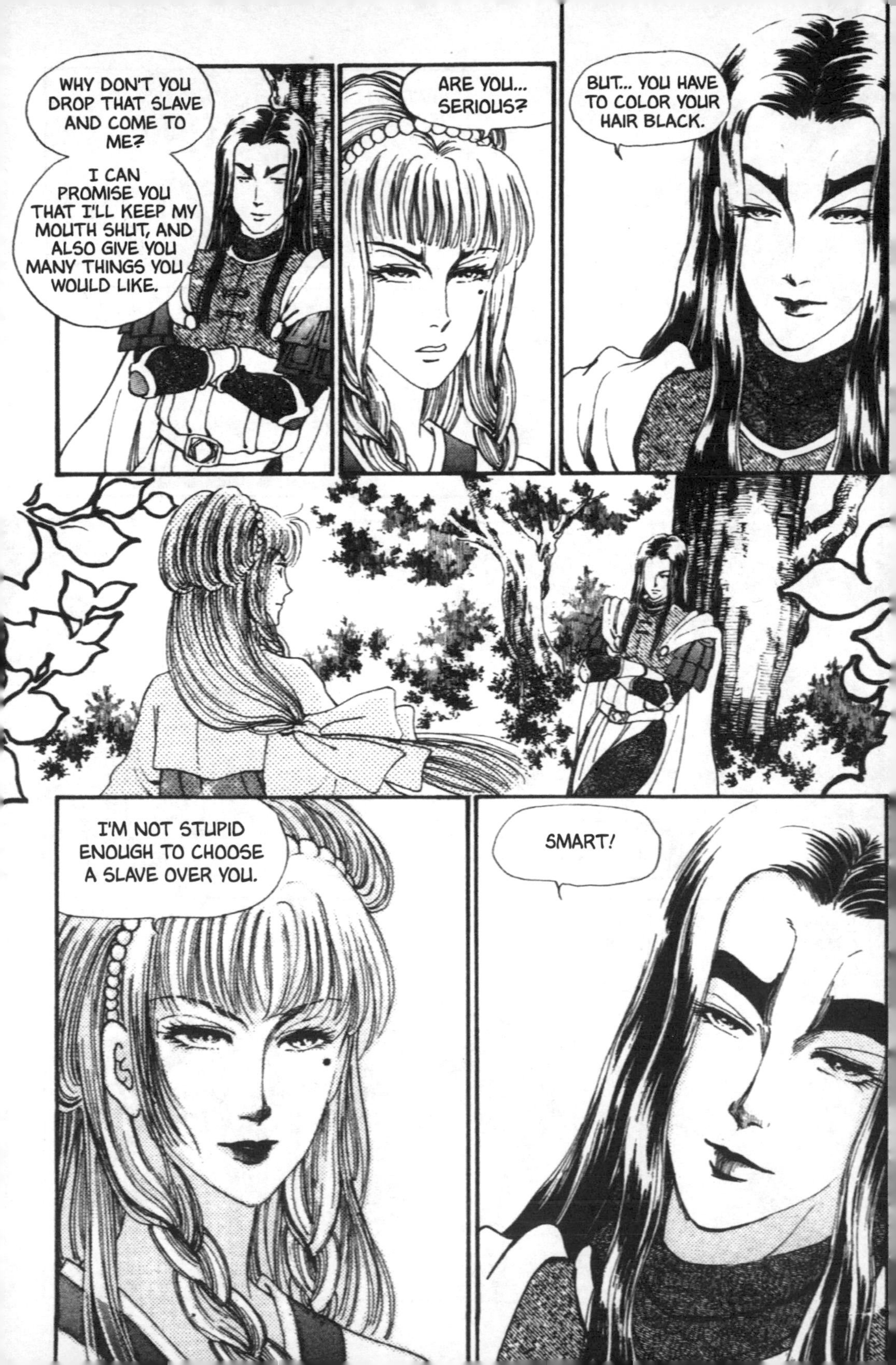
WHY DON'T YOU DROP THAT SLAVE AND COME TO ME?
I CAN PROMISE YOU THAT I'LL KEEP MY MOUTH SHUT, AND ALSO GIVE YOU MANY THINGS YOU WOULD LIKE.
ARE YOU... SERIOUS?
BUT... YOU HAVE TO COLOR YOUR HAIR BLACK.
I'M NOT STUPID ENOUGH TO CHOOSE A SLAVE OVER YOU.
SMART!

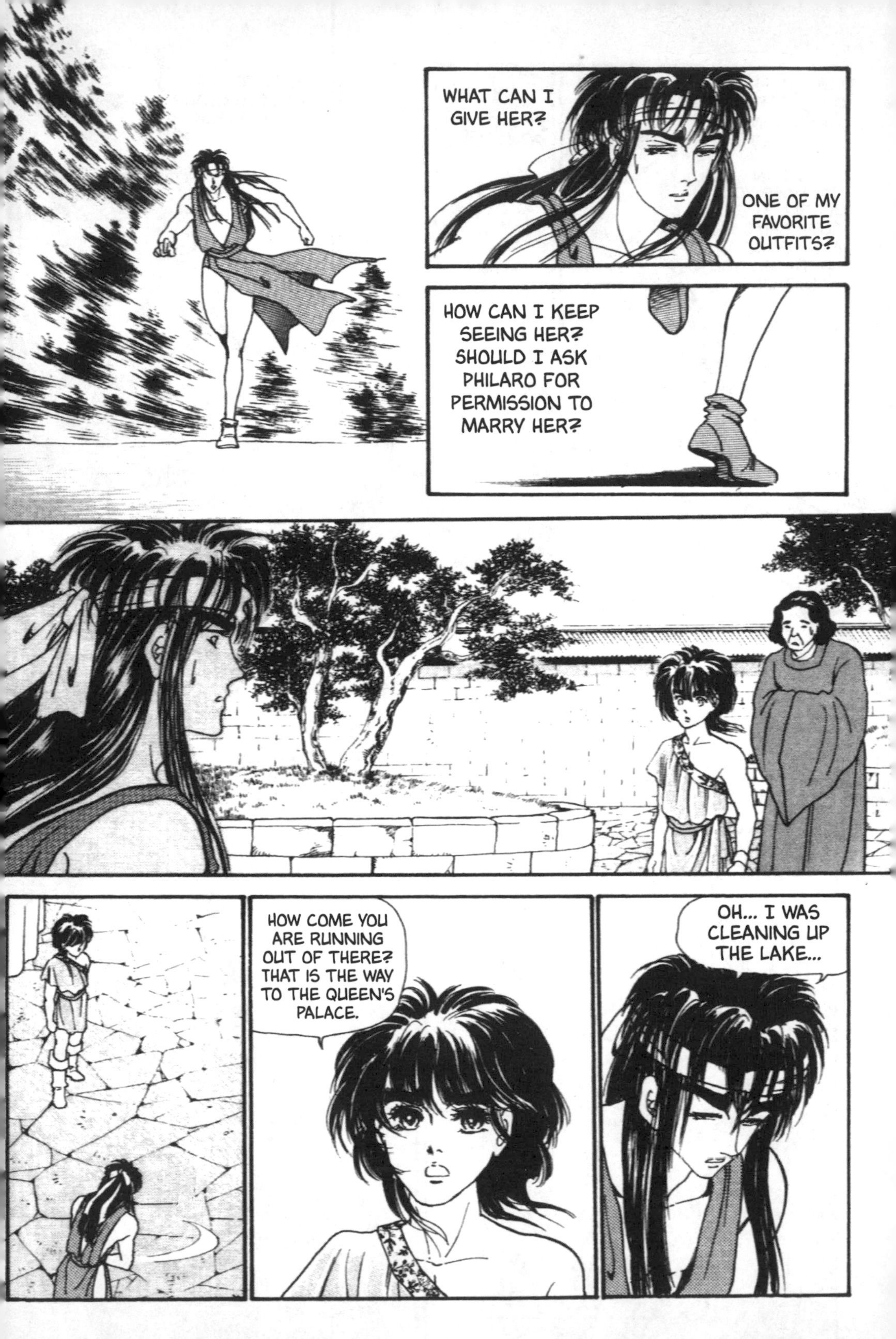
WHAT CAN I GIVE HER?
ONE OF MY FAVORITE OUTFITS?
HOW CAN I KEEP SEEING HER? SHOULD I ASK PHILARO FOR PERMISSION TO MARRY HER?
HOW COME YOU ARE RUNNING OUT OF THERE? THAT IS THE WAY TO THE QUEEN'S PALACE.
OH... I WAS CLEANING UP THE LAKE...

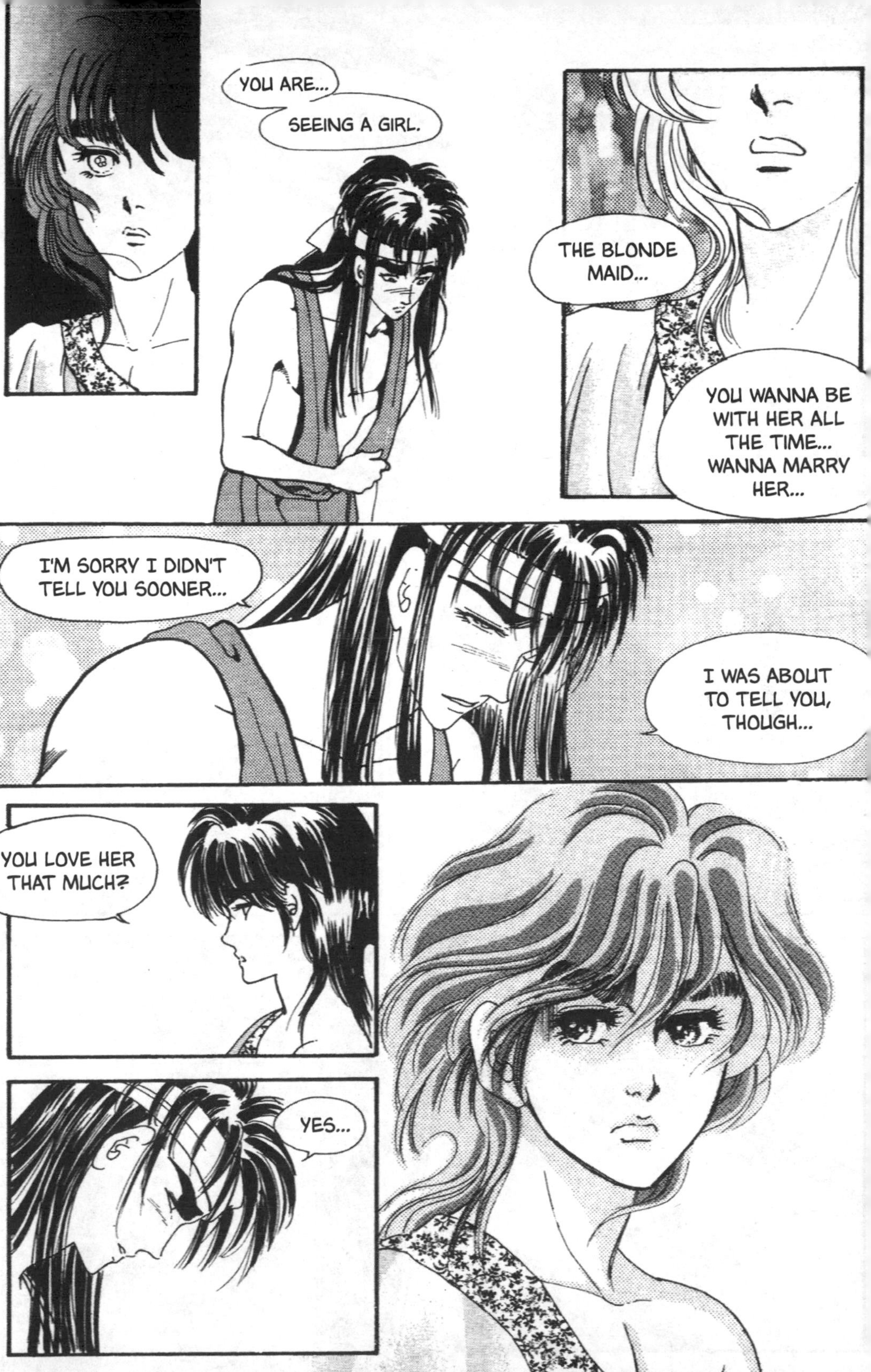
YOU ARE...
SEEING A GIRL.
THE BLONDE MAID...
YOU WANNA BE WITH HER ALL THE TIME... WANNA MARRY HER...
I'M SORRY I DIDN'T TELL YOU SOONER...
I WAS ABOUT TO TELL YOU, THOUGH...
YOU LOVE HER THAT MUCH?
YES...

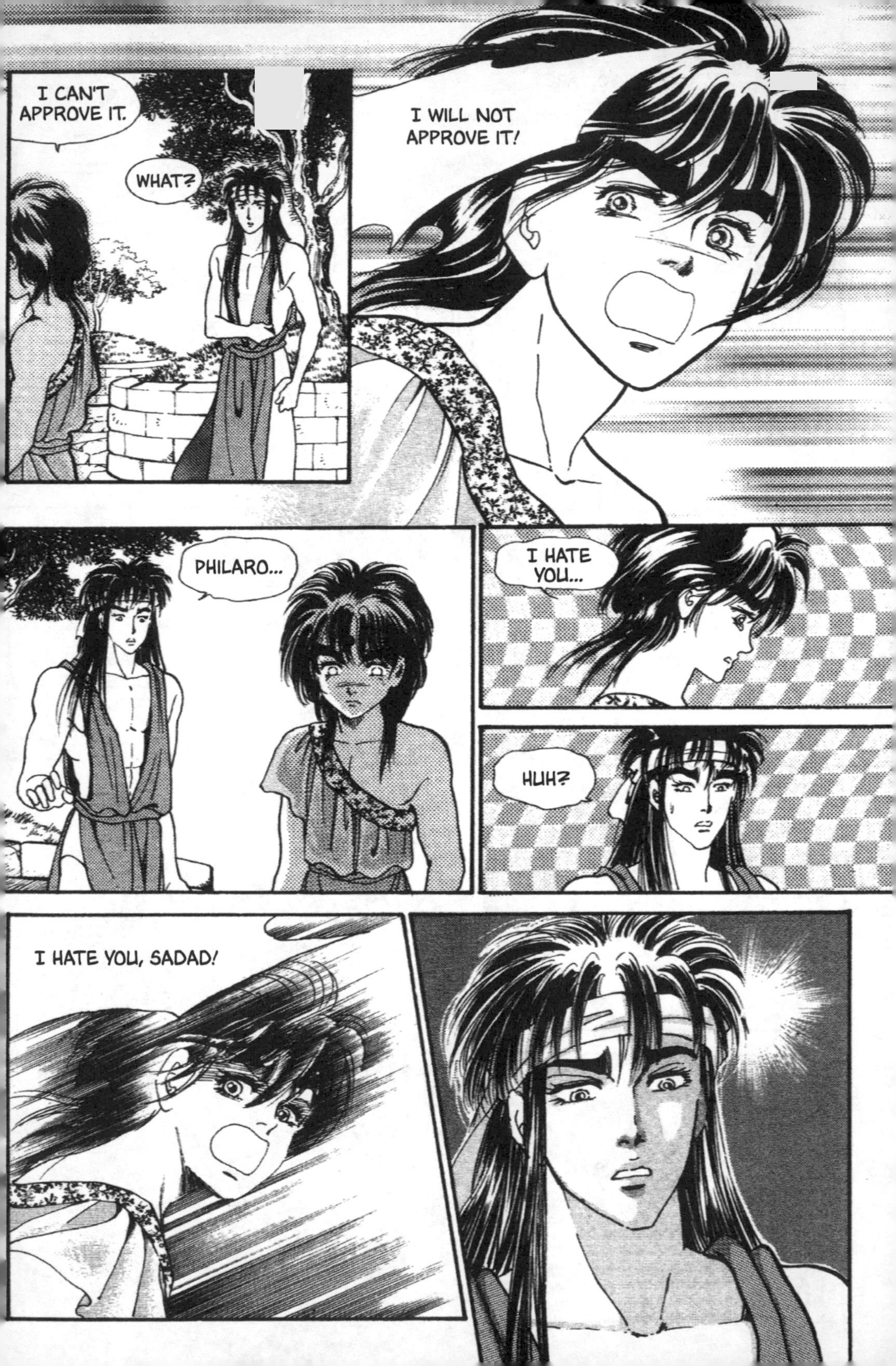
I CAN'T APPROVE IT.
WHAT?
I WILL NOT APPROVE IT!
PHILARO...
I HATE YOU...
HUH?
I HATE YOU, SADAD!

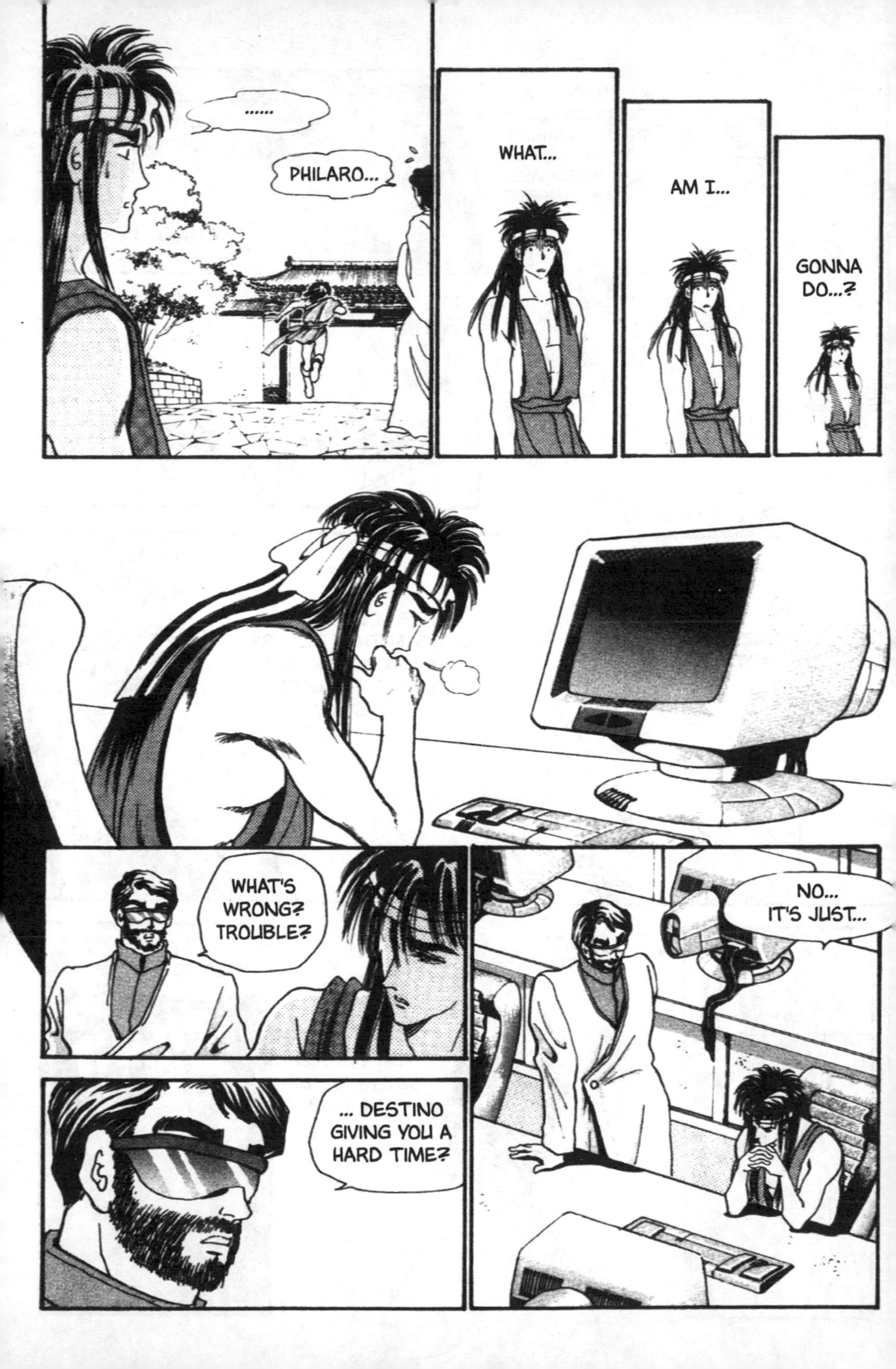
......
PHILARO...
WHAT...
AM I...
GONNA DO...?
WHAT'S WRONG? TROUBLE?
... DESTINO GIVING YOU A HARD TIME?
NO... IT'S JUST...

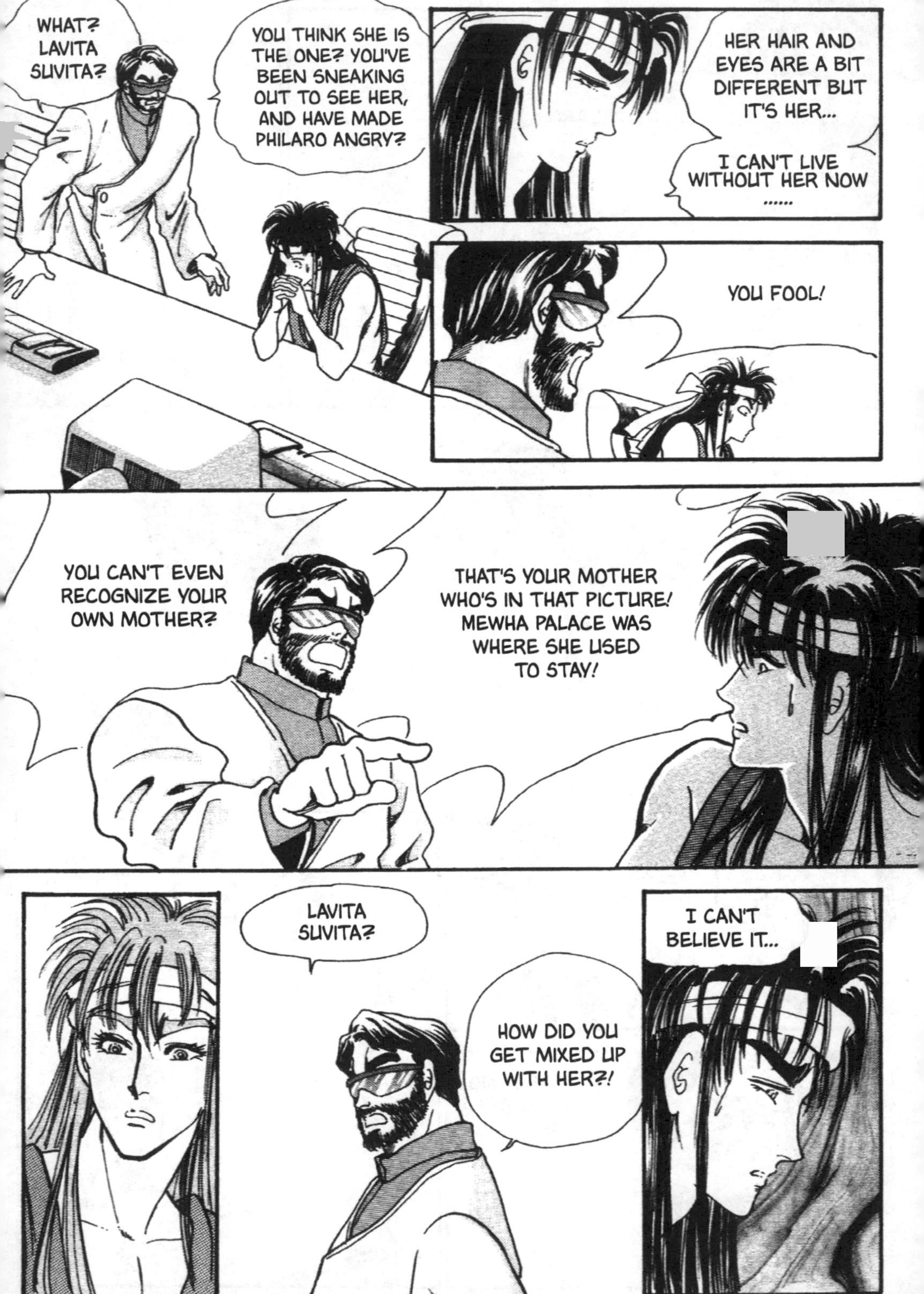
WHAT? LAVITA SUVITA?
YOU THINK SHE IS THE ONE? YOU'VE BEEN SNEAKING OUT TO SEE HER, AND HAVE MADE PHILARO ANGRY?
HER HAIR AND EYES ARE A BIT DIFFERENT BUT IT'S HER...
I CAN'T LIVE WITHOUT HER NOW ......
YOU FOOL!
YOU CAN'T EVEN RECOGNIZE YOUR OWN MOTHER?
THAT'S YOUR MOTHER WHO'S IN THAT PICTURE! MEWHA PALACE WAS WHERE SHE USED TO STAY!
LAVITA SUVITA?
HOW DID YOU GET MIXED UP WITH HER?!
I CAN'T BELIEVE IT...

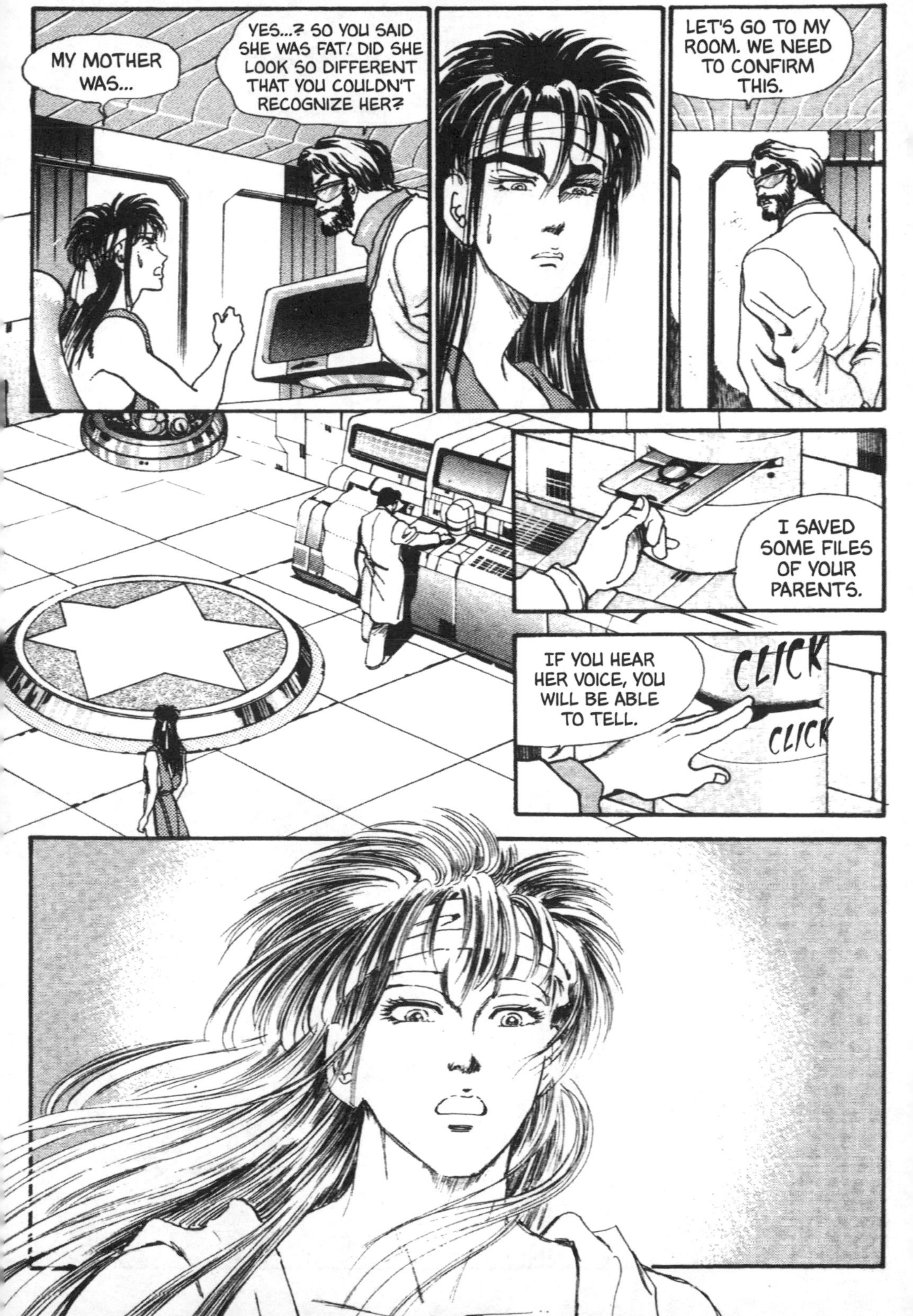
MY MOTHER WAS...
YES...? SO YOU SAID SHE WAS FAT! DID SHE LOOK SO DIFFERENT THAT YOU COULDN'T RECOGNIZE HER?
LET'S GO TO MY ROOM. WE NEED TO CONFIRM THIS.
I SAVED SOME FILES OF YOUR PARENTS.
IF YOU HEAR HER VOICE, YOU WILL BE ABLE TO TELL.
CLICK
CLICK

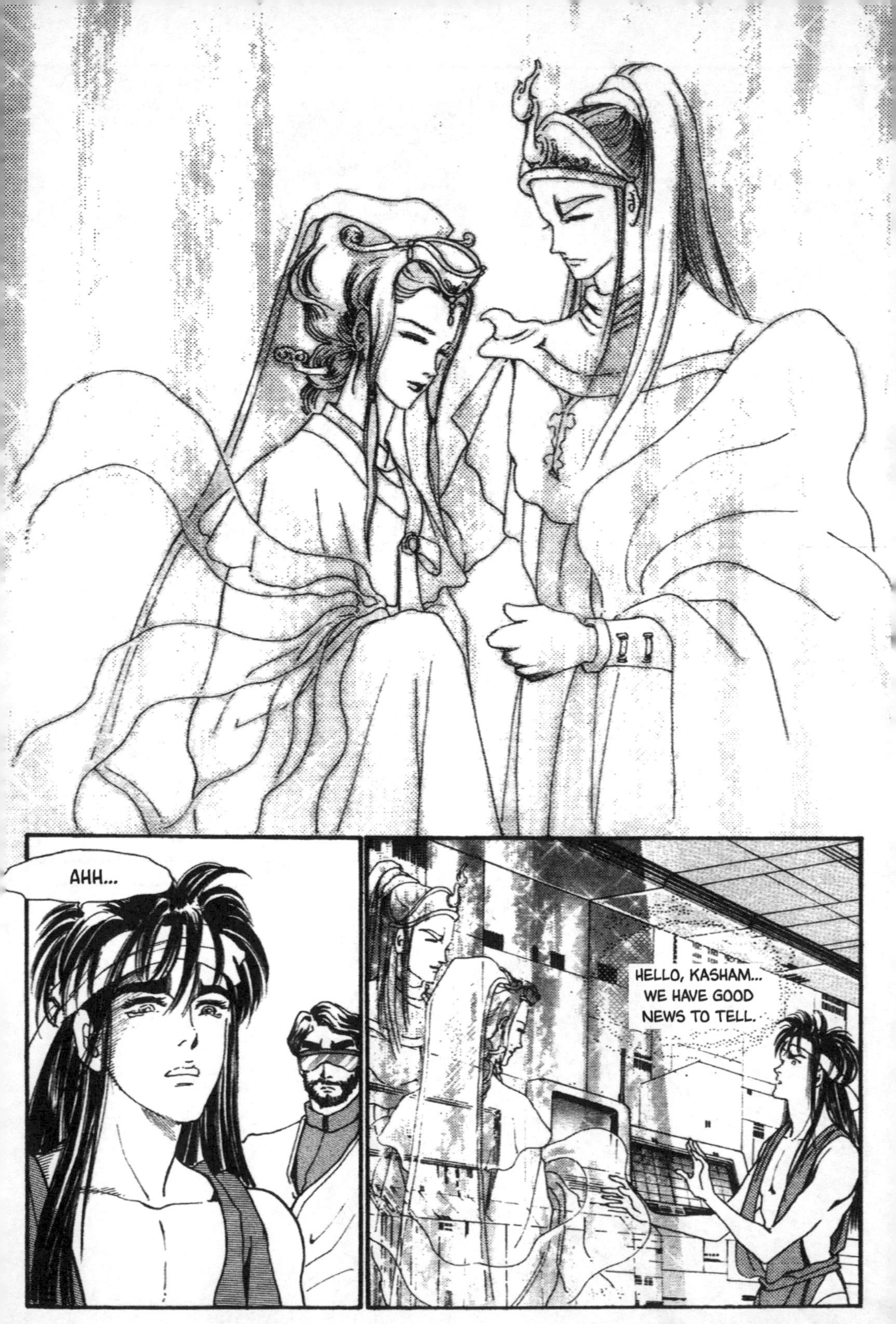
AHH...
HELLO, KASHAM... WE HAVE GOOD NEWS TO TELL.

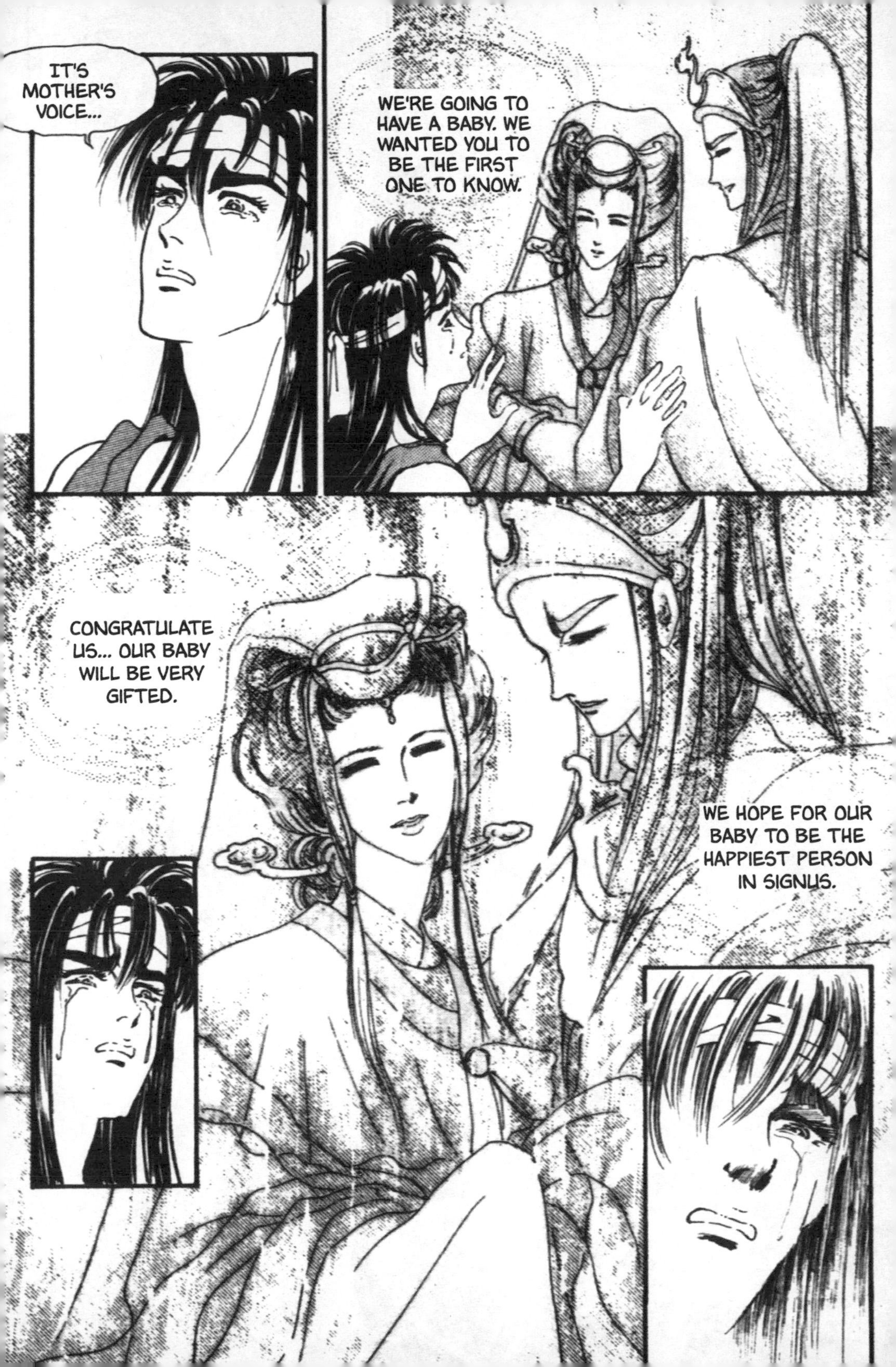
IT'S MOTHER'S VOICE...
WE'RE GOING TO HAVE A BABY. WE WANTED YOU TO BE THE FIRST ONE TO KNOW.
CONGRATULATE US... OUR BABY WILL BE VERY GIFTED.
WE HOPE FOR OUR BABY TO BE THE HAPPIEST PERSON IN SIGNUS.

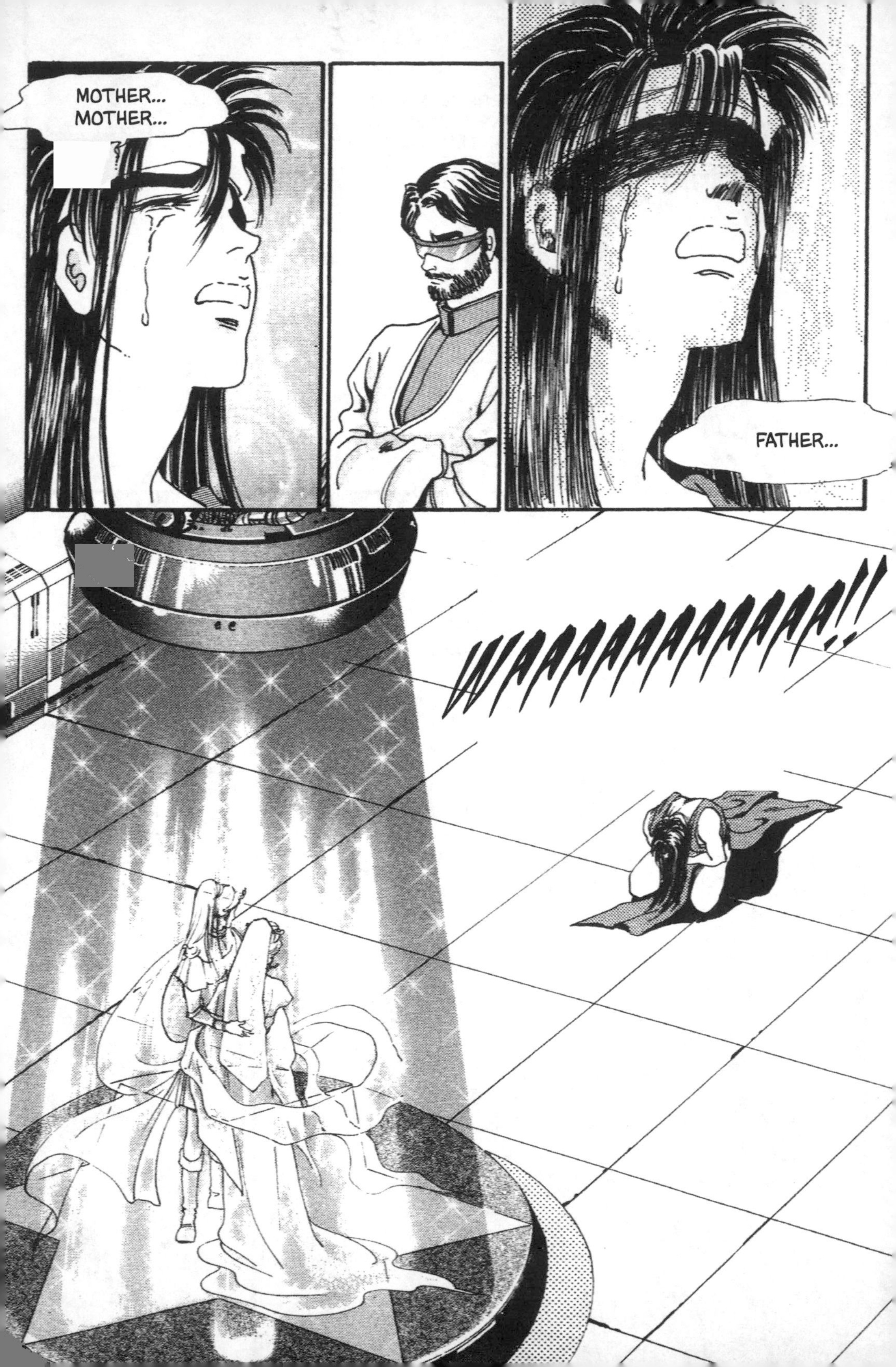
MOTHER... MOTHER...
FATHER...
WAAAAAAAAAAAAAA!!

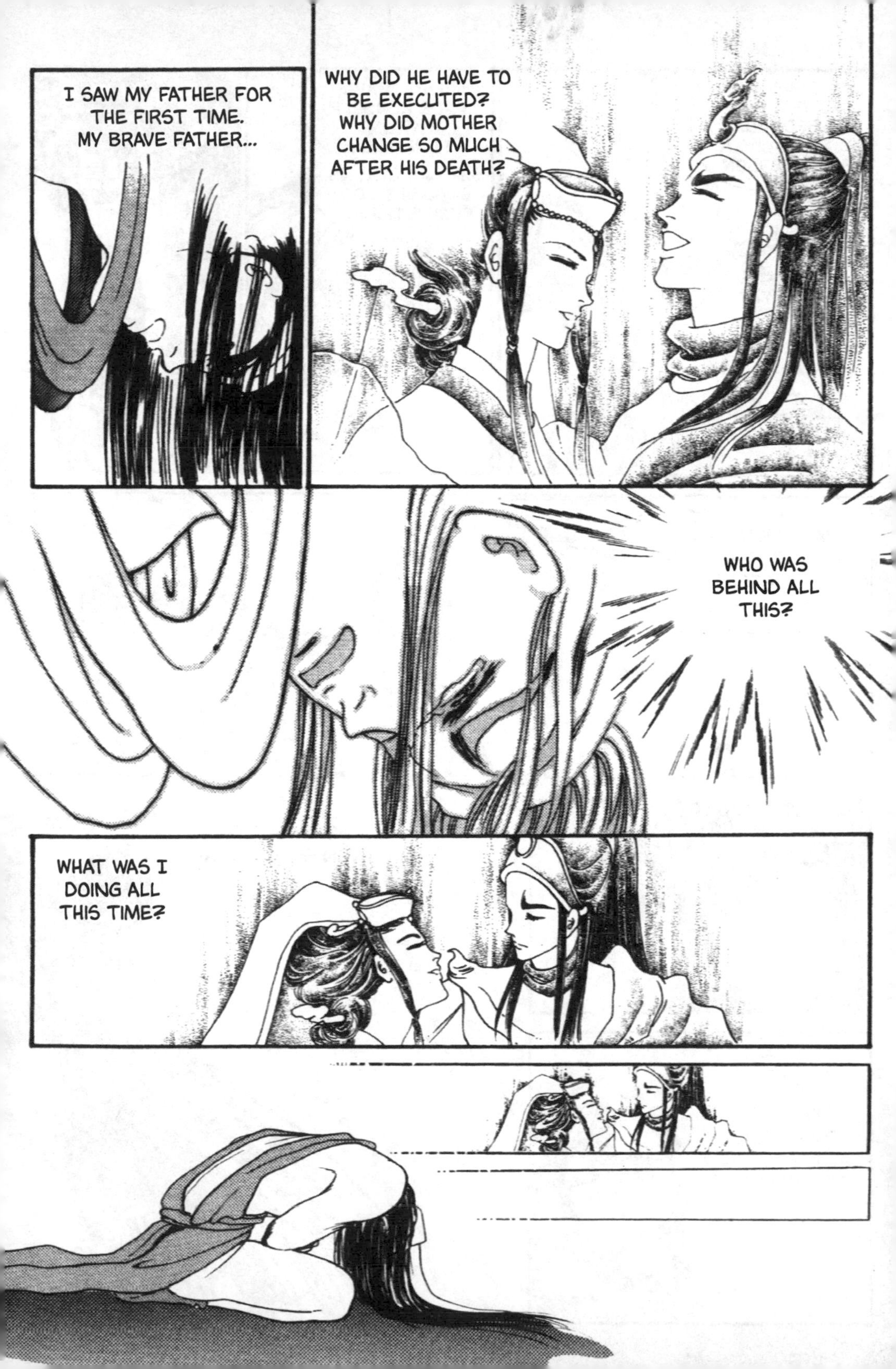
I SAW MY FATHER FOR THE FIRST TIME. MY BRAVE FATHER...
WHY DID HE HAVE TO BE EXECUTED? WHY DID MOTHER CHANGE SO MUCH AFTER HIS DEATH?
WHO WAS BEHIND ALL THIS?
WHAT WAS I DOING ALL THIS TIME?

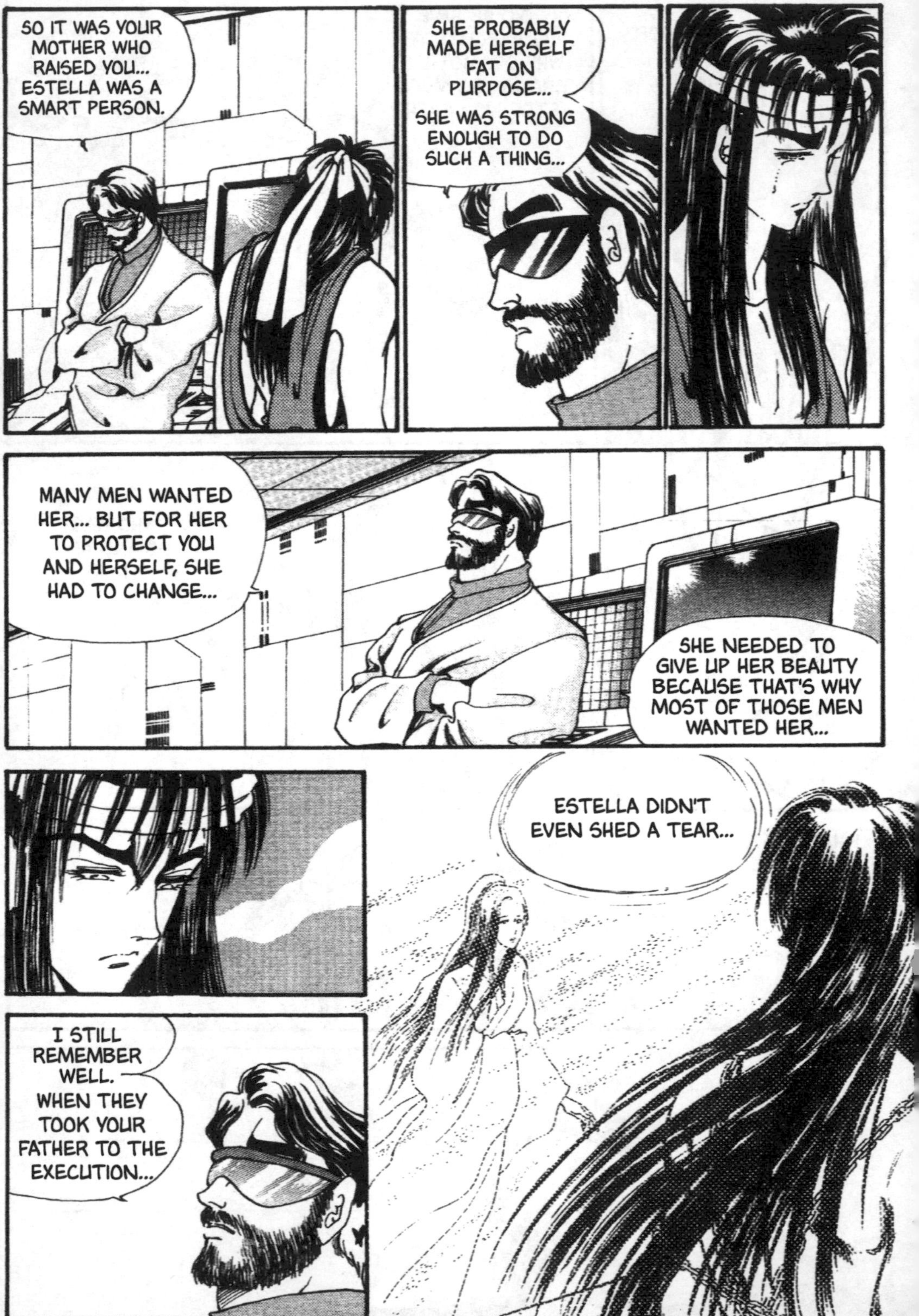
SO IT WAS YOUR MOTHER WHO RAISED YOU... ESTELLA WAS A SMART PERSON.
SHE PROBABLY MADE HERSELF FAT ON PURPOSE...
SHE WAS STRONG ENOUGH TO DO SUCH A THING...
MANY MEN WANTED HER... BUT FOR HER TO PROTECT YOU AND HERSELF, SHE HAD TO CHANGE...
SHE NEEDED TO GIVE UP HER BEAUTY BECAUSE THAT'S WHY MOST OF THOSE MEN WANTED HER...
ESTELLA DIDN'T EVEN SHED A TEAR...
I STILL REMEMBER WELL. WHEN THEY TOOK YOUR FATHER TO THE EXECUTION...

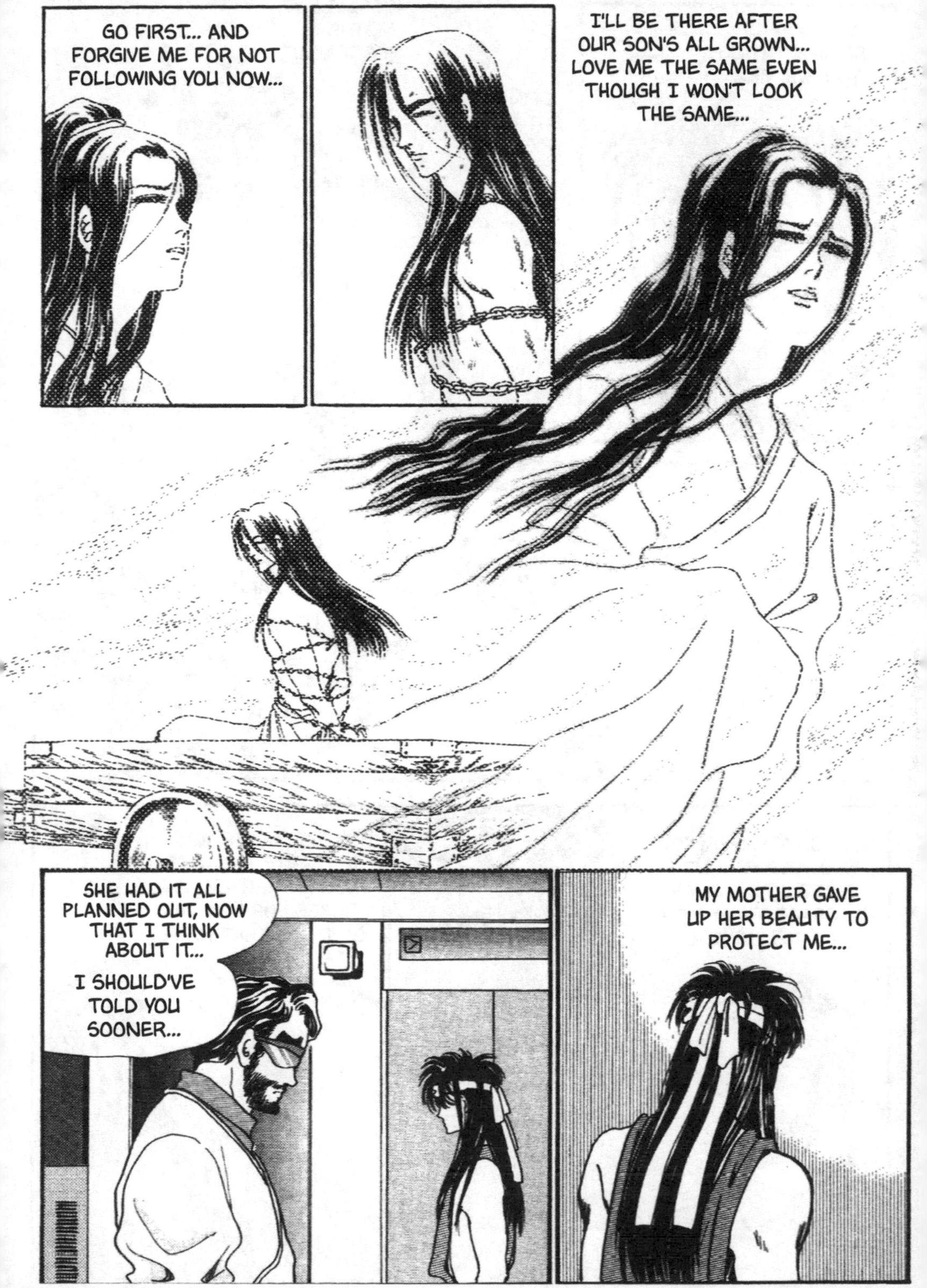
GO FIRST... AND FORGIVE ME FOR NOT FOLLOWING YOU NOW...
I'LL BE THERE AFTER OUR SON'S ALL GROWN... LOVE ME THE SAME EVEN THOUGH I WON'T LOOK THE SAME...
SHE HAD IT ALL PLANNED OUT, NOW THAT I THINK ABOUT IT...
I SHOULD'VE TOLD YOU SOONER...
MY MOTHER GAVE UP HER BEAUTY TO PROTECT ME...

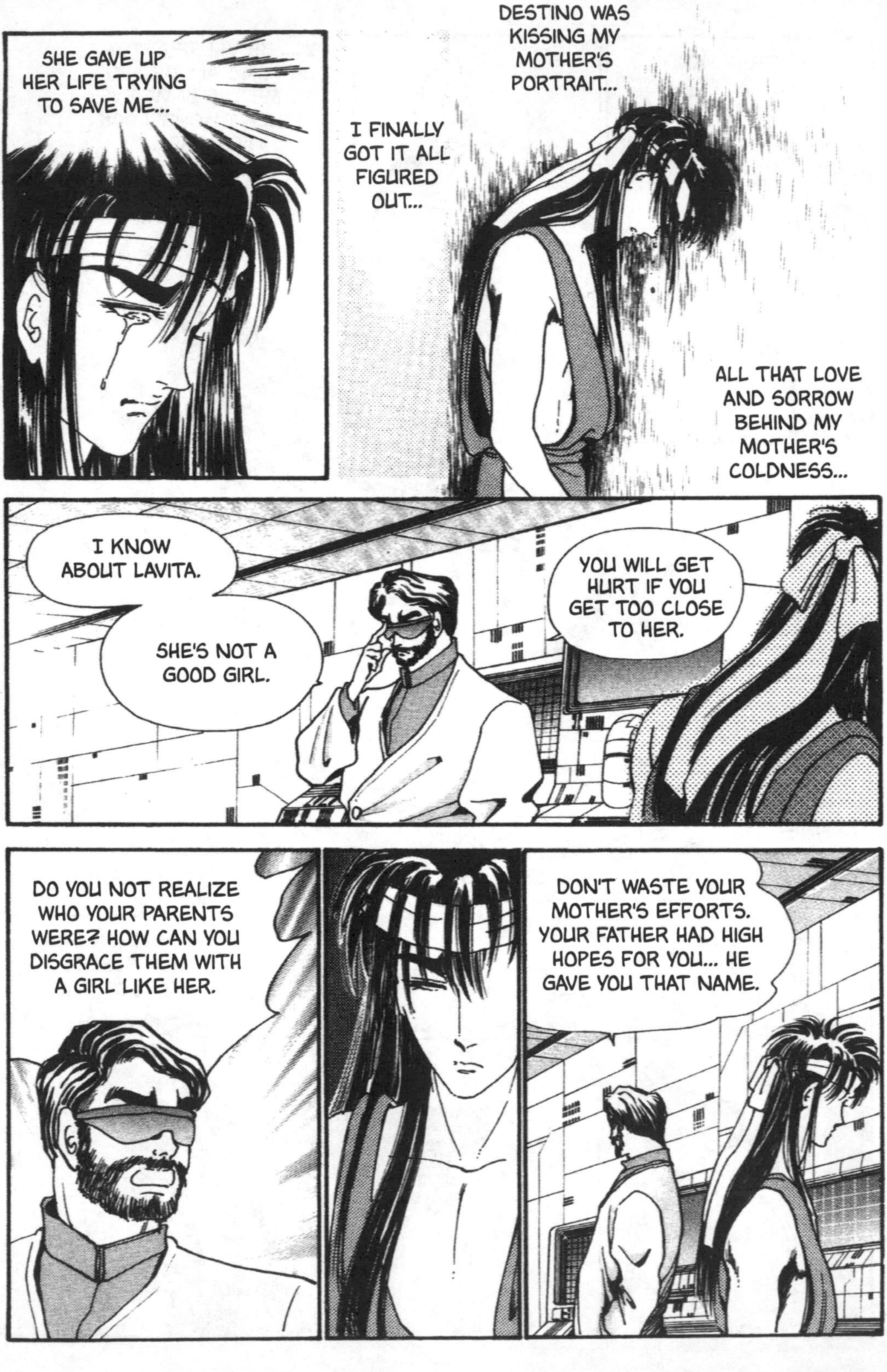
SHE GAVE UP HER LIFE TRYING TO SAVE ME...
DESTINO WAS KISSING MY MOTHER'S PORTRAIT...
I FINALLY GOT IT ALL FIGURED OUT...
ALL THAT LOVE AND SORROW BEHIND MY MOTHER'S COLDNESS...
I KNOW ABOUT LAVITA.
SHE'S NOT A GOOD GIRL.
YOU WILL GET HURT IF YOU GET TOO CLOSE TO HER.
DO YOU NOT REALIZE WHO YOUR PARENTS WERE? HOW CAN YOU DISGRACE THEM WITH A GIRL LIKE HER.
DON'T WASTE YOUR MOTHER'S EFFORTS. YOUR FATHER HAD HIGH HOPES FOR YOU... HE GAVE YOU THAT NAME.

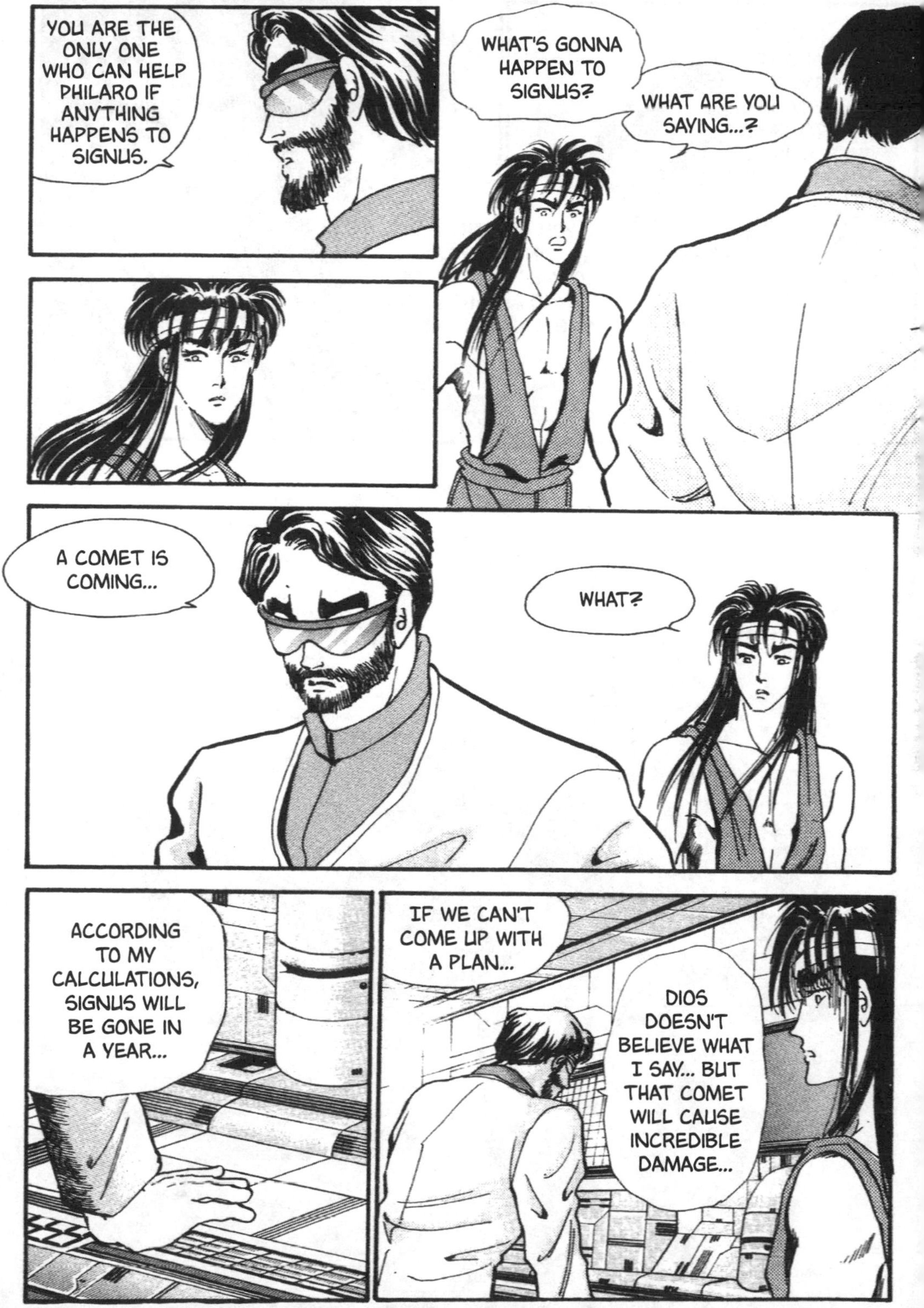
YOU ARE THE ONLY ONE WHO CAN HELP PHILARO IF ANYTHING HAPPENS TO SIGNUS.
WHAT'S GONNA HAPPEN TO SIGNUS?
WHAT ARE YOU SAYING...?
A COMET IS COMING...
WHAT?
ACCORDING TO MY CALCULATIONS, SIGNUS WILL BE GONE IN A YEAR...
IF WE CAN'T COME UP WITH A PLAN...
DIOS DOESN'T BELIEVE WHAT I SAY... BUT THAT COMET WILL CAUSE INCREDIBLE DAMAGE...

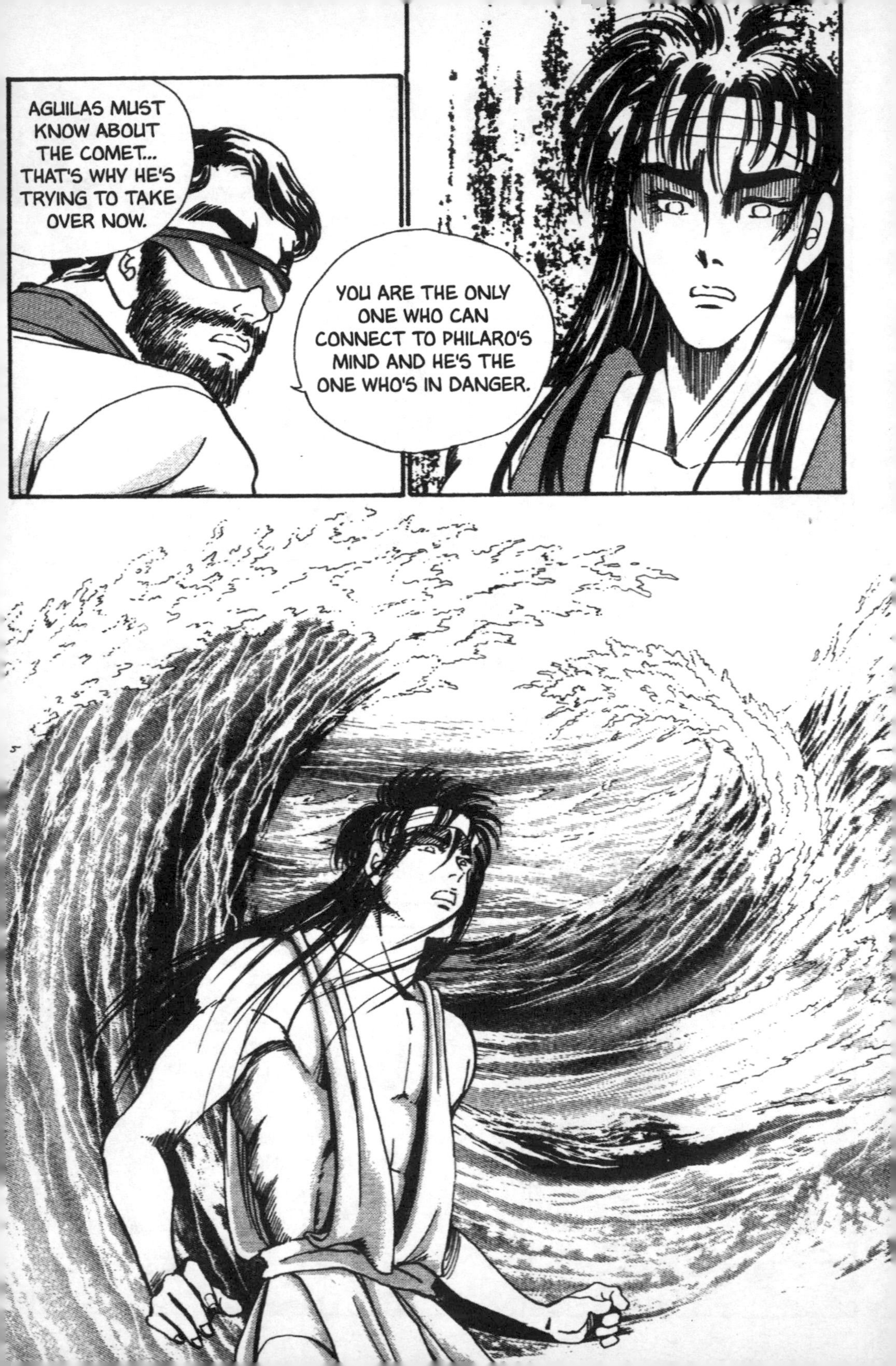
AGUILAS MUST KNOW ABOUT THE COMET... THAT'S WHY HE'S TRYING TO TAKE OVER NOW.
YOU ARE THE ONLY ONE WHO CAN CONNECT TO PHILARO'S MIND AND HE'S THE ONE WHO'S IN DANGER.

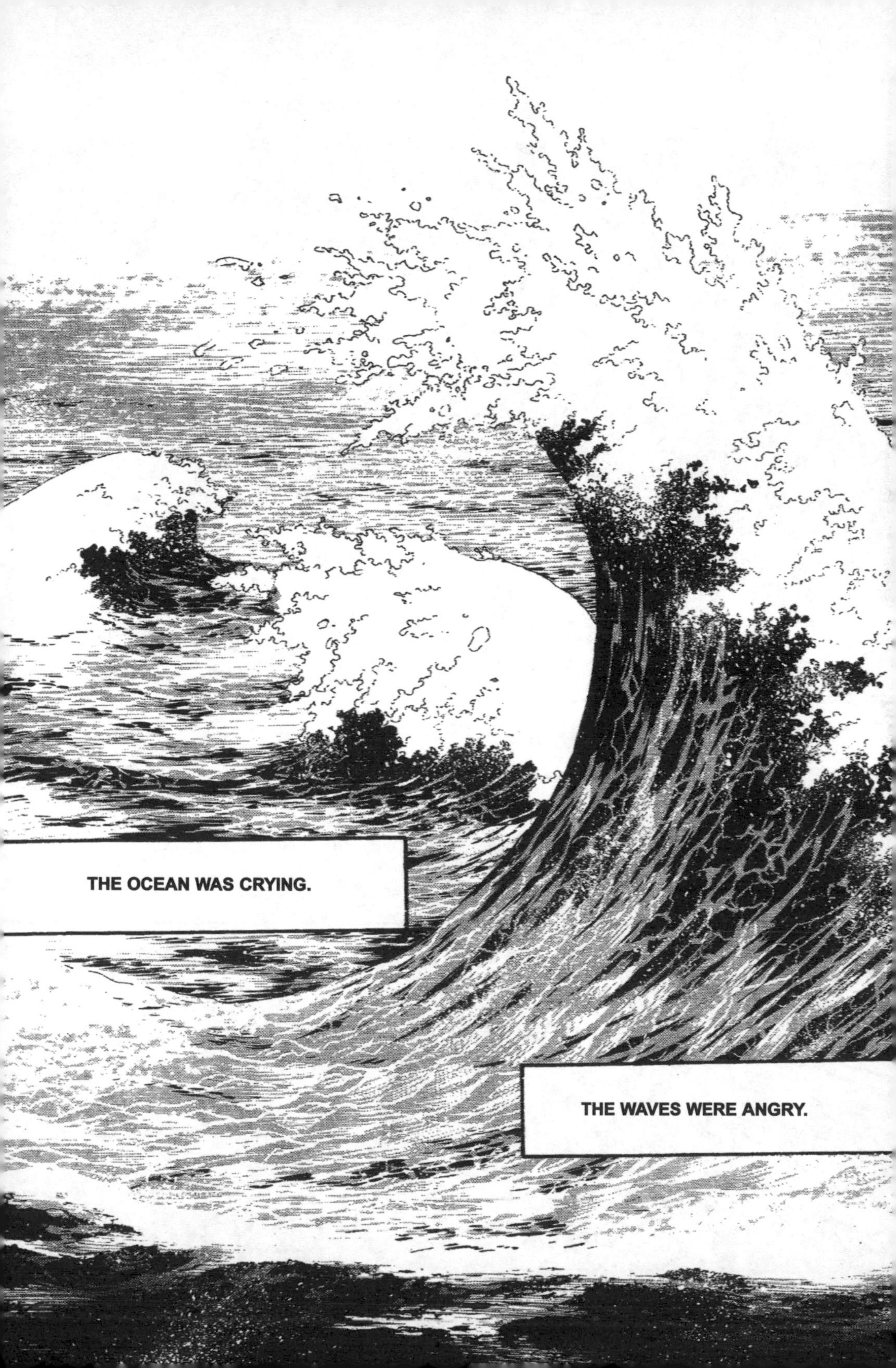
THE OCEAN WAS CRYING.
THE WAVES WERE ANGRY.

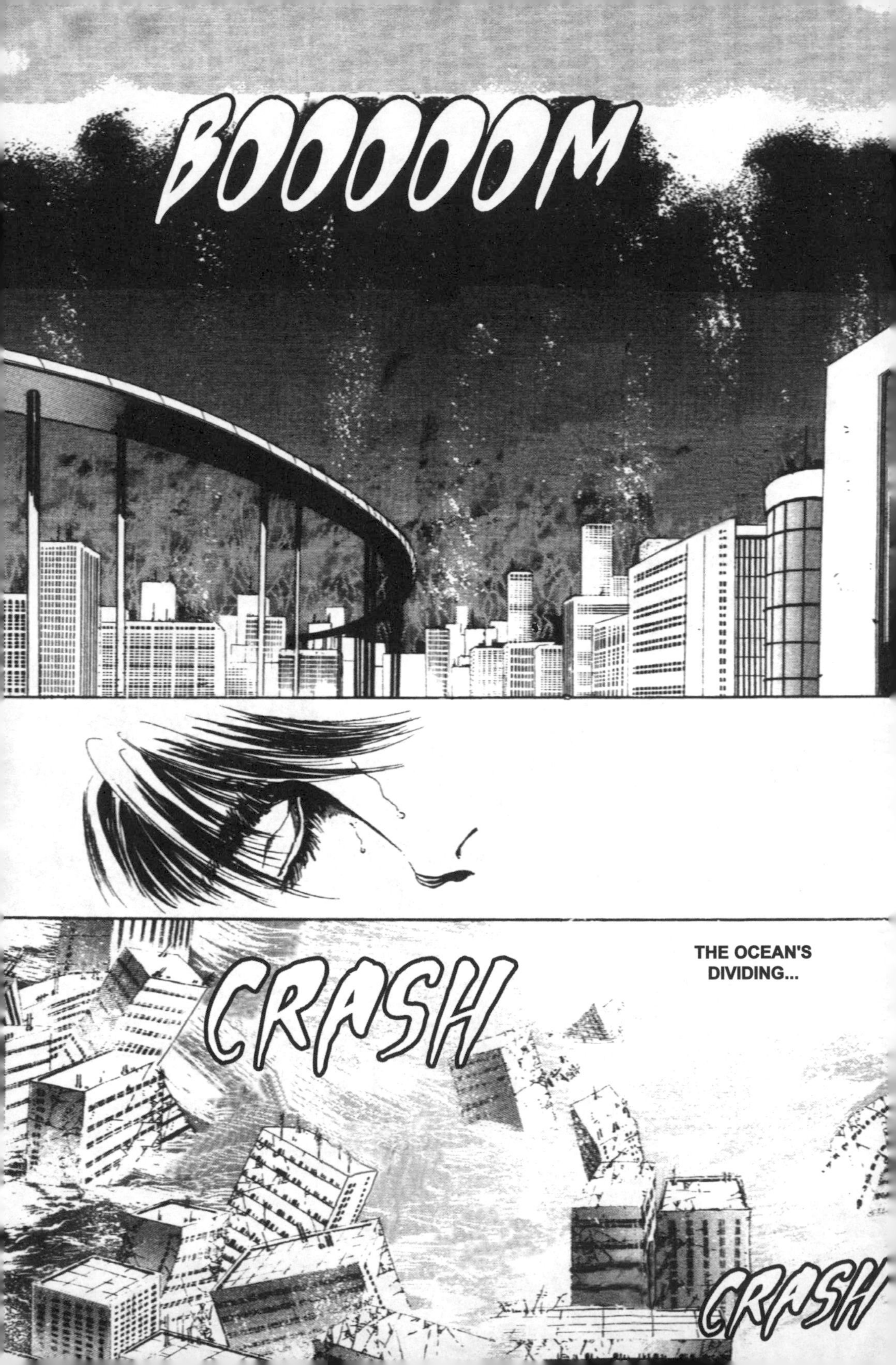
BOOOOOM
THE OCEAN'S DIVIDING...
CRASH
CRASH

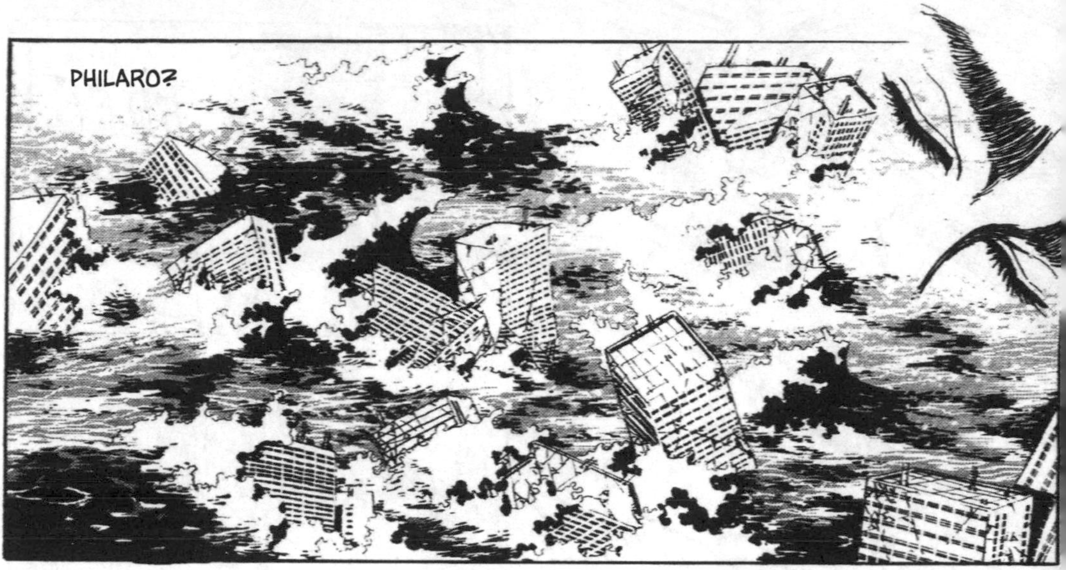
PHILARO?

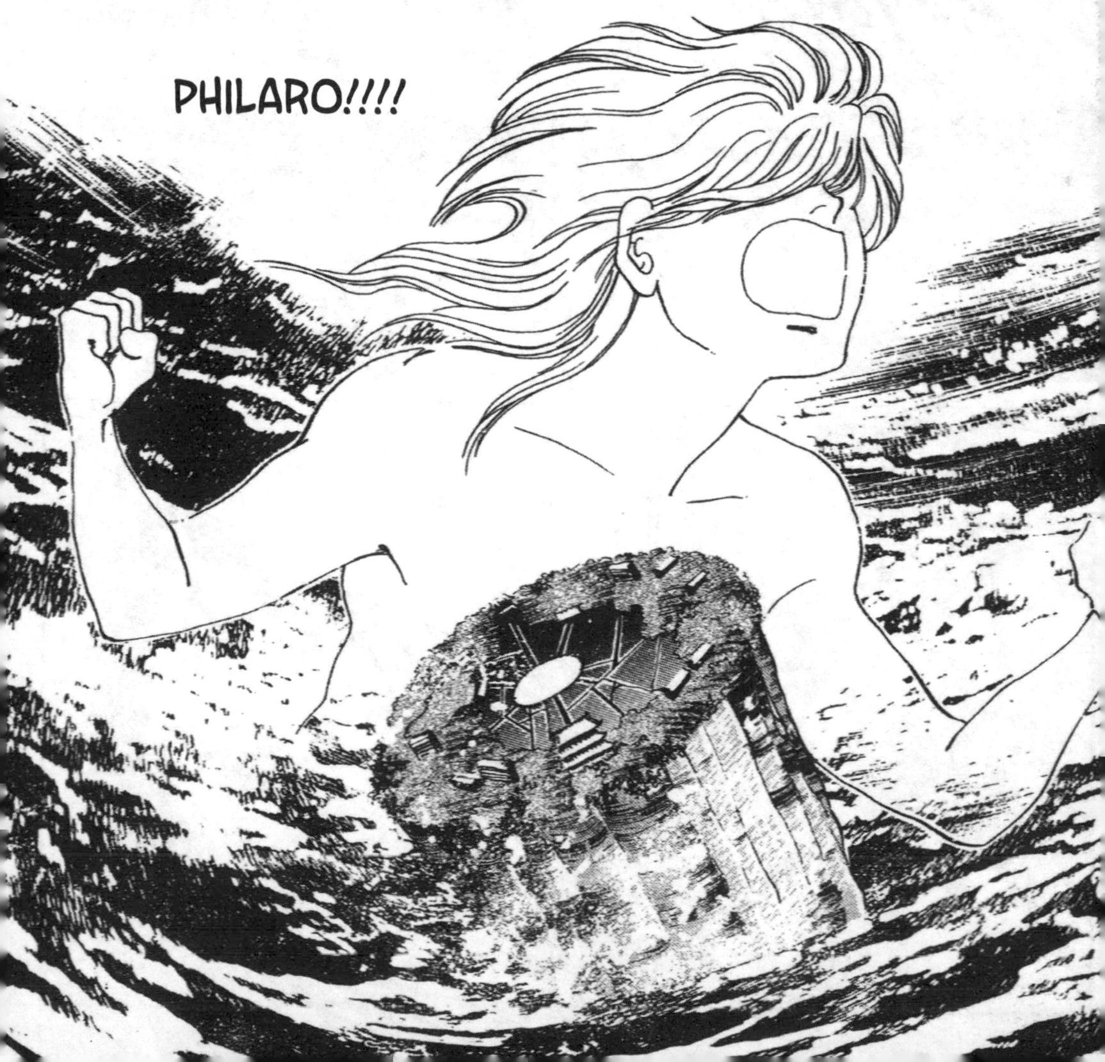
PHILARO!!!!

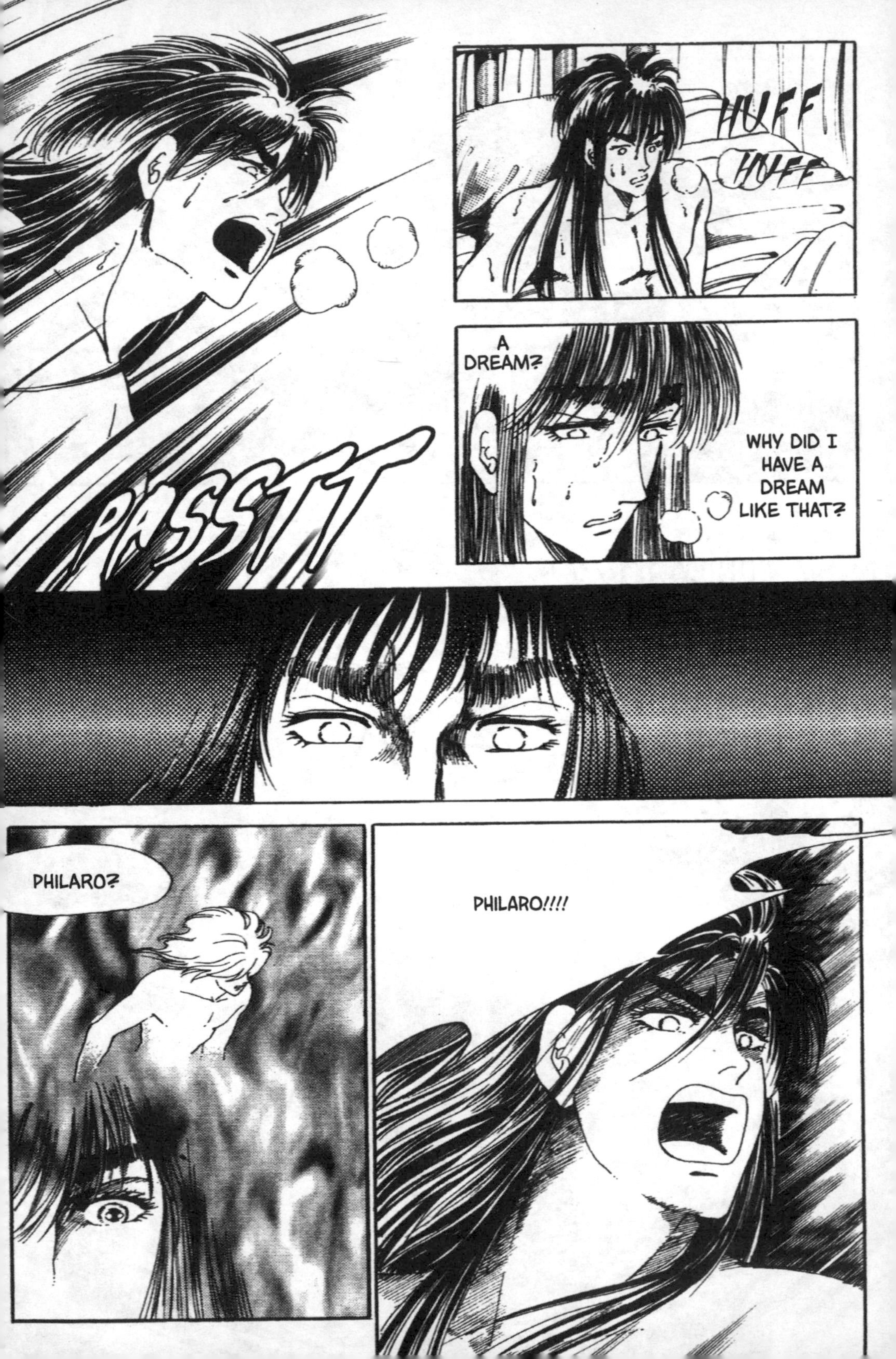
PASSTT
HUFF
HUFF
A DREAM?
WHY DID I HAVE A DREAM LIKE THAT?
PHILARO?
PHILARO!!!!

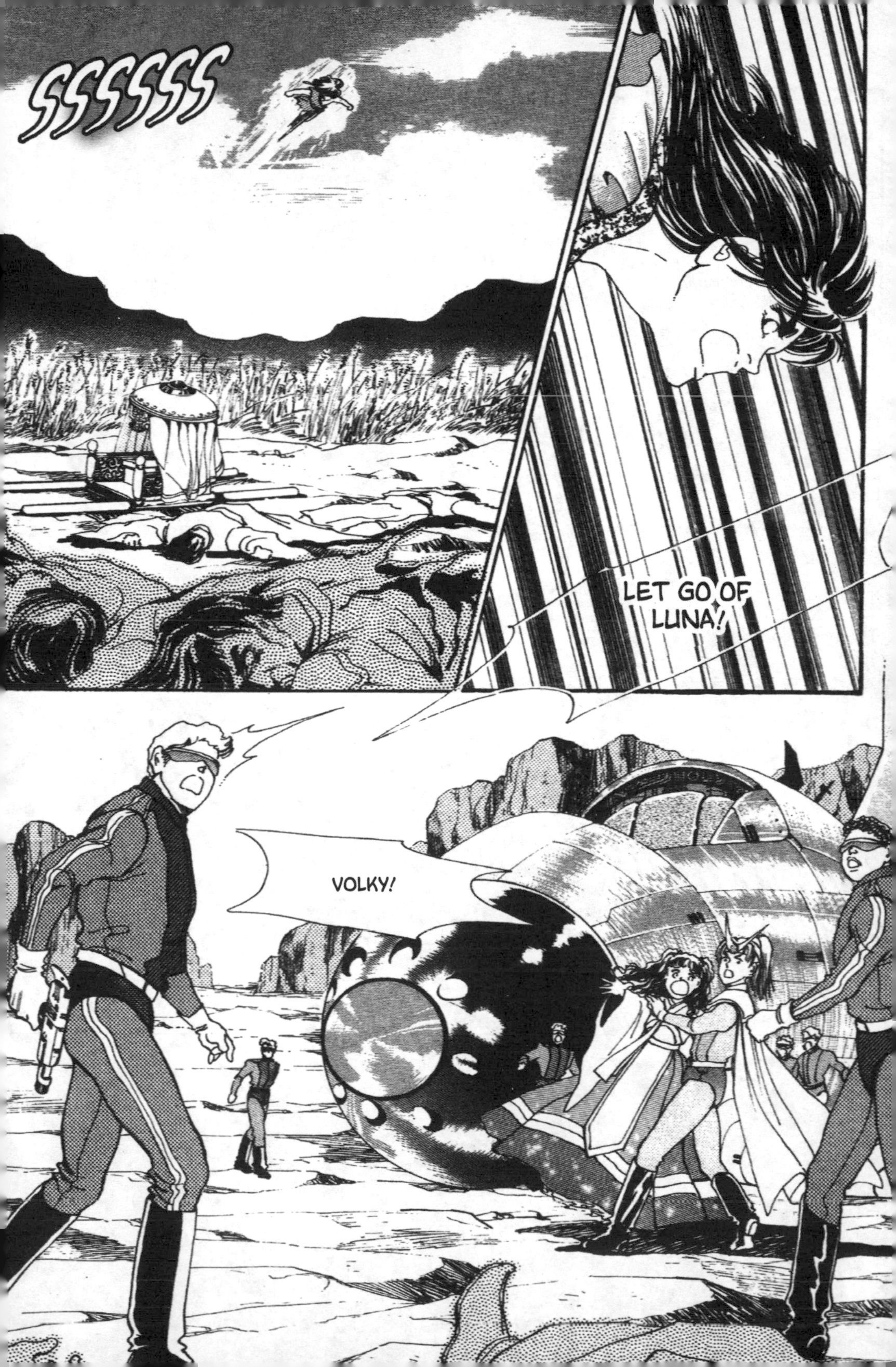
SSSSSS
LET GO OF LUNA!
VOLKY!

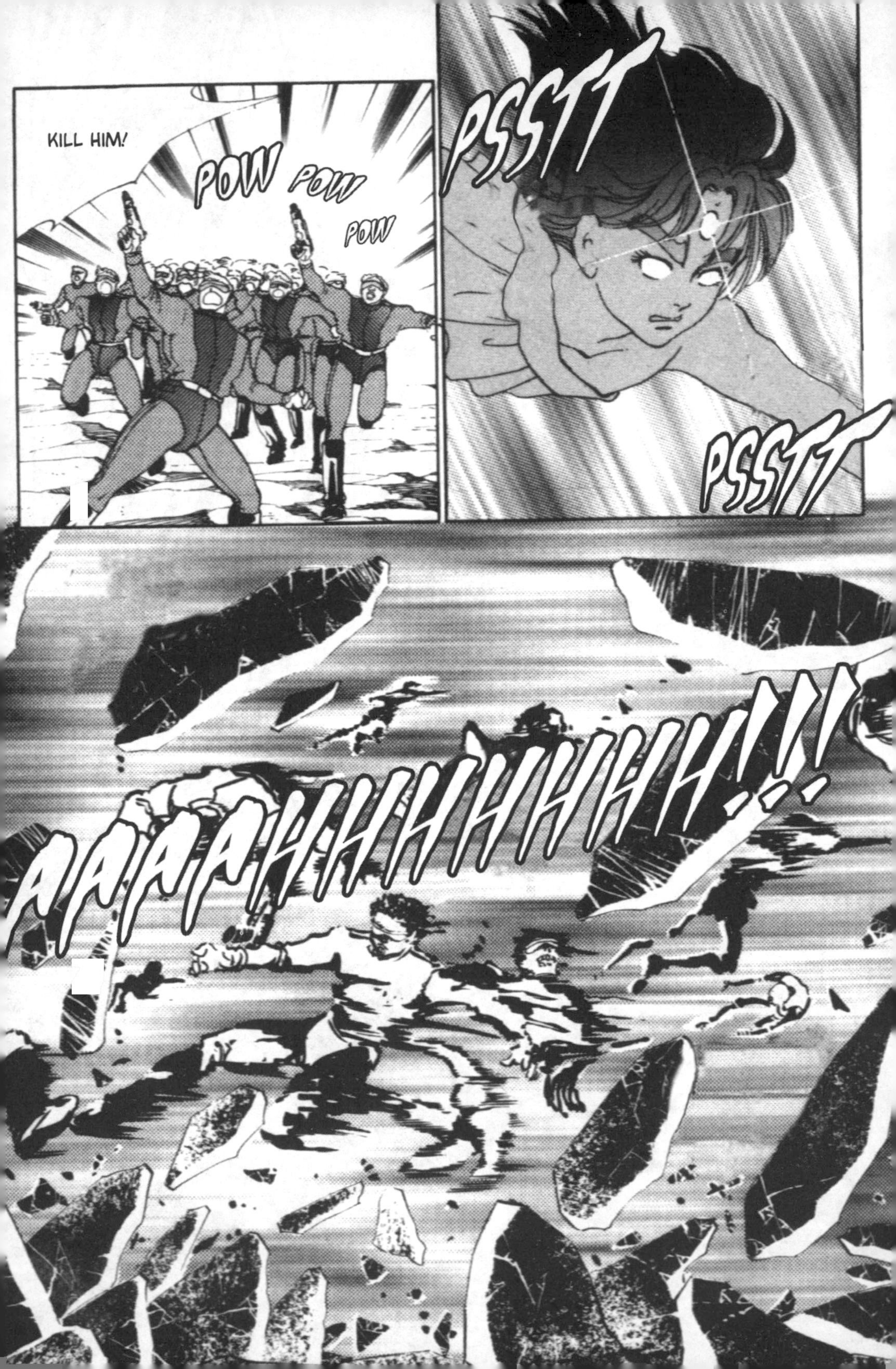
KILL HIM!
POW POW POW
PSSTT
PSSTT
AAAAHHHHHHHHH!!!

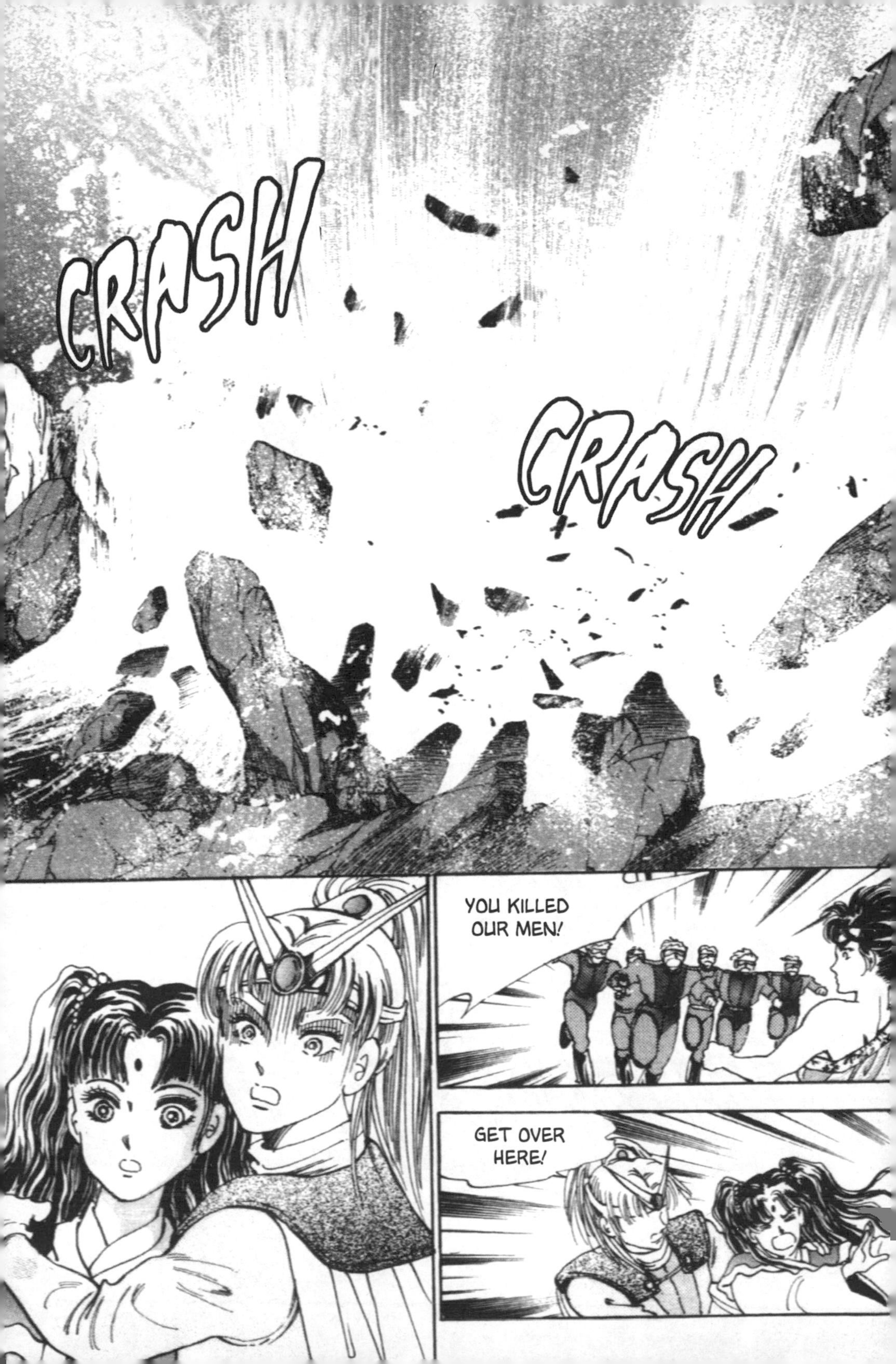
CRASH
CRASH
YOU KILLED OUR MEN!
GET OVER HERE!

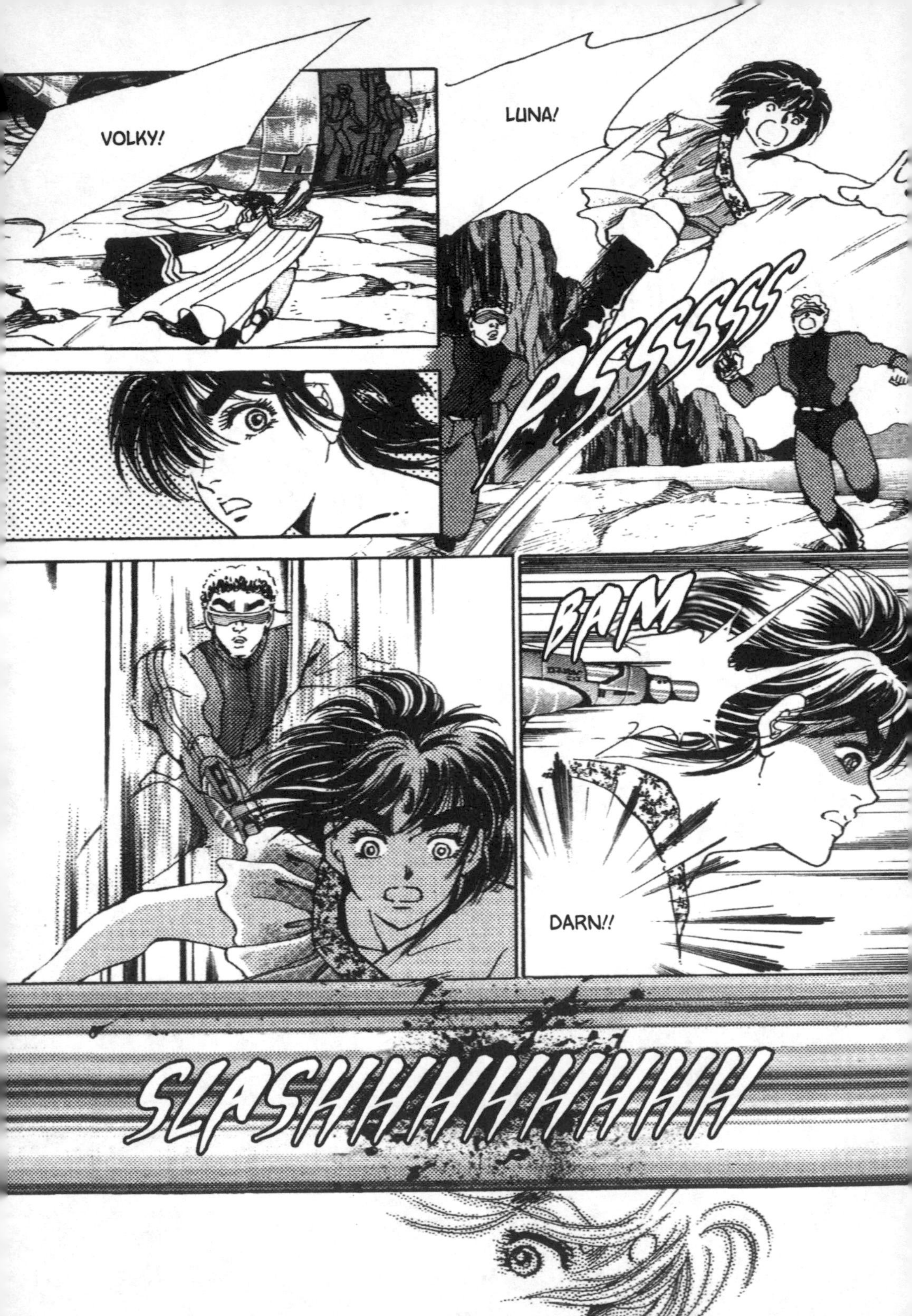
LUNA!
VOLKY!
PSSSSSS
BAM
DARN!!
SLASHHHHHHHHHH

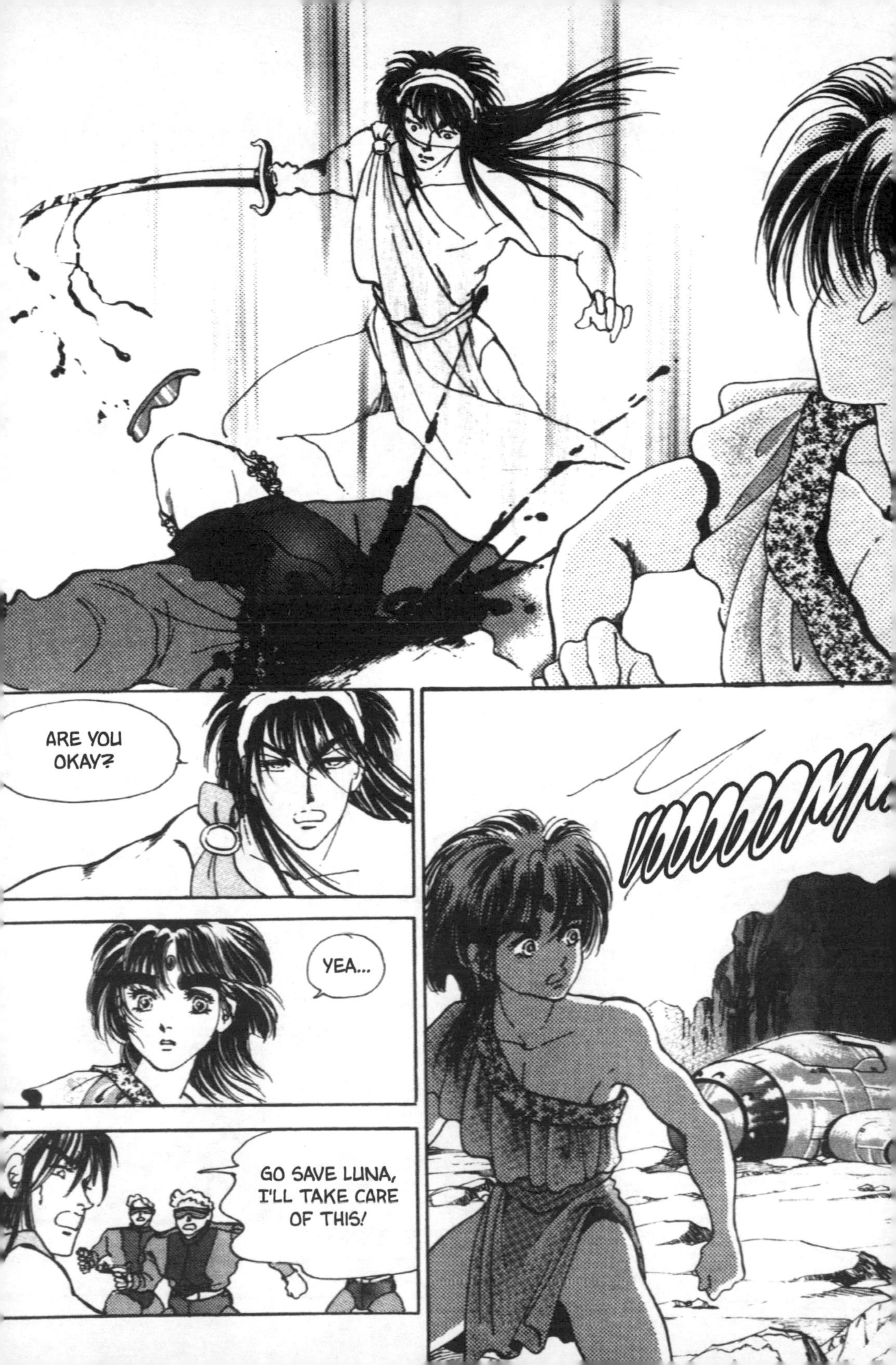
ARE YOU OKAY?
YEA...
GO SAVE LUNA, I'LL TAKE CARE OF THIS!
VVVVVOOMM

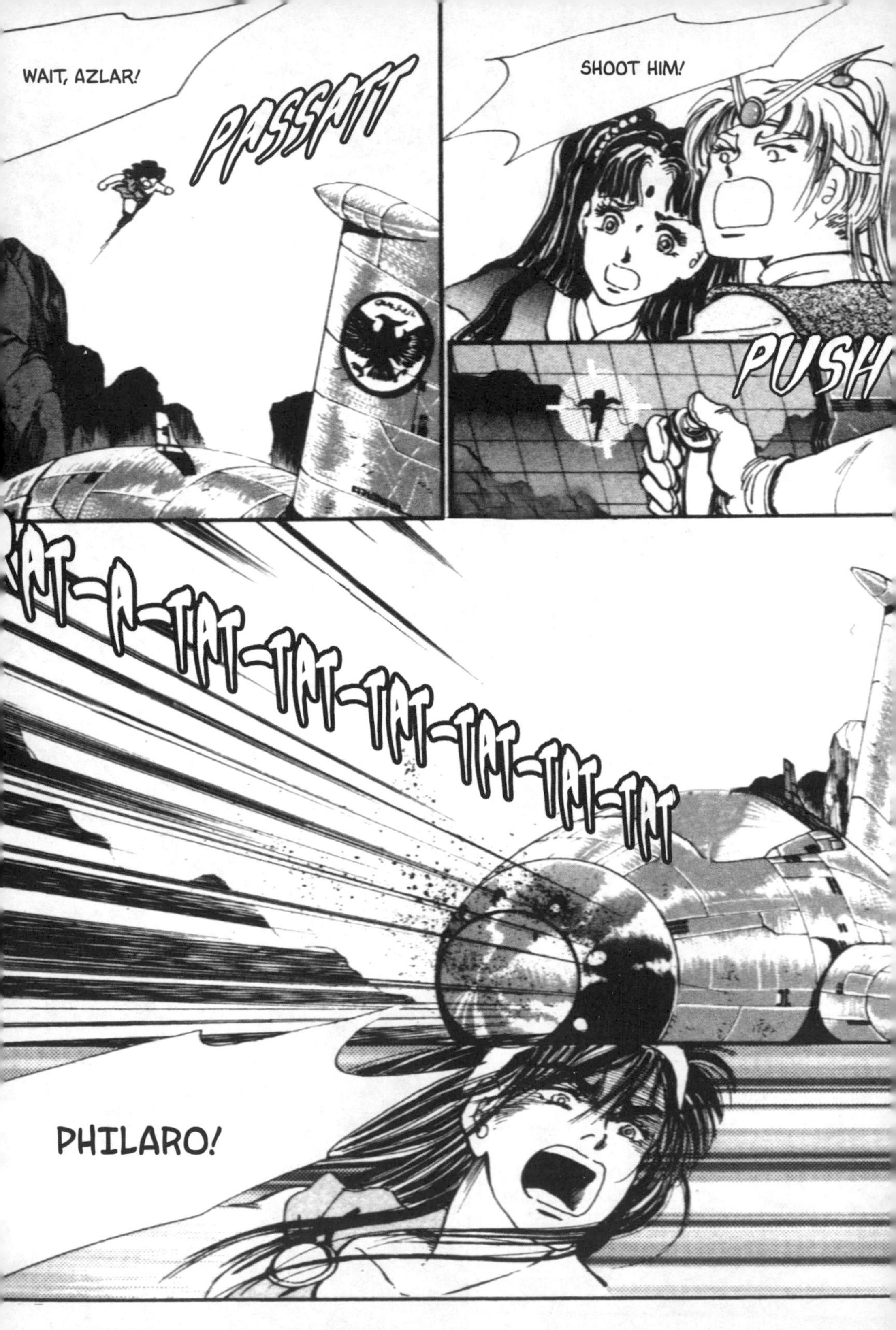
WAIT, AZLAR!
PASSATT
SHOOT HIM!
PUSH
RAT-A-TAT-TAT-TAT-TAT-TAT-TAT-TAT
PHILARO!

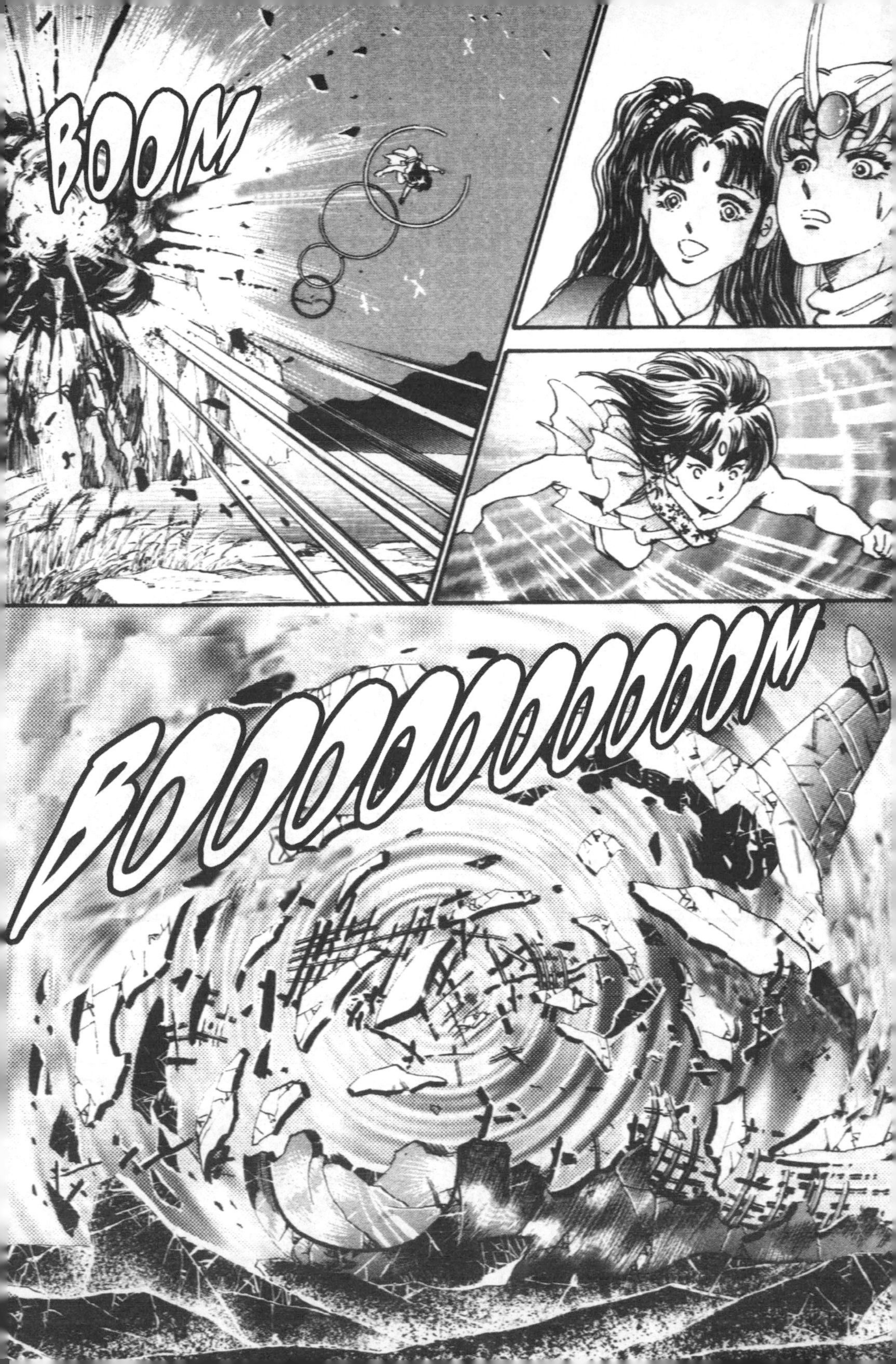
BOOM
BOOOOOOOOOM

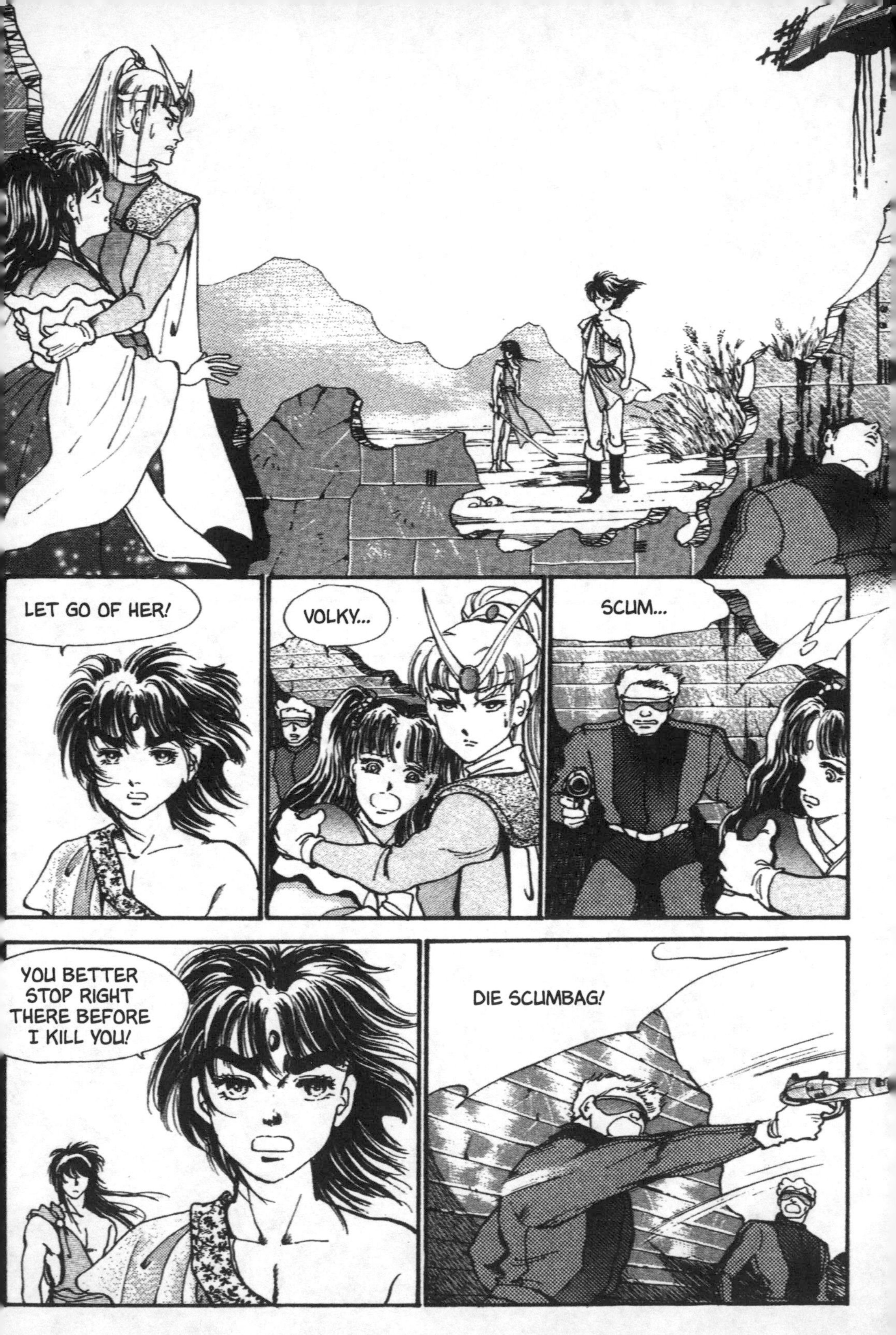
LET GO OF HER!
VOLKY...
SCUM...
YOU BETTER STOP RIGHT THERE BEFORE I KILL YOU!
DIE SCUMBAG!

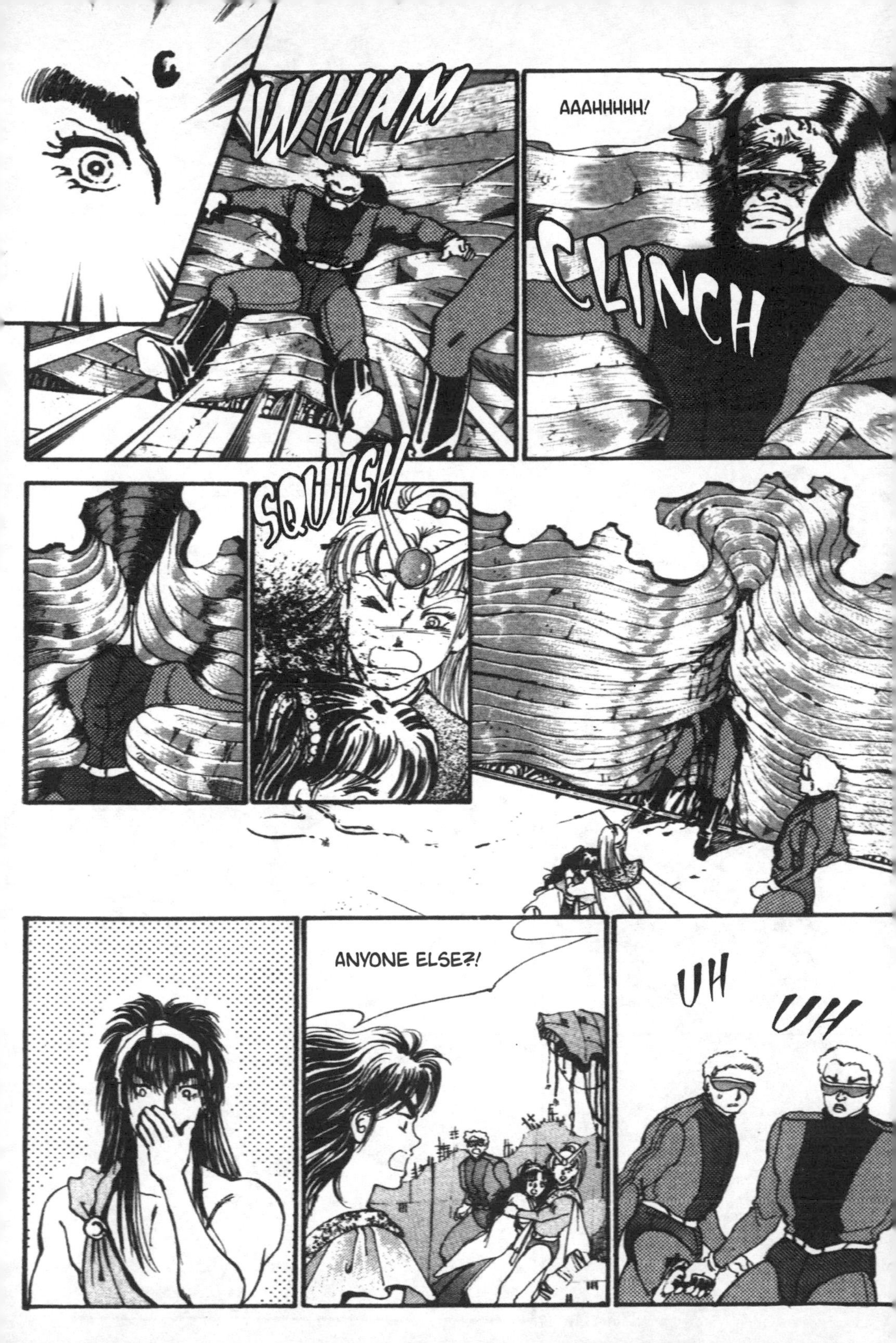
WHAM
AAAHHHHH!
CLINCH
SQUISH
ANYONE ELSE?!
UH
UH

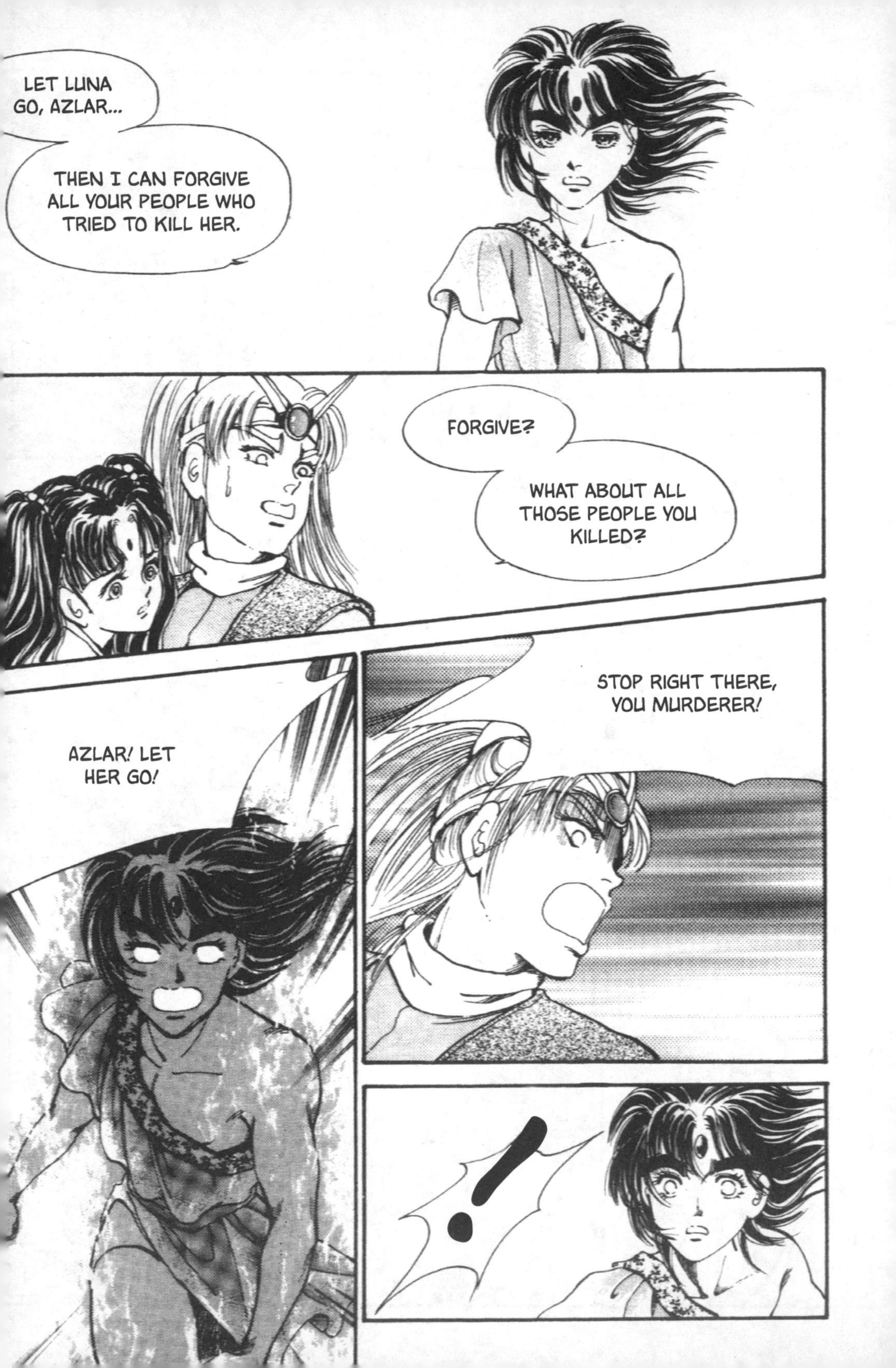
LET LUNA GO, AZLAR...
THEN I CAN FORGIVE ALL YOUR PEOPLE WHO TRIED TO KILL HER.
FORGIVE?
WHAT ABOUT ALL THOSE PEOPLE YOU KILLED?
AZLAR! LET HER GO!
STOP RIGHT THERE, YOU MURDERER!
!

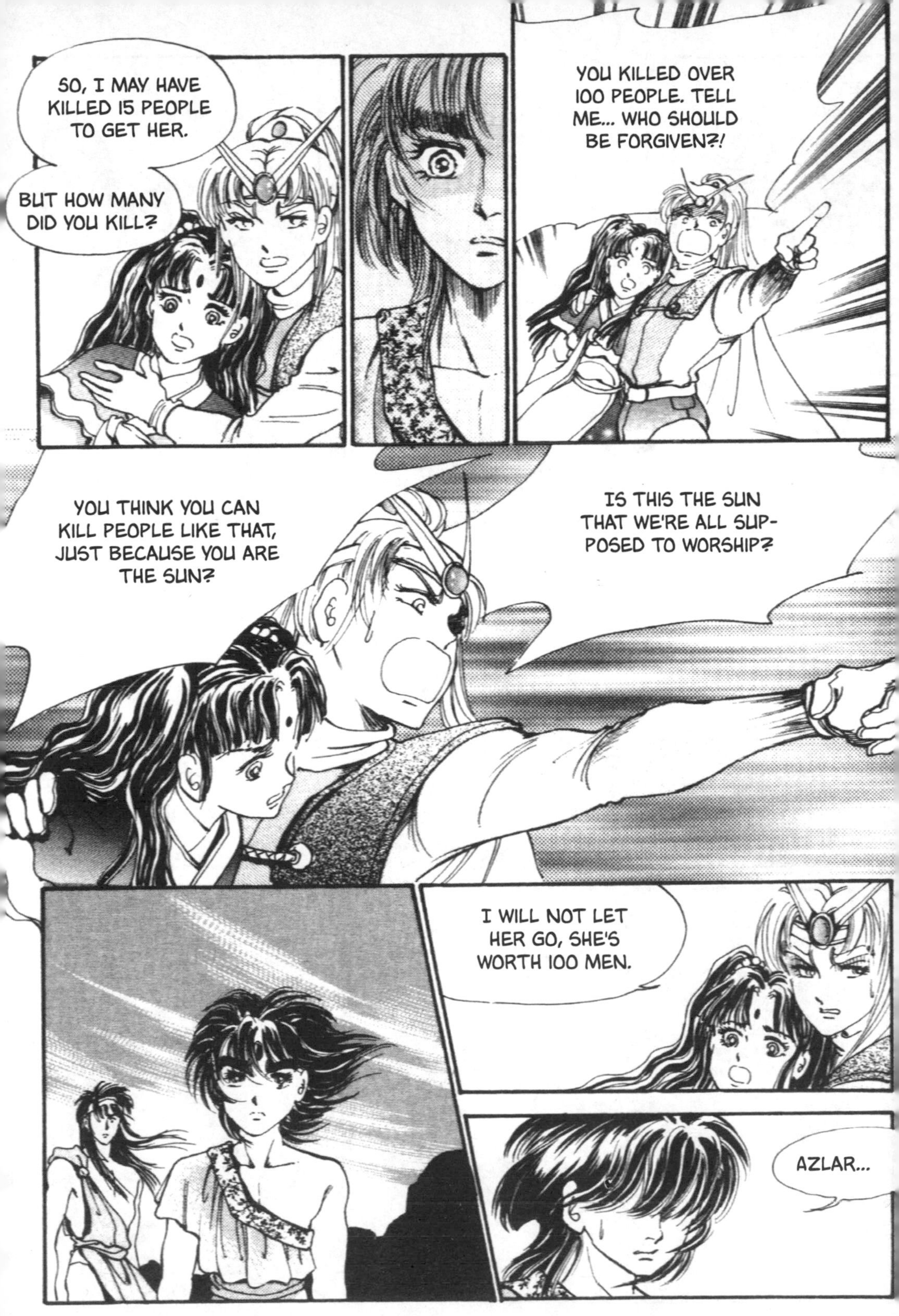
SO, I MAY HAVE KILLED 15 PEOPLE TO GET HER.
BUT HOW MANY DID YOU KILL?
YOU KILLED OVER 100 PEOPLE. TELL ME... WHO SHOULD BE FORGIVEN?!
YOU THINK YOU CAN KILL PEOPLE LIKE THAT, JUST BECAUSE YOU ARE THE SUN?
IS THIS THE SUN THAT WE'RE ALL SUP-POSED TO WORSHIP?
I WILL NOT LET HER GO, SHE'S WORTH 100 MEN.
AZLAR...

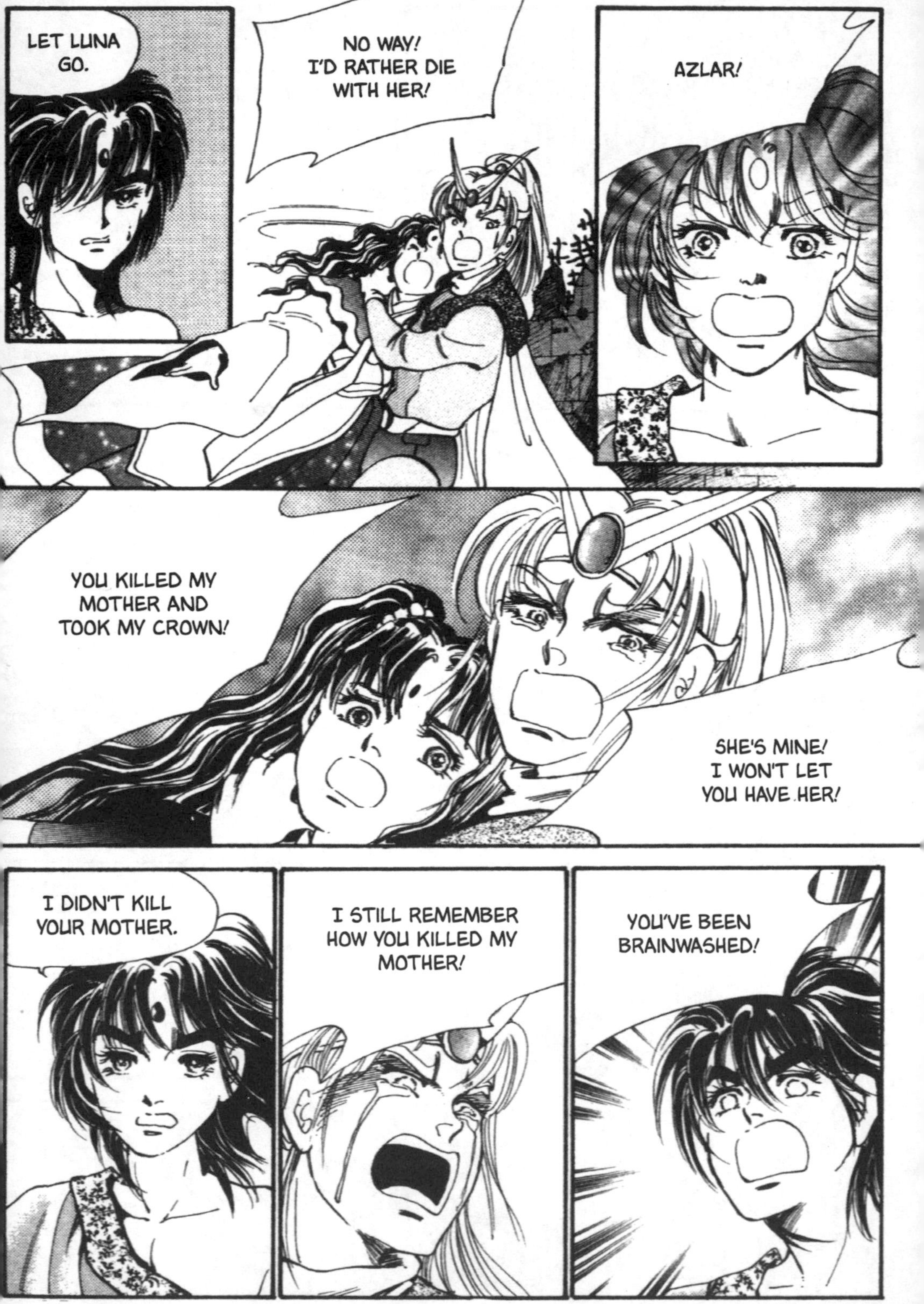
LET LUNA GO.
NO WAY! I'D RATHER DIE WITH HER!
AZLAR!
YOU KILLED MY MOTHER AND TOOK MY CROWN!
SHE'S MINE! I WON'T LET YOU HAVE HER!
I DIDN'T KILL YOUR MOTHER.
I STILL REMEMBER HOW YOU KILLED MY MOTHER!
YOU'VE BEEN BRAINWASHED!

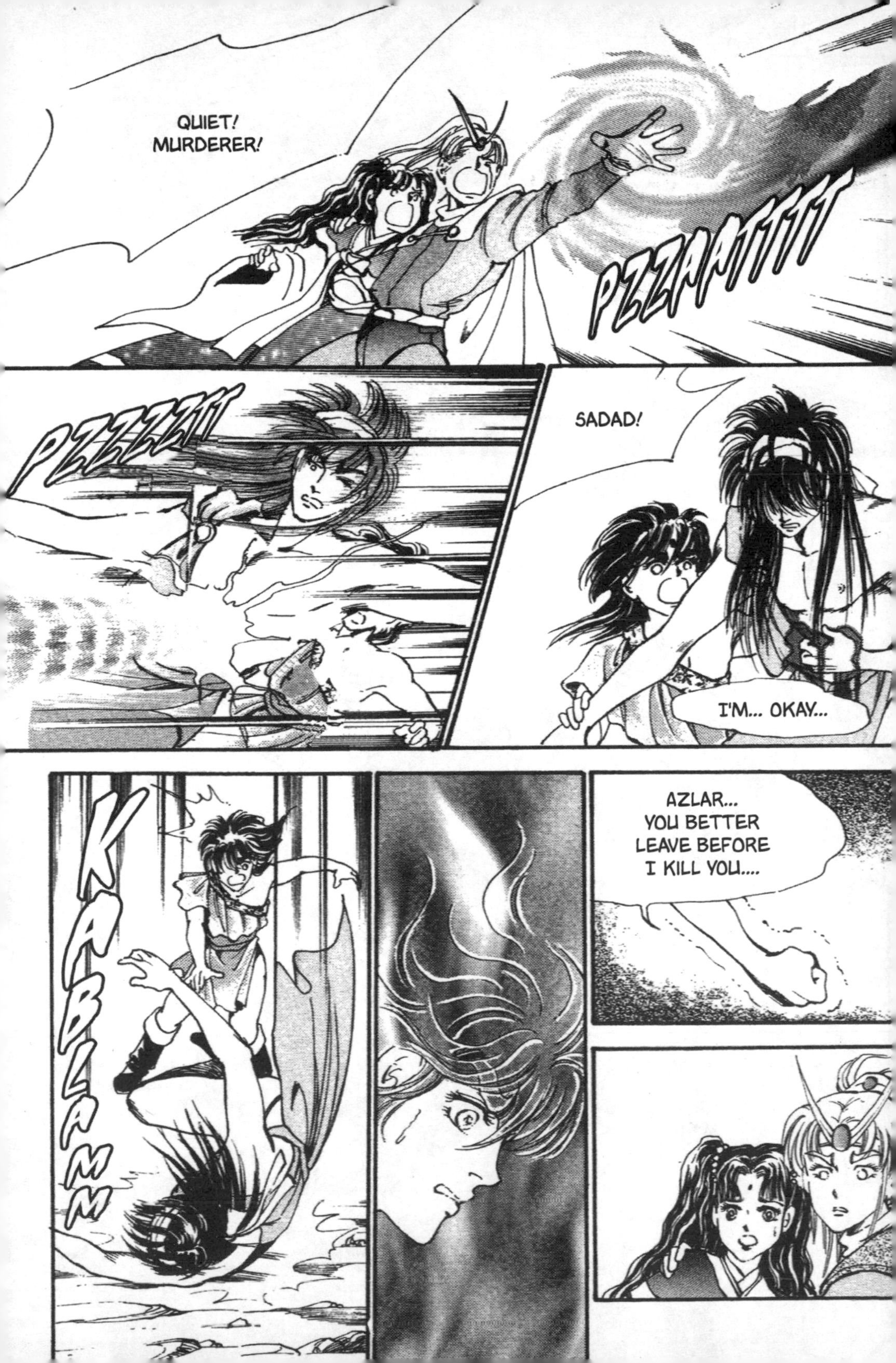
QUIET! MURDERER!
PZZAATTTTT
PZZZZZTT
SADAD!
I'M... OKAY...
KABLAMM
AZLAR... YOU BETTER LEAVE BEFORE I KILL YOU....

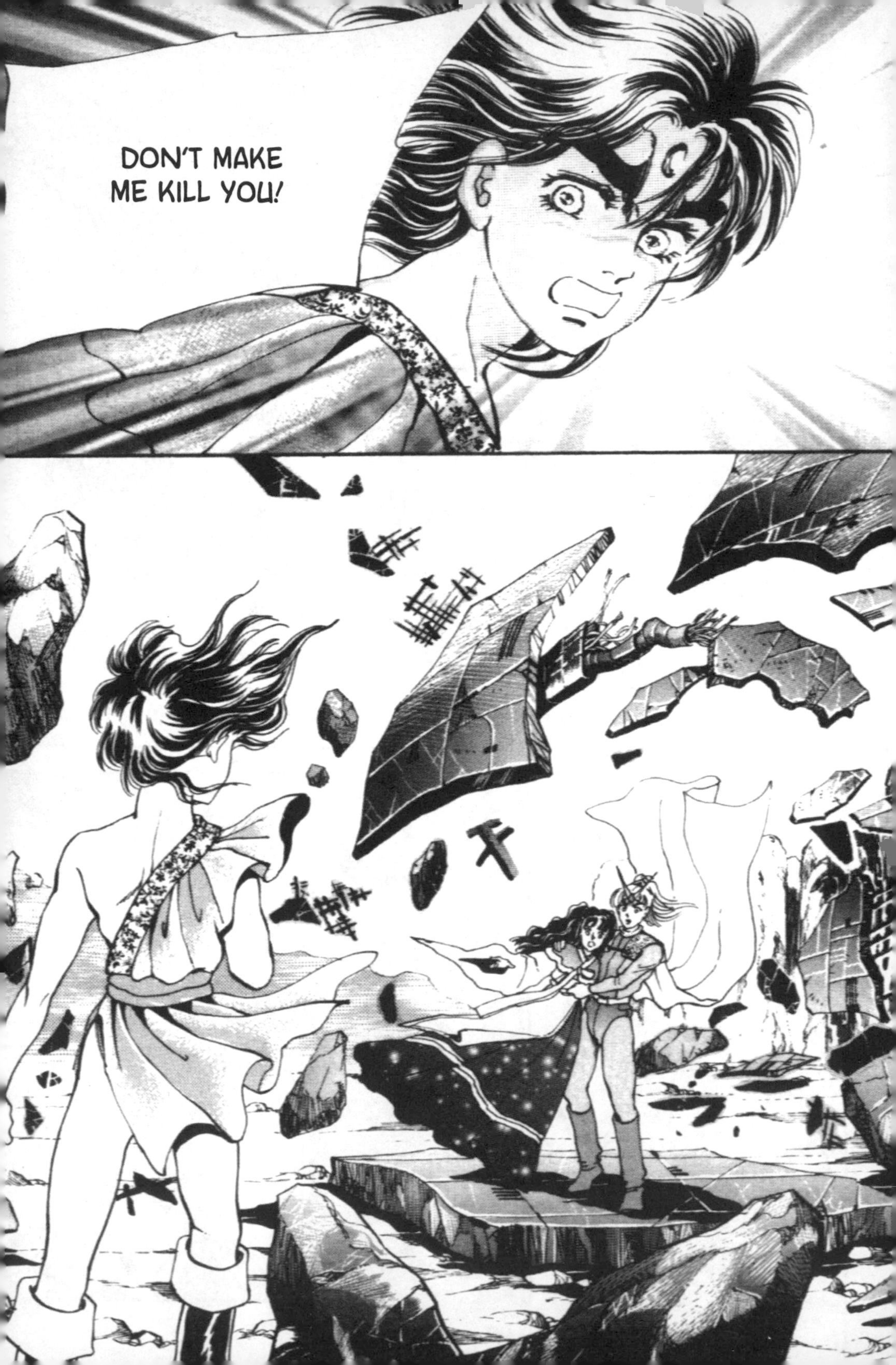
DON'T MAKE
ME KILL YOU!

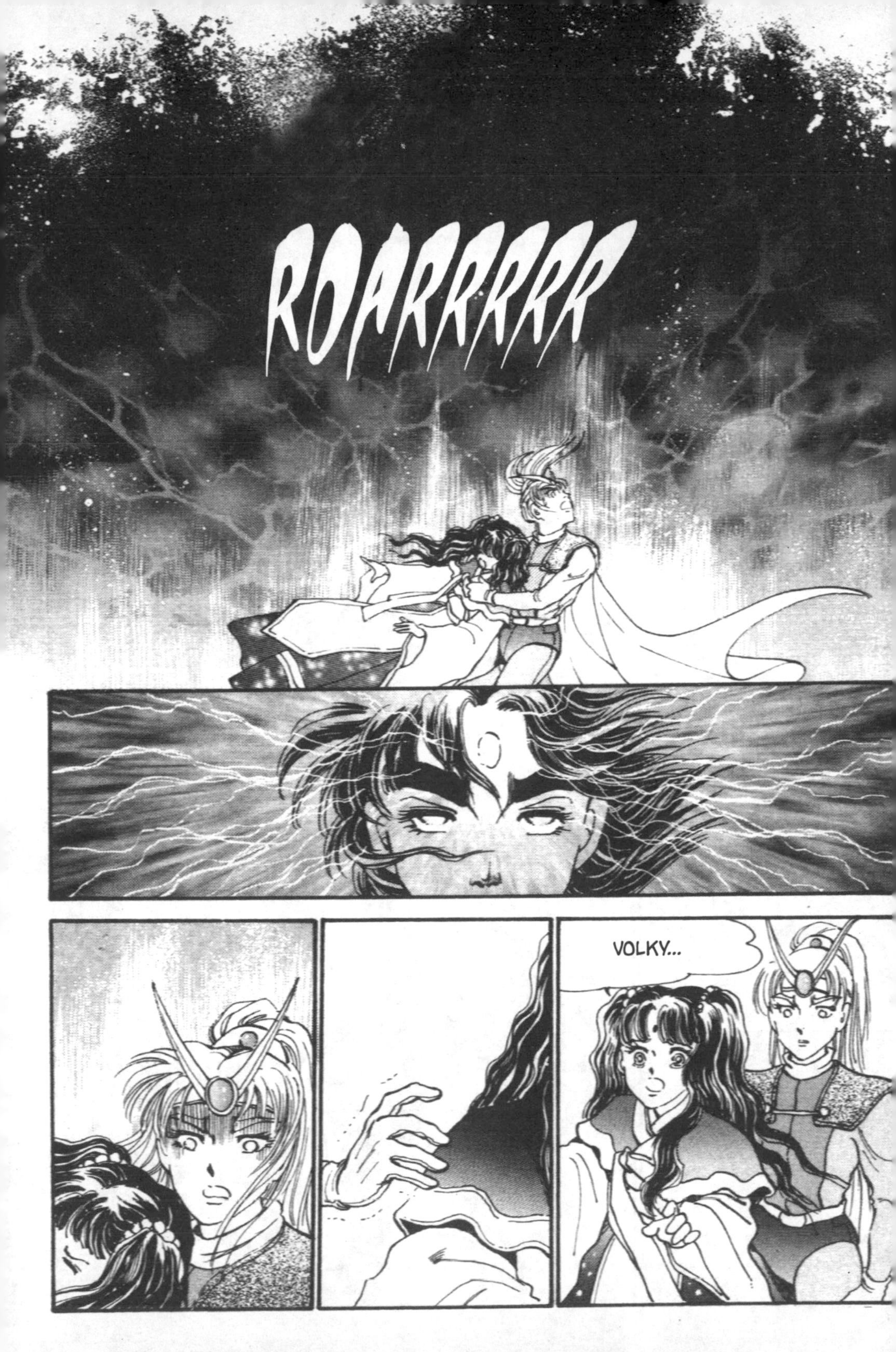
ROARRRRRR
VOLKY...

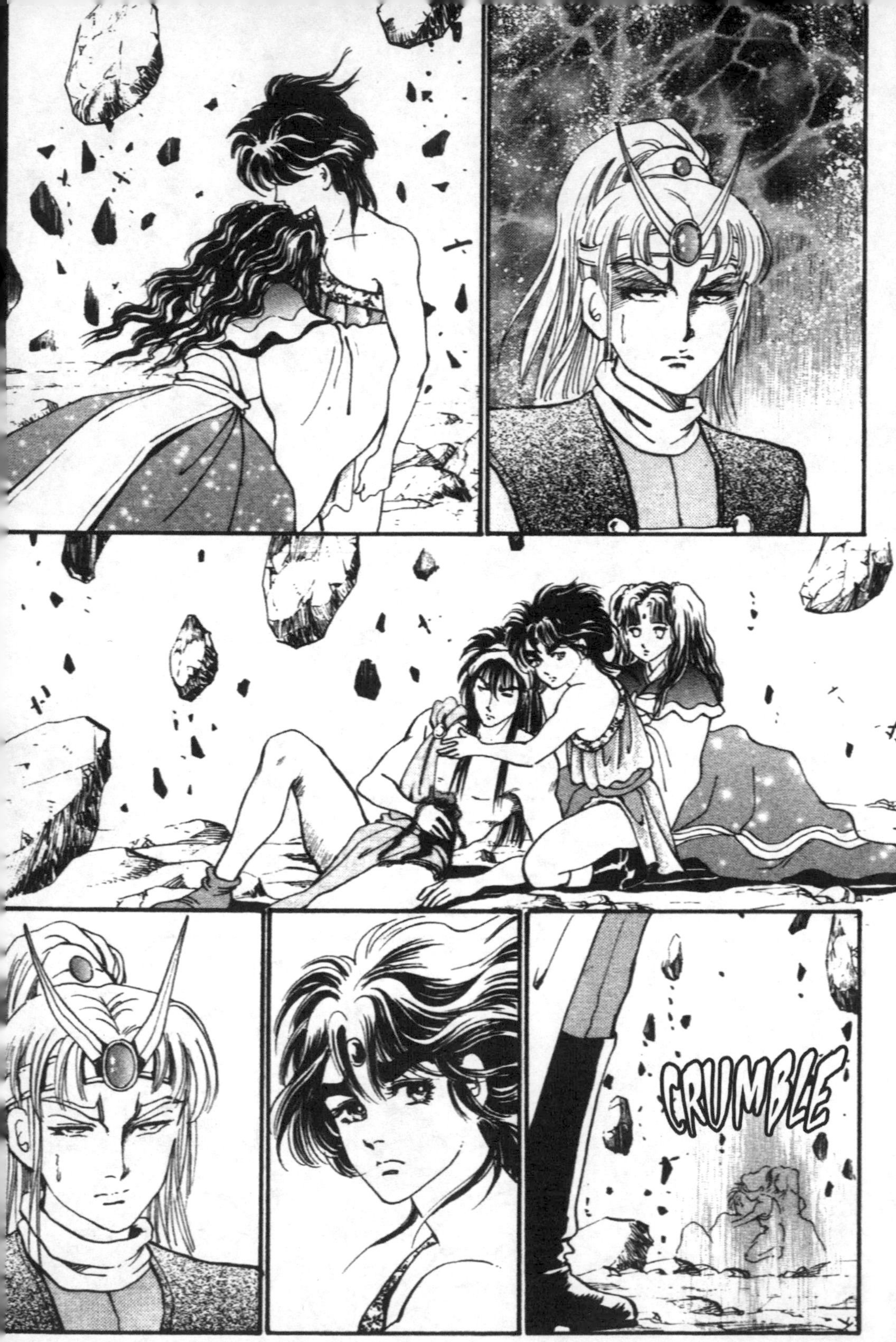
CRUMBLE

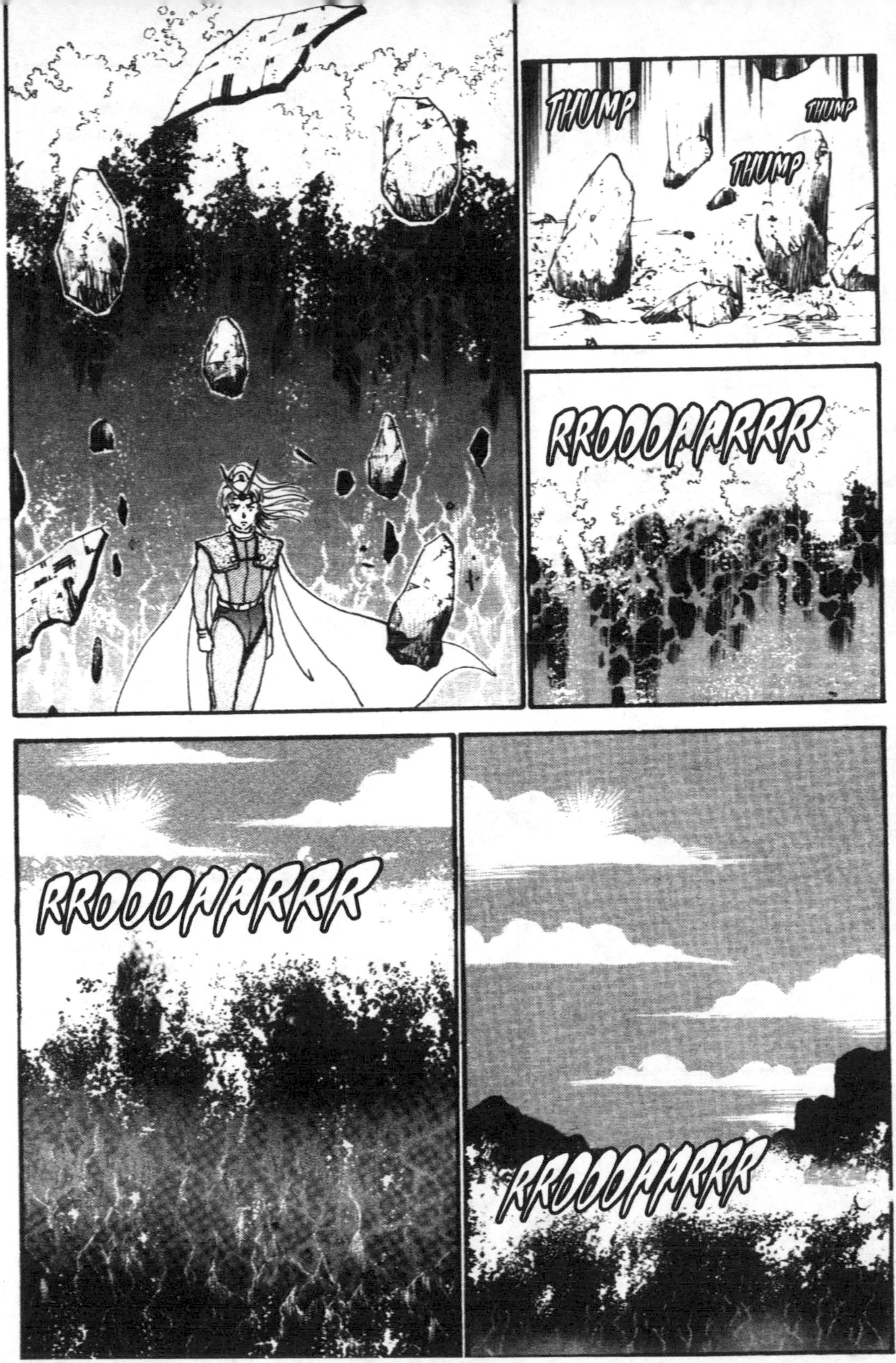
THUMP
THUMP
THUMP
RROOOAARRR
RROOOAARRR
RROOOARRR

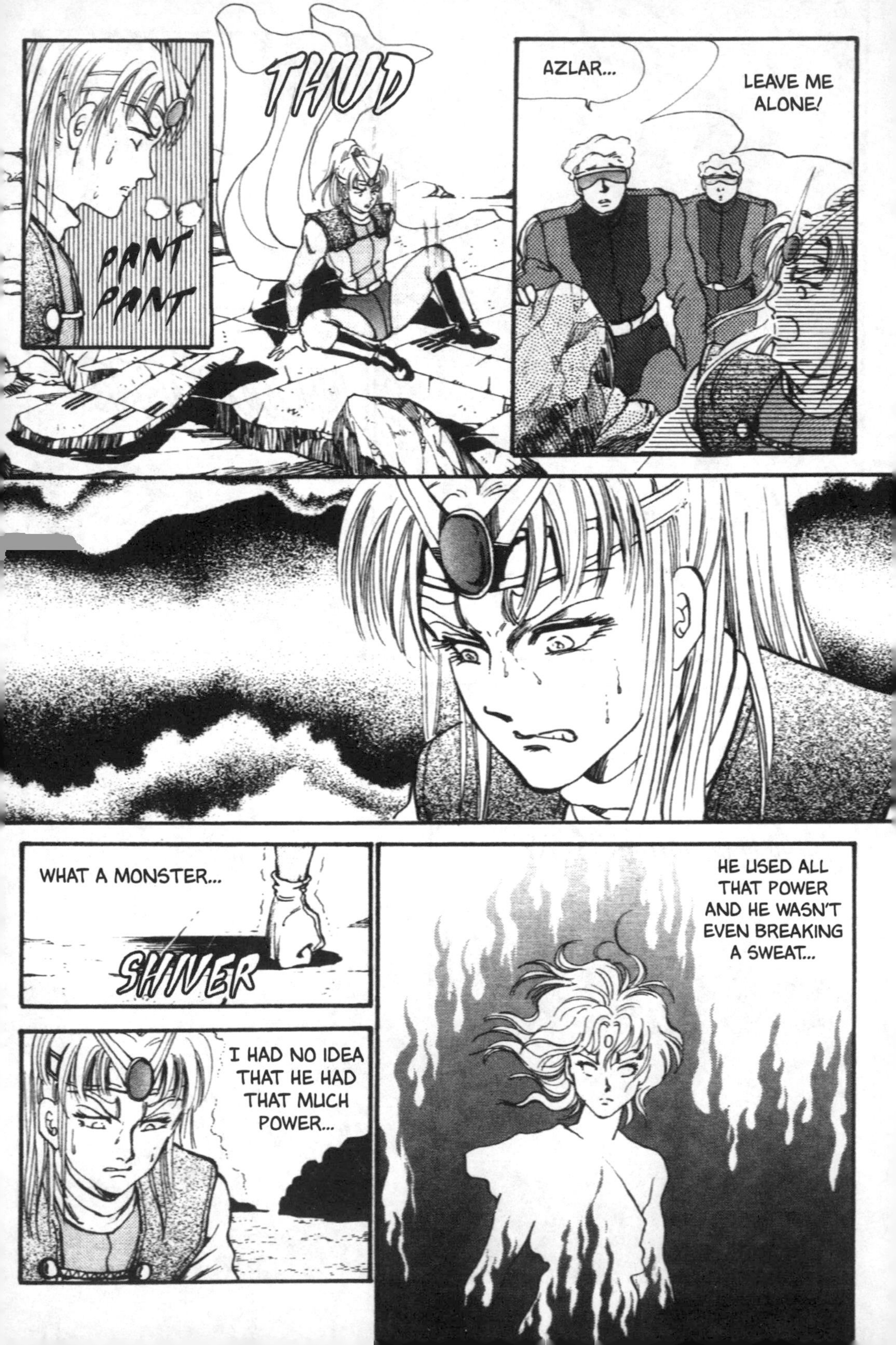
THUD
PANT PANT
AZLAR...
LEAVE ME ALONE!
WHAT A MONSTER...
SHIVER
I HAD NO IDEA THAT HE HAD THAT MUCH POWER...
HE USED ALL THAT POWER AND HE WASN'T EVEN BREAKING A SWEAT...

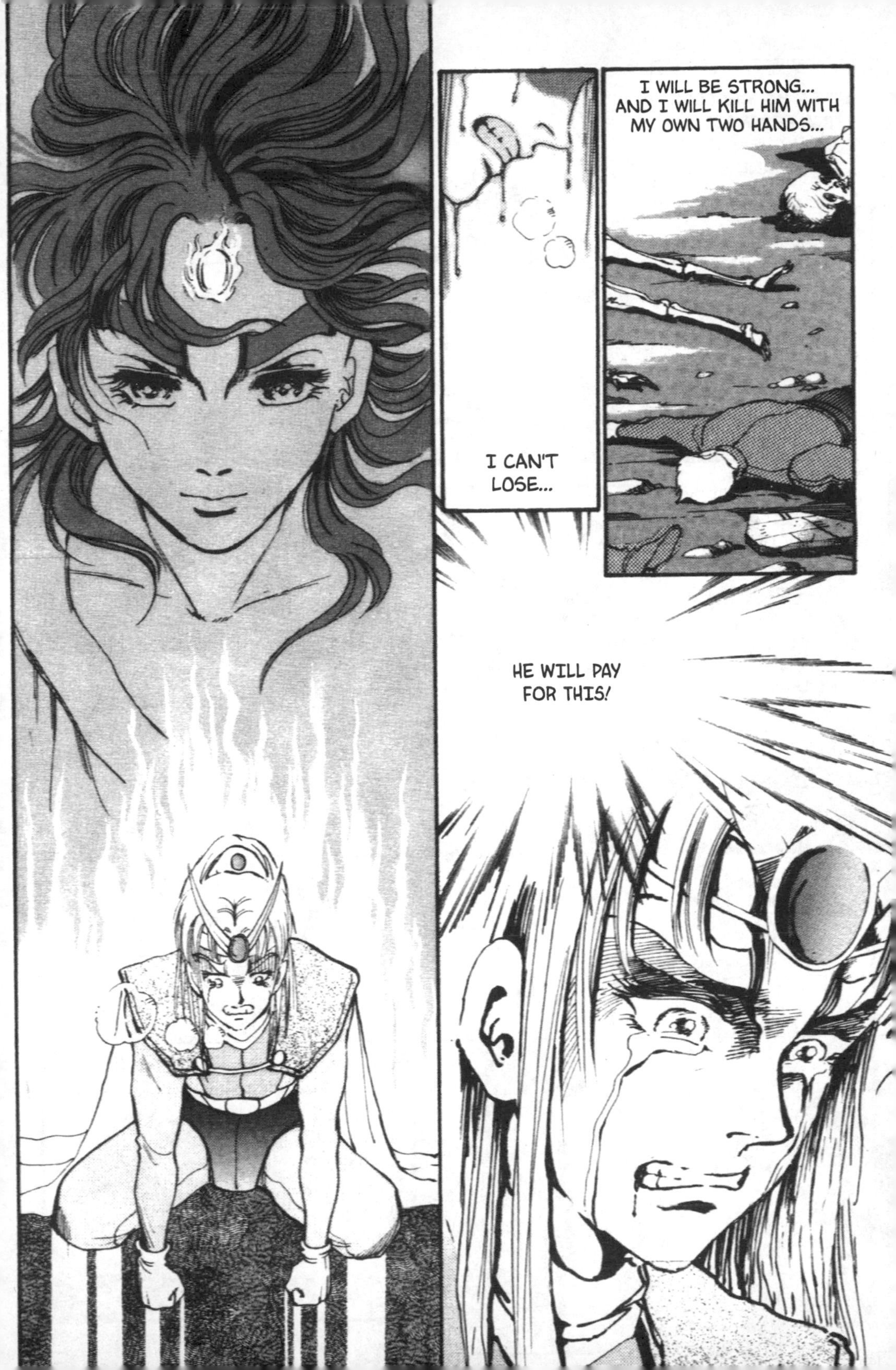
I CAN'T LOSE...
I WILL BE STRONG... AND I WILL KILL HIM WITH MY OWN TWO HANDS...
HE WILL PAY FOR THIS!

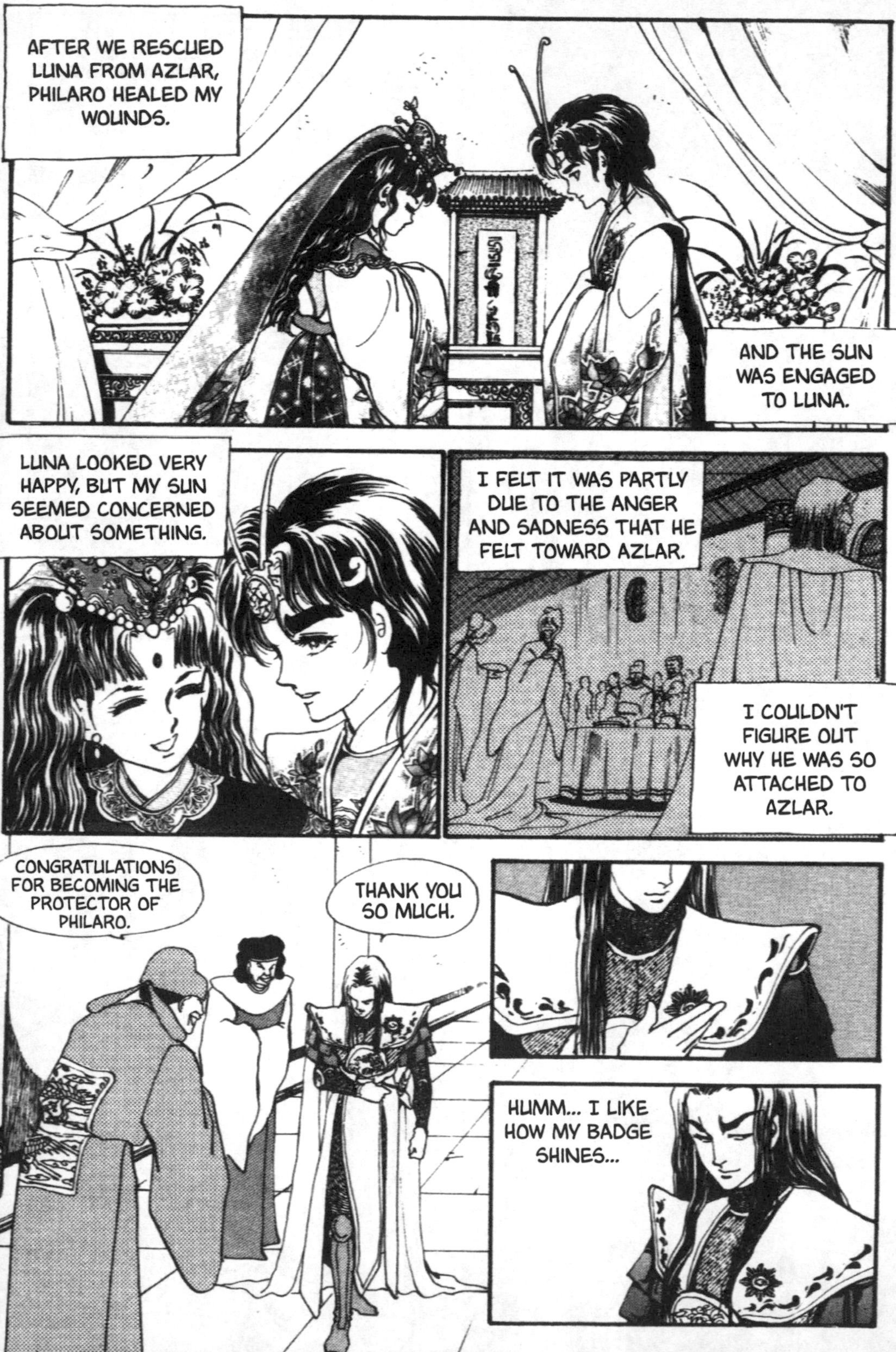
AFTER WE RESCUED LUNA FROM AZLAR, PHILARO HEALED MY WOUNDS.
AND THE SUN WAS ENGAGED TO LUNA.
LUNA LOOKED VERY HAPPY, BUT MY SUN SEEMED CONCERNED ABOUT SOMETHING.
I FELT IT WAS PARTLY DUE TO THE ANGER AND SADNESS THAT HE FELT TOWARD AZLAR.
I COULDN'T FIGURE OUT WHY HE WAS SO ATTACHED TO AZLAR.
CONGRATULATIONS FOR BECOMING THE PROTECTOR OF PHILARO.
THANK YOU SO MUCH.
HUMM... I LIKE HOW MY BADGE SHINES...

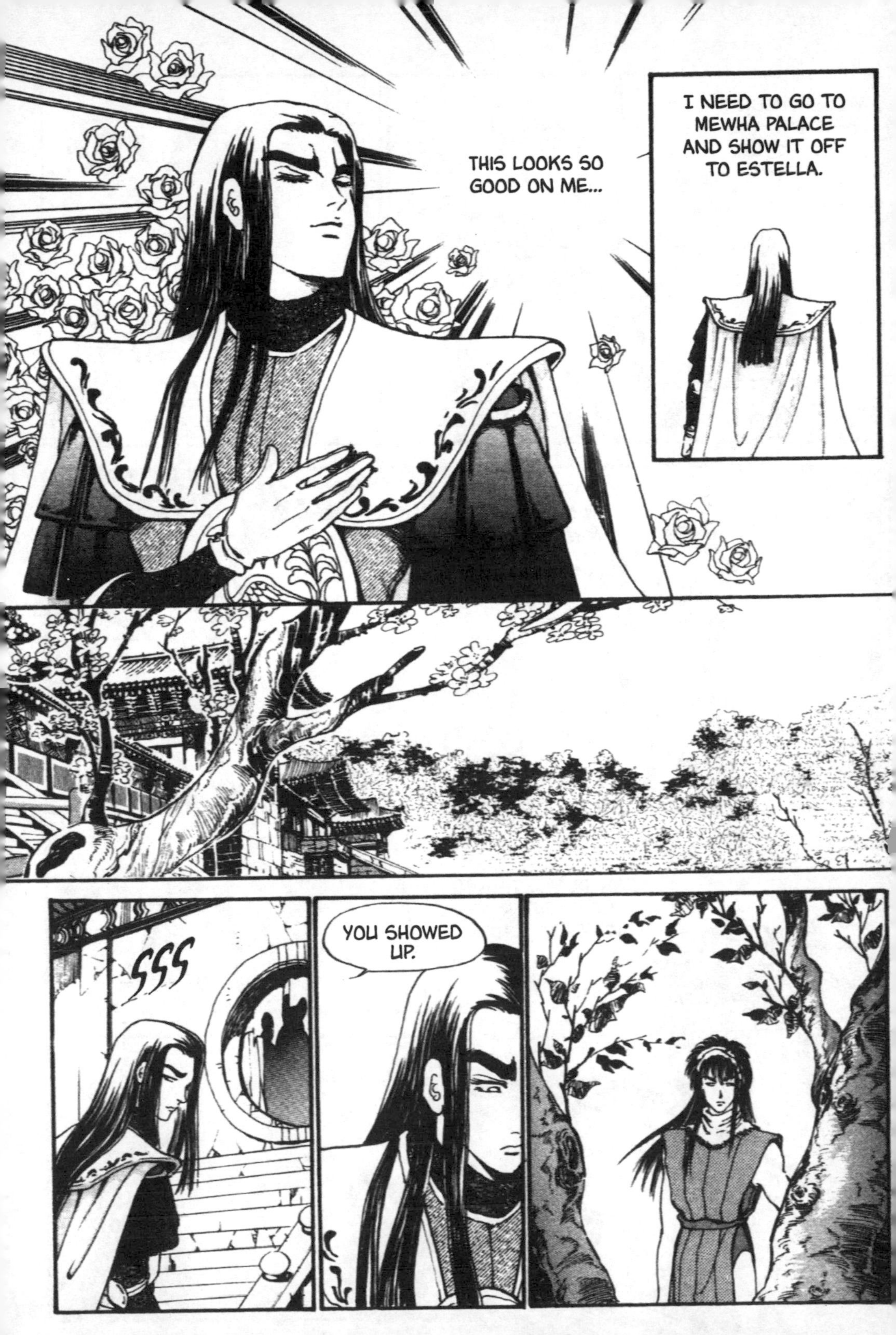
I NEED TO GO TO MEWHA PALACE AND SHOW IT OFF TO ESTELLA.
THIS LOOKS SO GOOD ON ME...
YOU SHOWED UP.
SSS

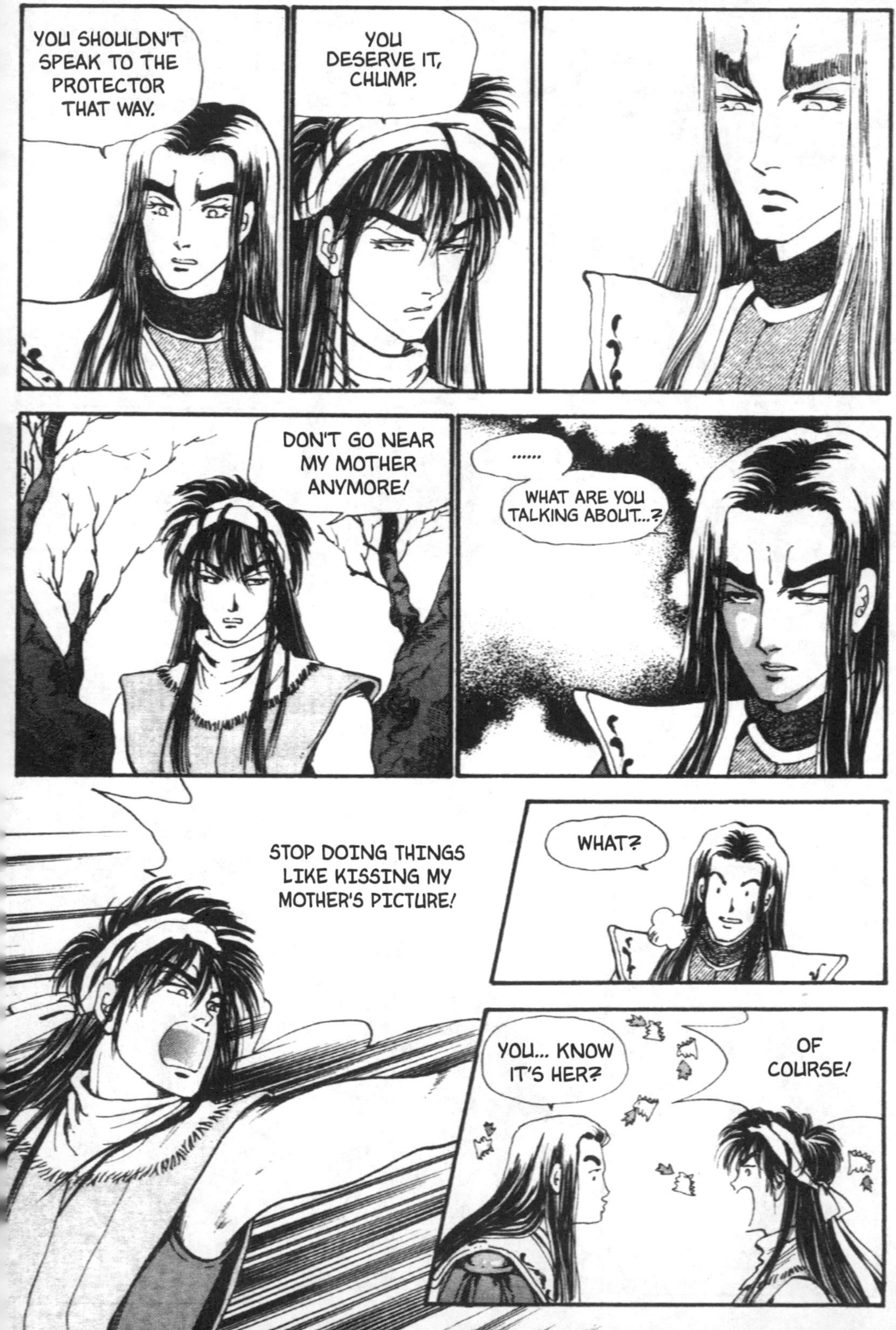
YOU SHOULDN'T SPEAK TO THE PROTECTOR THAT WAY.
YOU DESERVE IT, CHUMP.
DON'T GO NEAR MY MOTHER ANYMORE!
......
WHAT ARE YOU TALKING ABOUT...?
STOP DOING THINGS LIKE KISSING MY MOTHER'S PICTURE!
WHAT?
YOU... KNOW IT'S HER?
OF COURSE!

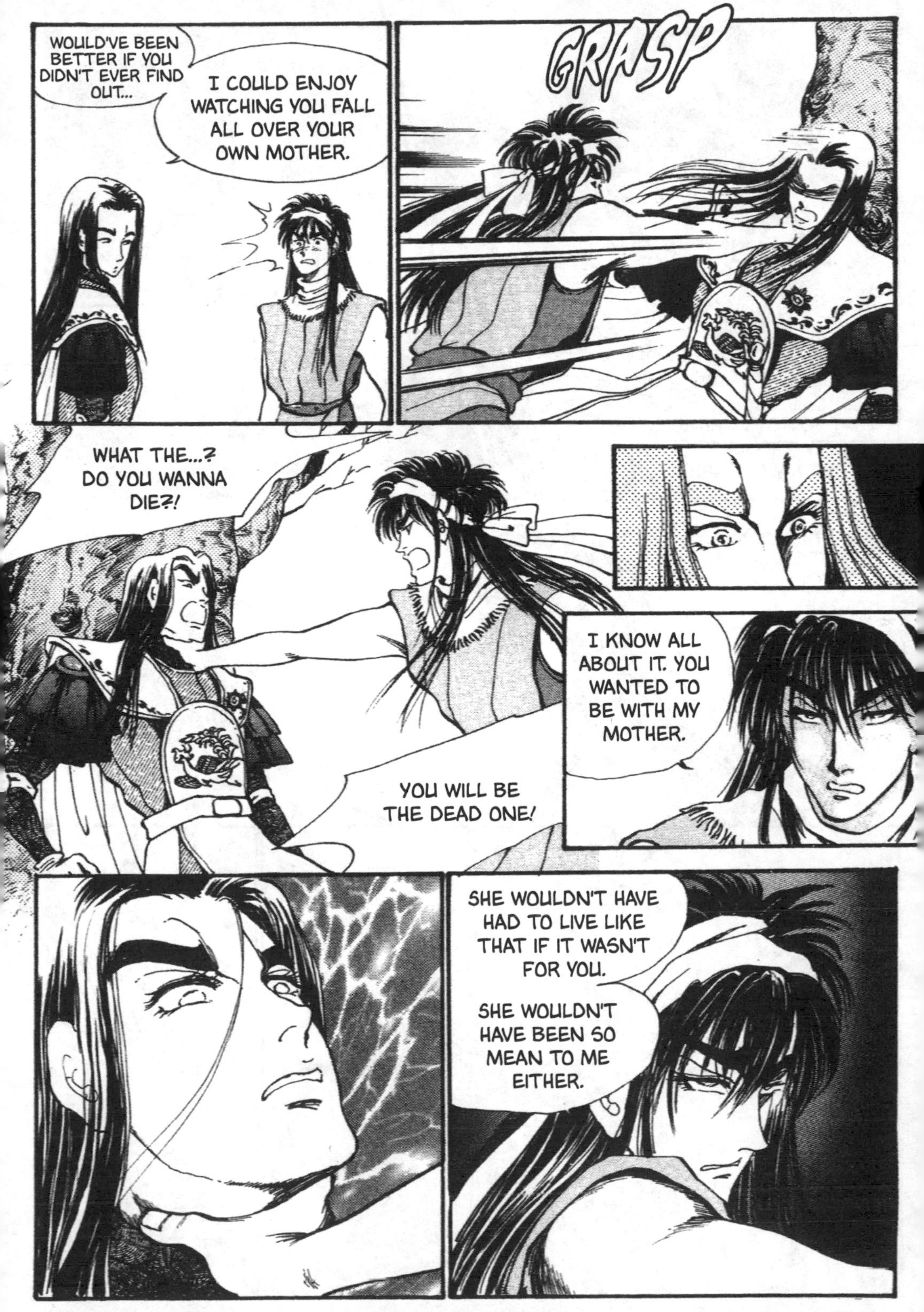
WOULD'VE BEEN BETTER IF YOU DIDN'T EVER FIND OUT...
I COULD ENJOY WATCHING YOU FALL ALL OVER YOUR OWN MOTHER.
GRASP
WHAT THE...?! DO YOU WANNA DIE?!
YOU WILL BE THE DEAD ONE!
I KNOW ALL ABOUT IT. YOU WANTED TO BE WITH MY MOTHER.
SHE WOULDN'T HAVE HAD TO LIVE LIKE THAT IF IT WASN'T FOR YOU.
SHE WOULDN'T HAVE BEEN SO MEAN TO ME EITHER.

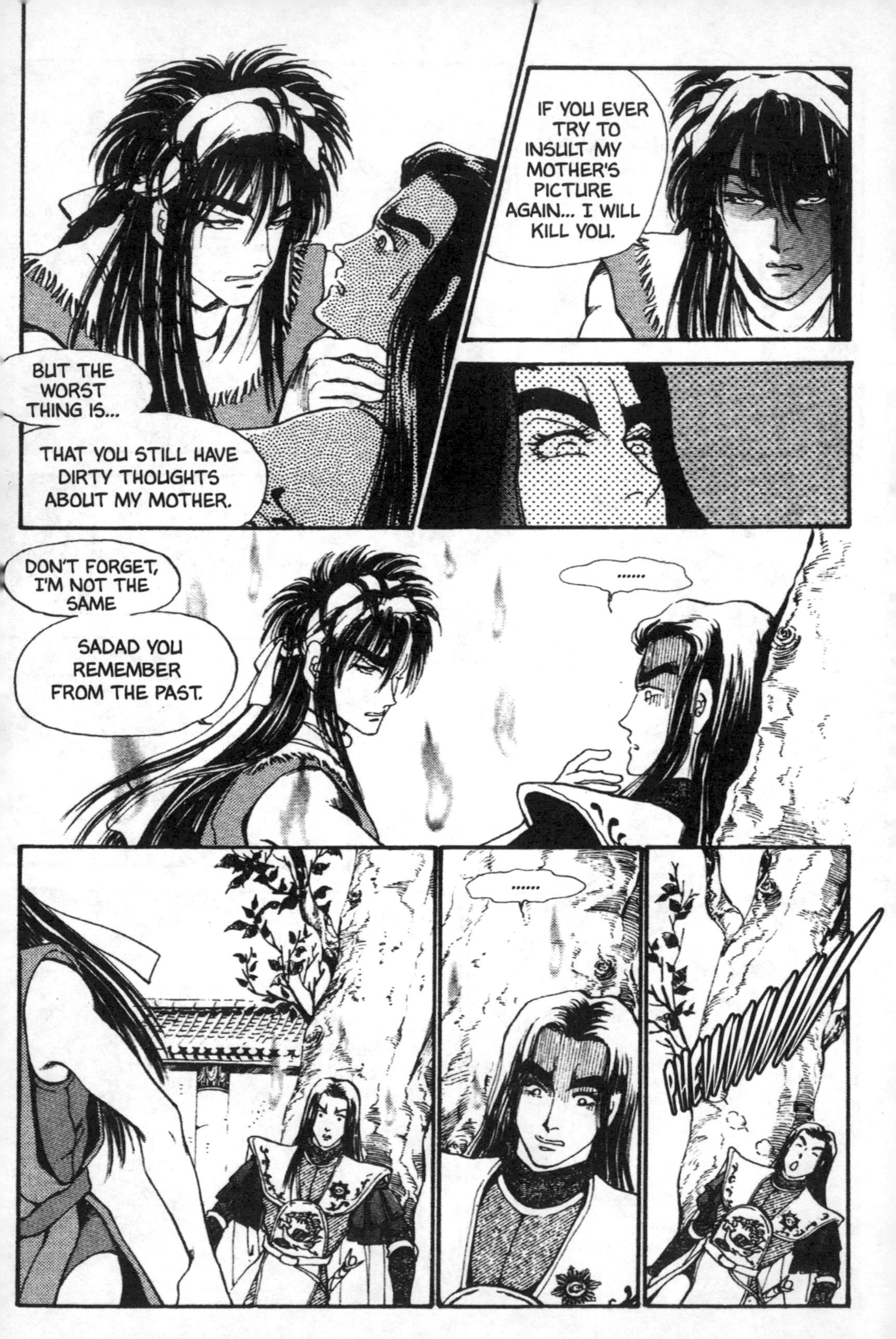
IF YOU EVER TRY TO INSULT MY MOTHER'S PICTURE AGAIN... I WILL KILL YOU.
BUT THE WORST THING IS...
THAT YOU STILL HAVE DIRTY THOUGHTS ABOUT MY MOTHER.
DON'T FORGET, I'M NOT THE SAME
SADAD YOU REMEMBER FROM THE PAST.
......
......

I THOUGHT HE WAS GONNA KILL ME FOR HAVING HIS FATHER EXECUTED.

IDIOT... WHO IS HE TRYING TO MESS WITH?

I'M STILL GONNA GO LOOK AT THE PICTURE...

......

I'LL SEE YOU LATER...

......

DAMN HIM... WHAT WOULD HAPPEN IF HE FOUND OUT ABOUT HIS FATHER?

THAT MEANS... I MAY JUST HAVE TO KILL HIM...

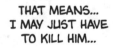

HMMM

DON'T FORGET, I'M NOT THE SAME SADAD YOU REMEMBER FROM THE PAST.

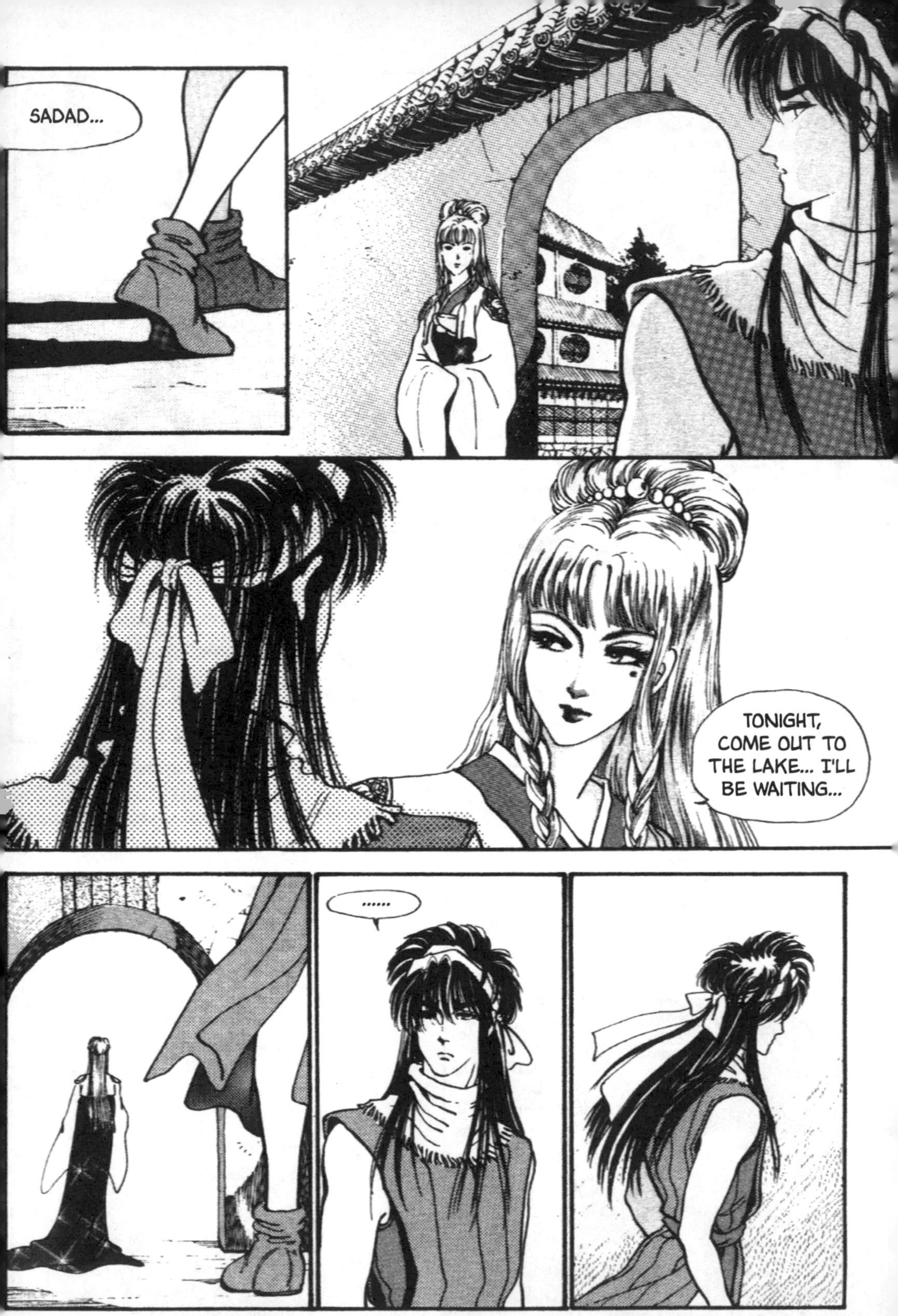
SADAD...
TONIGHT, COME OUT TO THE LAKE... I'LL BE WAITING...
......

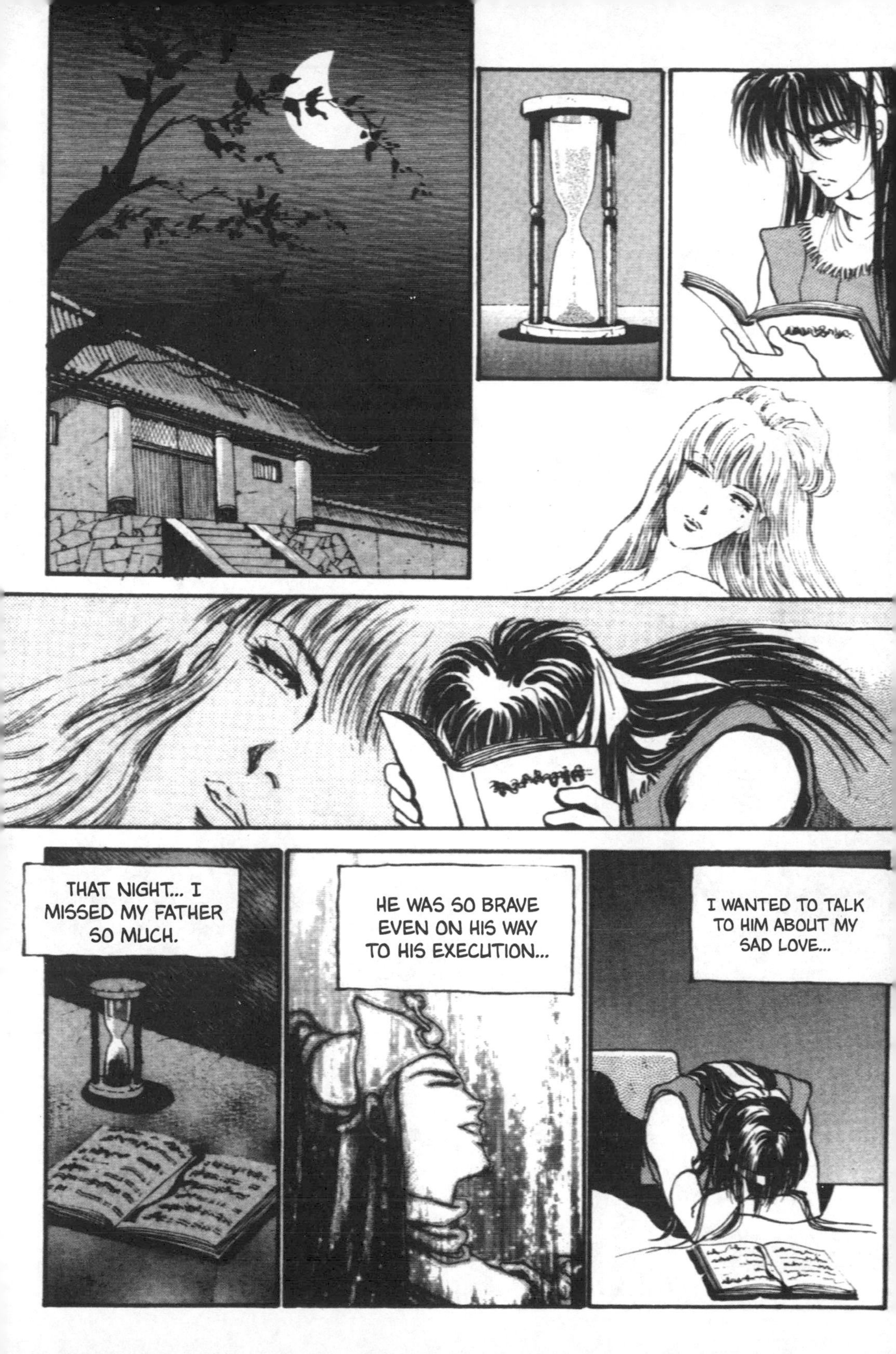
THAT NIGHT... I MISSED MY FATHER SO MUCH.
HE WAS SO BRAVE EVEN ON HIS WAY TO HIS EXECUTION...
I WANTED TO TALK TO HIM ABOUT MY SAD LOVE...

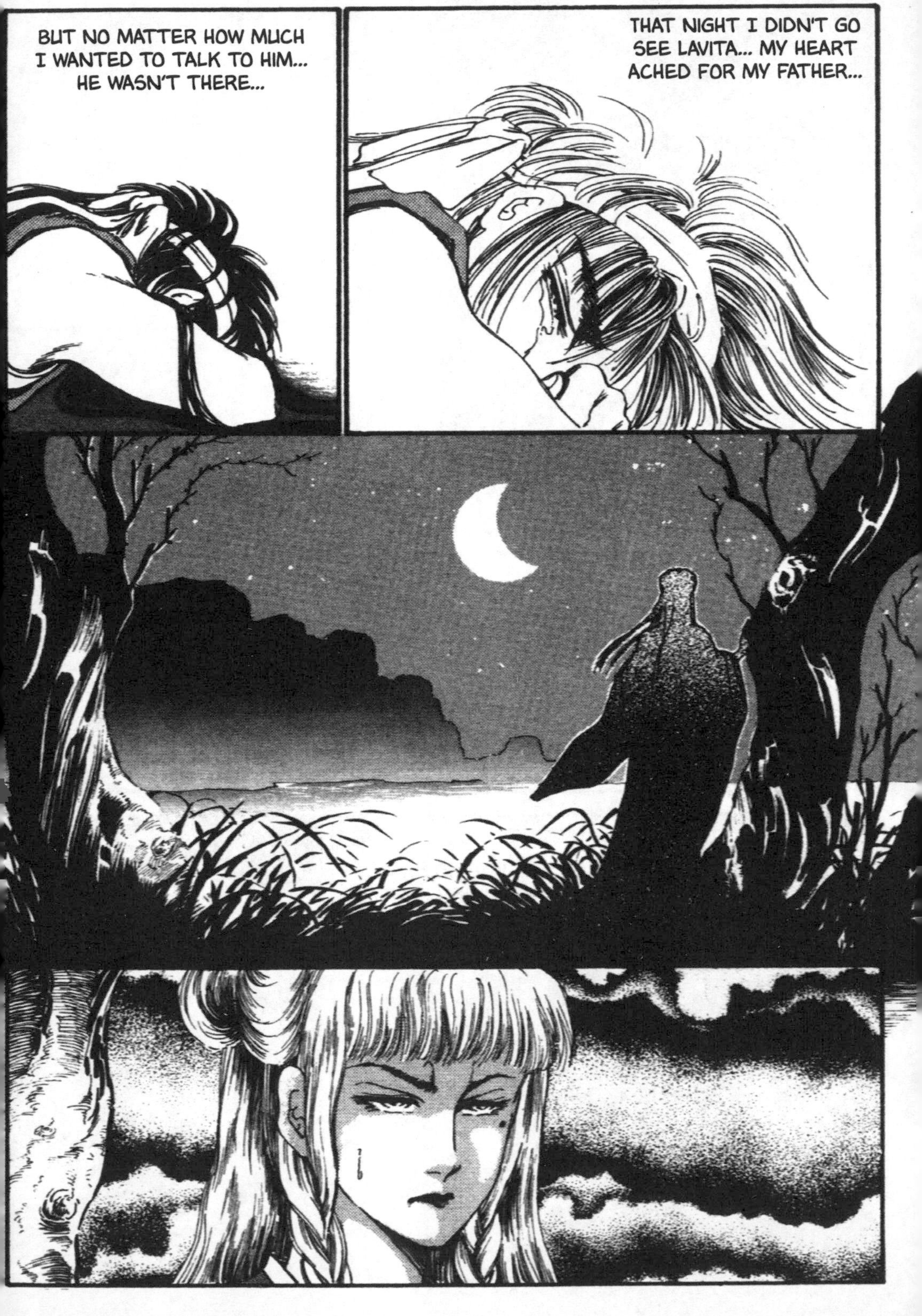
BUT NO MATTER HOW MUCH I WANTED TO TALK TO HIM... HE WASN'T THERE...
THAT NIGHT I DIDN'T GO SEE LAVITA... MY HEART ACHED FOR MY FATHER...

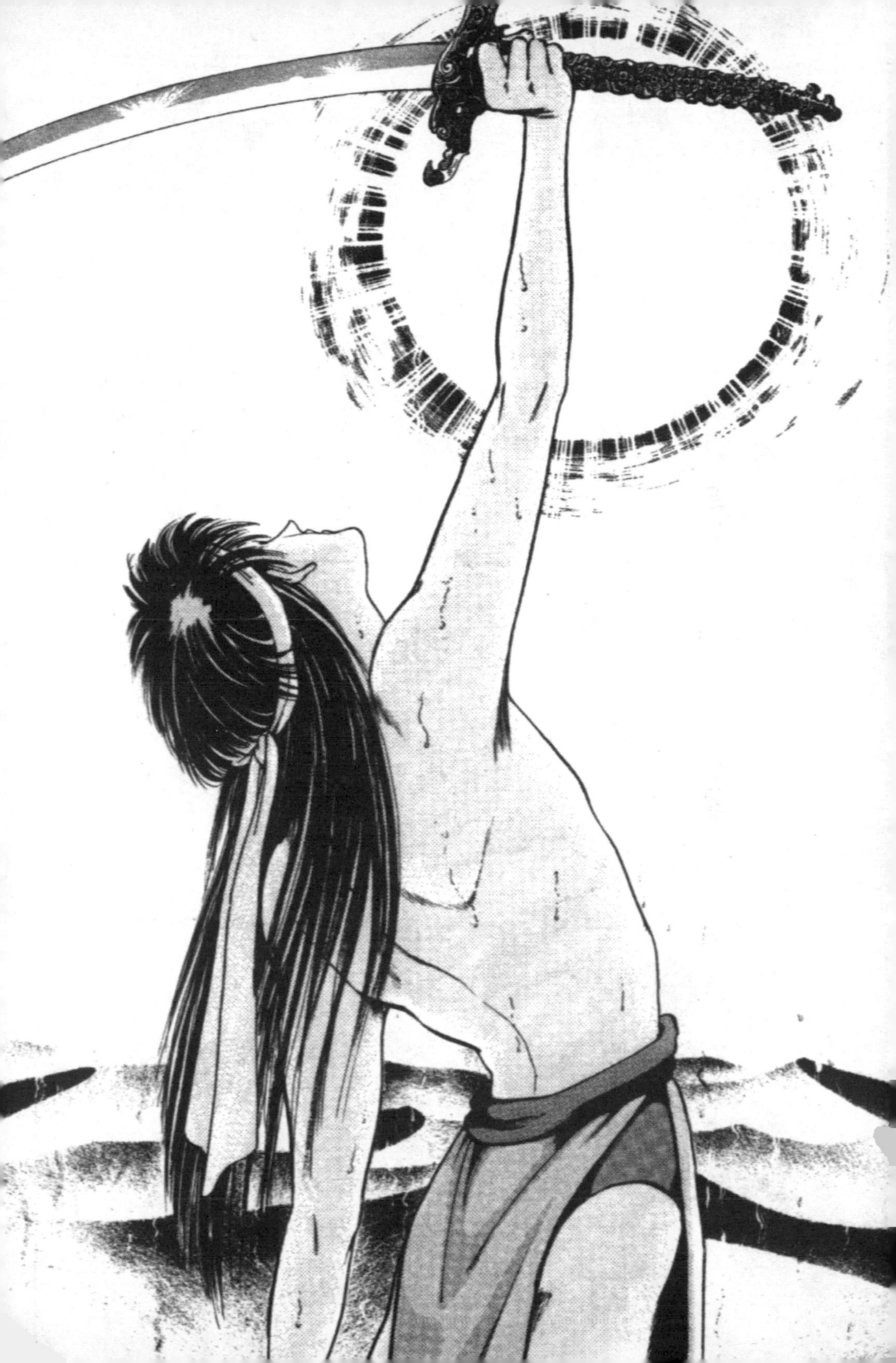

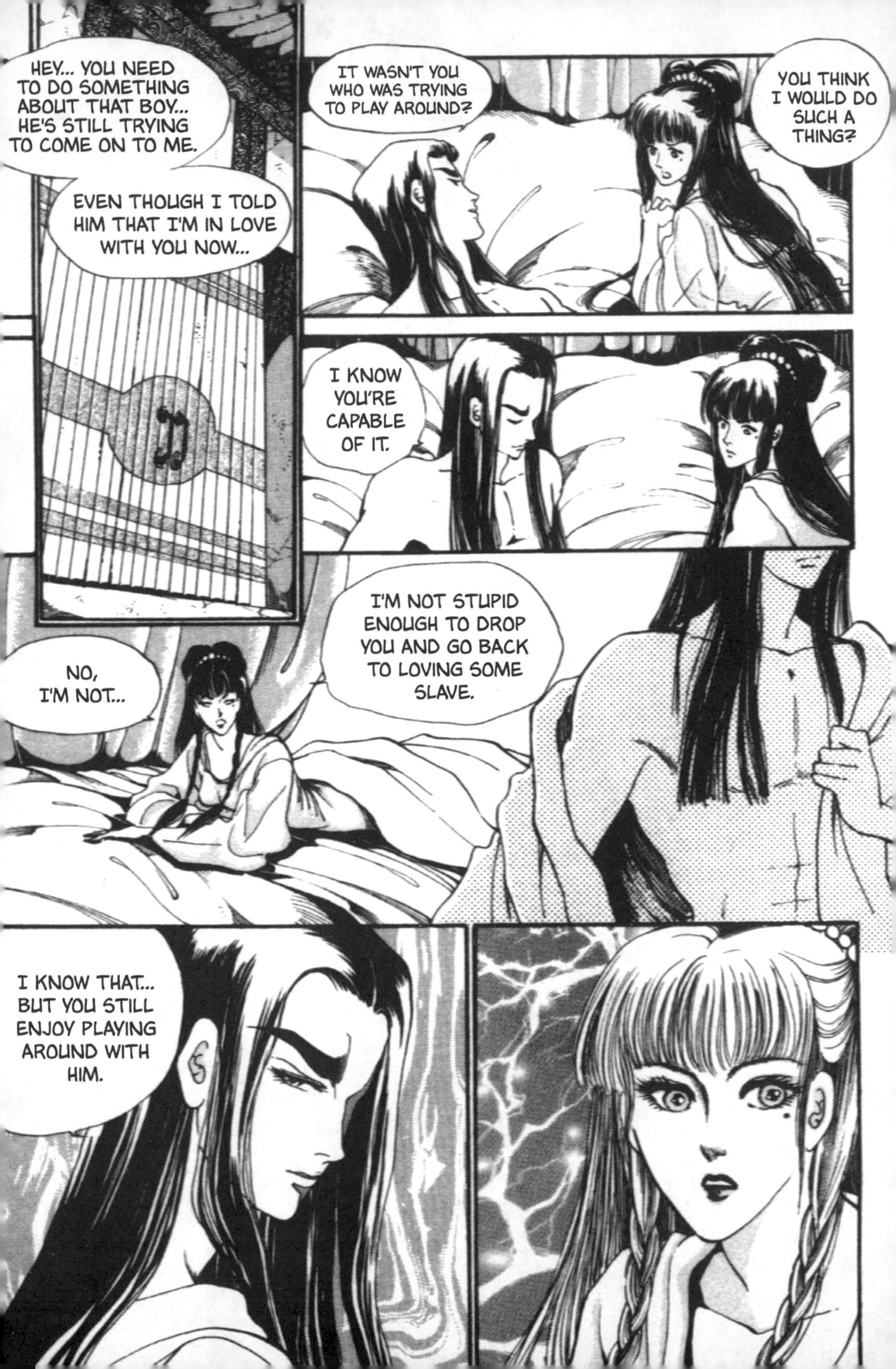
HEY... YOU NEED TO DO SOMETHING ABOUT THAT BOY... HE'S STILL TRYING TO COME ON TO ME.
EVEN THOUGH I TOLD HIM THAT I'M IN LOVE WITH YOU NOW...
IT WASN'T YOU WHO WAS TRYING TO PLAY AROUND?
YOU THINK I WOULD DO SUCH A THING?
I KNOW YOU'RE CAPABLE OF IT.
NO, I'M NOT...
I'M NOT STUPID ENOUGH TO DROP YOU AND GO BACK TO LOVING SOME SLAVE.
I KNOW THAT... BUT YOU STILL ENJOY PLAYING AROUND WITH HIM.

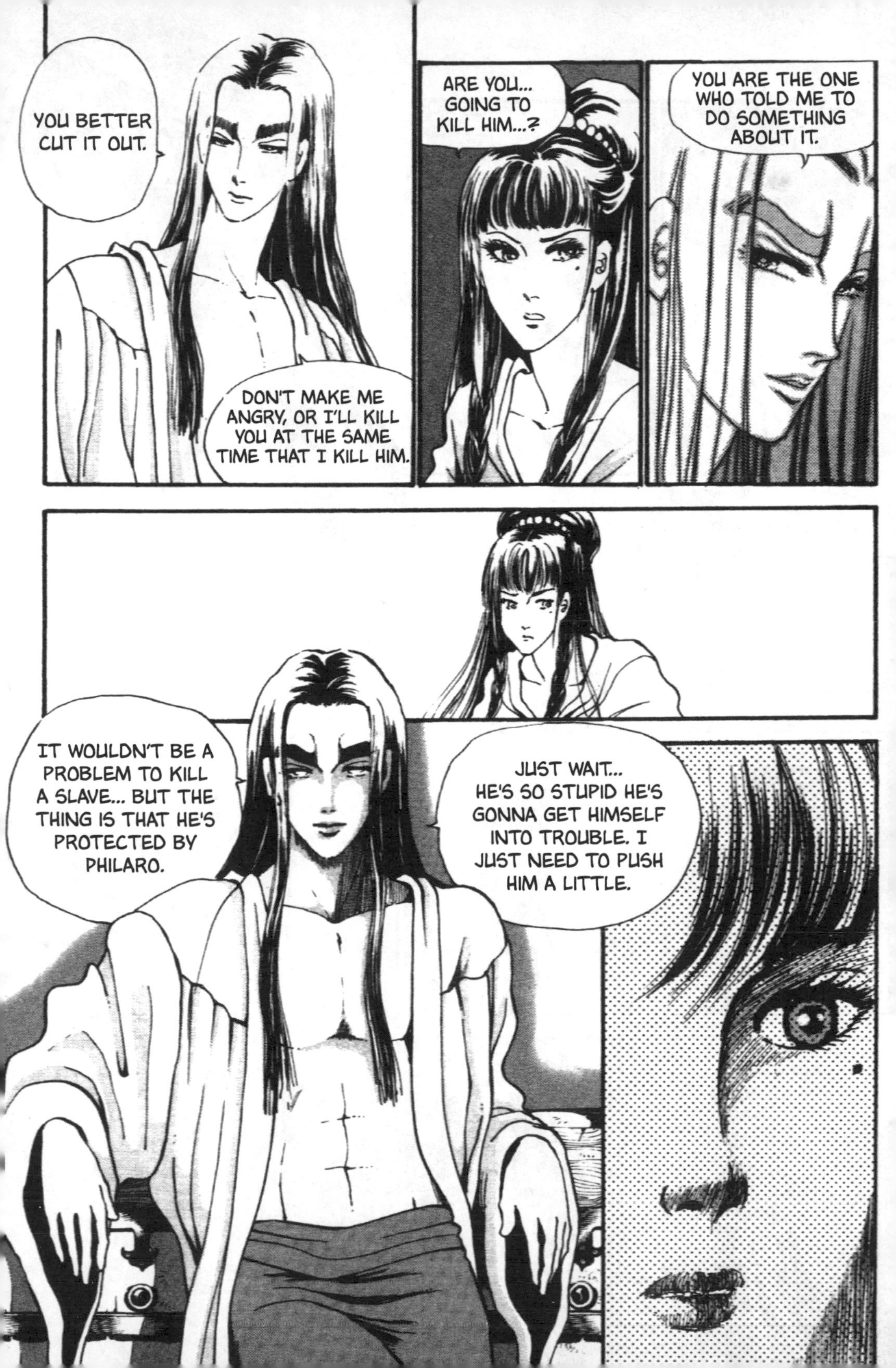
YOU BETTER CUT IT OUT.
DON'T MAKE ME ANGRY, OR I'LL KILL YOU AT THE SAME TIME THAT I KILL HIM.
ARE YOU... GOING TO KILL HIM...?
YOU ARE THE ONE WHO TOLD ME TO DO SOMETHING ABOUT IT.
IT WOULDN'T BE A PROBLEM TO KILL A SLAVE... BUT THE THING IS THAT HE'S PROTECTED BY PHILARO.
JUST WAIT... HE'S SO STUPID HE'S GONNA GET HIMSELF INTO TROUBLE. I JUST NEED TO PUSH HIM A LITTLE.

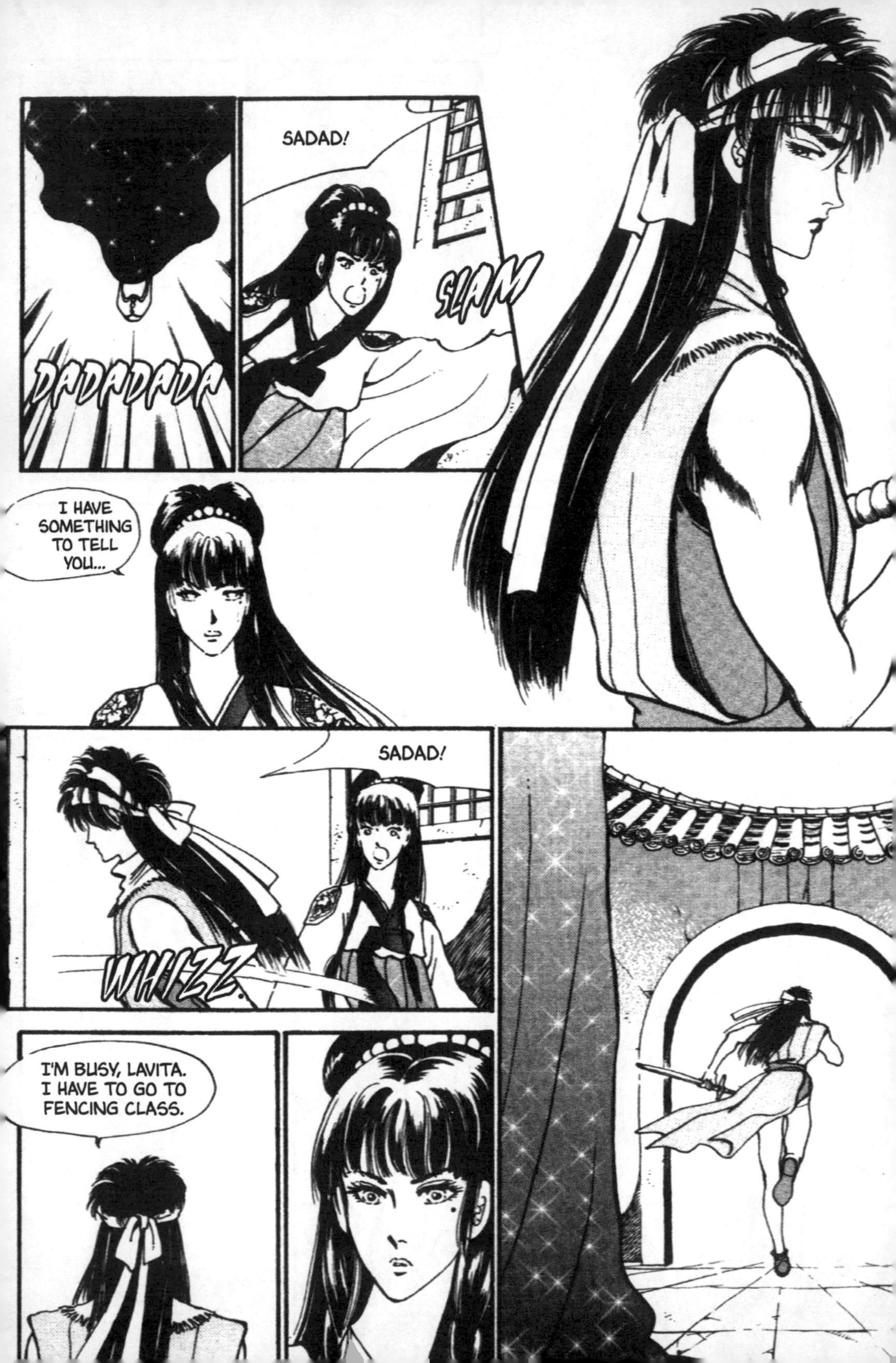
DADADADA
SADAD!
SLAM
I HAVE SOMETHING TO TELL YOU...
SADAD!
WHIZZ
I'M BUSY, LAVITA. I HAVE TO GO TO FENCING CLASS.

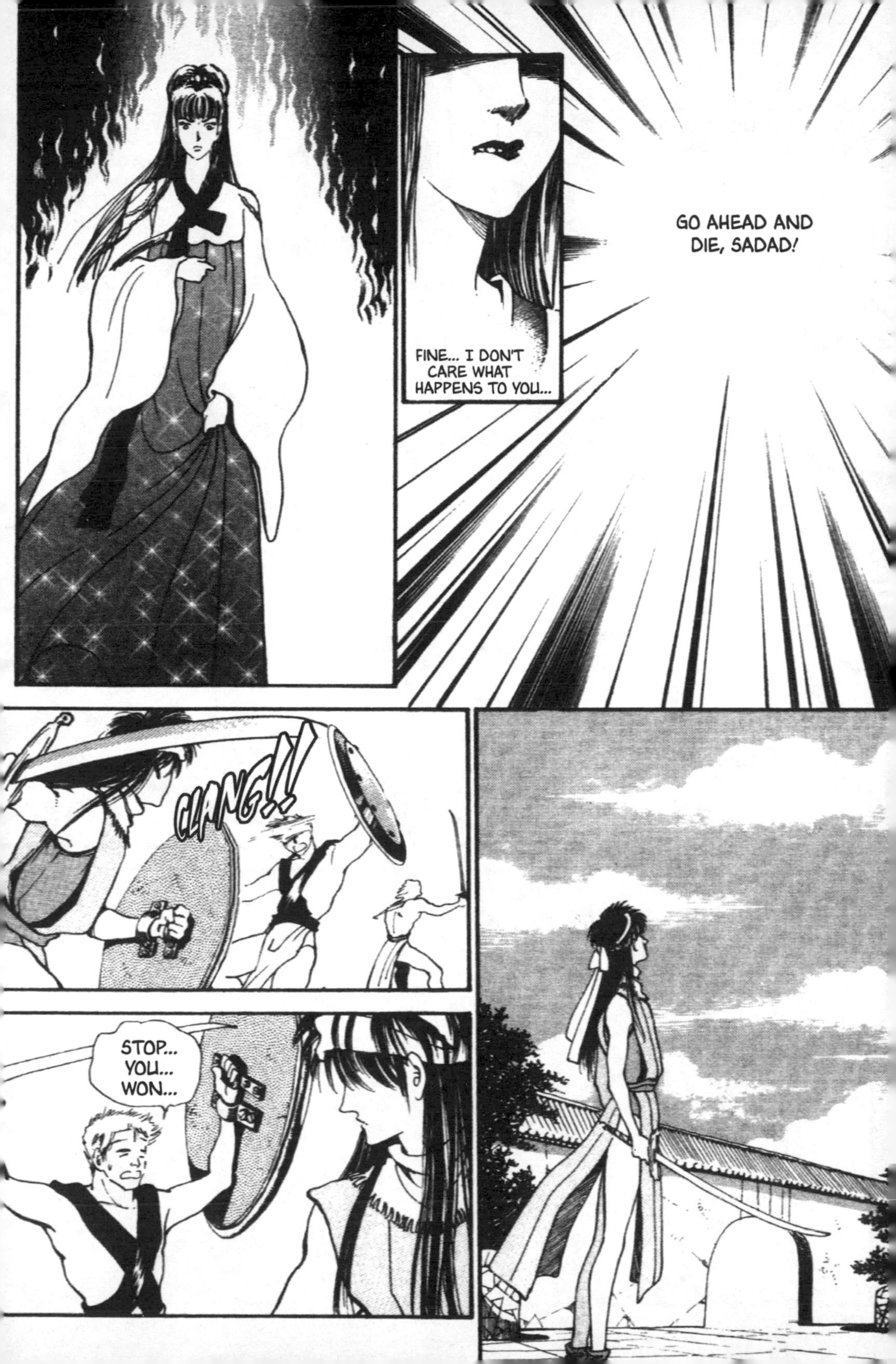
FINE... I DON'T CARE WHAT HAPPENS TO YOU...
GO AHEAD AND DIE, SADAD!
CLANG!!
STOP... YOU... WON...

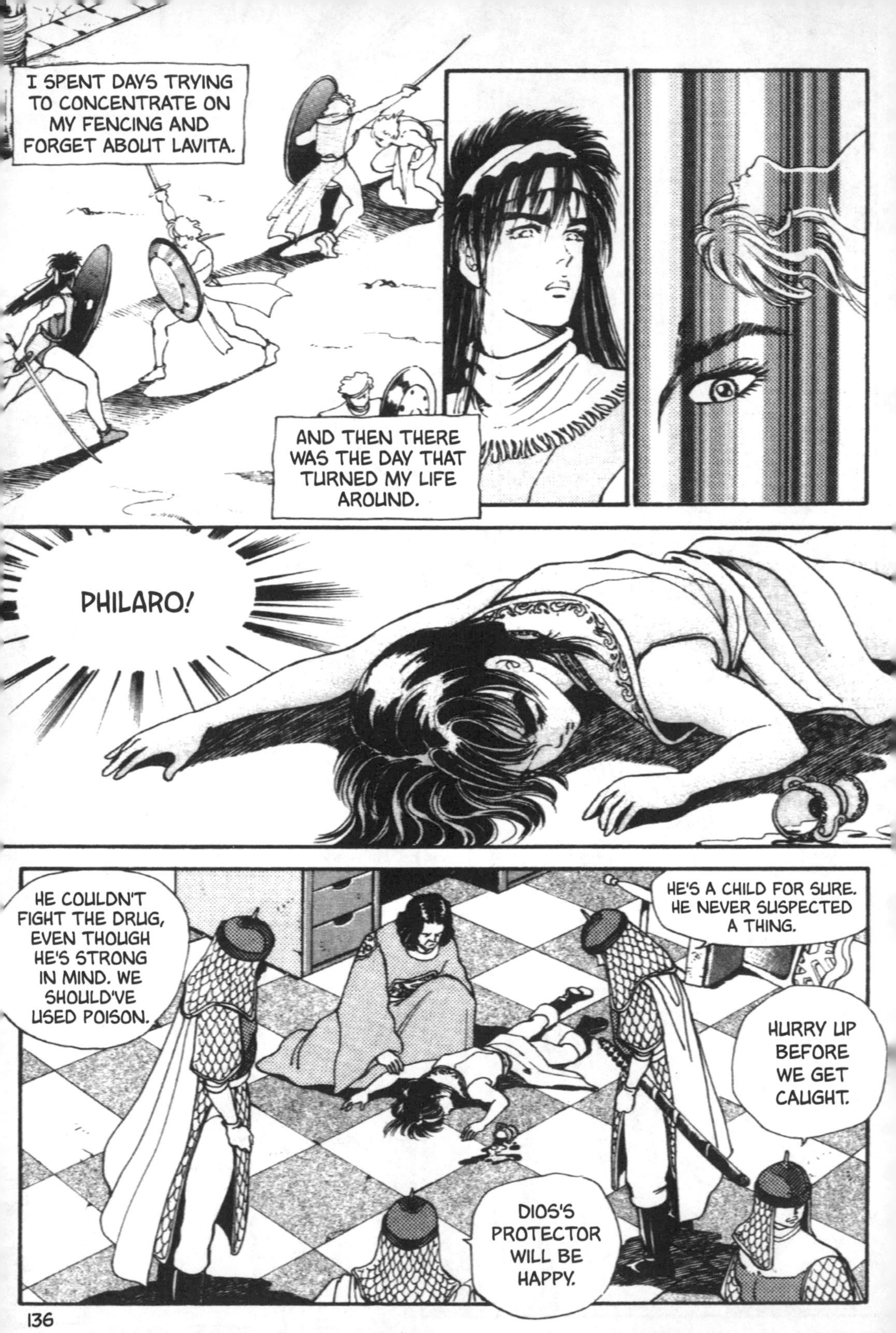
I SPENT DAYS TRYING TO CONCENTRATE ON MY FENCING AND FORGET ABOUT LAVITA.
AND THEN THERE WAS THE DAY THAT TURNED MY LIFE AROUND.
PHILARO!
HE COULDN'T FIGHT THE DRUG, EVEN THOUGH HE'S STRONG IN MIND. WE SHOULD'VE USED POISON.
HE'S A CHILD FOR SURE. HE NEVER SUSPECTED A THING.
HURRY UP BEFORE WE GET CAUGHT.
DIOS'S PROTECTOR WILL BE HAPPY.

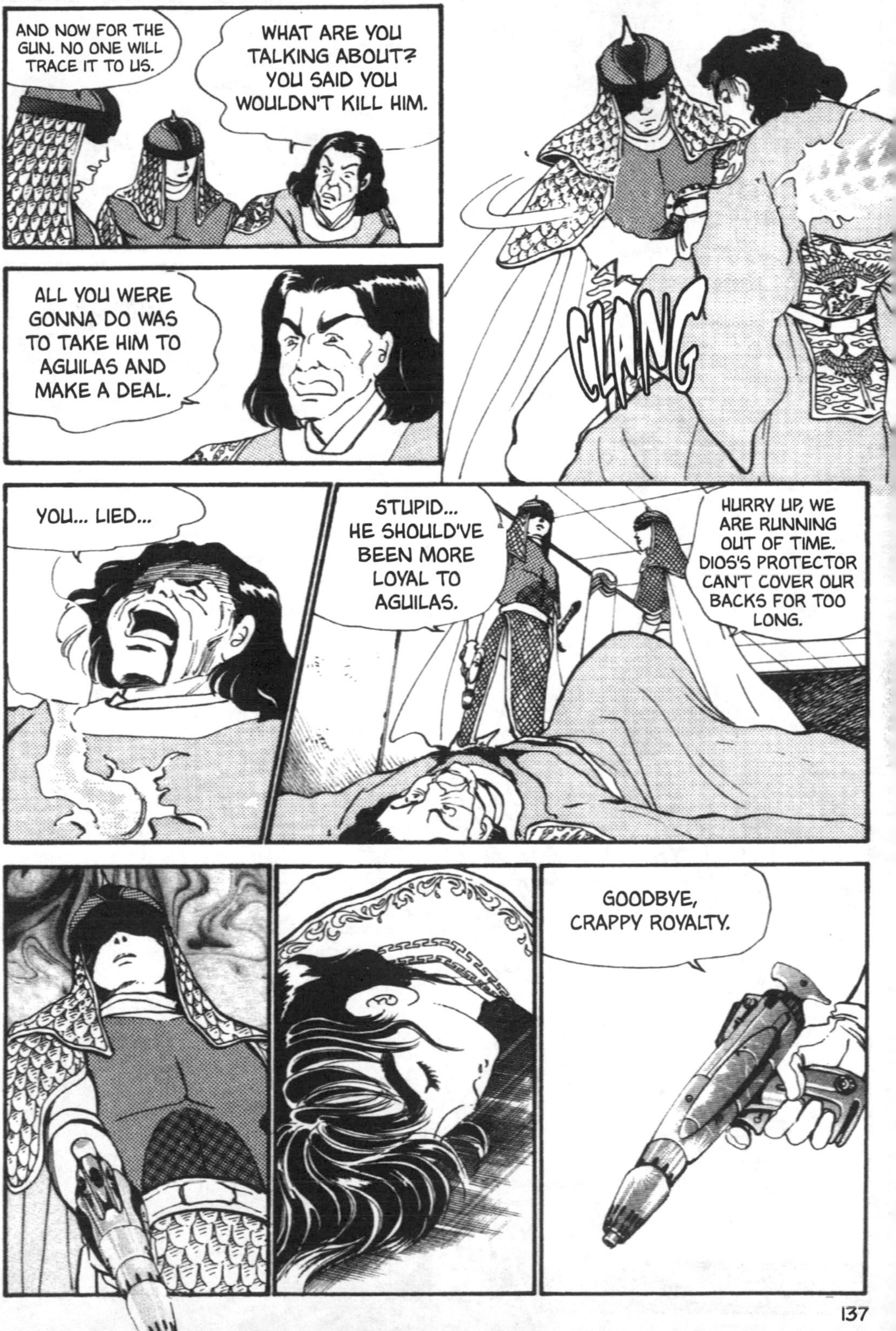
AND NOW FOR THE GUN. NO ONE WILL TRACE IT TO US.
WHAT ARE YOU TALKING ABOUT? YOU SAID YOU WOULDN'T KILL HIM.
ALL YOU WERE GONNA DO WAS TO TAKE HIM TO AGUILAS AND MAKE A DEAL.
CLANG
YOU... LIED...
STUPID... HE SHOULD'VE BEEN MORE LOYAL TO AGUILAS.
HURRY UP, WE ARE RUNNING OUT OF TIME. DIOS'S PROTECTOR CAN'T COVER OUR BACKS FOR TOO LONG.
GOODBYE, CRAPPY ROYALTY.

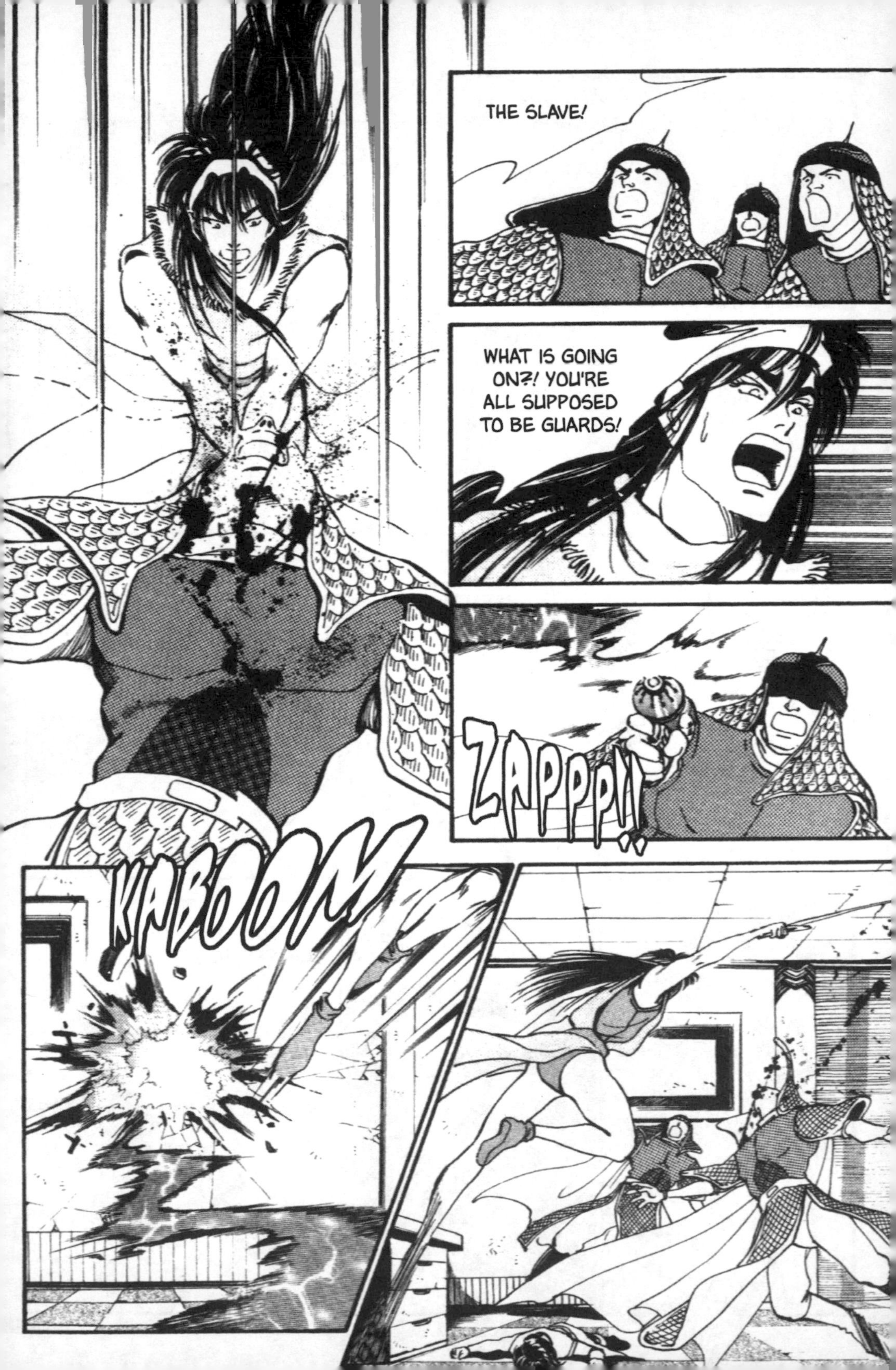
THE SLAVE!
WHAT IS GOING ON?! YOU'RE ALL SUPPOSED TO BE GUARDS!
ZAPPP!!
KABOOM

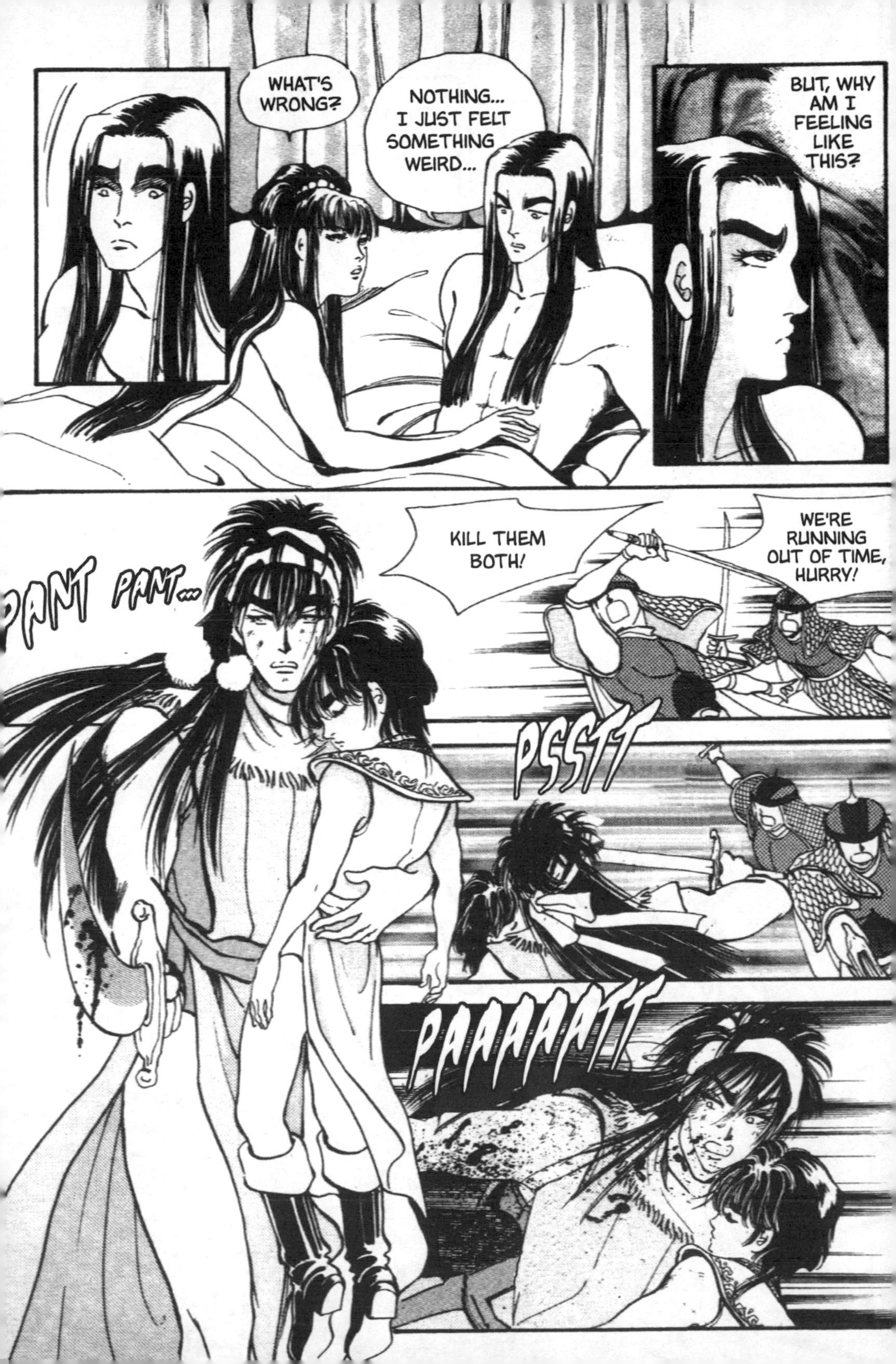
WHAT'S WRONG?
NOTHING... I JUST FELT SOMETHING WEIRD...
BUT, WHY AM I FEELING LIKE THIS?
PANT PANT...
KILL THEM BOTH!
WE'RE RUNNING OUT OF TIME, HURRY!
PSSTT
PAAAAATT

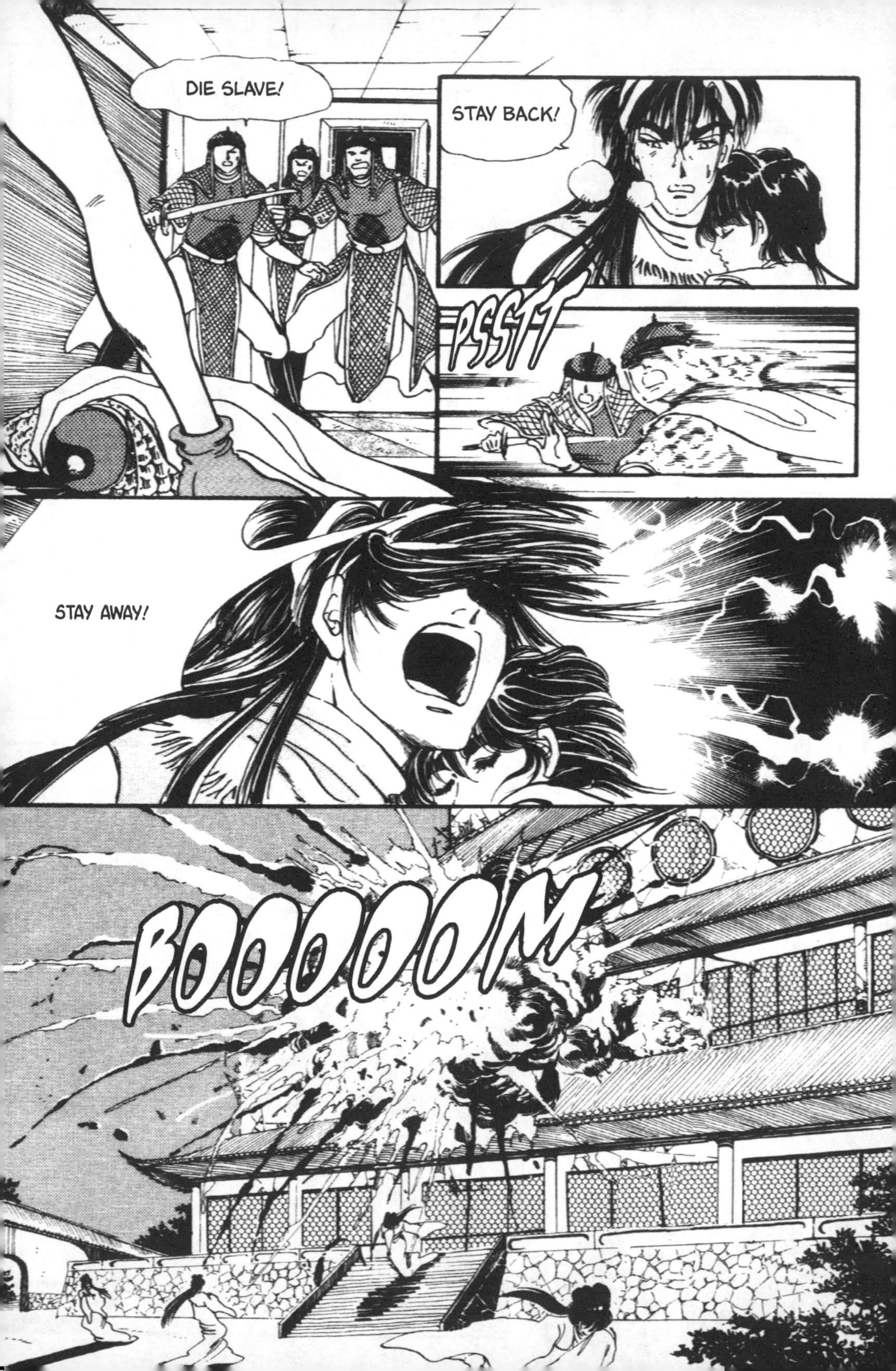

DIE SLAVE!
STAY BACK!
PSSTT
STAY AWAY!
BOOOOOM

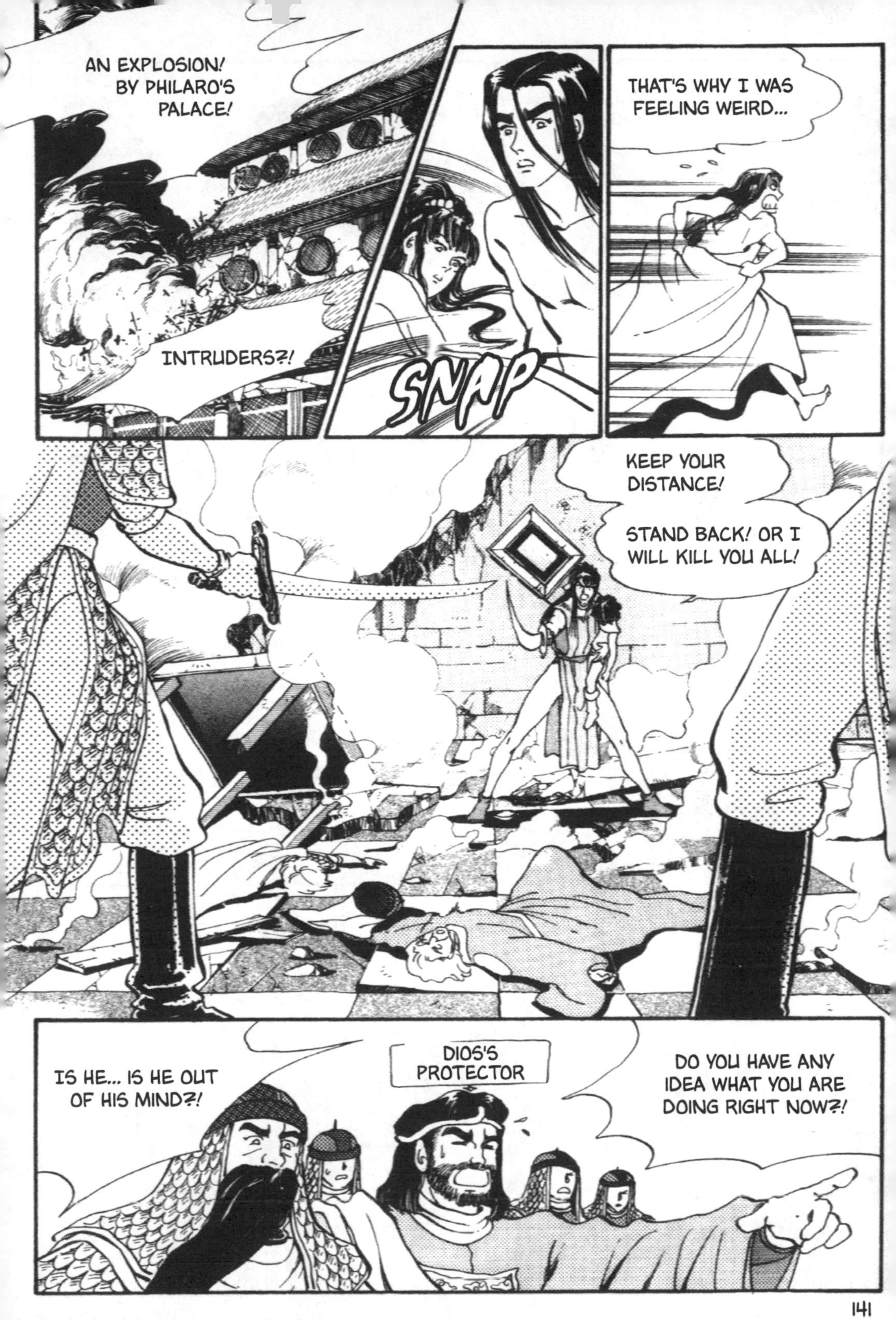
AN EXPLOSION! BY PHILARO'S PALACE!
INTRUDERS?!
SNAP
THAT'S WHY I WAS FEELING WEIRD...
KEEP YOUR DISTANCE!
STAND BACK! OR I WILL KILL YOU ALL!
IS HE... IS HE OUT OF HIS MIND?!
DIOS'S PROTECTOR
DO YOU HAVE ANY IDEA WHAT YOU ARE DOING RIGHT NOW?!

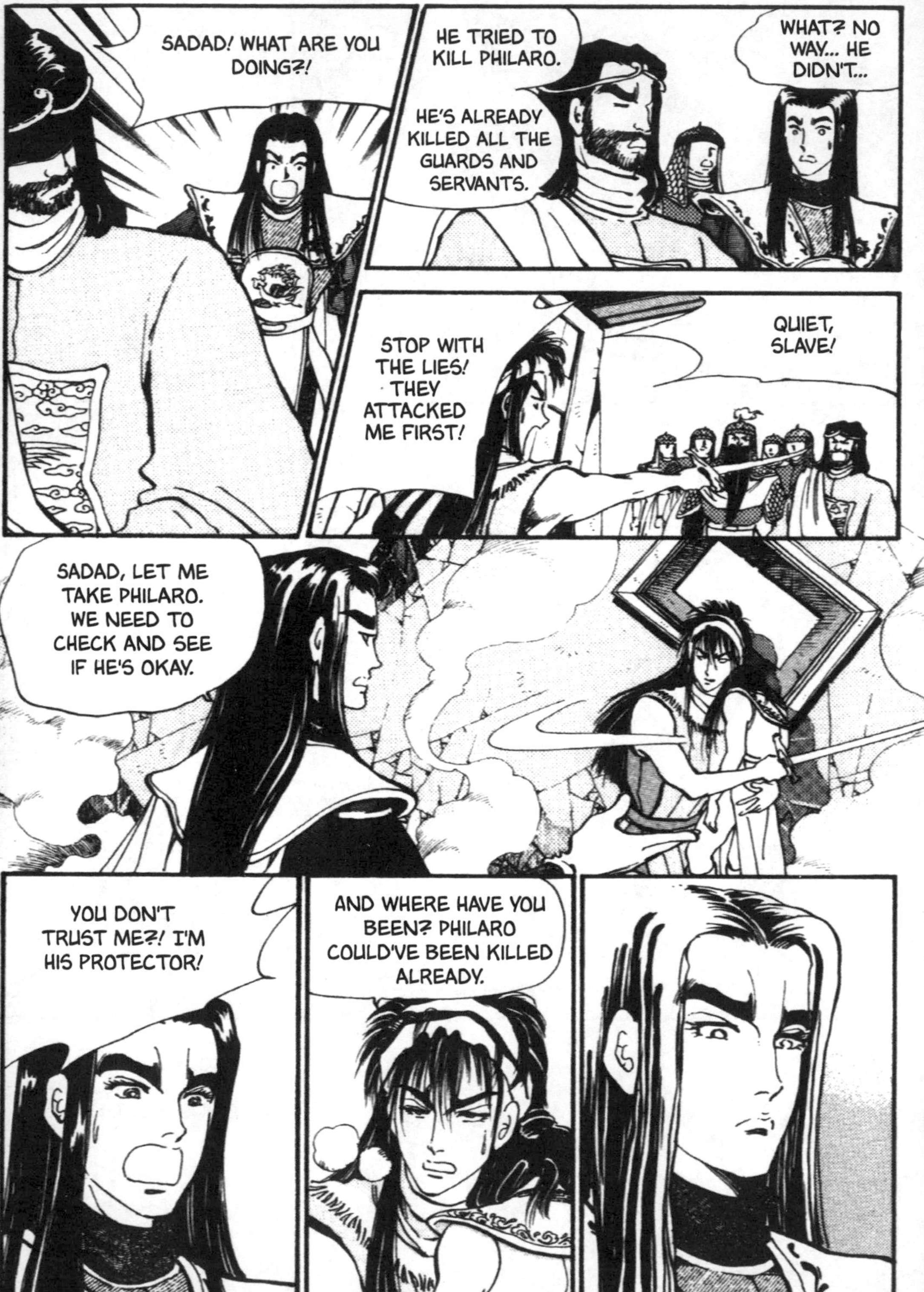

SADAD! WHAT ARE YOU DOING?!
HE TRIED TO KILL PHILARO.
HE'S ALREADY KILLED ALL THE GUARDS AND SERVANTS.
WHAT? NO WAY... HE DIDN'T...
QUIET, SLAVE!
STOP WITH THE LIES! THEY ATTACKED ME FIRST!
SADAD, LET ME TAKE PHILARO. WE NEED TO CHECK AND SEE IF HE'S OKAY.
YOU DON'T TRUST ME?! I'M HIS PROTECTOR!
AND WHERE HAVE YOU BEEN? PHILARO COULD'VE BEEN KILLED ALREADY.

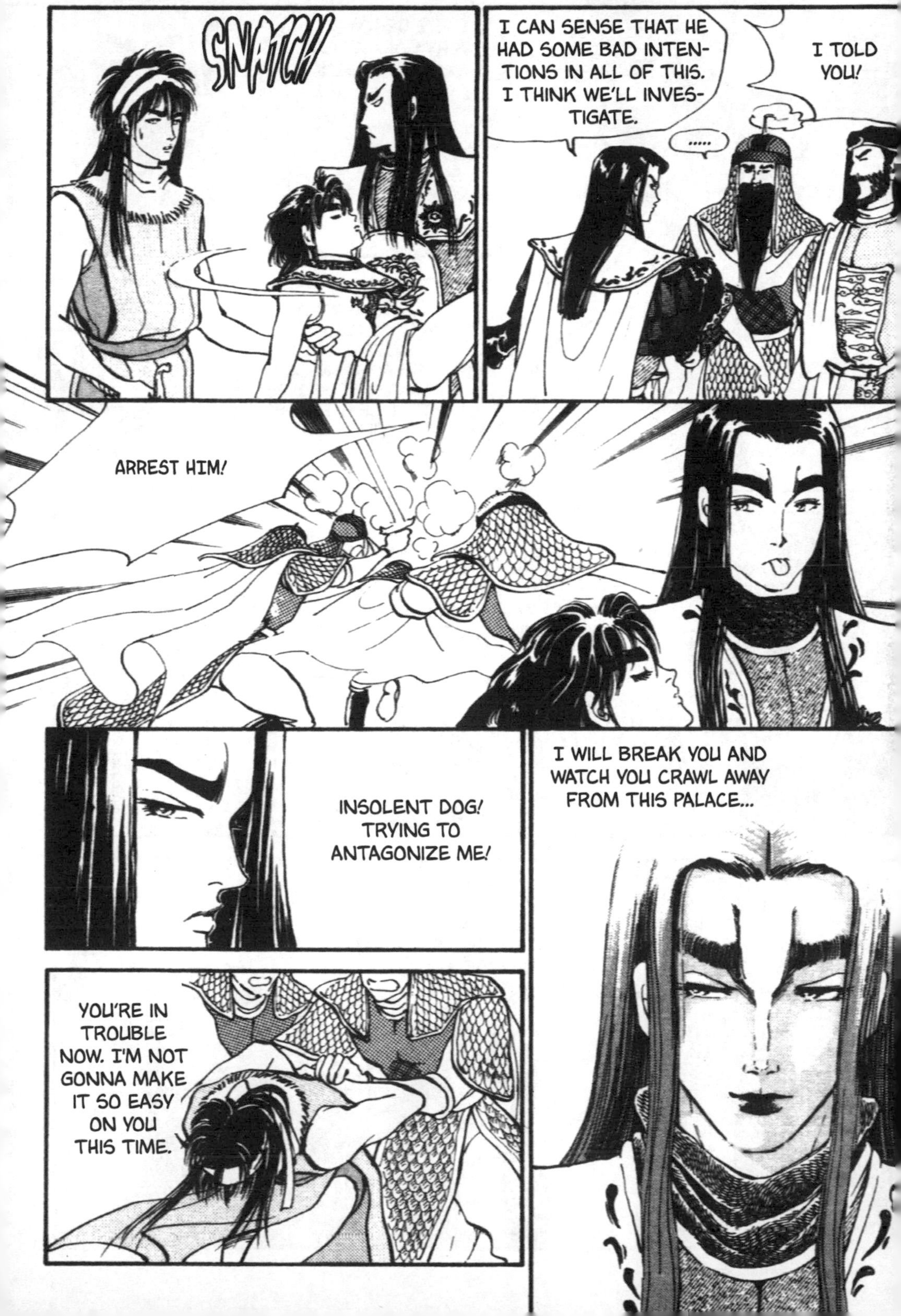
SNATCH!
I CAN SENSE THAT HE HAD SOME BAD INTENTIONS IN ALL OF THIS. I THINK WE'LL INVESTIGATE.
......
I TOLD YOU!
ARREST HIM!
INSOLENT DOG! TRYING TO ANTAGONIZE ME!
I WILL BREAK YOU AND WATCH YOU CRAWL AWAY FROM THIS PALACE...
YOU'RE IN TROUBLE NOW. I'M NOT GONNA MAKE IT SO EASY ON YOU THIS TIME.

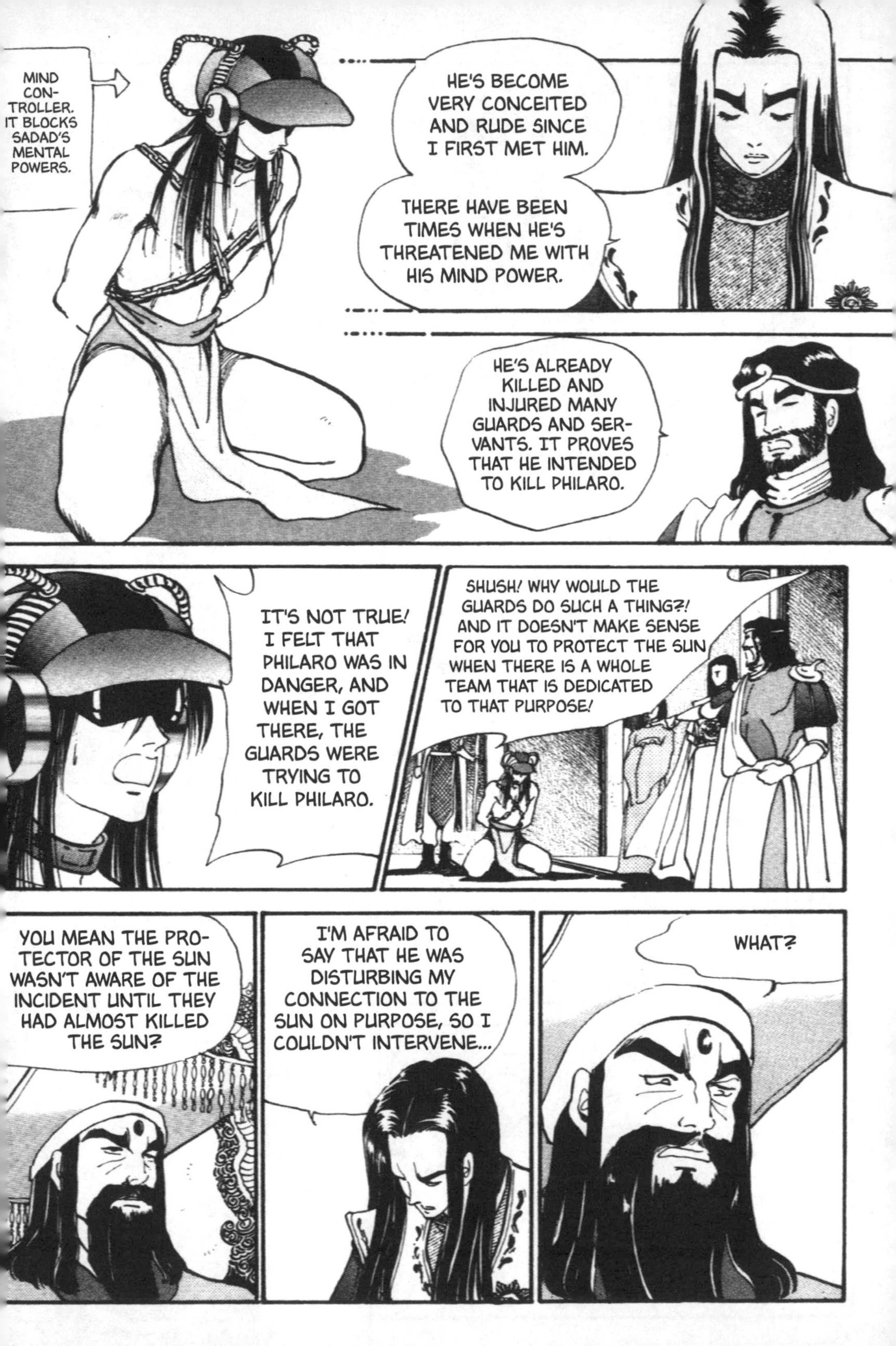
MIND CON-TROLLER. IT BLOCKS SADAD'S MENTAL POWERS.
HE'S BECOME VERY CONCEITED AND RUDE SINCE I FIRST MET HIM.
THERE HAVE BEEN TIMES WHEN HE'S THREATENED ME WITH HIS MIND POWER.
HE'S ALREADY KILLED AND INJURED MANY GUARDS AND SER-VANTS. IT PROVES THAT HE INTENDED TO KILL PHILARO.
IT'S NOT TRUE! I FELT THAT PHILARO WAS IN DANGER, AND WHEN I GOT THERE, THE GUARDS WERE TRYING TO KILL PHILARO.
SHUSH! WHY WOULD THE GUARDS DO SUCH A THING?! AND IT DOESN'T MAKE SENSE FOR YOU TO PROTECT THE SUN WHEN THERE IS A WHOLE TEAM THAT IS DEDICATED TO THAT PURPOSE!
YOU MEAN THE PRO-TECTOR OF THE SUN WASN'T AWARE OF THE INCIDENT UNTIL THEY HAD ALMOST KILLED THE SUN?
I'M AFRAID TO SAY THAT HE WAS DISTURBING MY CONNECTION TO THE SUN ON PURPOSE, SO I COULDN'T INTERVENE...
WHAT?

WE SHOULDN'T LET HIM LIVE THIS TIME. HE'S ALREADY HURT SO MANY PEOPLE...

AND AS A TRAITOR'S SON, HE CAN ONLY BE A TRAITOR HIMSELF.

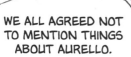

WE ALL AGREED NOT TO MENTION THINGS ABOUT AURELLO.

WHAT MADE YOU BRING UP HIS NAME?

DON'T YOU GET IT, DIOS?! IT'S HIS REVENGE! HE WILL KILL OUR SUN AND KILL YOU, TOO!

I DIDN'T KNOW THIS AT THE TIME BUT DIOS'S PROTECTOR AND MANY OTHER GUARDS HAD ALREADY BECOME SUPPORTERS OF AGUILAS.

DIOS, WE KNOW YOU WILL USE YOUR BEST JUDGEMENT!

THEY NEEDED TO ACCUSE SOMEBODY... THEY NEEDED A SCAPEGOAT.

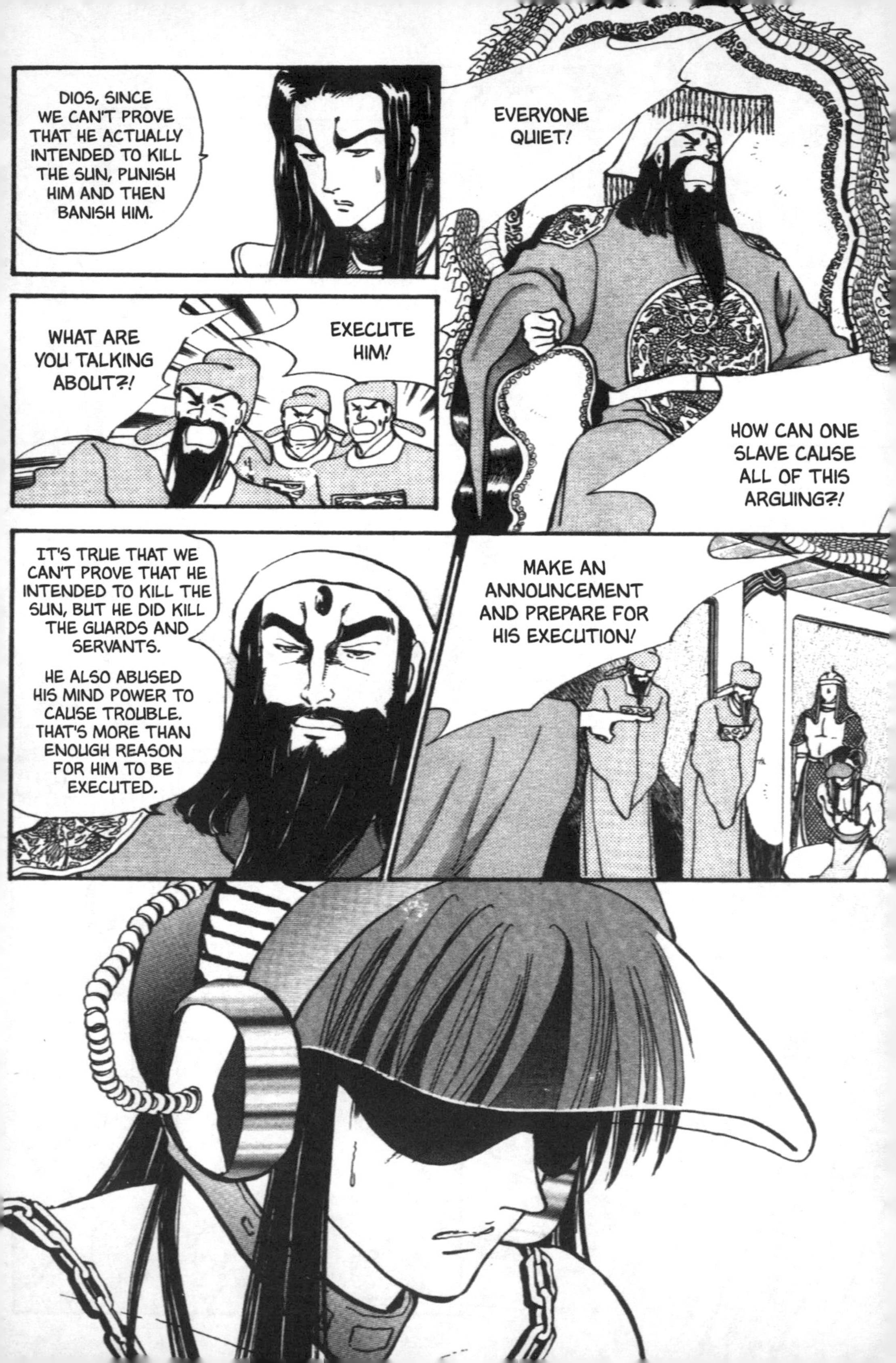
DIOS, SINCE WE CAN'T PROVE THAT HE ACTUALLY INTENDED TO KILL THE SUN, PUNISH HIM AND THEN BANISH HIM.
EVERYONE QUIET!
WHAT ARE YOU TALKING ABOUT?!
EXECUTE HIM!
HOW CAN ONE SLAVE CAUSE ALL OF THIS ARGUING?!
IT'S TRUE THAT WE CAN'T PROVE THAT HE INTENDED TO KILL THE SUN, BUT HE DID KILL THE GUARDS AND SERVANTS.
HE ALSO ABUSED HIS MIND POWER TO CAUSE TROUBLE. THAT'S MORE THAN ENOUGH REASON FOR HIM TO BE EXECUTED.
MAKE AN ANNOUNCEMENT AND PREPARE FOR HIS EXECUTION!

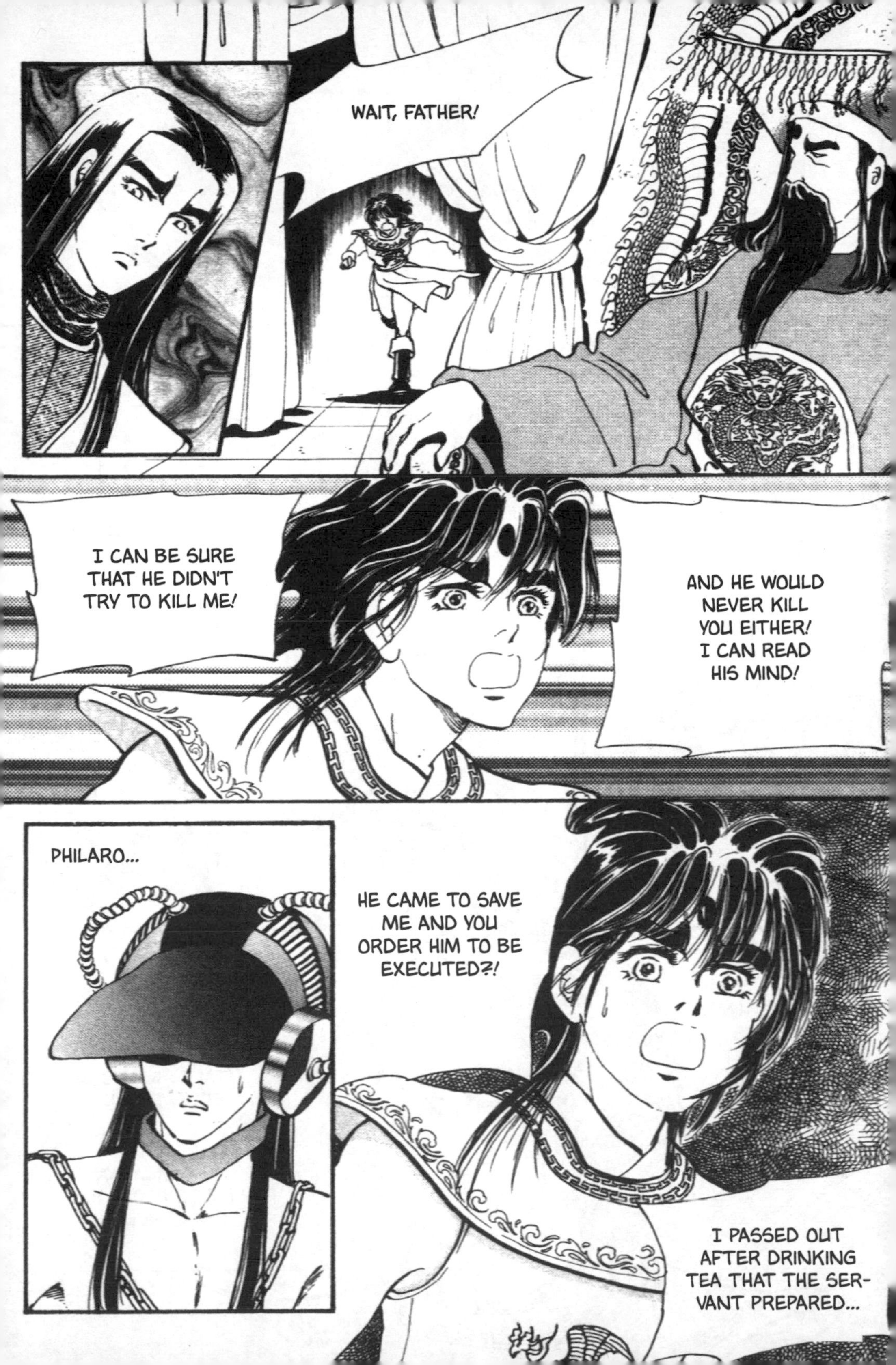
WAIT, FATHER!
I CAN BE SURE THAT HE DIDN'T TRY TO KILL ME!
AND HE WOULD NEVER KILL YOU EITHER! I CAN READ HIS MIND!
PHILARO...
HE CAME TO SAVE ME AND YOU ORDER HIM TO BE EXECUTED?!
I PASSED OUT AFTER DRINKING TEA THAT THE SER-VANT PREPARED...

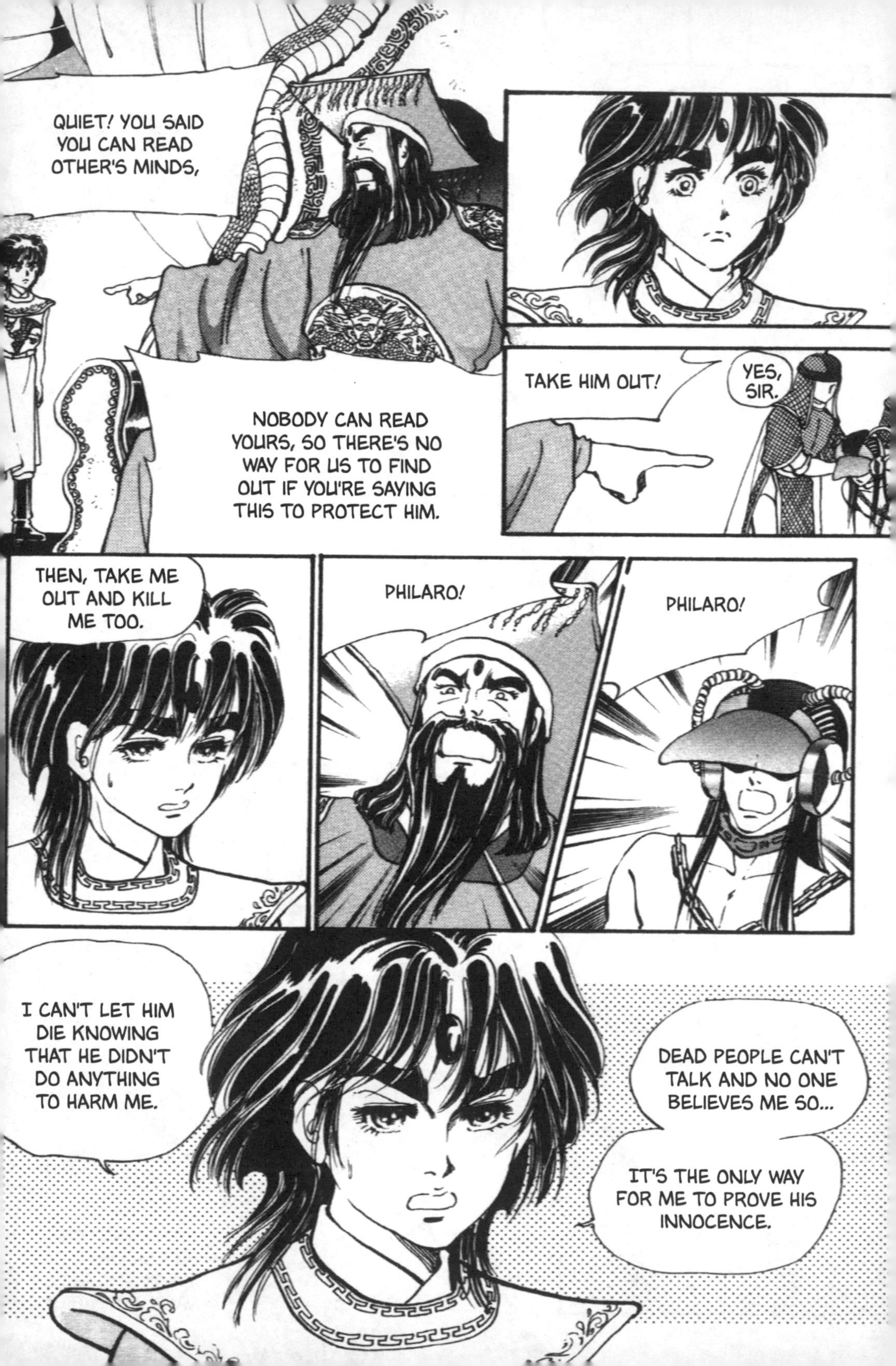
QUIET! YOU SAID YOU CAN READ OTHER'S MINDS,
NOBODY CAN READ YOURS, SO THERE'S NO WAY FOR US TO FIND OUT IF YOU'RE SAYING THIS TO PROTECT HIM.
TAKE HIM OUT!
YES, SIR.
THEN, TAKE ME OUT AND KILL ME TOO.
PHILARO!
PHILARO!
I CAN'T LET HIM DIE KNOWING THAT HE DIDN'T DO ANYTHING TO HARM ME.
DEAD PEOPLE CAN'T TALK AND NO ONE BELIEVES ME SO...
IT'S THE ONLY WAY FOR ME TO PROVE HIS INNOCENCE.

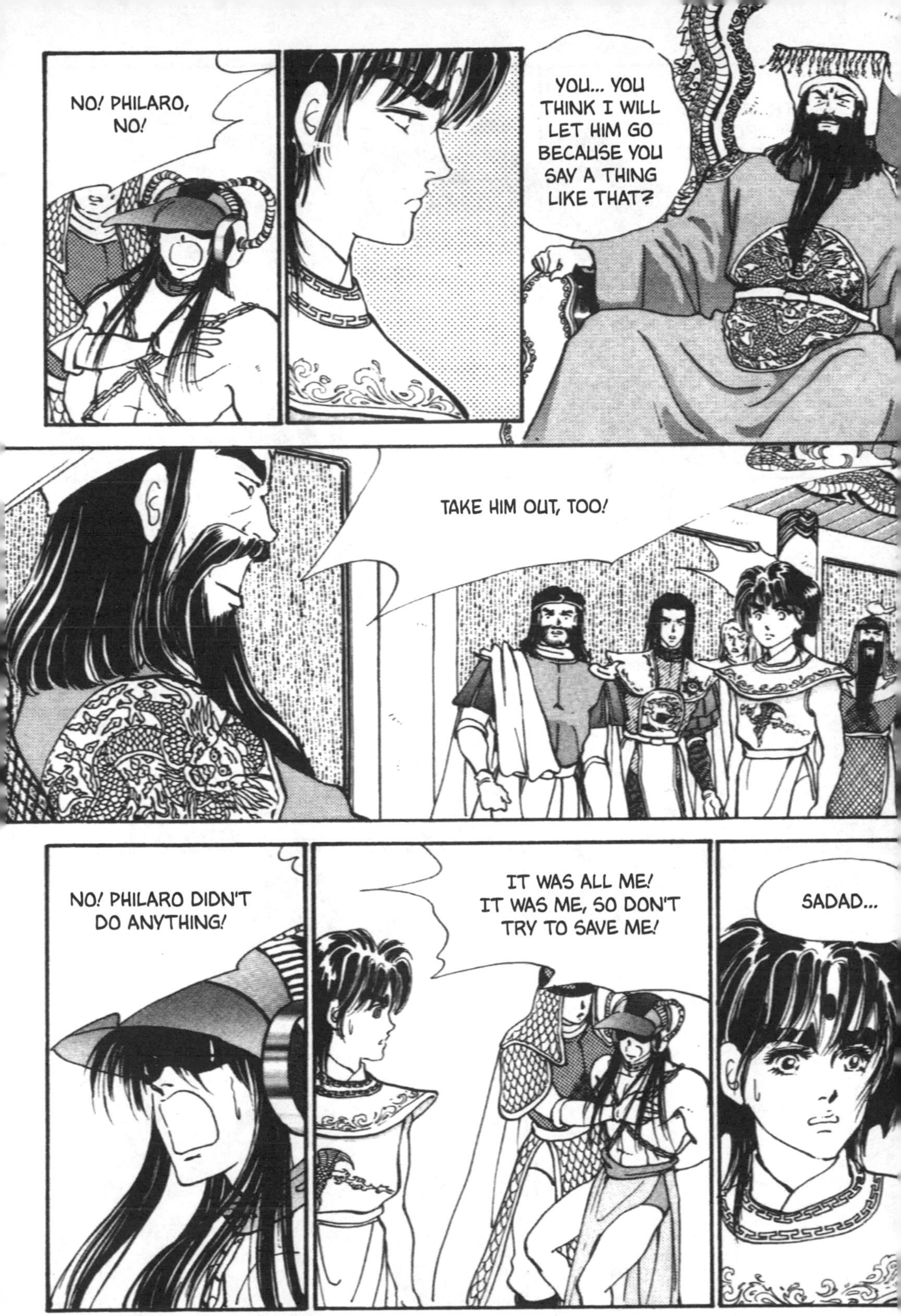
NO! PHILARO, NO!
YOU... YOU THINK I WILL LET HIM GO BECAUSE YOU SAY A THING LIKE THAT?
TAKE HIM OUT, TOO!
NO! PHILARO DIDN'T DO ANYTHING!
IT WAS ALL ME! IT WAS ME, SO DON'T TRY TO SAVE ME!
SADAD...

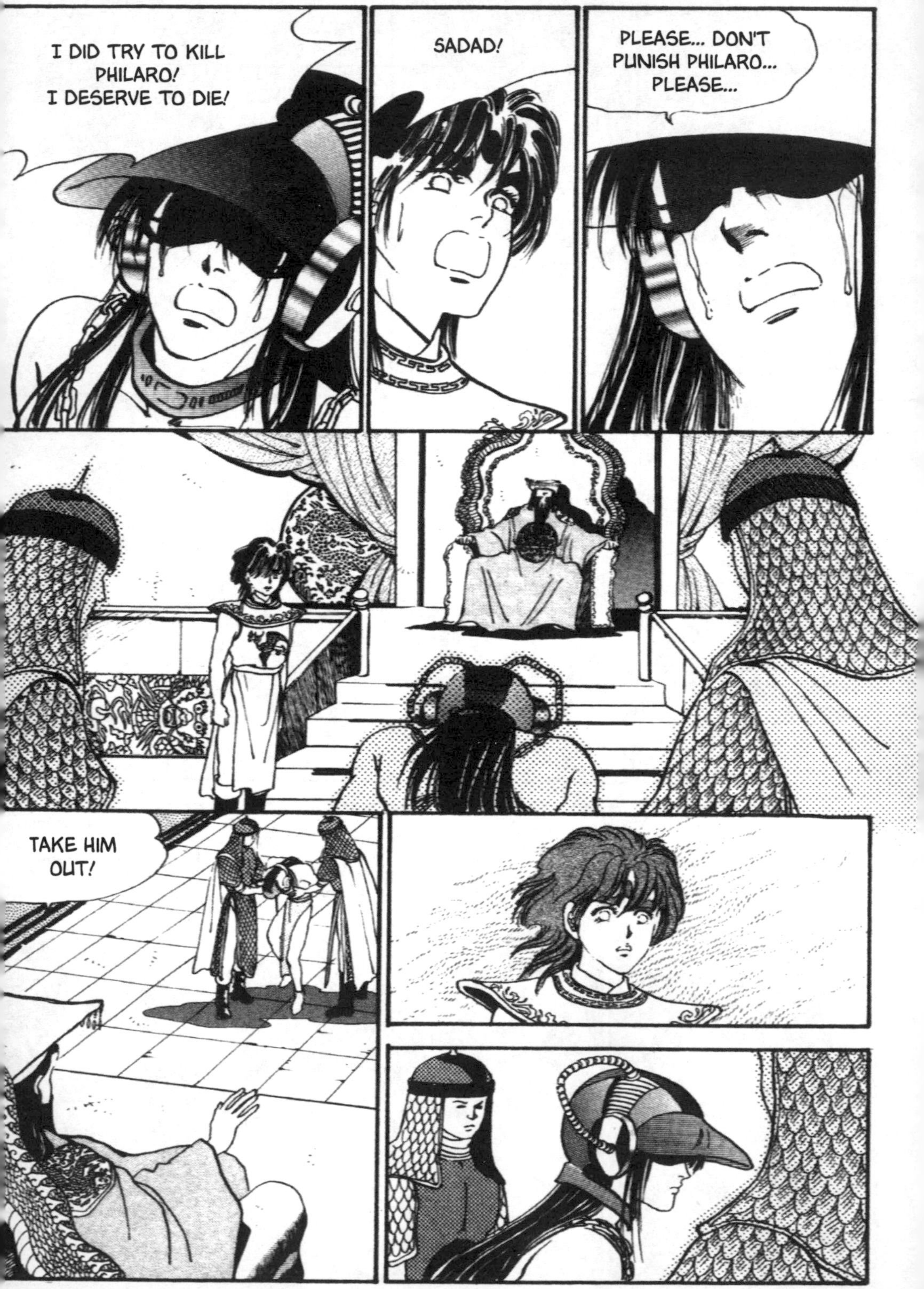
I DID TRY TO KILL PHILARO! I DESERVE TO DIE!
SADAD!
PLEASE... DON'T PUNISH PHILARO... PLEASE...
TAKE HIM OUT!

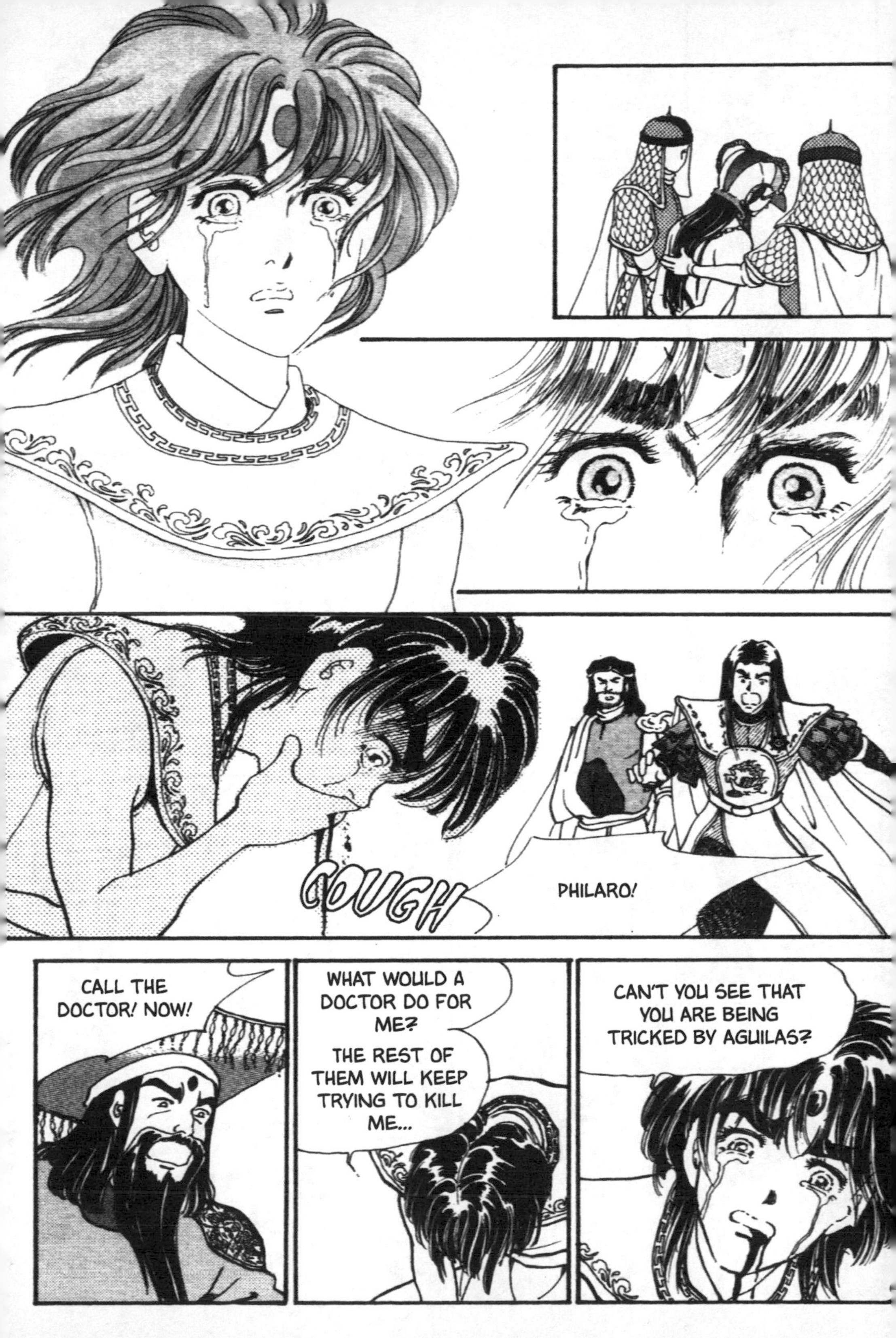
COUGH
PHILARO!
CALL THE DOCTOR! NOW!
WHAT WOULD A DOCTOR DO FOR ME?
THE REST OF THEM WILL KEEP TRYING TO KILL ME...
CAN'T YOU SEE THAT YOU ARE BEING TRICKED BY AGUILAS?

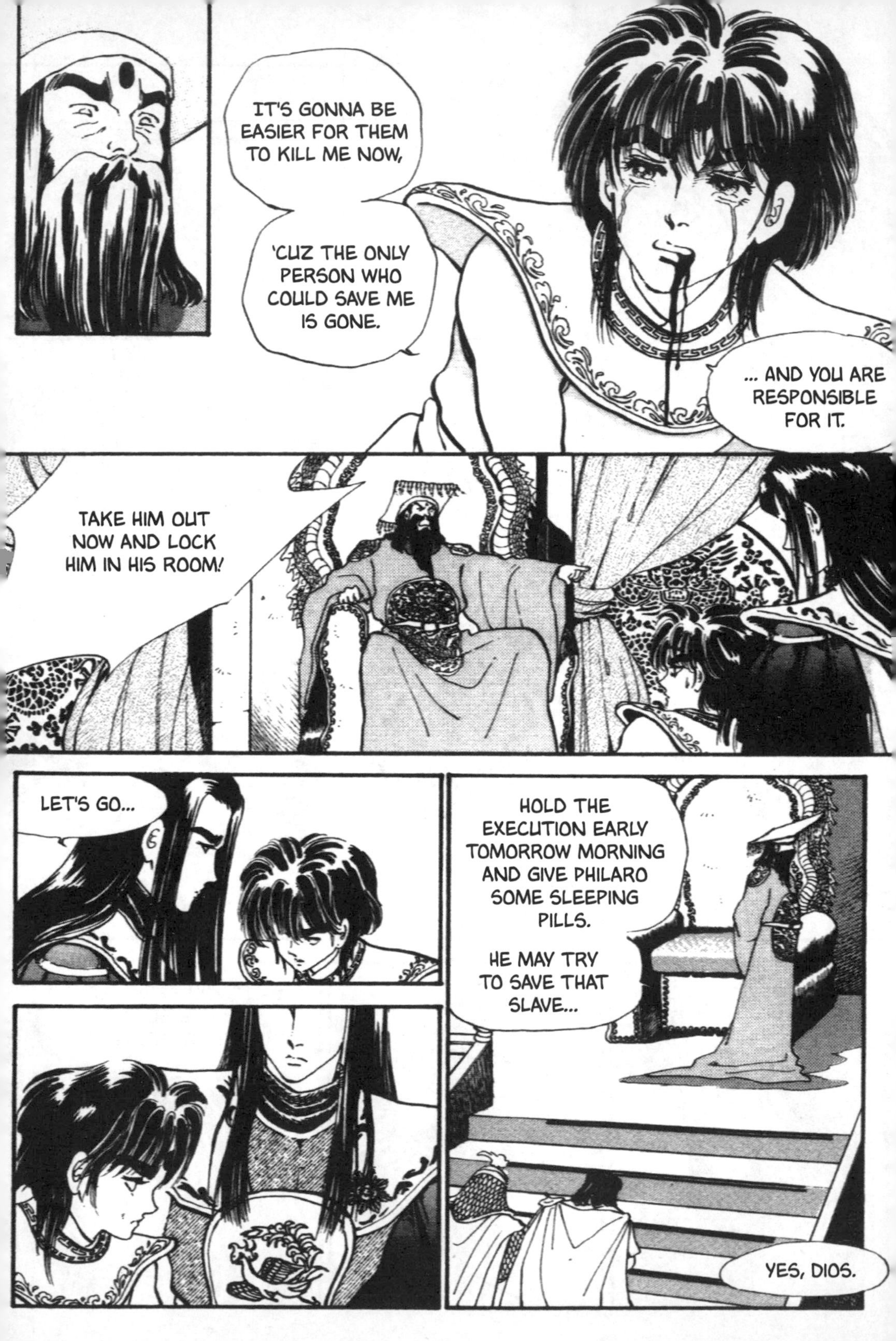

IT'S GONNA BE EASIER FOR THEM TO KILL ME NOW,
'CUZ THE ONLY PERSON WHO COULD SAVE ME IS GONE.
... AND YOU ARE RESPONSIBLE FOR IT.
TAKE HIM OUT NOW AND LOCK HIM IN HIS ROOM!
LET'S GO...
HOLD THE EXECUTION EARLY TOMORROW MORNING AND GIVE PHILARO SOME SLEEPING PILLS.
HE MAY TRY TO SAVE THAT SLAVE...
YES, DIOS.

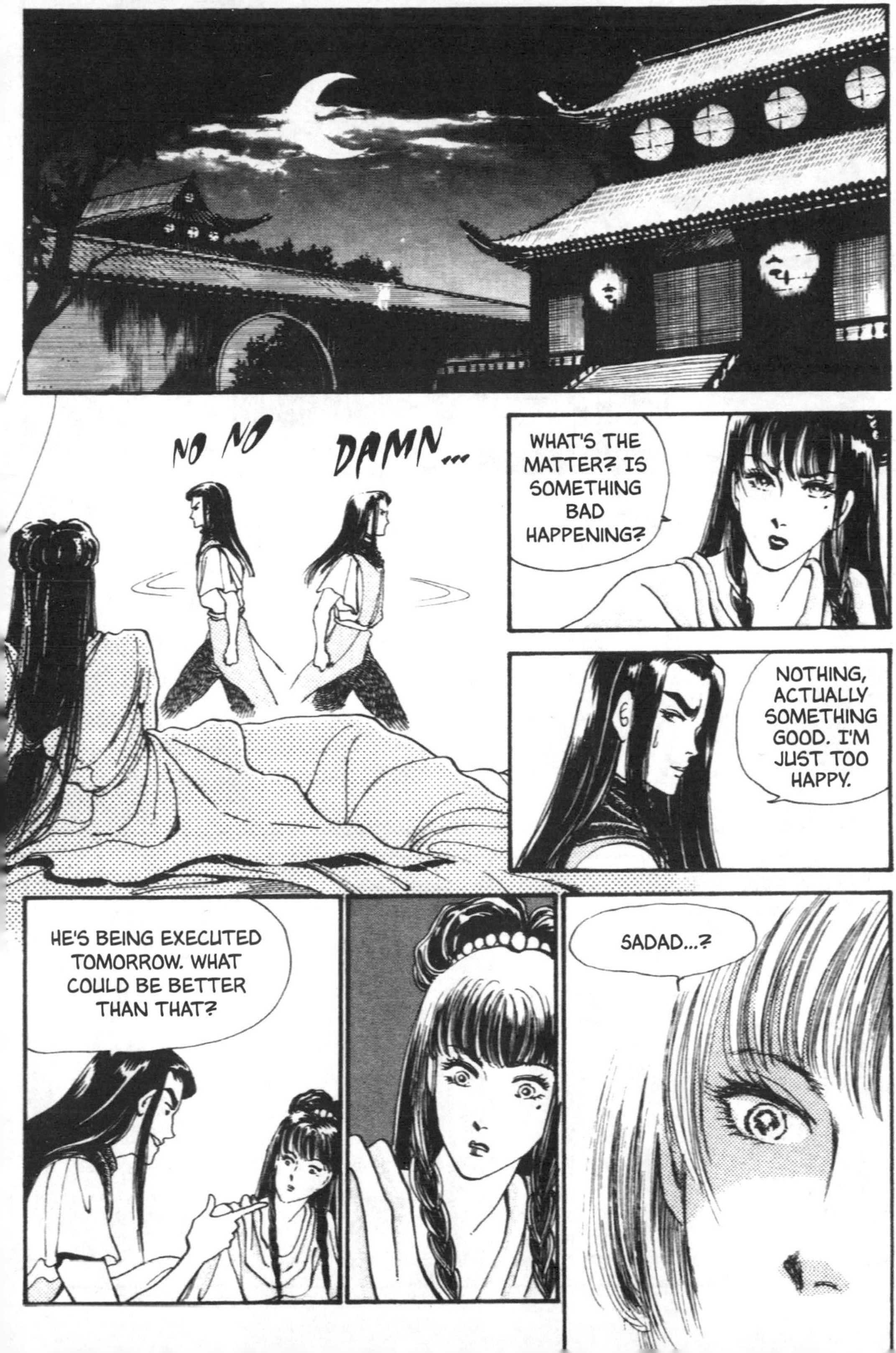
NO NO
DAMN...
WHAT'S THE MATTER? IS SOMETHING BAD HAPPENING?
NOTHING, ACTUALLY SOMETHING GOOD. I'M JUST TOO HAPPY.
HE'S BEING EXECUTED TOMORROW. WHAT COULD BE BETTER THAN THAT?
SADAD...?

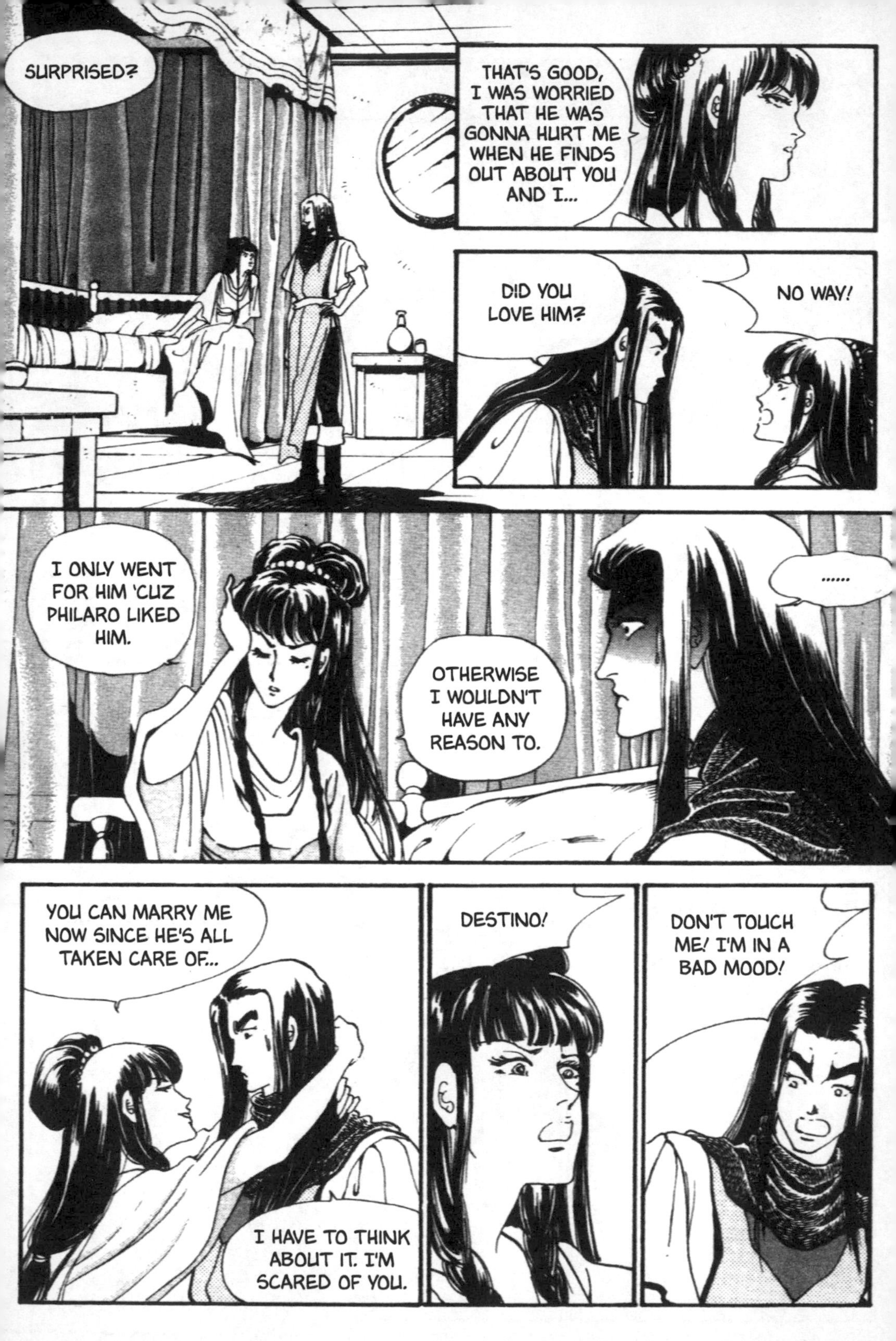
SURPRISED?
THAT'S GOOD, I WAS WORRIED THAT HE WAS GONNA HURT ME WHEN HE FINDS OUT ABOUT YOU AND I...
DID YOU LOVE HIM?
NO WAY!
I ONLY WENT FOR HIM 'CUZ PHILARO LIKED HIM.
OTHERWISE I WOULDN'T HAVE ANY REASON TO.
......
YOU CAN MARRY ME NOW SINCE HE'S ALL TAKEN CARE OF...
I HAVE TO THINK ABOUT IT. I'M SCARED OF YOU.
DESTINO!
DON'T TOUCH ME! I'M IN A BAD MOOD!

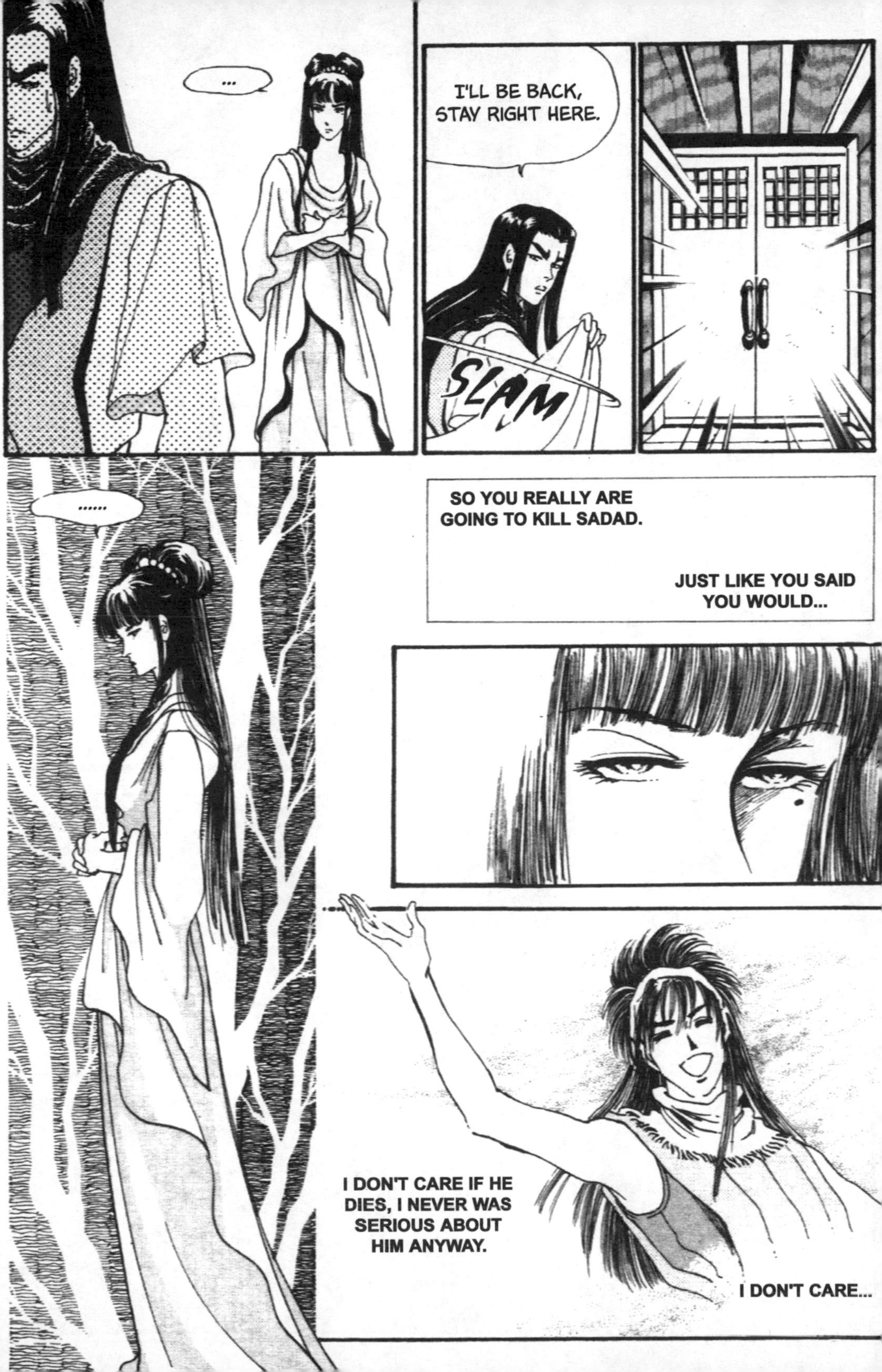
...
I'LL BE BACK, STAY RIGHT HERE.
SLAM
......
SO YOU REALLY ARE GOING TO KILL SADAD.
JUST LIKE YOU SAID YOU WOULD...
I DON'T CARE IF HE DIES, I NEVER WAS SERIOUS ABOUT HIM ANYWAY.
I DON'T CARE...

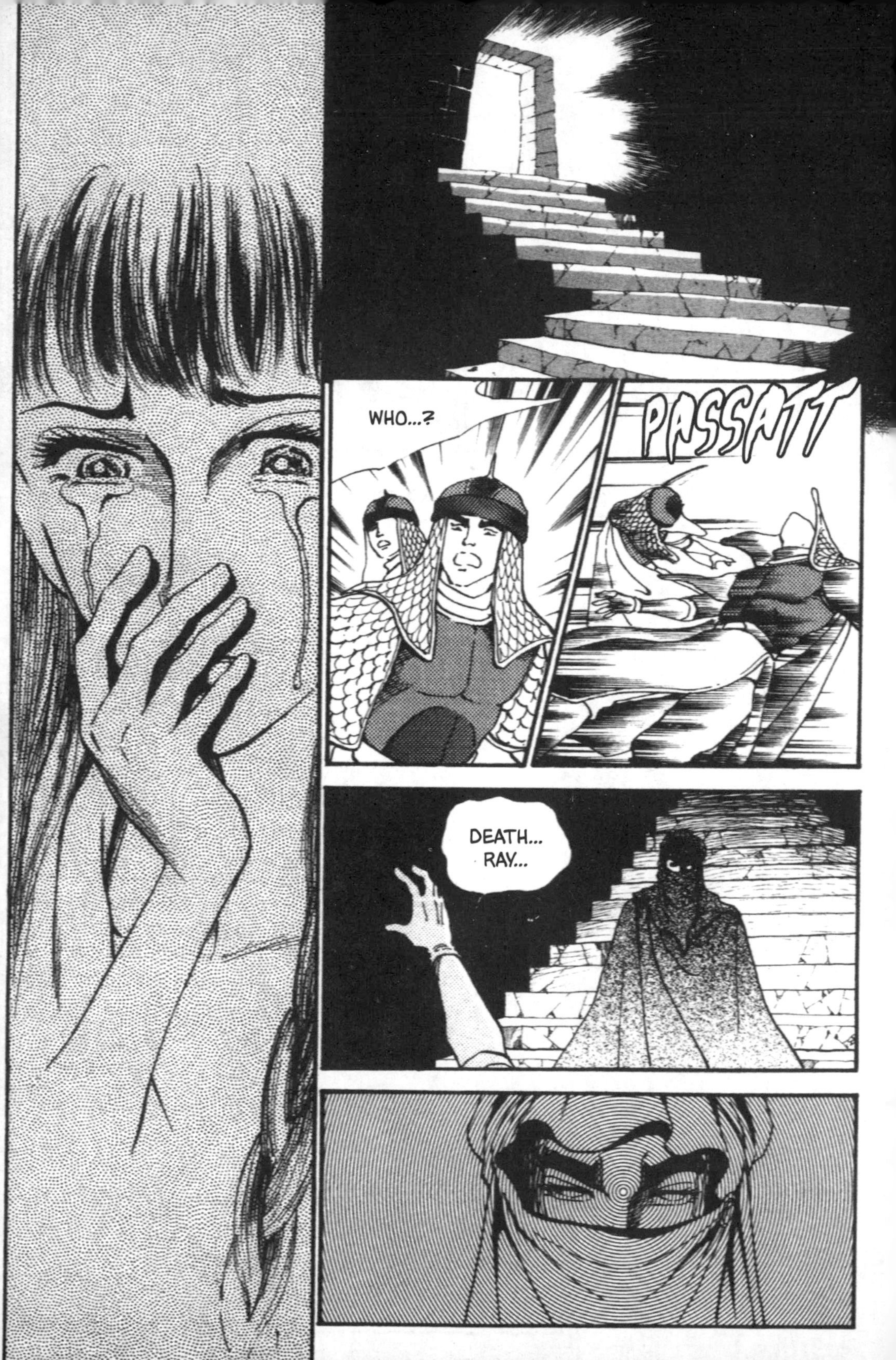
WHO...?
PASSATT
DEATH... RAY...

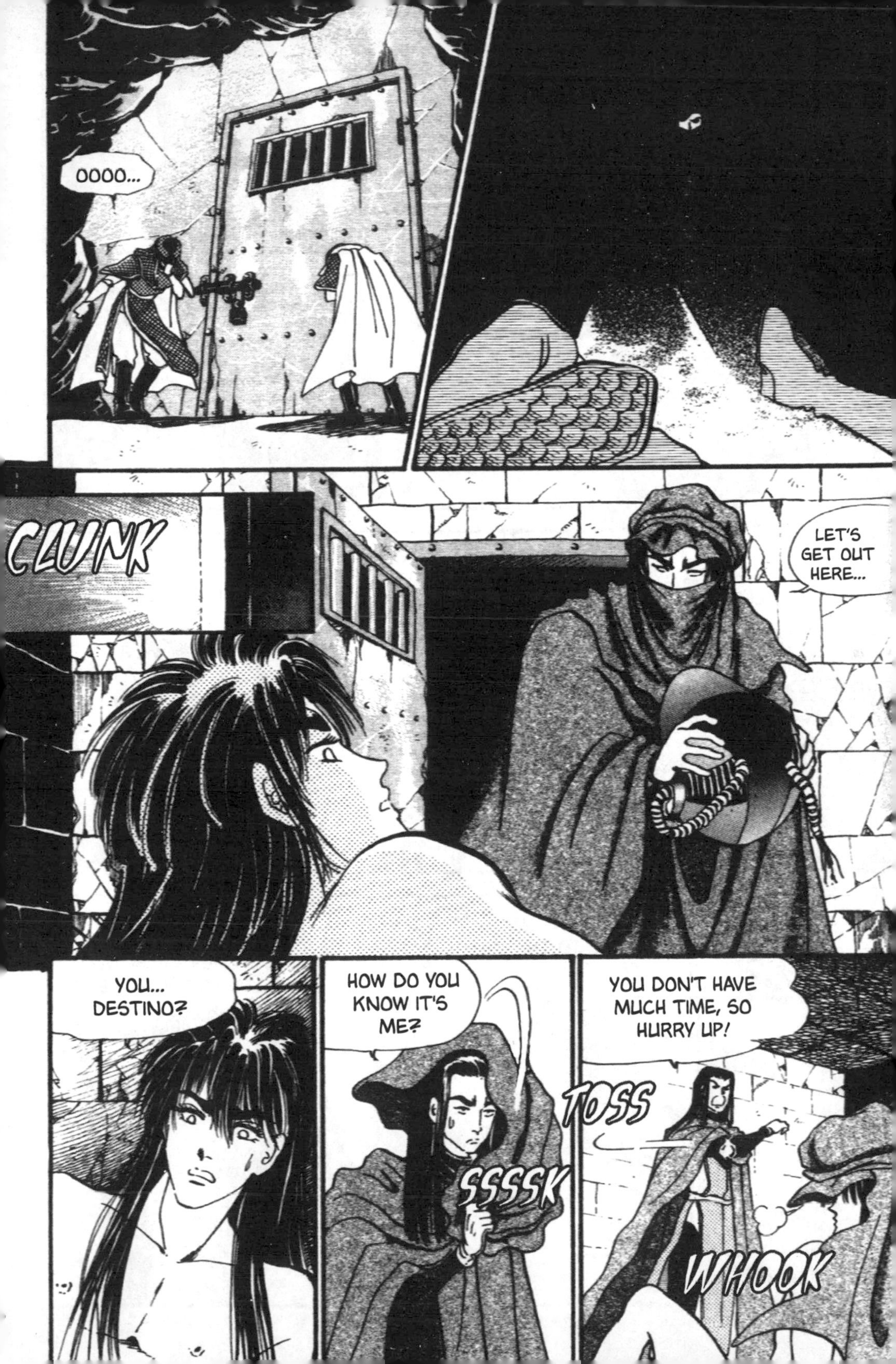
OOOO...
CLUNK
LET'S GET OUT HERE...
YOU... DESTINO?
HOW DO YOU KNOW IT'S ME?
SSSSK
YOU DON'T HAVE MUCH TIME, SO HURRY UP!
TOSS
WHOOK

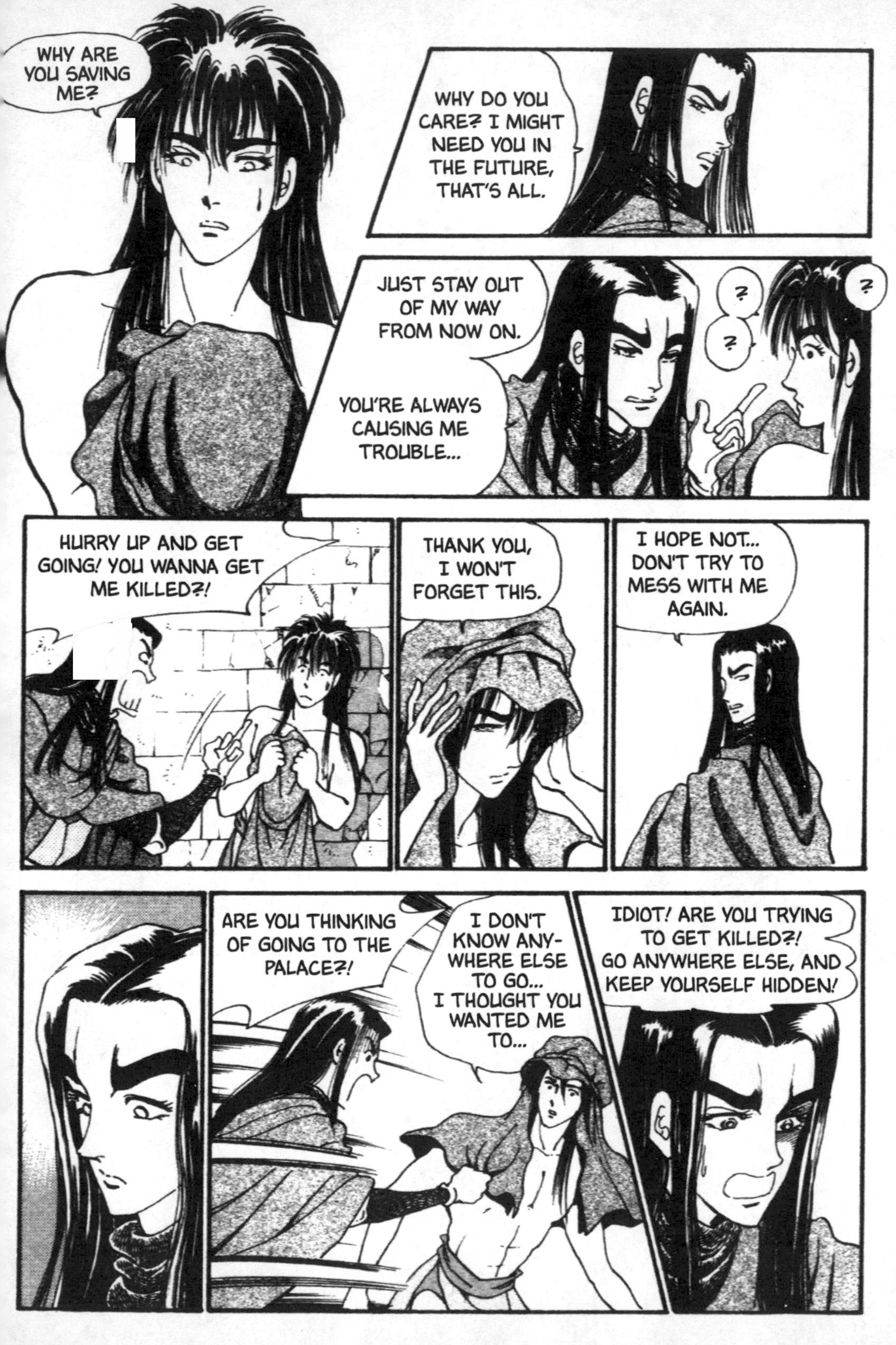
WHY ARE YOU SAVING ME?
WHY DO YOU CARE? I MIGHT NEED YOU IN THE FUTURE, THAT'S ALL.
JUST STAY OUT OF MY WAY FROM NOW ON.
YOU'RE ALWAYS CAUSING ME TROUBLE...
?
?
?
HURRY UP AND GET GOING! YOU WANNA GET ME KILLED?!
THANK YOU, I WON'T FORGET THIS.
I HOPE NOT... DON'T TRY TO MESS WITH ME AGAIN.
ARE YOU THINKING OF GOING TO THE PALACE?!
I DON'T KNOW ANY-WHERE ELSE TO GO... I THOUGHT YOU WANTED ME TO...
IDIOT! ARE YOU TRYING TO GET KILLED?! GO ANYWHERE ELSE, AND KEEP YOURSELF HIDDEN!

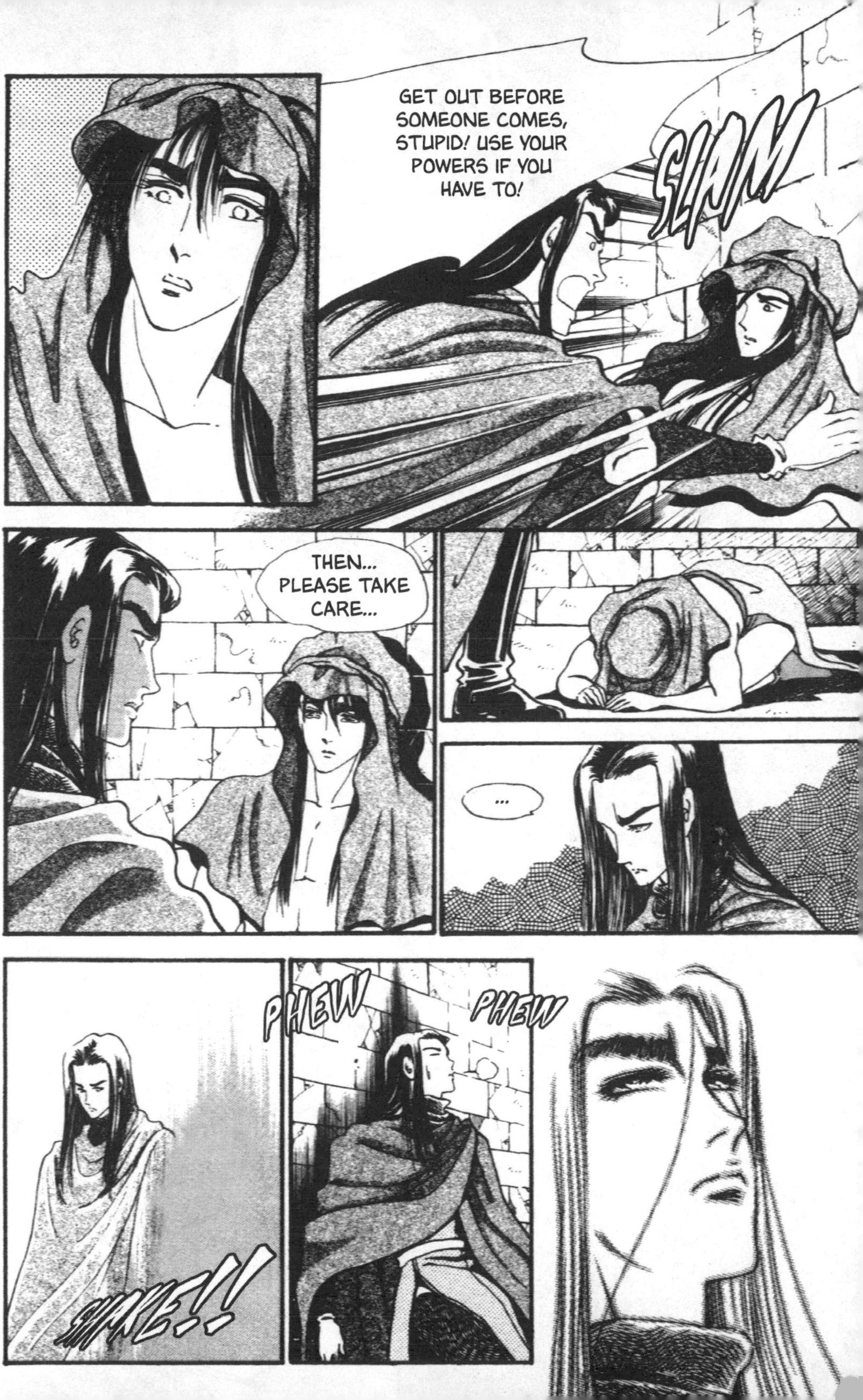
GET OUT BEFORE SOMEONE COMES, STUPID! USE YOUR POWERS IF YOU HAVE TO!
SLAM
THEN... PLEASE TAKE CARE...
...
PHEW
PHEW

I KEPT MY PROMISE, ESTELLA...
I DIDN'T KILL YOUR SON..
WHERE SHOULD I GO?
WHAT SHOULD I DO NOW?

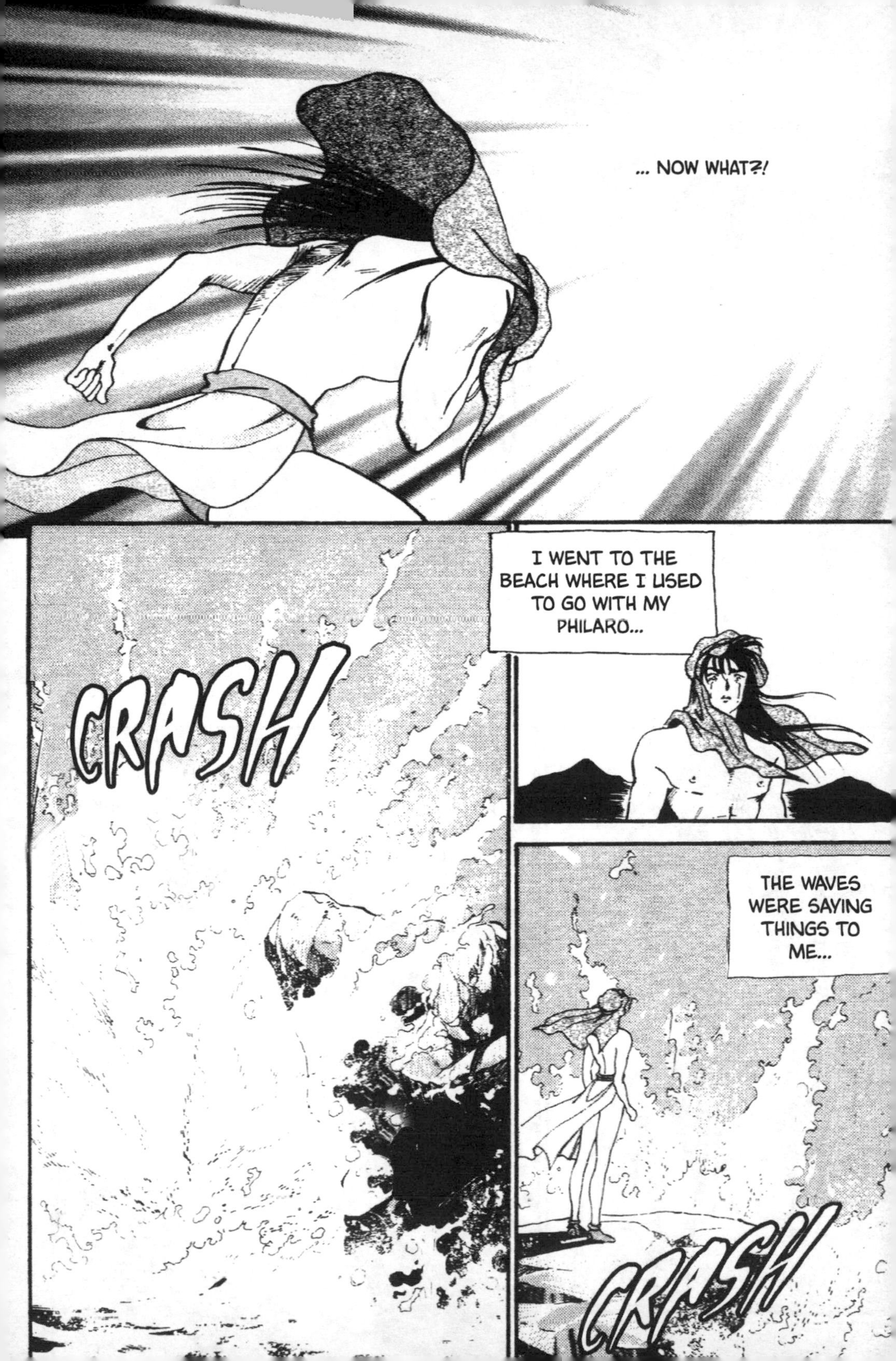
... NOW WHAT?!
I WENT TO THE BEACH WHERE I USED TO GO WITH MY PHILARO...
CRASH
THE WAVES WERE SAYING THINGS TO ME...
CRASH

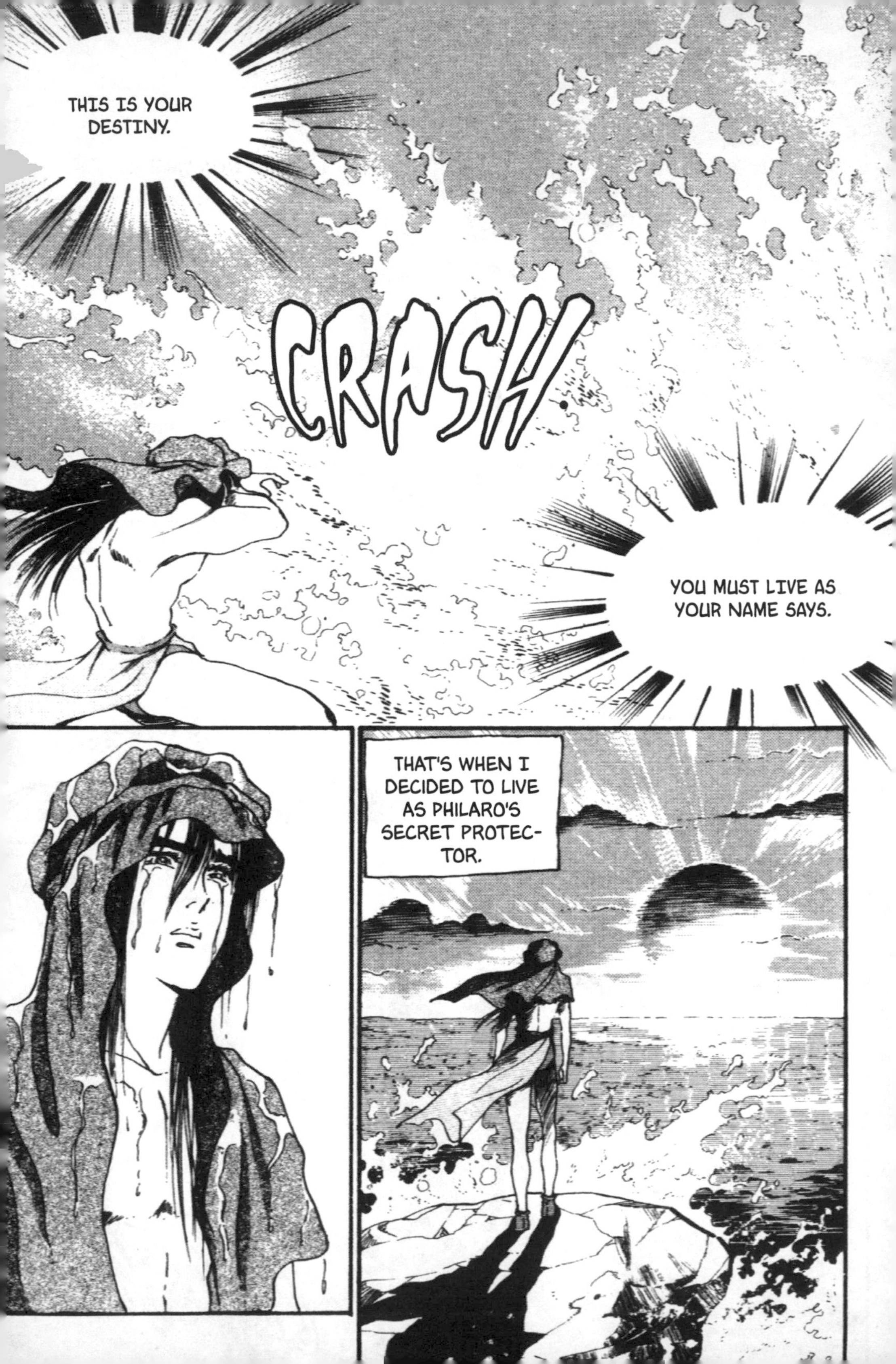
THIS IS YOUR DESTINY.
CRASH
YOU MUST LIVE AS YOUR NAME SAYS.
THAT'S WHEN I DECIDED TO LIVE AS PHILARO'S SECRET PROTEC-TOR.

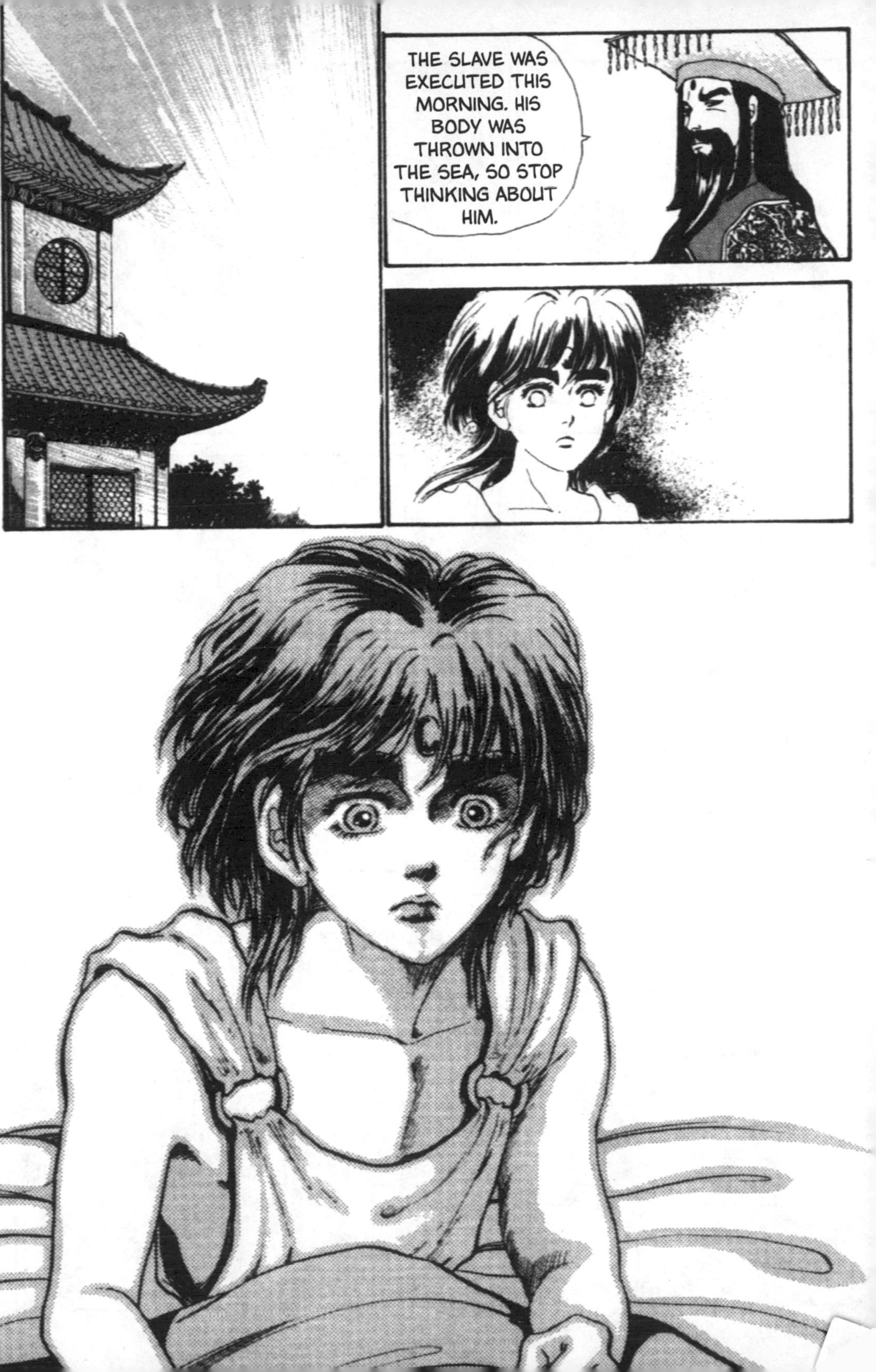
THE SLAVE WAS EXECUTED THIS MORNING. HIS BODY WAS THROWN INTO THE SEA, SO STOP THINKING ABOUT HIM.

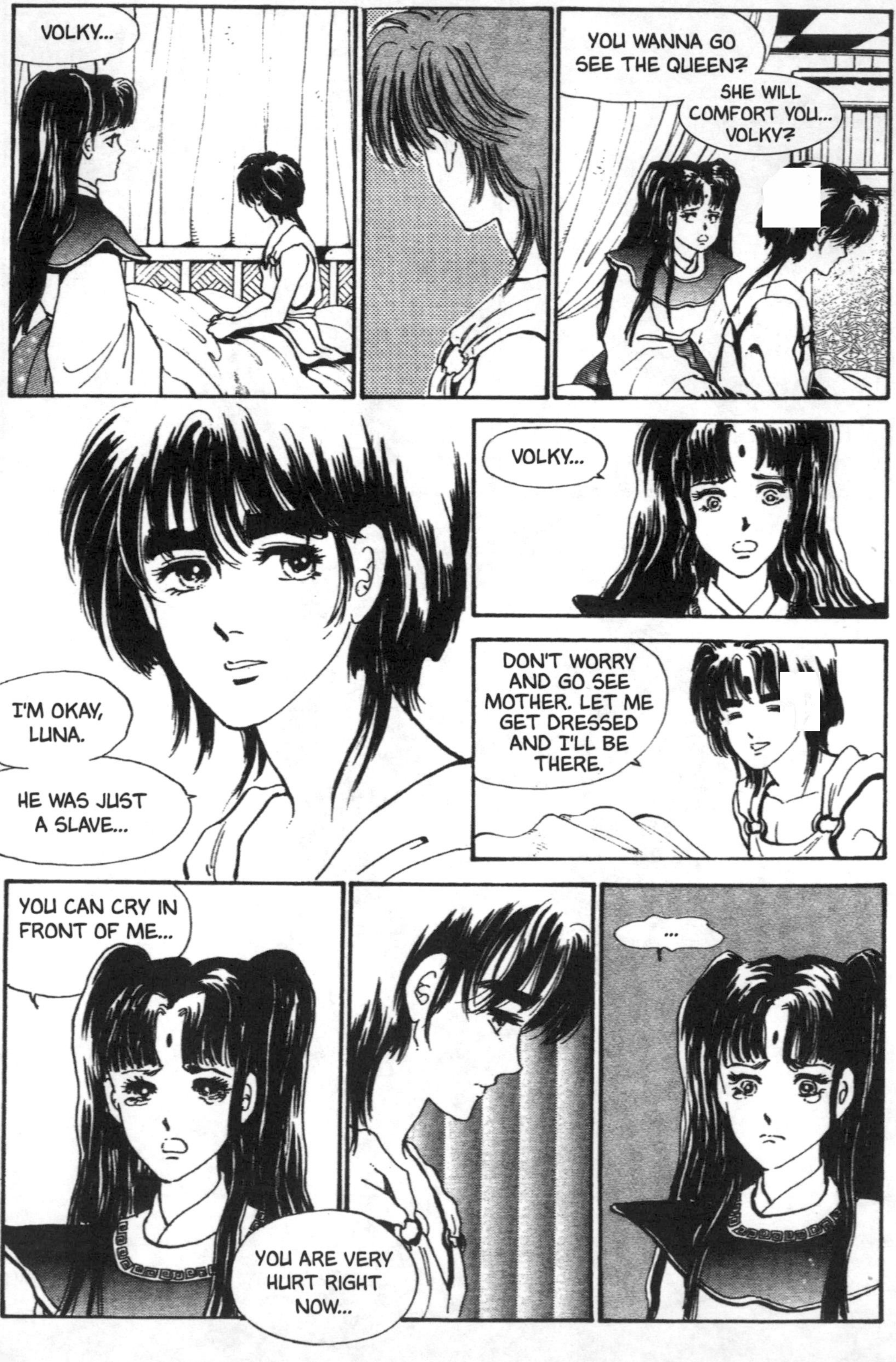
VOLKY...
YOU WANNA GO SEE THE QUEEN?
SHE WILL COMFORT YOU... VOLKY?
I'M OKAY, LUNA.
HE WAS JUST A SLAVE...
VOLKY...
DON'T WORRY AND GO SEE MOTHER. LET ME GET DRESSED AND I'LL BE THERE.
YOU CAN CRY IN FRONT OF ME...
YOU ARE VERY HURT RIGHT NOW...
...

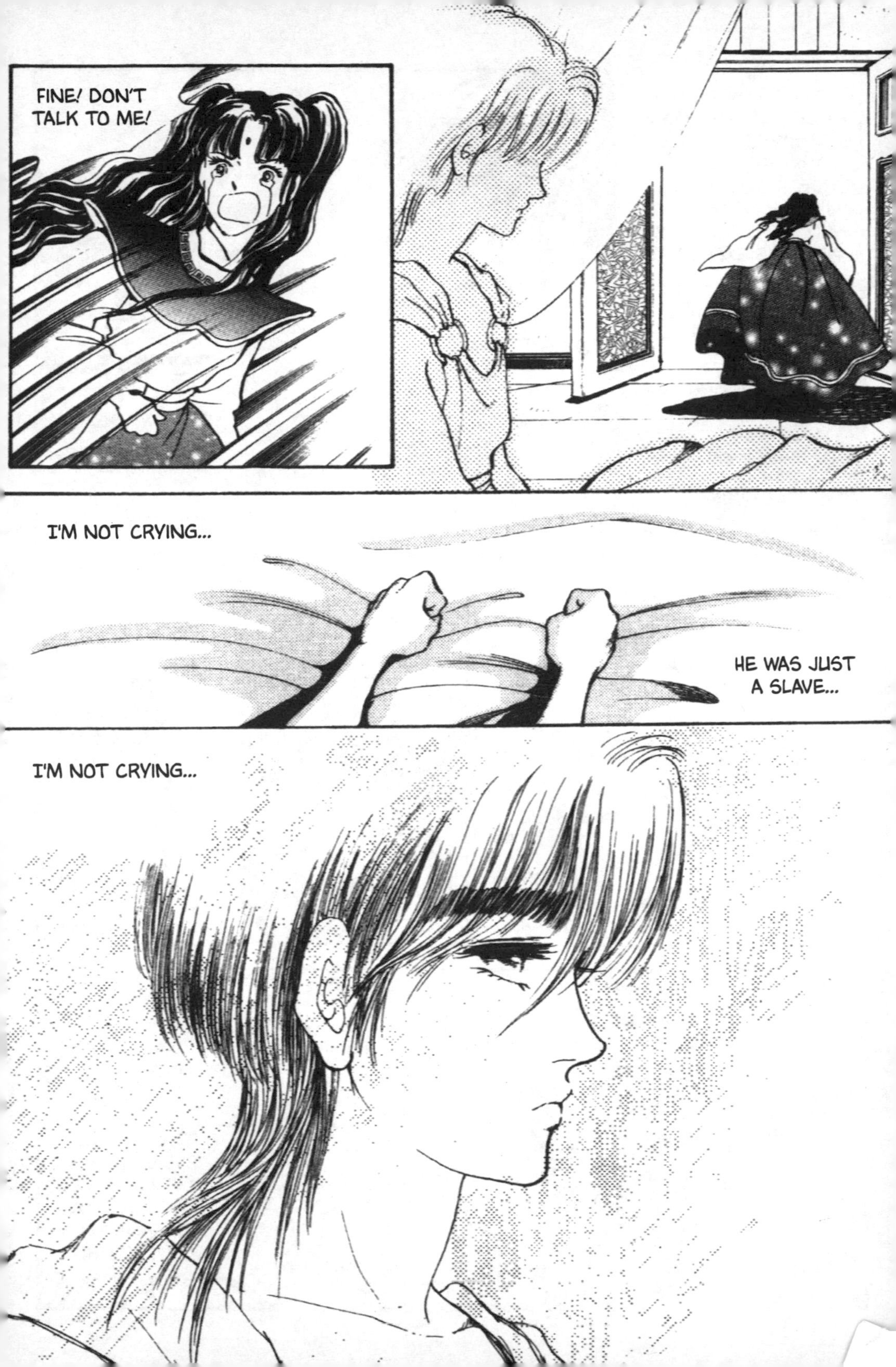
FINE! DON'T TALK TO ME!
I'M NOT CRYING...
HE WAS JUST A SLAVE...
I'M NOT CRYING...

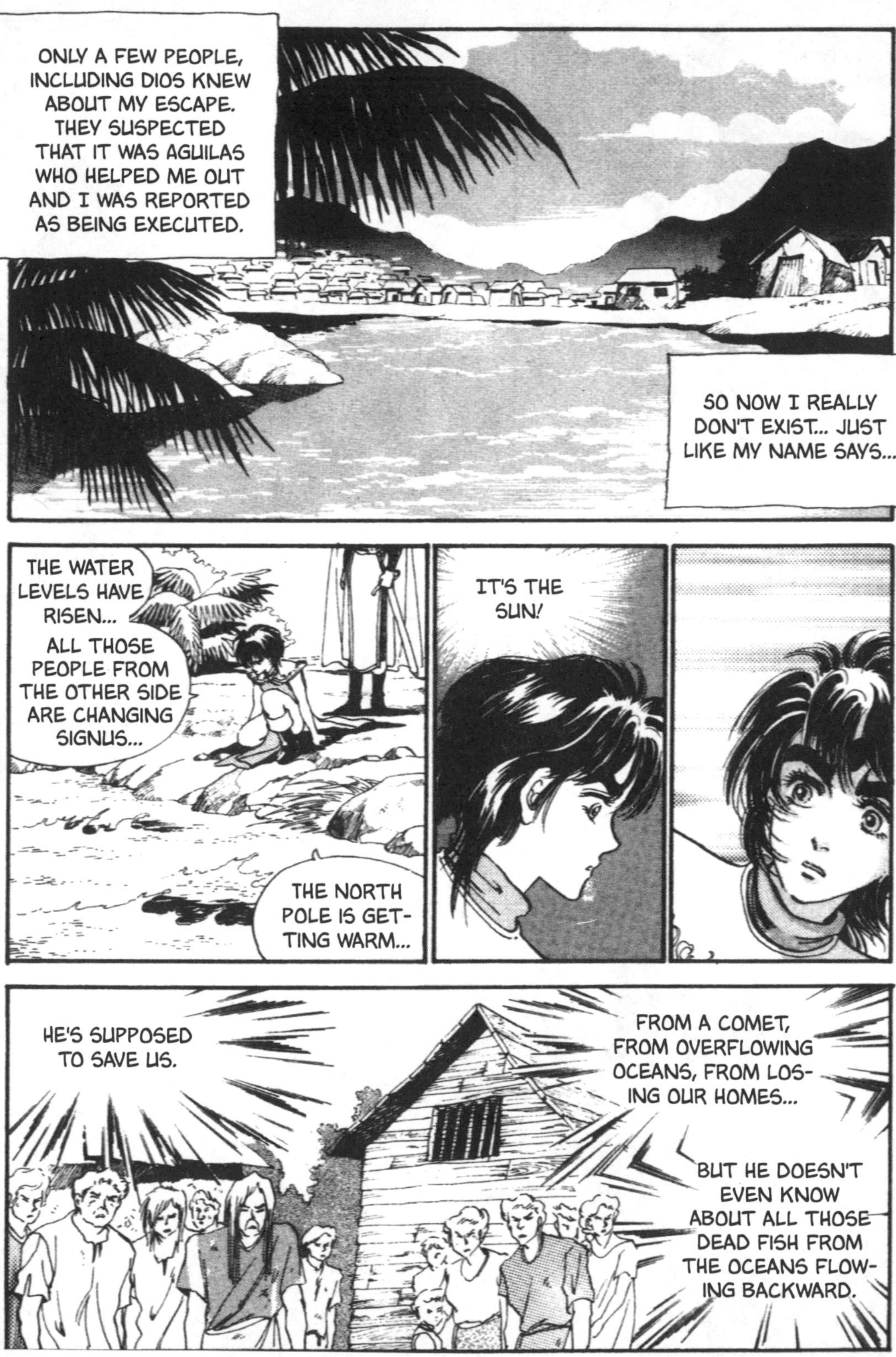

ONLY A FEW PEOPLE, INCLUDING DIOS KNEW ABOUT MY ESCAPE. THEY SUSPECTED THAT IT WAS AGUILAS WHO HELPED ME OUT AND I WAS REPORTED AS BEING EXECUTED.
SO NOW I REALLY DON'T EXIST... JUST LIKE MY NAME SAYS...
THE WATER LEVELS HAVE RISEN...
ALL THOSE PEOPLE FROM THE OTHER SIDE ARE CHANGING SIGNUS...
THE NORTH POLE IS GETTING WARM...
IT'S THE SUN!
HE'S SUPPOSED TO SAVE US.
FROM A COMET, FROM OVERFLOWING OCEANS, FROM LOSING OUR HOMES...
BUT HE DOESN'T EVEN KNOW ABOUT ALL THOSE DEAD FISH FROM THE OCEANS FLOWING BACKWARD.

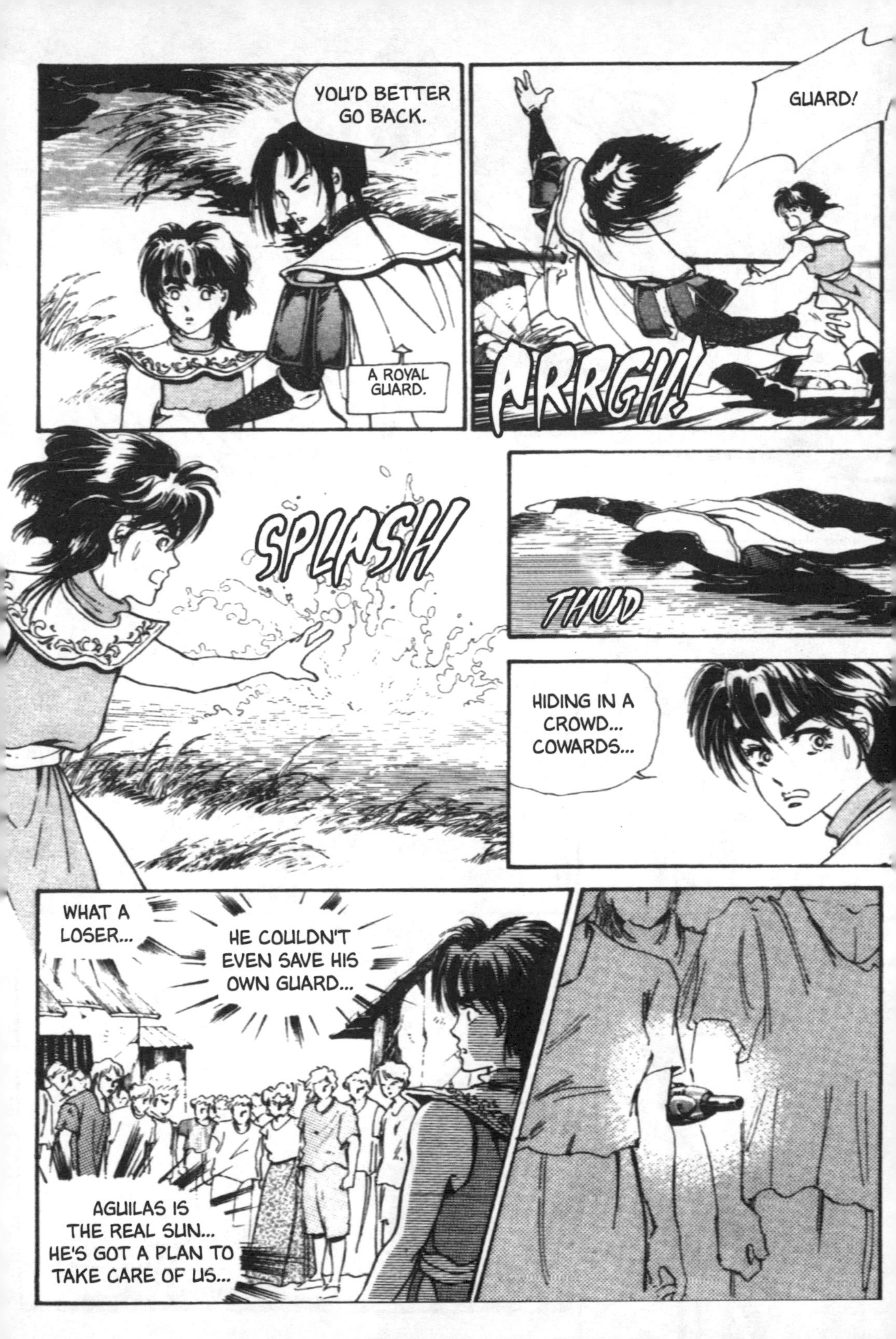
YOU'D BETTER GO BACK.
A ROYAL GUARD.
GUARD!
ARRGH!
SPLASH
THUD
HIDING IN A CROWD... COWARDS...
WHAT A LOSER...
HE COULDN'T EVEN SAVE HIS OWN GUARD...
AGUILAS IS THE REAL SUN... HE'S GOT A PLAN TO TAKE CARE OF US...

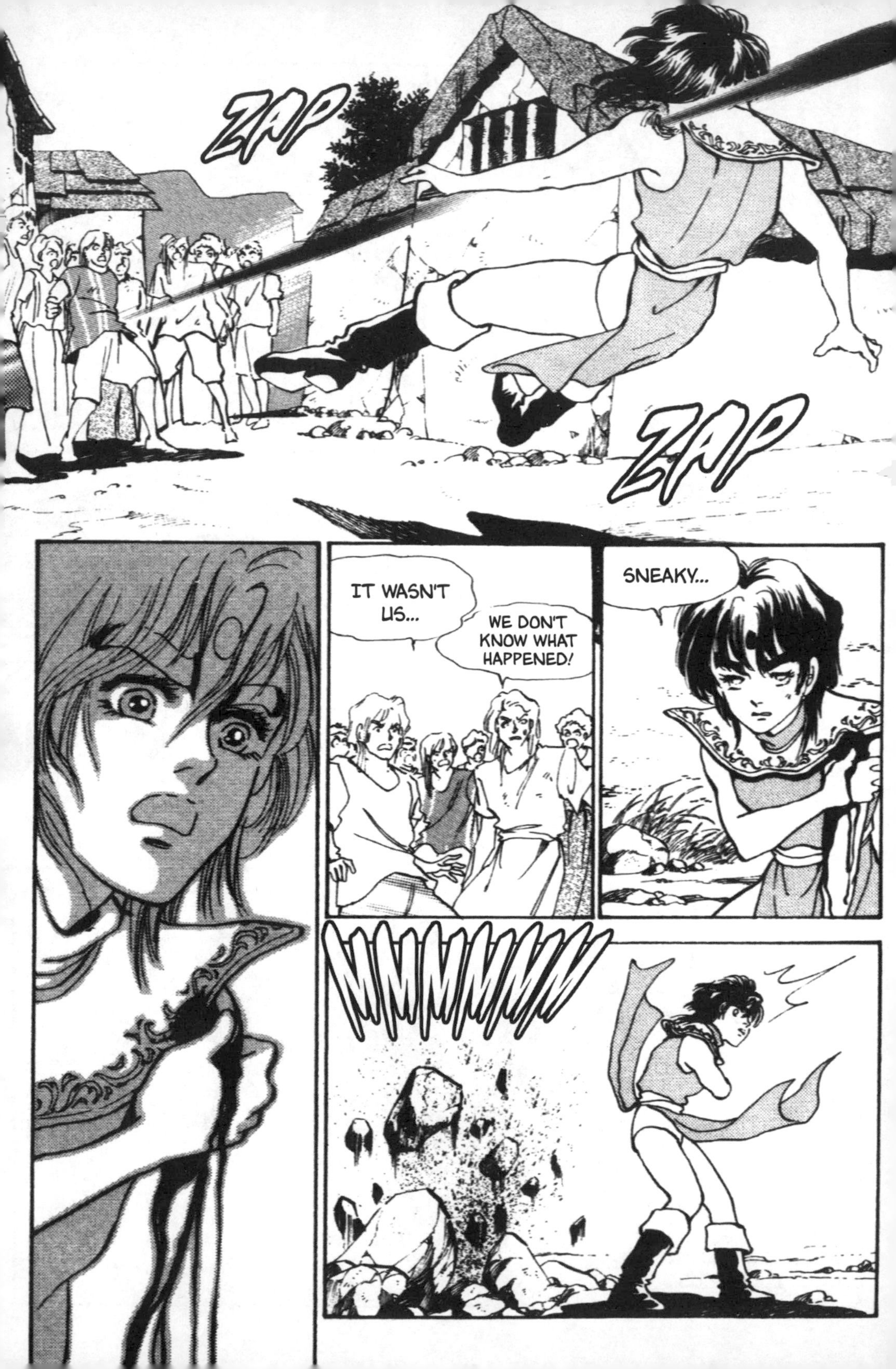
ZAP
ZAP
IT WASN'T US...
WE DON'T KNOW WHAT HAPPENED!
SNEAKY...
MMMMMM

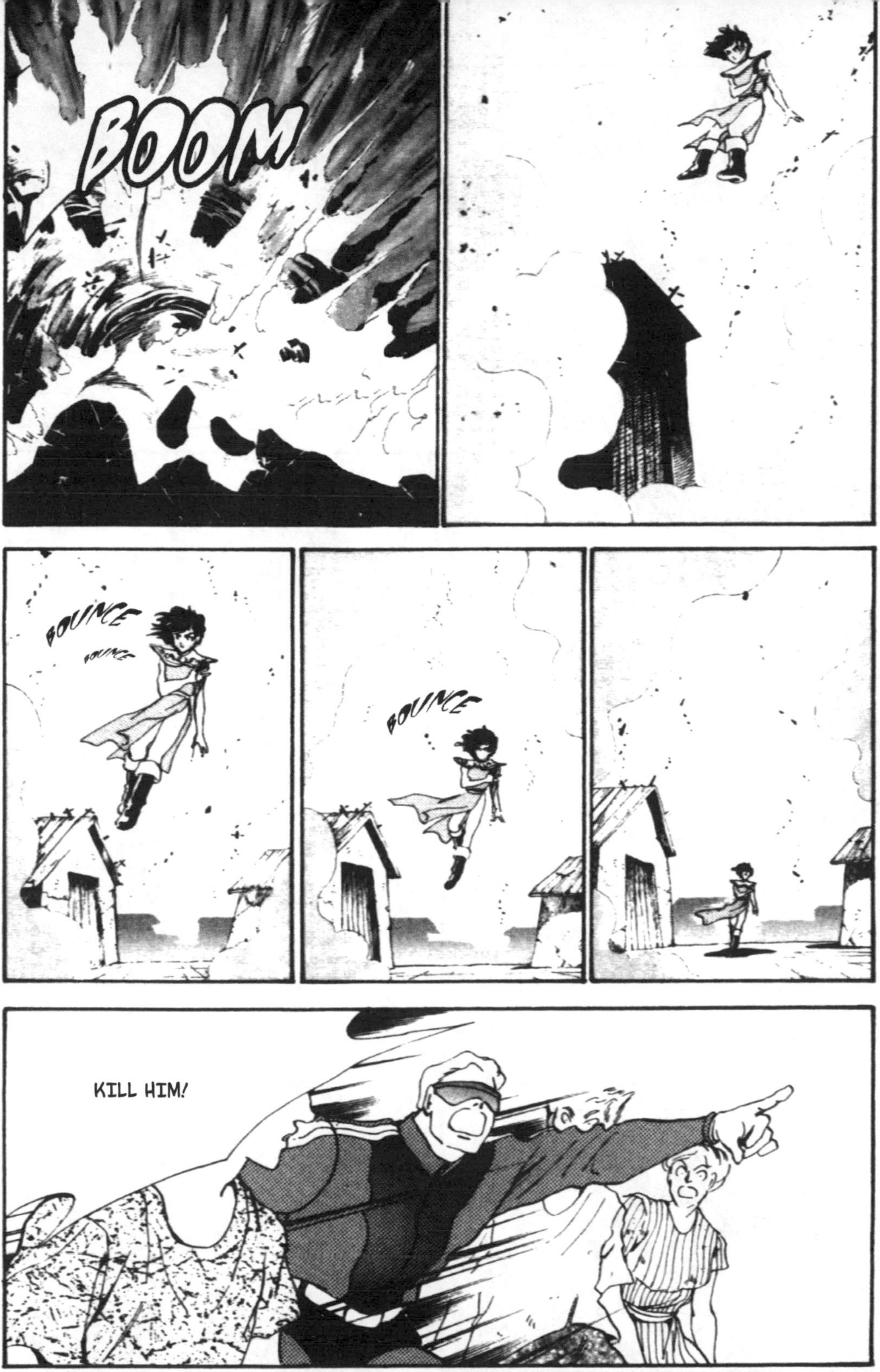
BOOM
BOUNCE
BOUNCE
BOUNCE
KILL HIM!

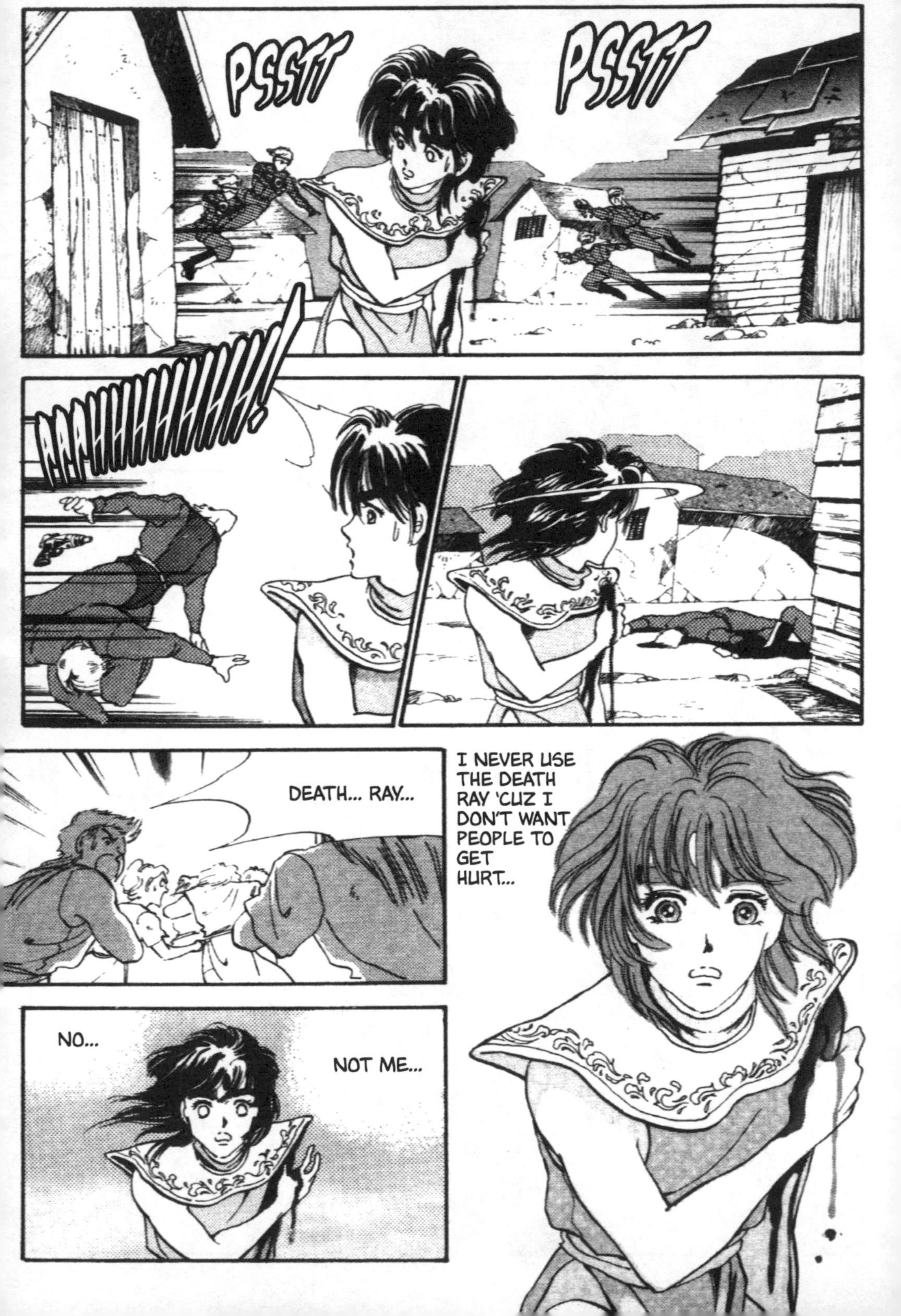
PSSTT
PSSTT
AAAHHHHHHHHH!
DEATH... RAY...
I NEVER USE THE DEATH RAY 'CUZ I DON'T WANT PEOPLE TO GET HURT...
NO...
NOT ME...

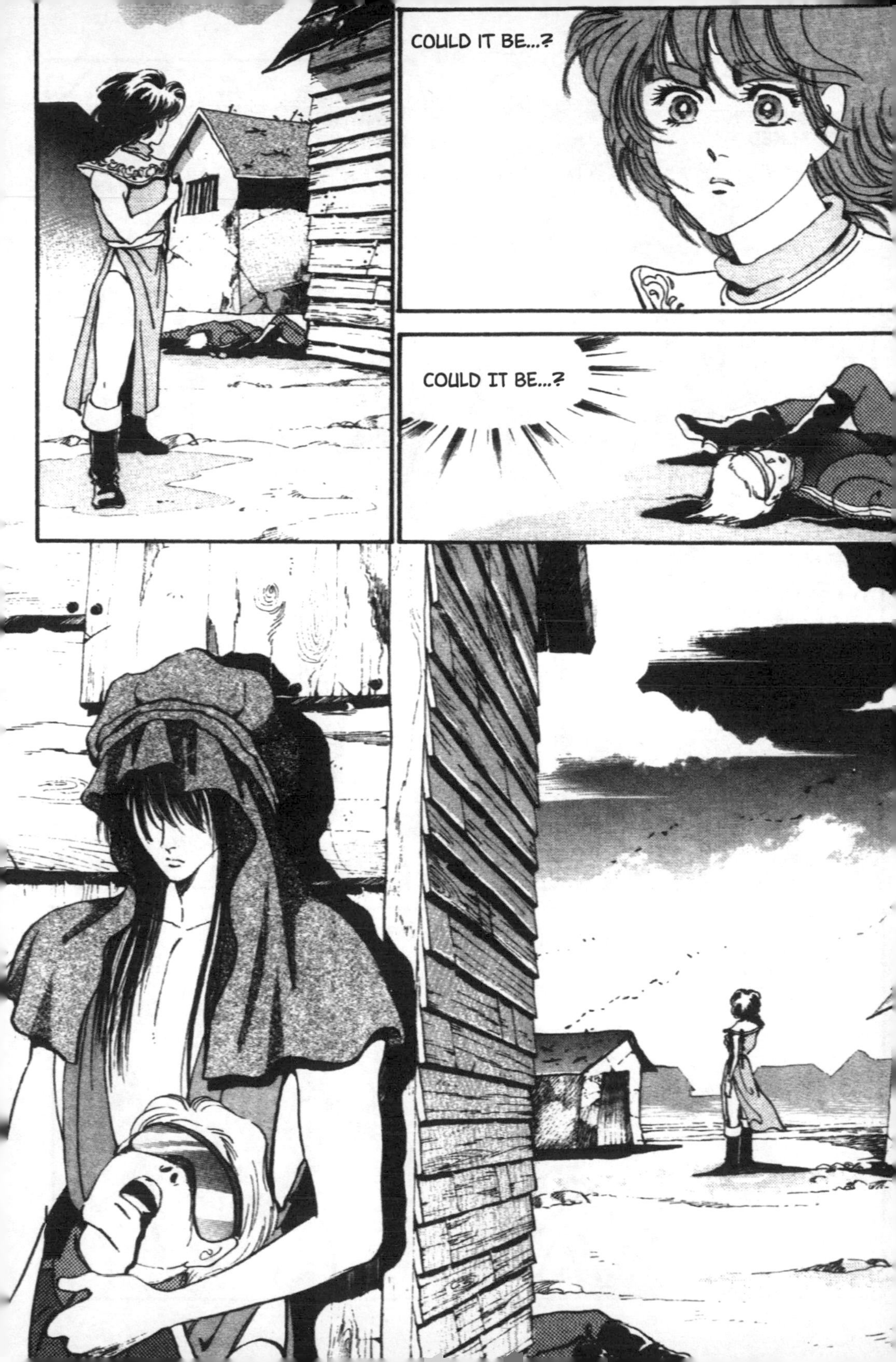
COULD IT BE...?
COULD IT BE...?

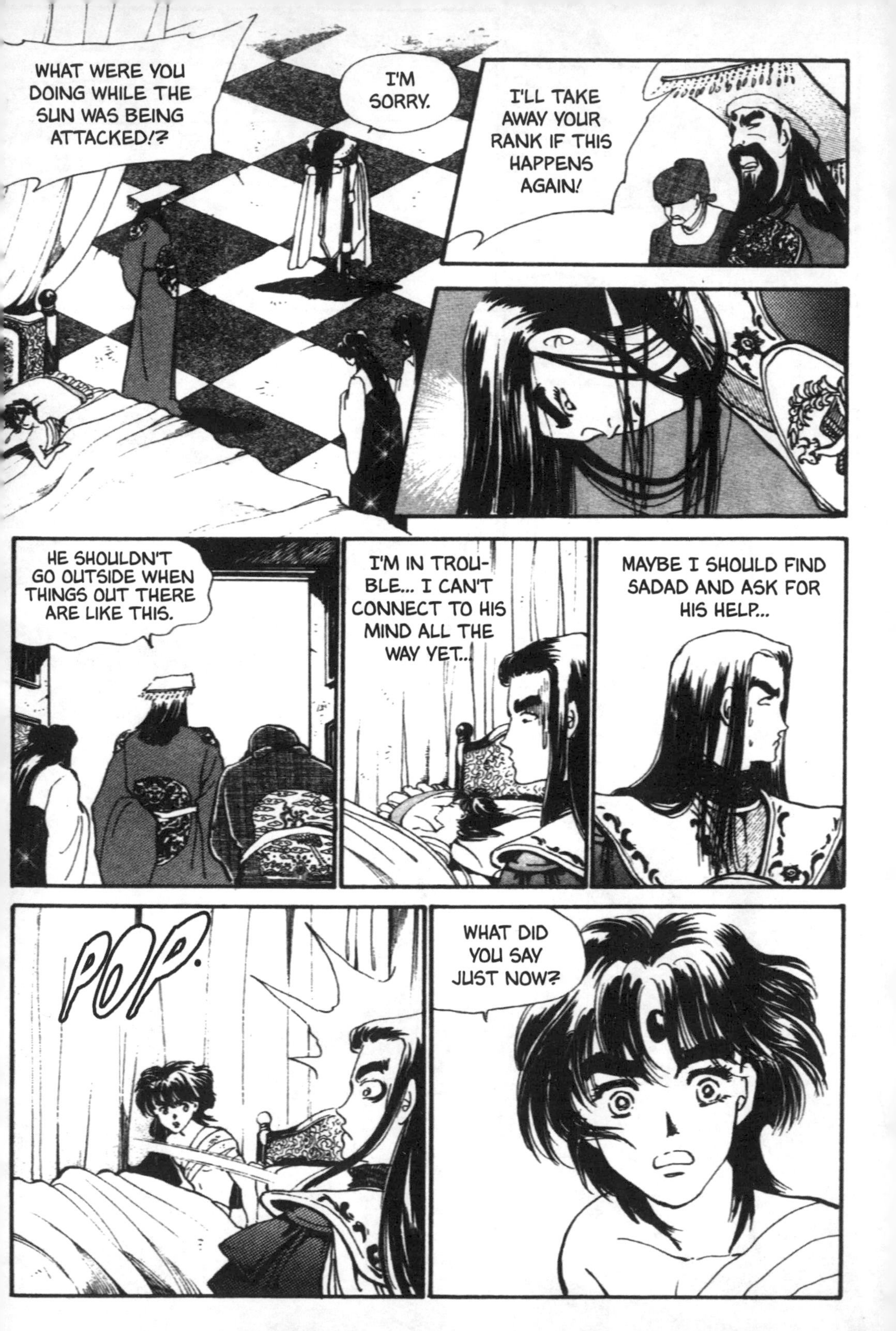
WHAT WERE YOU DOING WHILE THE SUN WAS BEING ATTACKED!?
I'M SORRY.
I'LL TAKE AWAY YOUR RANK IF THIS HAPPENS AGAIN!
HE SHOULDN'T GO OUTSIDE WHEN THINGS OUT THERE ARE LIKE THIS.
I'M IN TROU-BLE... I CAN'T CONNECT TO HIS MIND ALL THE WAY YET...
MAYBE I SHOULD FIND SADAD AND ASK FOR HIS HELP...
POP.
WHAT DID YOU SAY JUST NOW?

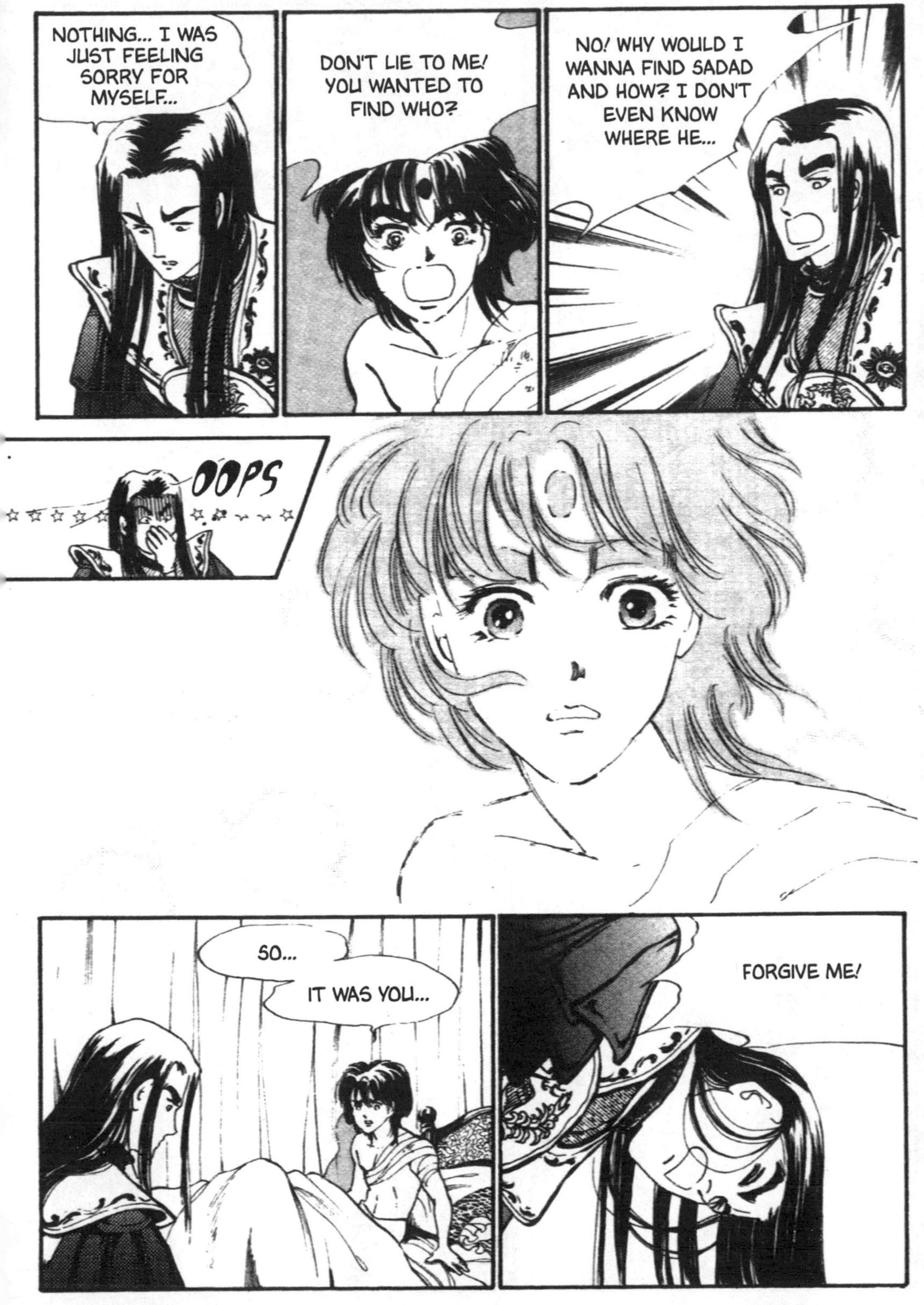
NOTHING... I WAS JUST FEELING SORRY FOR MYSELF...
DON'T LIE TO ME! YOU WANTED TO FIND WHO?
NO! WHY WOULD I WANNA FIND SADAD AND HOW? I DON'T EVEN KNOW WHERE HE...
OOPS
SO...
IT WAS YOU...
FORGIVE ME!

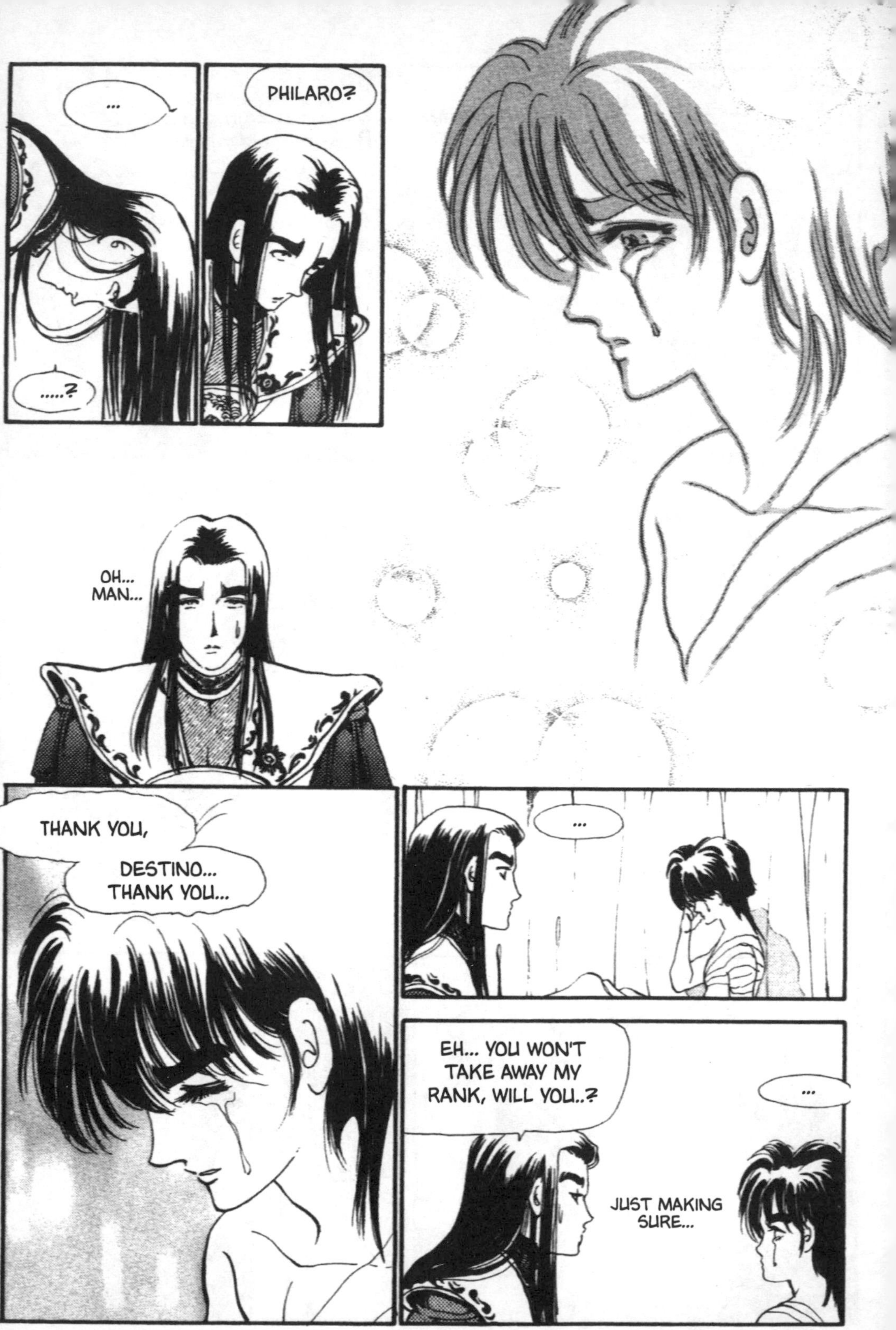
...
.....?
PHILARO?
OH... MAN...
THANK YOU,
DESTINO... THANK YOU...
...
EH... YOU WON'T TAKE AWAY MY RANK, WILL YOU..?
...
JUST MAKING SURE...

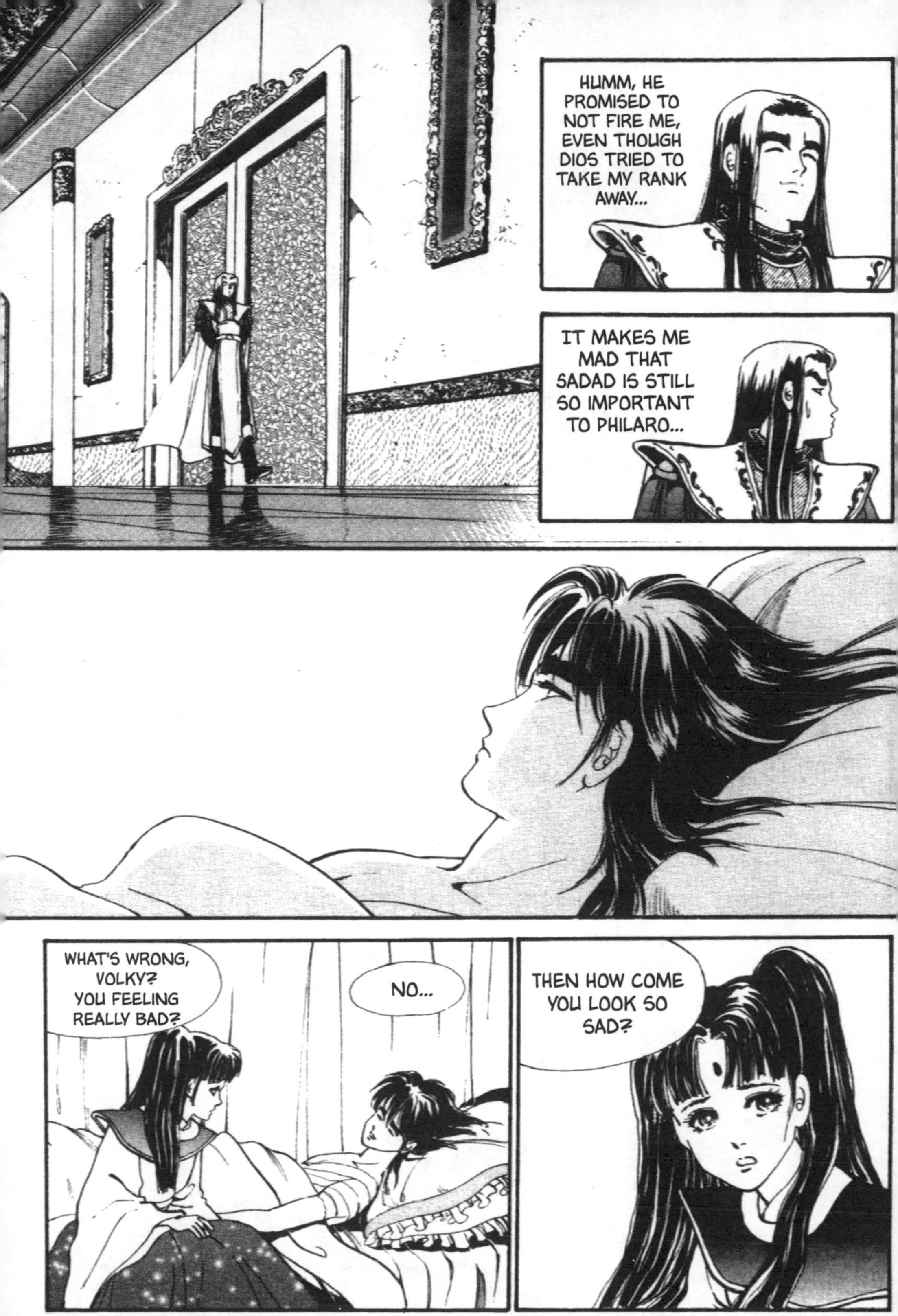
HUMM, HE PROMISED TO NOT FIRE ME, EVEN THOUGH DIOS TRIED TO TAKE MY RANK AWAY...
IT MAKES ME MAD THAT SADAD IS STILL SO IMPORTANT TO PHILARO...
WHAT'S WRONG, VOLKY? YOU FEELING REALLY BAD?
NO...
THEN HOW COME YOU LOOK SO SAD?

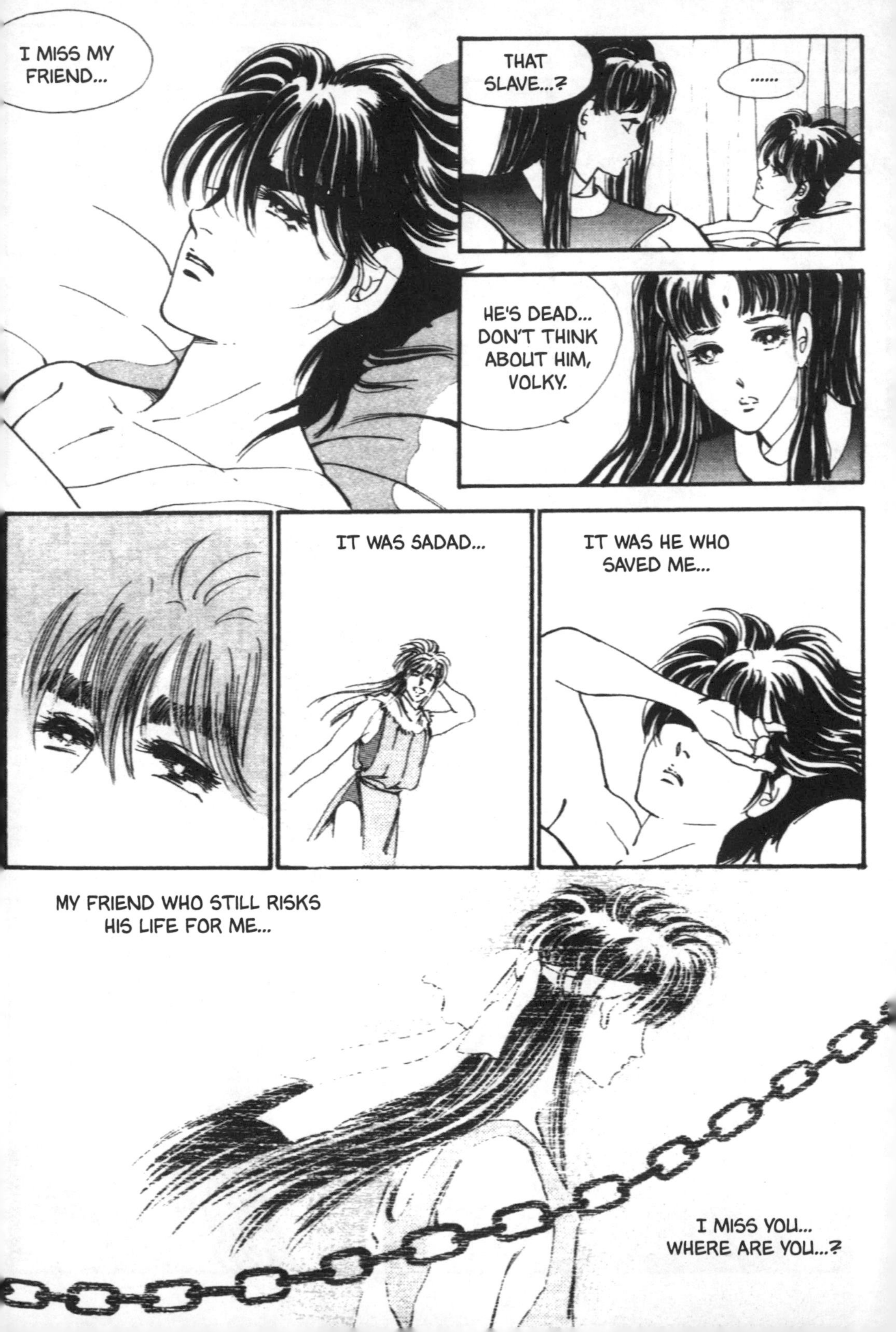
I MISS MY FRIEND...
THAT SLAVE...?
......
HE'S DEAD... DON'T THINK ABOUT HIM, VOLKY.
IT WAS SADAD...
IT WAS HE WHO SAVED ME...
MY FRIEND WHO STILL RISKS HIS LIFE FOR ME...
I MISS YOU... WHERE ARE YOU...?

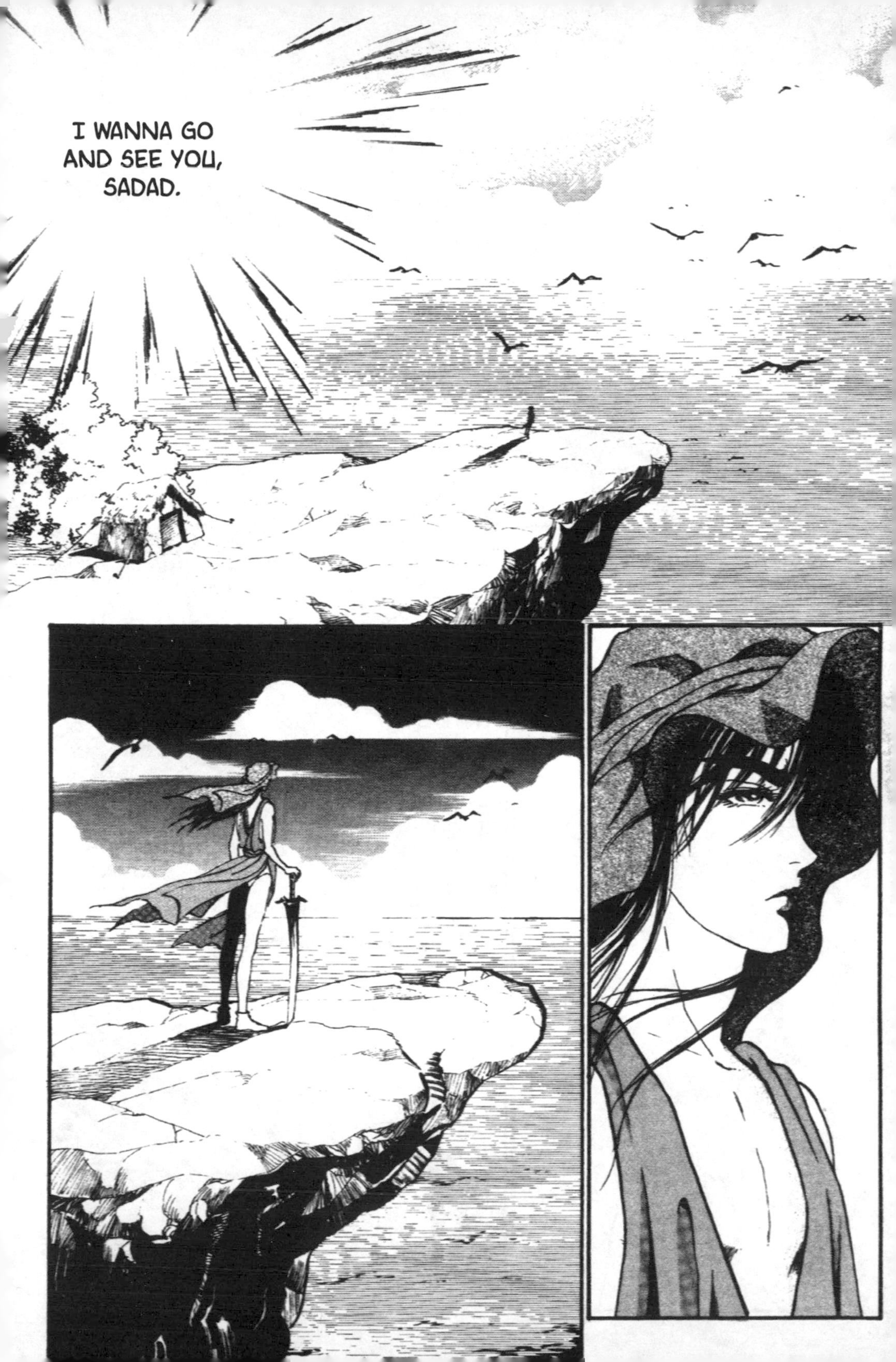
I WANNA GO AND SEE YOU, SADAD.

HUMMMMMMMMMMM

AZLAR'S RECONNAISSANCE PLANES.

LOOK AND SEE IF THERE ARE ANY FIGHTERS.

WE COULDN'T PASS THIS ZONE IN THE PAST.

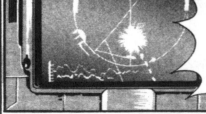

ACK! SOME-THING'S COMING STRAIGHT AHEAD AT 6 O'CLOCK!

WATCH OUT!

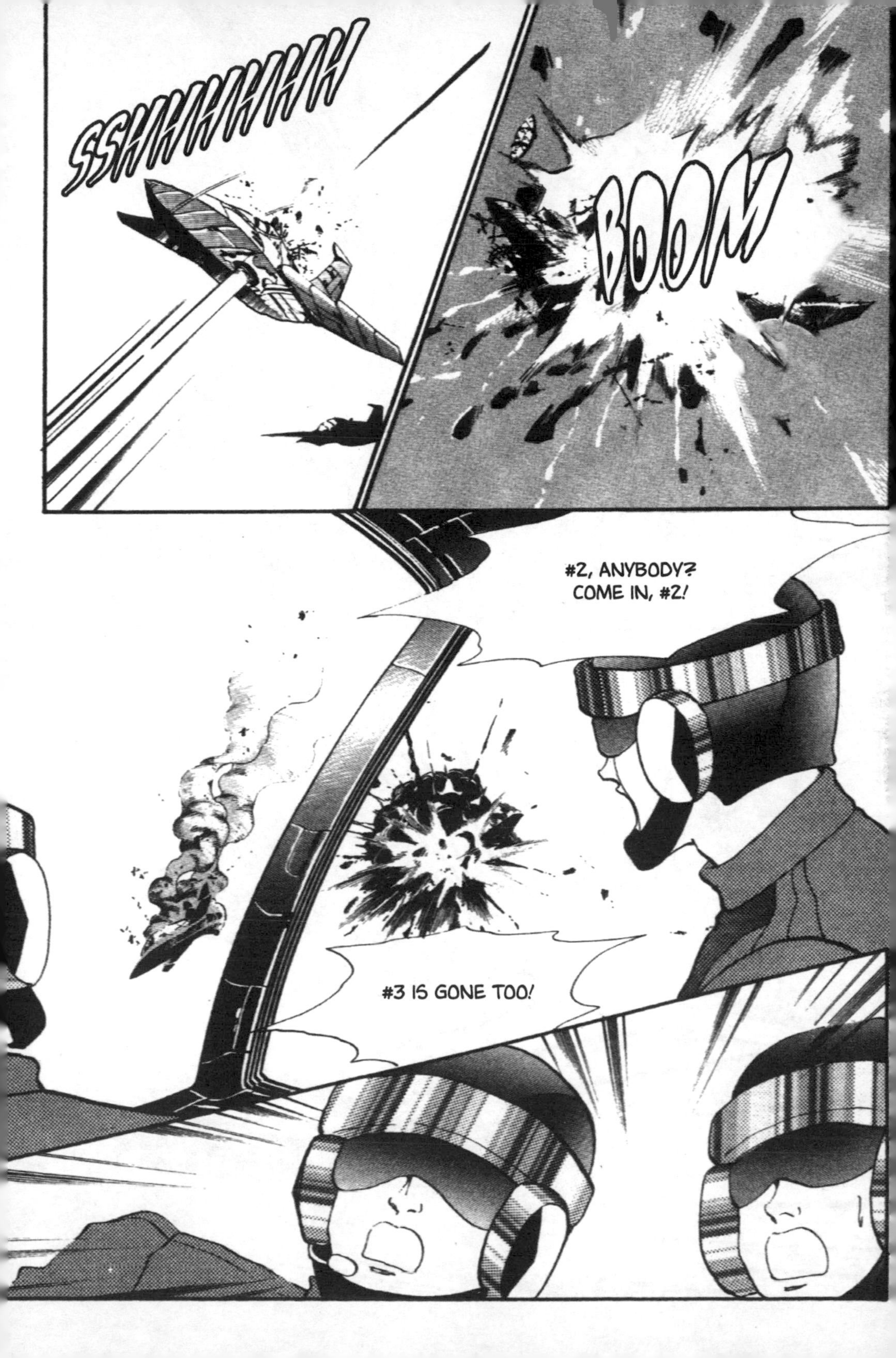
SSHHHHHHH
BOOM
#2, ANYBODY? COME IN, #2!
#3 IS GONE TOO!

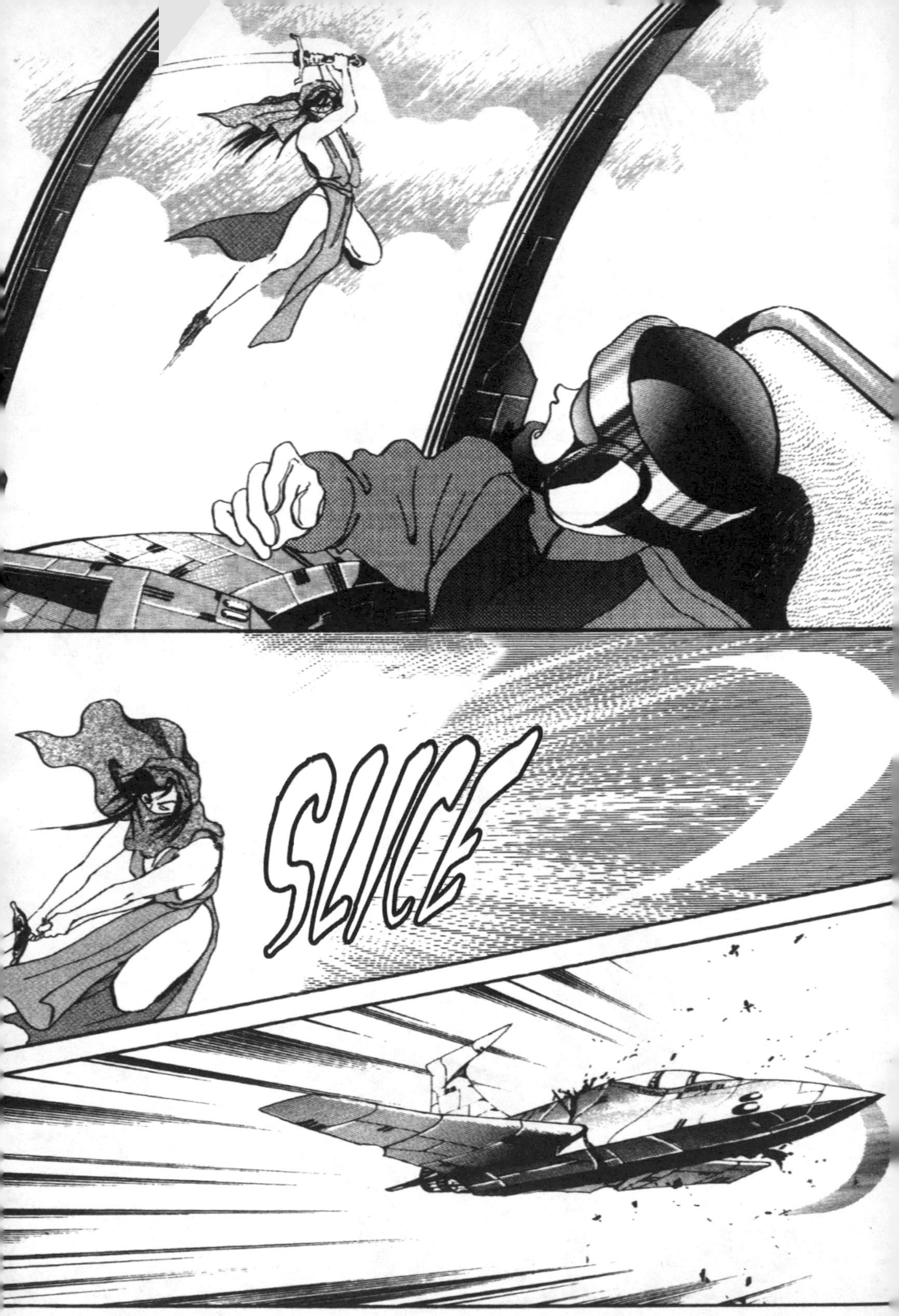
SLICE

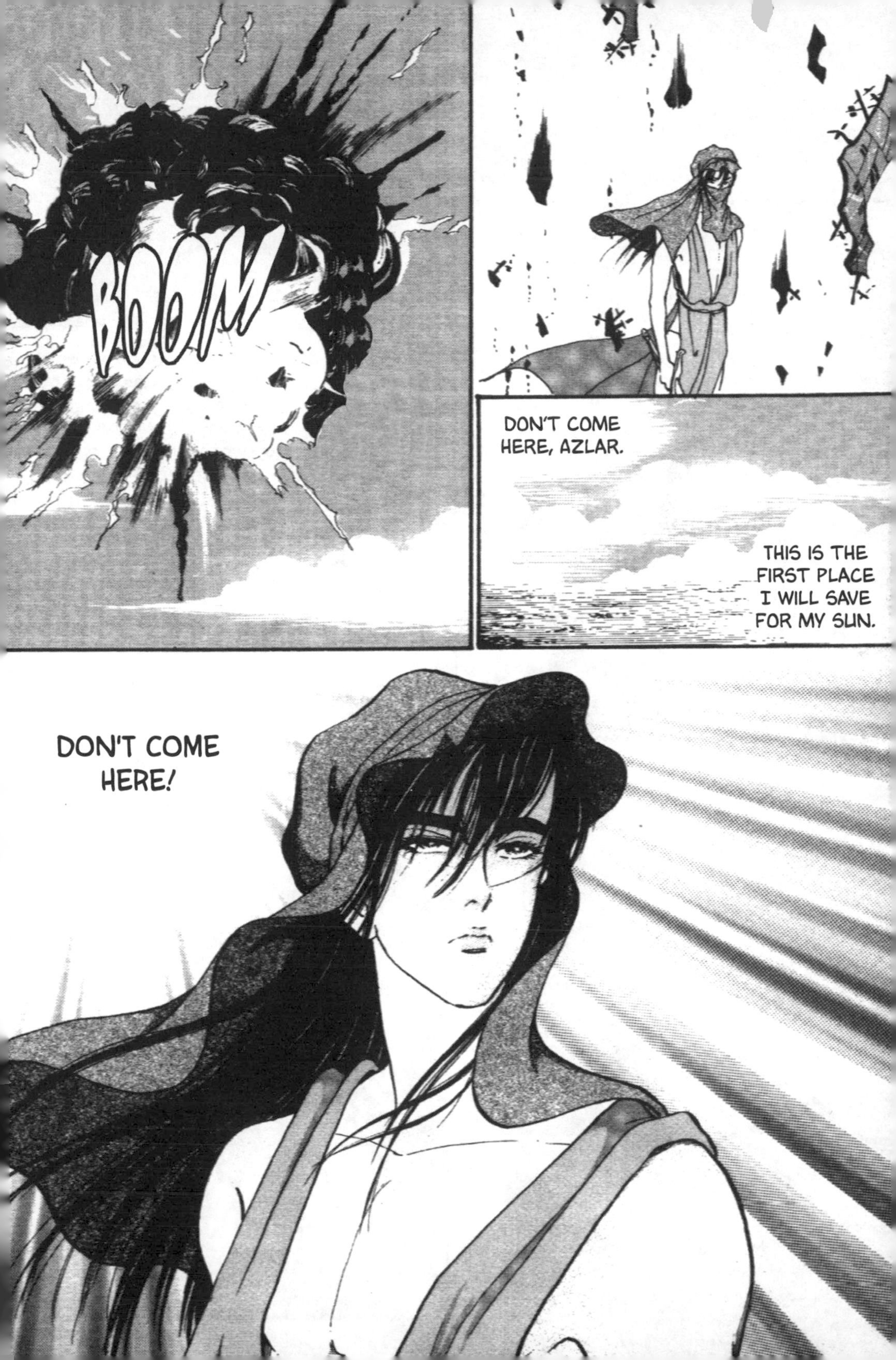
BOOM
DON'T COME HERE, AZLAR.
THIS IS THE FIRST PLACE I WILL SAVE FOR MY SUN.
DON'T COME HERE!

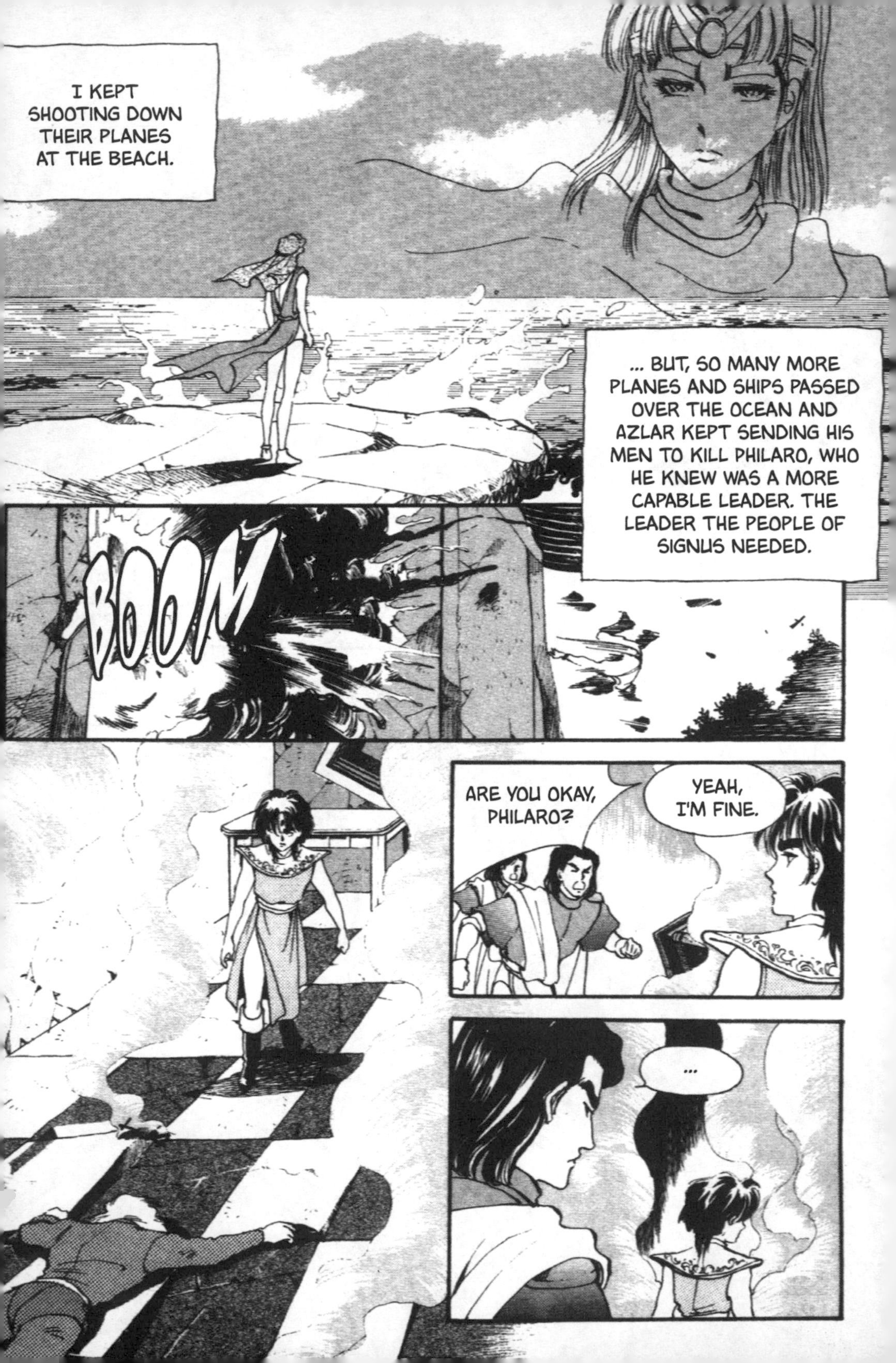
I KEPT SHOOTING DOWN THEIR PLANES AT THE BEACH.
... BUT, SO MANY MORE PLANES AND SHIPS PASSED OVER THE OCEAN AND AZLAR KEPT SENDING HIS MEN TO KILL PHILARO, WHO HE KNEW WAS A MORE CAPABLE LEADER. THE LEADER THE PEOPLE OF SIGNUS NEEDED.
BOOM
ARE YOU OKAY, PHILARO?
YEAH, I'M FINE.
...

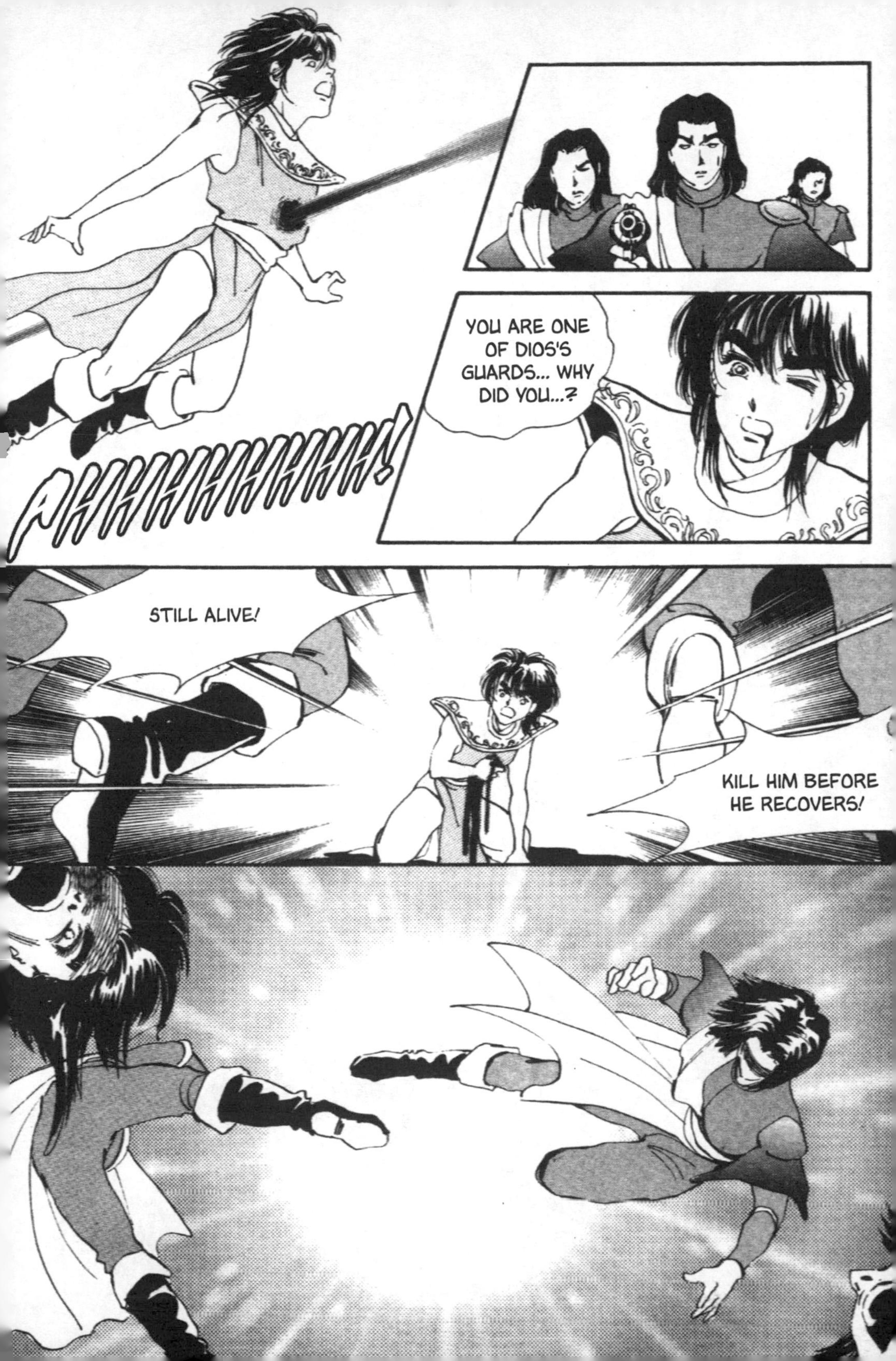
PHHHHHHHHHH!
YOU ARE ONE OF DIOS'S GUARDS... WHY DID YOU...?
STILL ALIVE!
KILL HIM BEFORE HE RECOVERS!

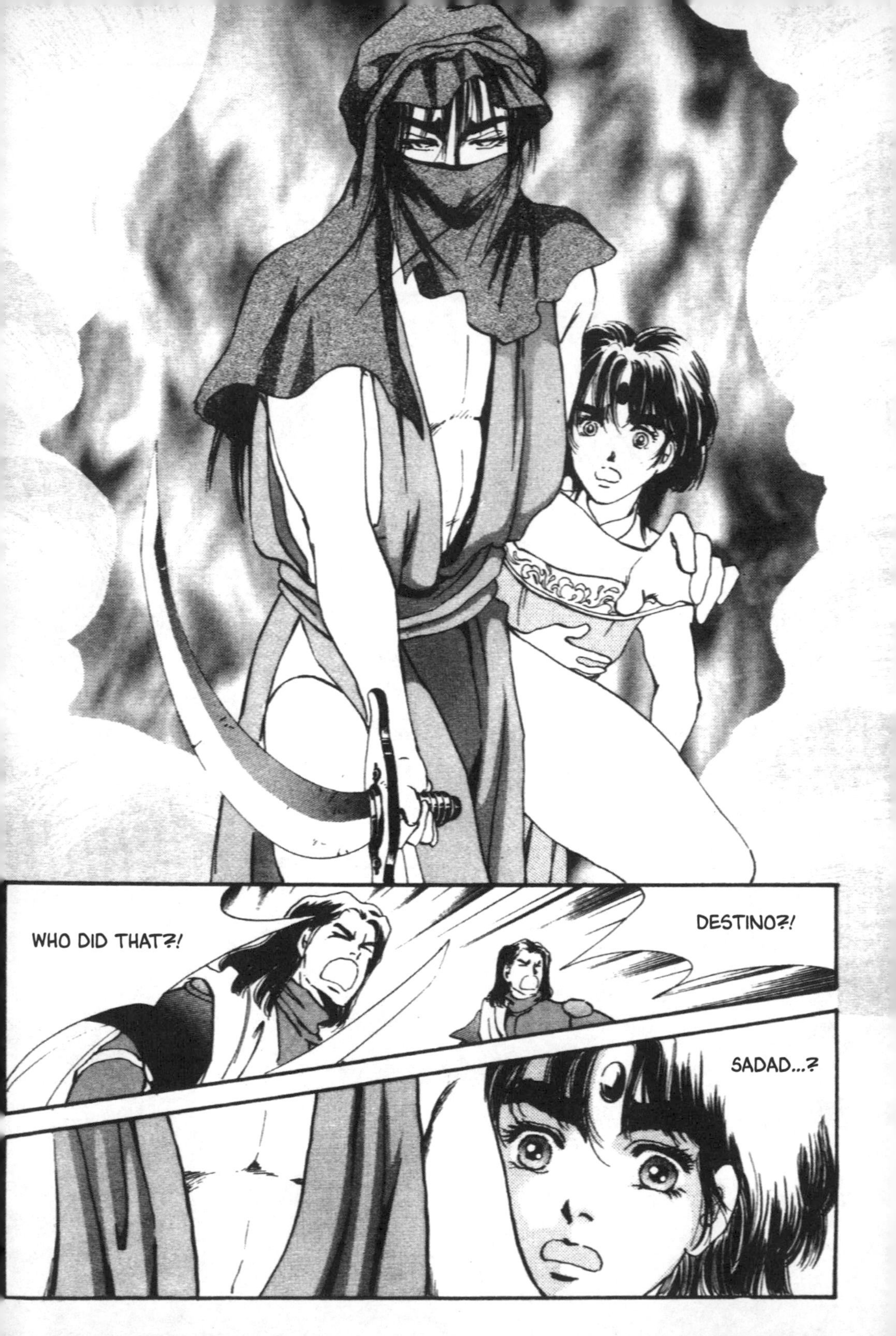
DESTINO?!
WHO DID THAT?!
SADAD...?

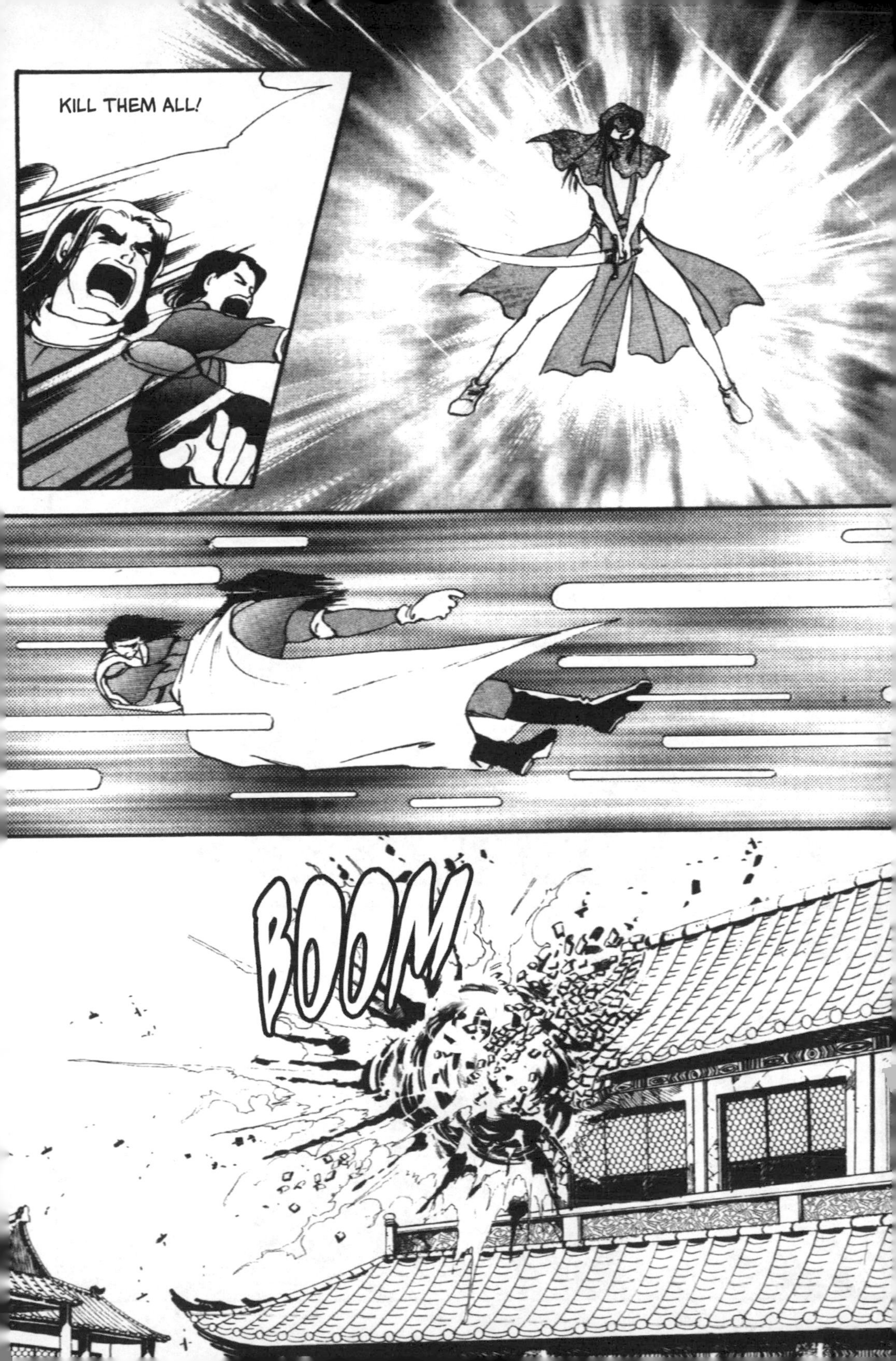
KILL THEM ALL!
BOOM

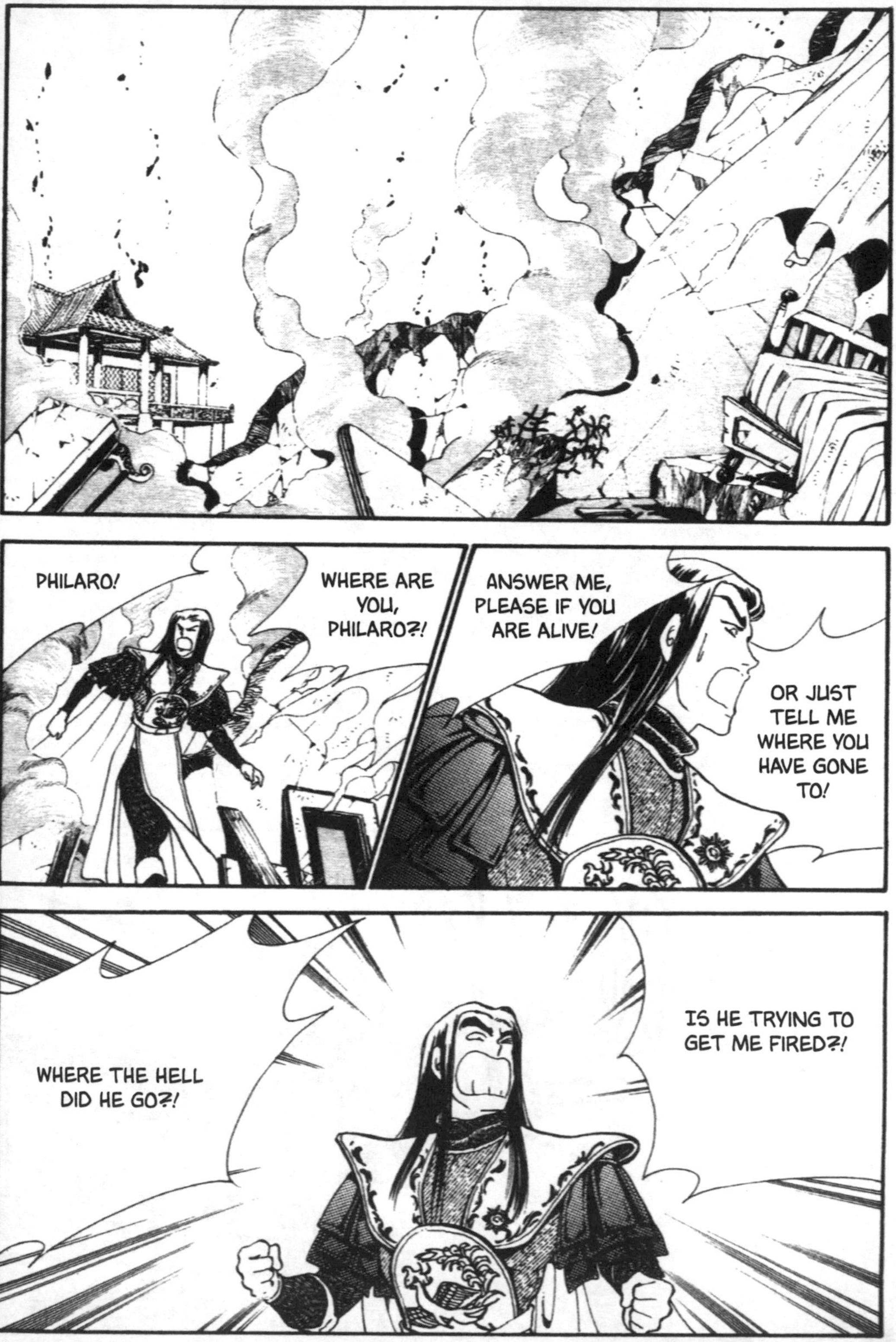
PHILARO!
WHERE ARE YOU, PHILARO?!
ANSWER ME, PLEASE IF YOU ARE ALIVE!
OR JUST TELL ME WHERE YOU HAVE GONE TO!
WHERE THE HELL DID HE GO?!
IS HE TRYING TO GET ME FIRED?!

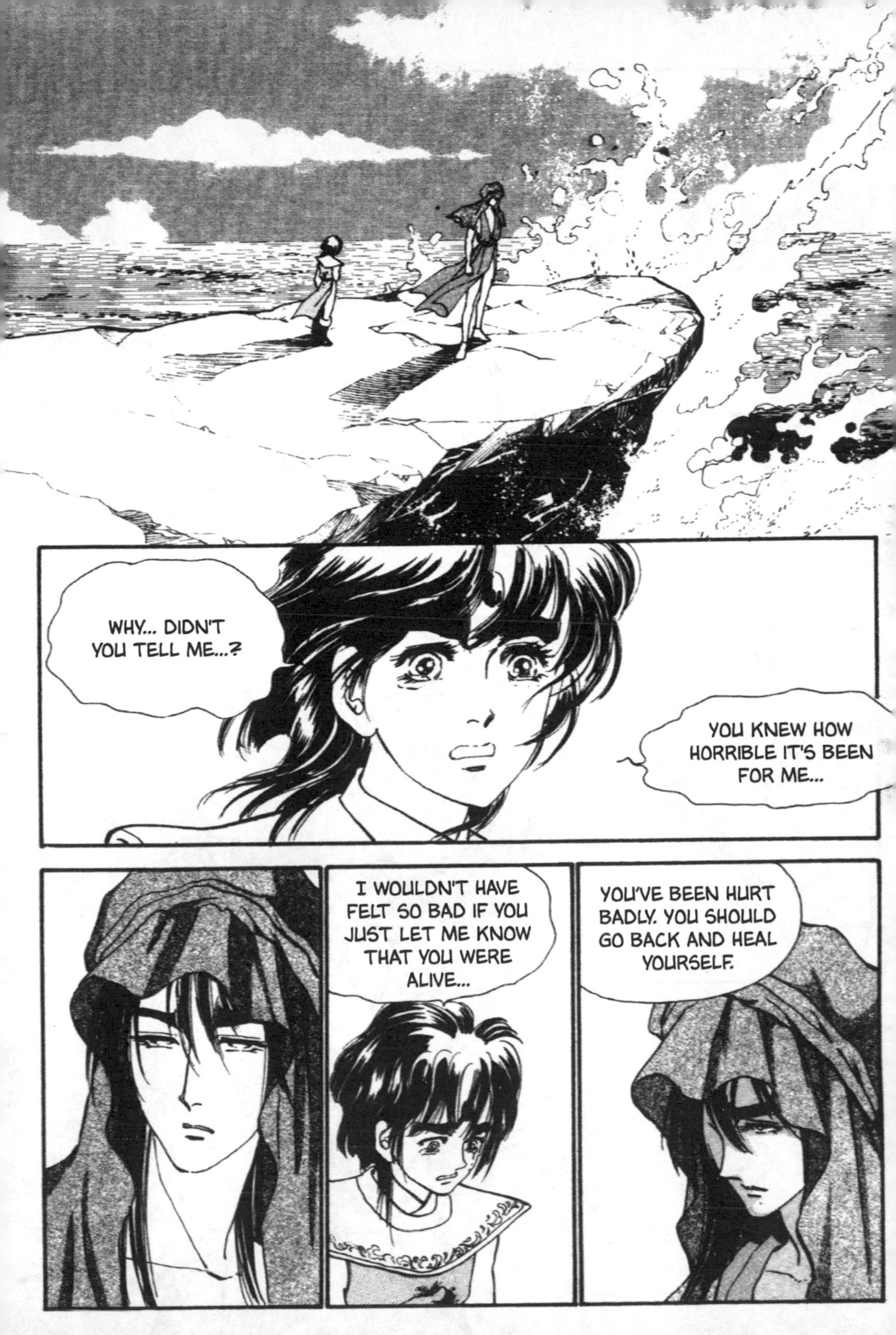
WHY... DIDN'T YOU TELL ME...?
YOU KNEW HOW HORRIBLE IT'S BEEN FOR ME...
I WOULDN'T HAVE FELT SO BAD IF YOU JUST LET ME KNOW THAT YOU WERE ALIVE...
YOU'VE BEEN HURT BADLY. YOU SHOULD GO BACK AND HEAL YOURSELF.

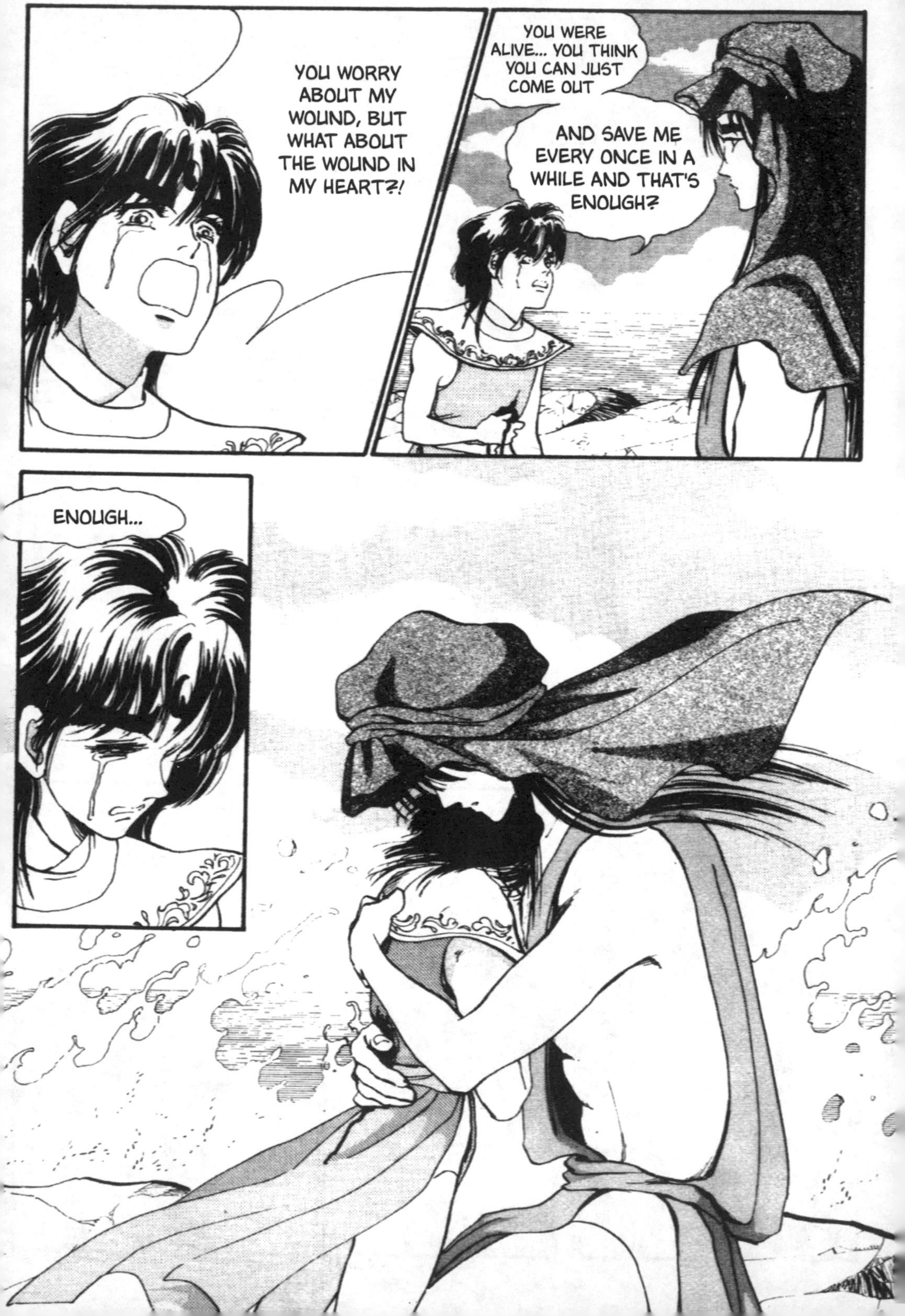
YOU WORRY ABOUT MY WOUND, BUT WHAT ABOUT THE WOUND IN MY HEART?!
YOU WERE ALIVE... YOU THINK YOU CAN JUST COME OUT
AND SAVE ME EVERY ONCE IN A WHILE AND THAT'S ENOUGH?
ENOUGH...

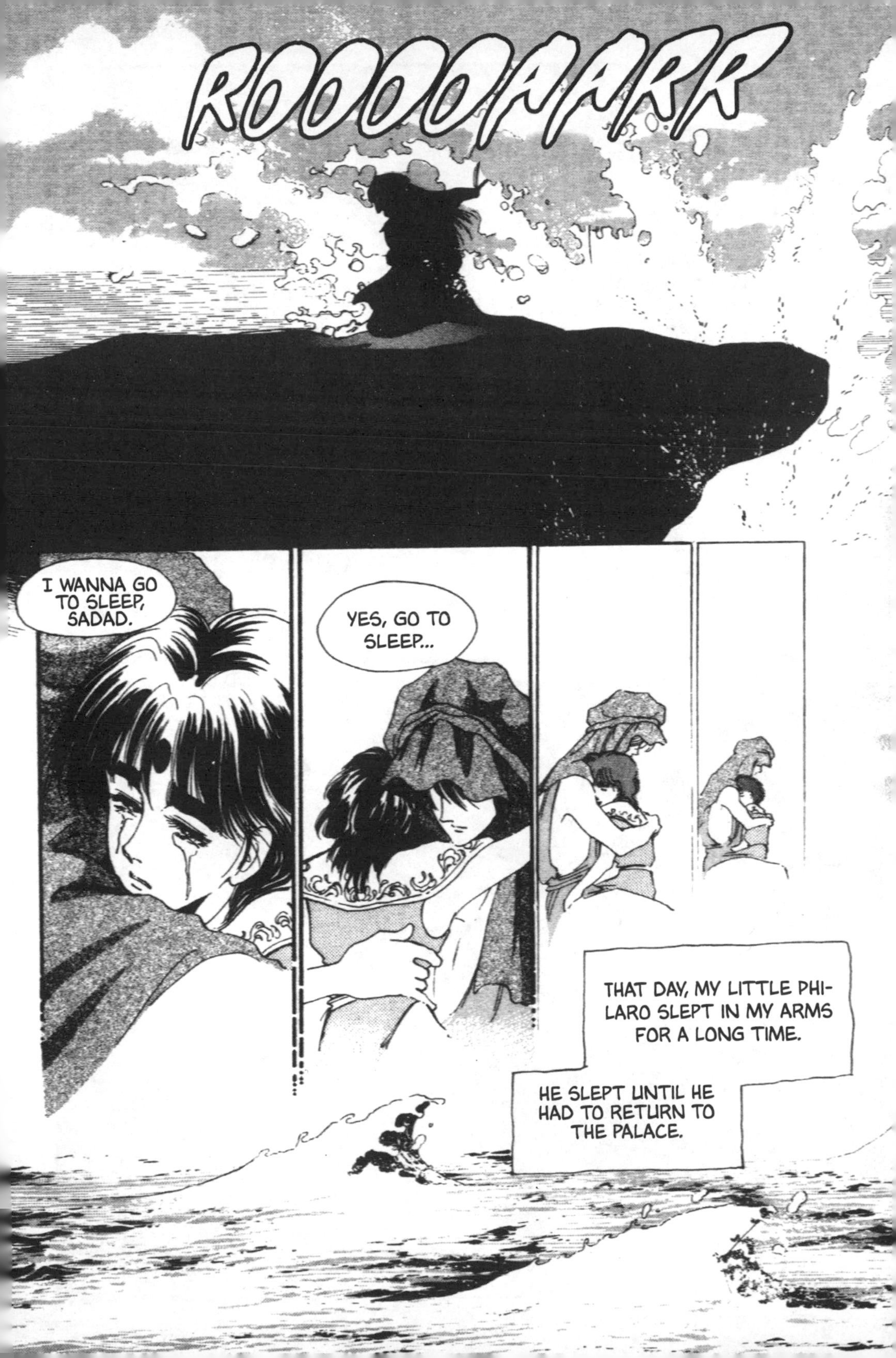
ROOOOAARR
I WANNA GO TO SLEEP, SADAD.
YES, GO TO SLEEP...
THAT DAY, MY LITTLE PHI-LARO SLEPT IN MY ARMS FOR A LONG TIME.
HE SLEPT UNTIL HE HAD TO RETURN TO THE PALACE.

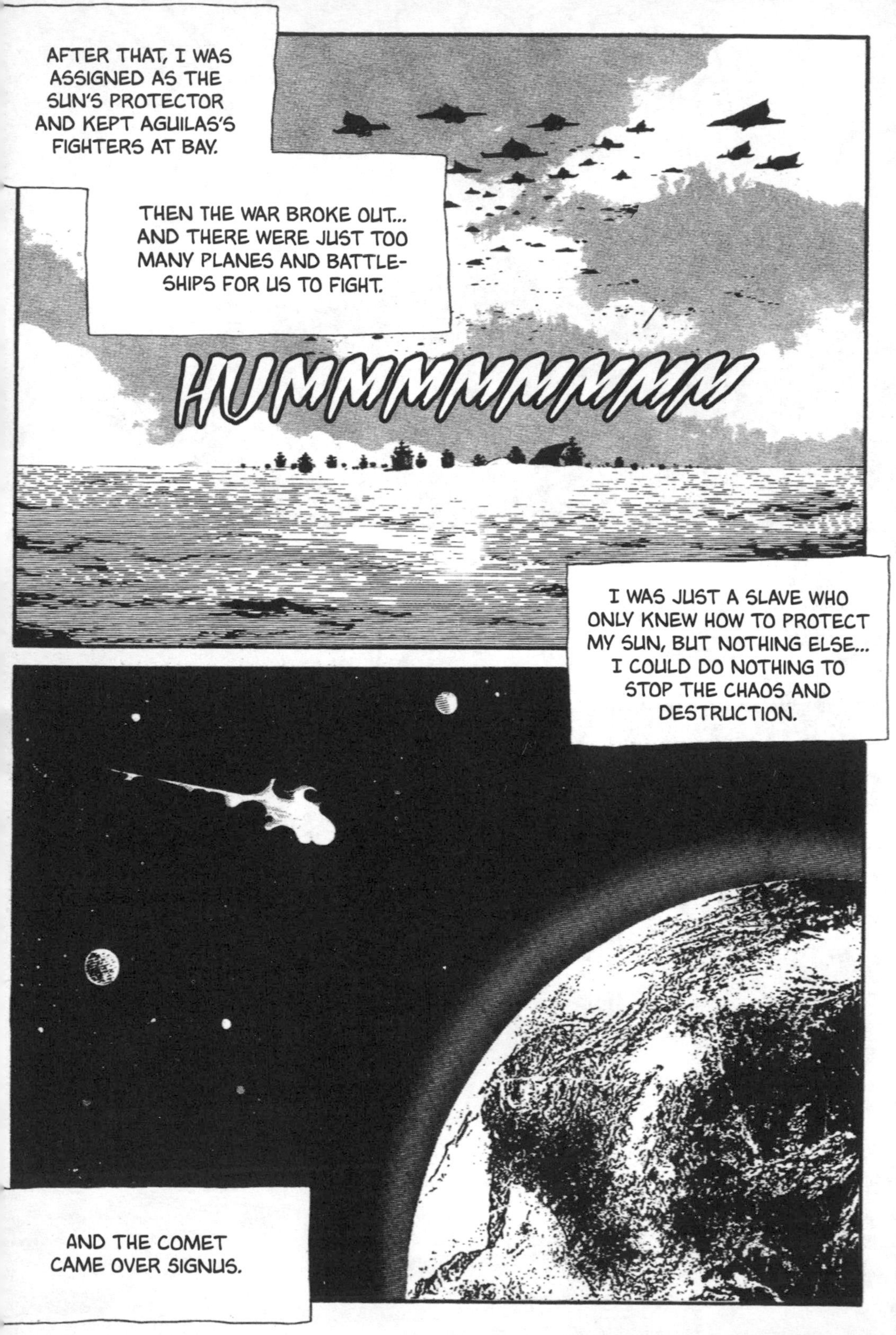
AFTER THAT, I WAS ASSIGNED AS THE SUN'S PROTECTOR AND KEPT AGUILAS'S FIGHTERS AT BAY.
THEN THE WAR BROKE OUT... AND THERE WERE JUST TOO MANY PLANES AND BATTLE-SHIPS FOR US TO FIGHT.
HUMMMMMMMMM
I WAS JUST A SLAVE WHO ONLY KNEW HOW TO PROTECT MY SUN, BUT NOTHING ELSE... I COULD DO NOTHING TO STOP THE CHAOS AND DESTRUCTION.
AND THE COMET CAME OVER SIGNUS.

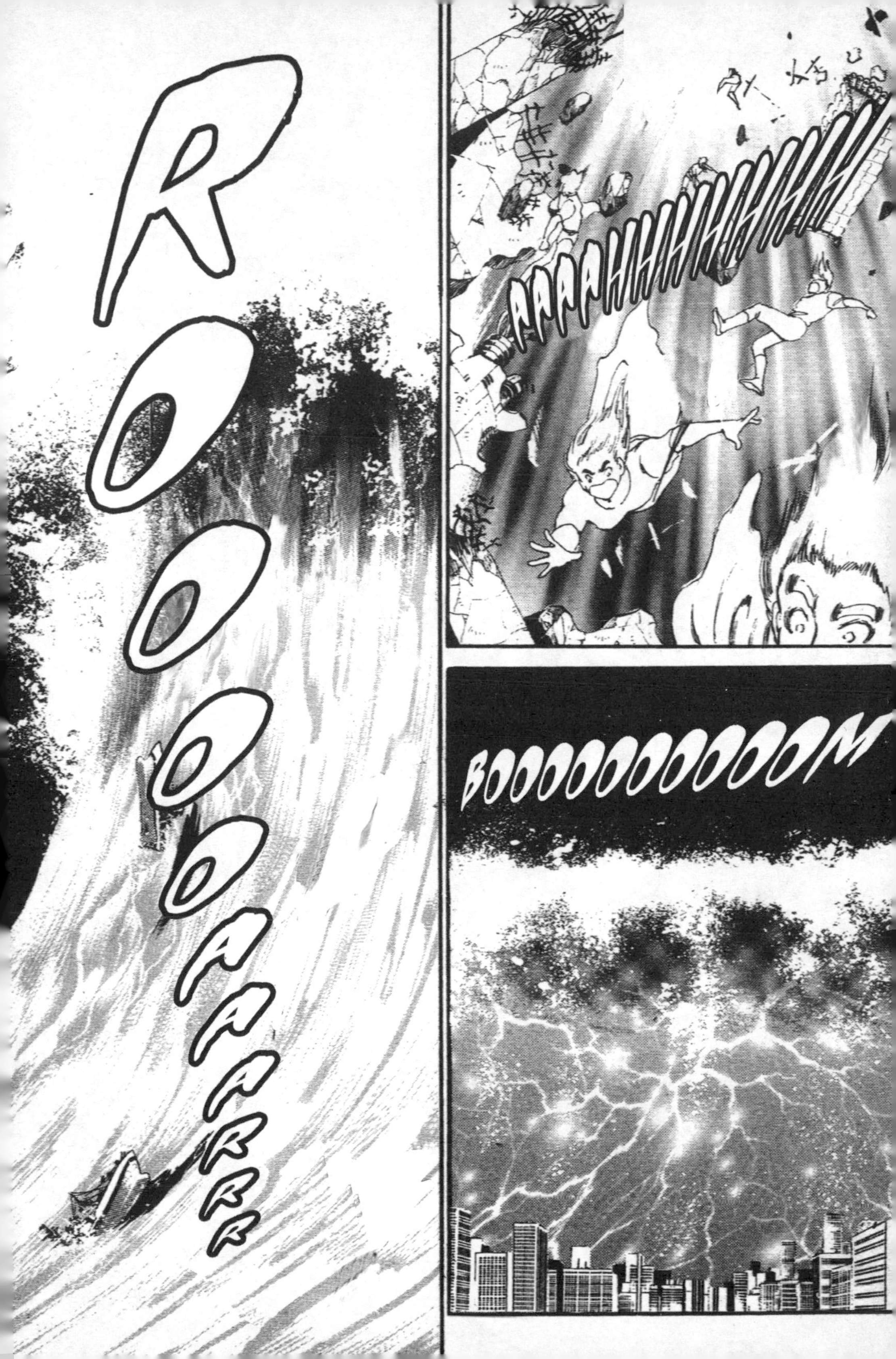
ROOOOAAARRR
AAAAHHHHHHHHHHHHH
BOOOOOOOOOOOM

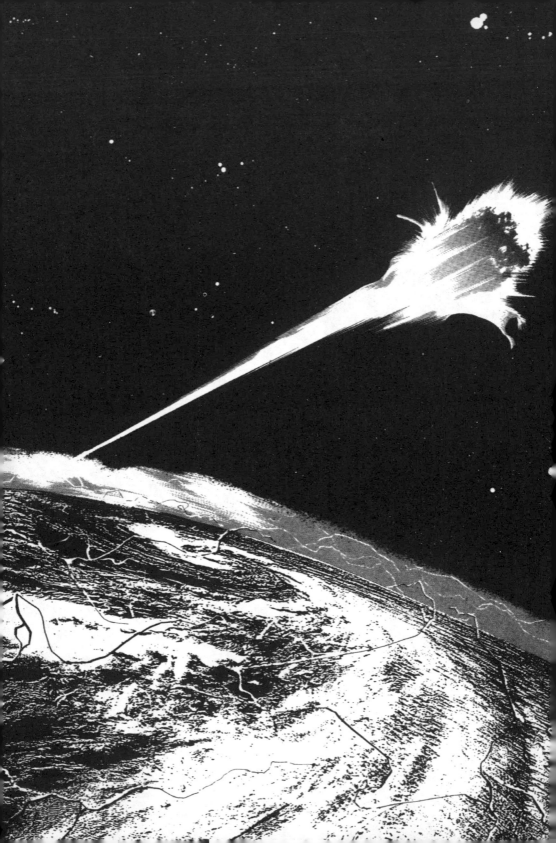

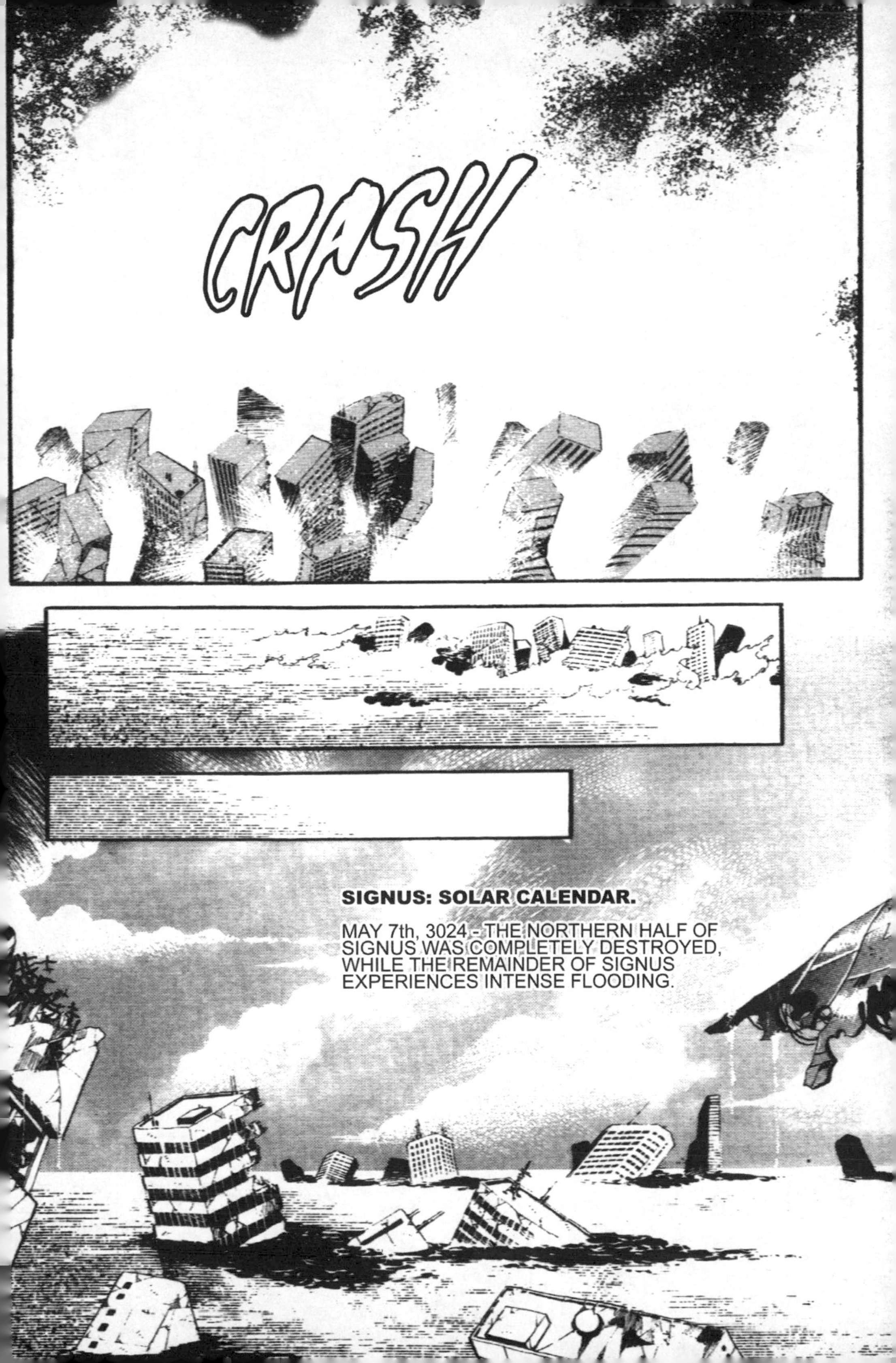
CRASH
SIGNUS: SOLAR CALENDAR.
MAY 7th, 3024 - THE NORTHERN HALF OF SIGNUS WAS COMPLETELY DESTROYED, WHILE THE REMAINDER OF SIGNUS EXPERIENCES INTENSE FLOODING.

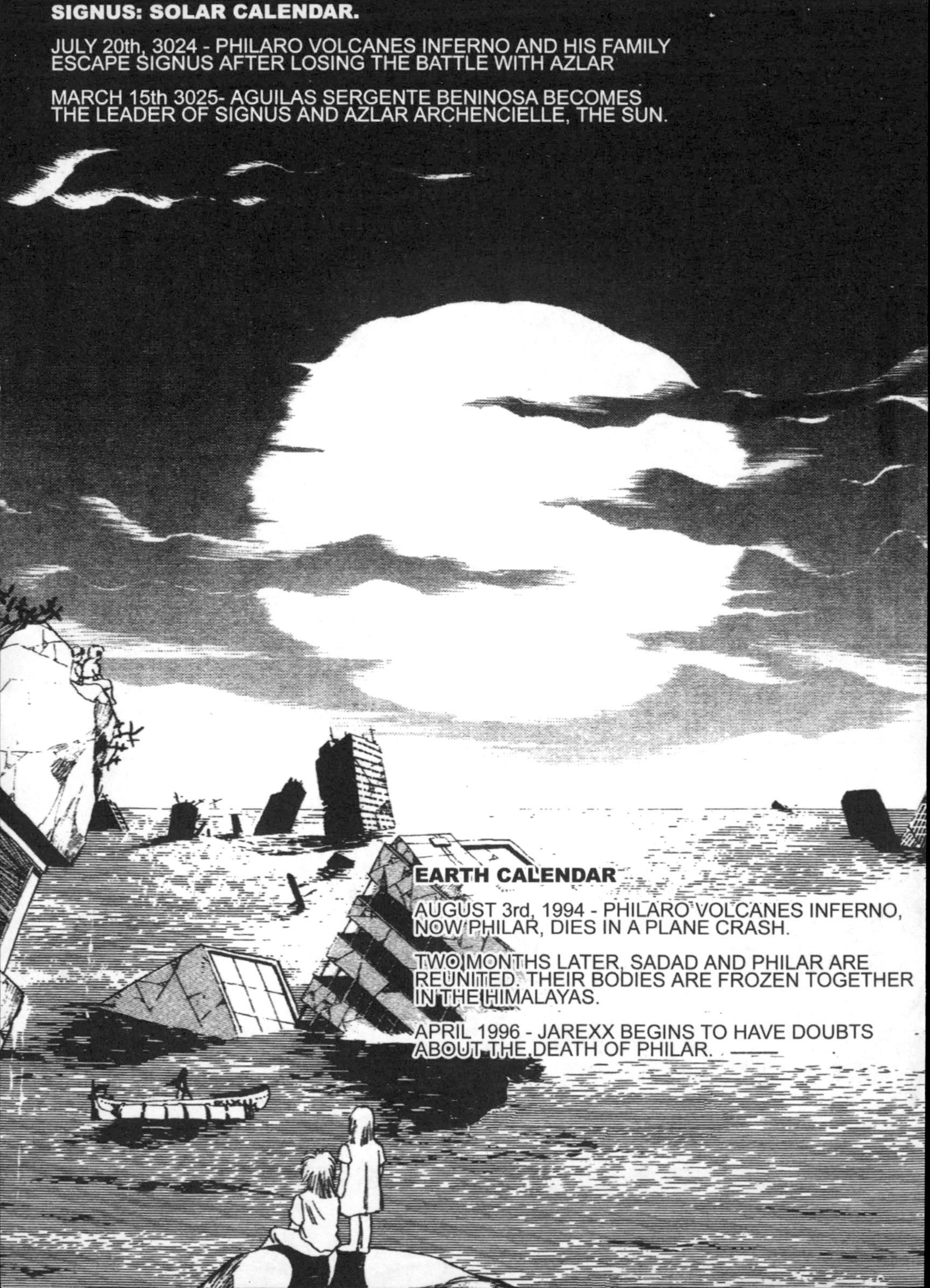
SIGNUS: SOLAR CALENDAR.
JULY 20th, 3024 - PHILARO VOLCANES INFERNO AND HIS FAMILY ESCAPE SIGNUS AFTER LOSING THE BATTLE WITH AZLAR
MARCH 15th 3025- AGUILAS SERGENTE BENINOSA BECOMES THE LEADER OF SIGNUS AND AZLAR ARCHENCIELLE, THE SUN.
EARTH CALENDAR
AUGUST 3rd, 1994 - PHILARO VOLCANES INFERNO, NOW PHILAR, DIES IN A PLANE CRASH.
TWO MONTHS LATER, SADAD AND PHILAR ARE REUNITED. THEIR BODIES ARE FROZEN TOGETHER IN THE HIMALAYAS.
APRIL 1996 - JAREXX BEGINS TO HAVE DOUBTS ABOUT THE DEATH OF PHILAR.

KAZAN

Kazan is the last surviving member of a nomad tribe known as The Red Sand. When his village is wiped out by a vicious Water Demon, and his best friend Elsie is kidnapped, Kazan begins a journey to uncover answers that will span 10 years! Befriending a water woman, a cranky old lady, and a bizarre white Eagle, Kazan sets out for the legendary land of Goldene. Get ready for an action-packed ride through the desert as nomads, assassins, slave traders, thieves, and even giant centipedes cross paths with the young hero and his sharp-edged knife...

5 vols - 200+ pages B&W
Hardcopy US $9.95 each
eBook US $2.95 each

Wounded Man

By: Kazuo Koike & Ryoichi Ikegami

Keisuke Ibaraki is not a man to be trifled
with and the pornography company, G.P.X.,
makes a grave mistake when they kidnap
his high school sweetheart, force her to do
unspeakable acts and then make her com-
mit suicide. Keisuke is now on a mission of
vengeance and will stop at nothing until he
vindicates the memory of his girlfriend.
Travel with him through the jungles of Brazil
as he exacts his revenge and tries to avoid
a pure-as-white reporter out to get the story
that will make her famous.

From the creators of *Crying Freeman*
Recommended for mature readers

9 vols -2- 400+ pages B&W
US $9.95-14.95 each

www.comicsone.com

Maico 2010

By: Toshimitsu Shimizu

4 vols - 200+ pages B&W
Hardcopy US $9.95 each
eBook US $2.95 each

Maico's more than just an adorable radio DJ, she's also the wacky scientist Masudamasu's creation! Maico was designed to save Japan Radio from plummeting popularity, as well as to probe the intricacies and weaknesses of the human heart--so you can imagine what kind of trouble she gets into. Whether she's entangled in human/android love triangles, or trying to protect her friends (and her own cute little tail) from the deadly advances of a batch of evil robots,
she always comes out on top!
Recommended for mature readers

www.comicsone.com

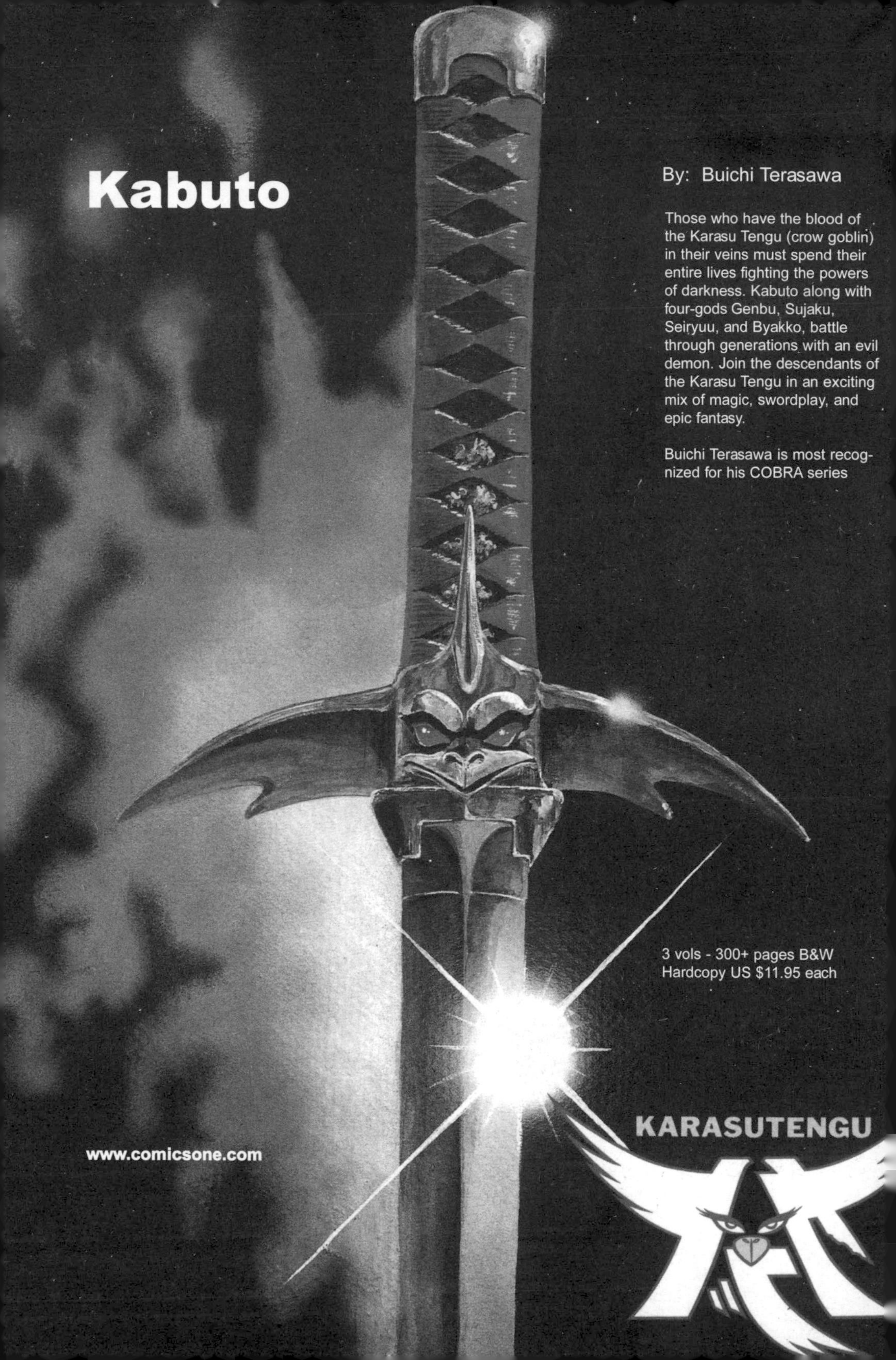
Kabuto
By: Buichi Terasawa
Those who have the blood of the Karasu Tengu (crow goblin) in their veins must spend their entire lives fighting the powers of darkness. Kabuto along with four-gods Genbu, Sujaku, Seiryuu, and Byakko, battle through generations with an evil demon. Join the descendants of the Karasu Tengu in an exciting mix of magic, swordplay, and epic fantasy.
Buichi Terasawa is most recognized for his COBRA series
3 vols - 300+ pages B&W
Hardcopy US $11.95 each
KARASUTENGU
www.comicsone.com